SECOND EDITION

W9-BTN-200

IMPROVING READING

A HANDBOOK OF STRATEGIES

JERRY L. JOHNS
NORTHERN ILLINOIS UNIVERSITY

SUSAN DAVIS LENSKI
ILLINOIS STATE UNIVERSITY

KENDALL/HUNT PUBLISHING COMPANY
4050 Westmark Drive   Dubuque, Iowa 52002

Books by Jerry L. Johns

Basic Reading Inventory (seven editions)
Balanced Reading Instruction: Teachers' Visions and Voices (edited with Laurie Elish-Piper)
Secondary & College Reading Inventory (two editions)
Literacy for Diverse Learners (edited)
Handbook for Remediation of Reading Difficulties
Informal Reading Inventories: An Annotated Reference Guide (compiled)
Literacy: Celebration and Challenge (edited)
Spanish Reading Inventory

Books by Jerry L. Johns and Susan Davis Lenski

Celebrate Literacy! The Joy of Reading and Writing (with June E. Barnhart, James H. Moss, and
    Thomas E. Wheat)
Language Arts for Gifted Middle School Students

Author Addresses

Jerry L. Johns
Northern Illinois University
Reading Clinic—119 Graham
DeKalb, IL 60115
E-mail: jjohns@niu.edu
815-753-8484

Susan Davis Lenski
Illinois State University
239 DeGarmo Hall
Normal, IL 61790
E-mail: sjlensk@ilstu.edu
309-438-3028

Address for Orders

Kendall/Hunt Publishing Company
4050 Westmark Drive P.O. Box 1840
Dubuque, IA 52004-0810

Telephone for Orders

800-228-0810

Photos by Susan Johns and Gary Meader

Copyright © 1994, 1997 by Kendall/Hunt Publishing Company

ISBN 0-7872-2881-8

Printed in the United States of America
10 9 8 7

Contents

Preface

The second edition of *Improving Reading: A Handbook of Strategies* builds upon the many favorable comments we have received from classroom teachers, reading teachers, and students studying in undergraduate and graduate programs. Professionals use the many teaching suggestions and activities to assist a diverse group of students. Some of these students just need a little extra assistance in reading. Other students are struggling with reading and need more intensive help from classroom teachers and specialists. The *Handbook* is an ideal resource for all types of learners.

We have maintained the convenient size and basic organization. Teachers have appreciated the Quick Reference Guide inside the front and back covers, noting that it makes the *Handbook* easy to use. The full page resource materials following each chapter are ready for photocopying. We have made additions throughout the *Handbook* based on our review of the literature or ideas shared by teachers and reading specialists.

A number of suggestions for using writing to strengthen reading are contained in a new chapter and integrated at appropriate places throughout the book. Teachers have told us they like information readily available so we have put it where it fits best. We have also repeated an idea in more than one place if it's appropriate.

The *Handbook* can be applied or adapted in ways that fit your needs and the needs of your students. We know the ideas shared work with students, and we encourage you to experience the joy of assisting all students to become more effective and efficient readers.

■　■　■

Acknowledgments

It's a great feeling to be approached by teachers or reading specialists at a conference, in a school, or following a presentation and be told that the *Handbook* is making a positive contribution to their teaching. Professors at colleges and university have shared similar comments. We sincerely thank all of you who have found ways to use the *Handbook* to enhance your teaching.

Special thanks are again extended to Barb Meredith, a wonderful, talented secretary of six years, for her expertise in assisting with numerous revisions. Julie Mossberg, a new secretary, also helped with the typing. Laurie Elish-Piper, an energetic colleague in Reading, graciously agreed to prepare a new chapter on writing. And Linda Hursh, a first-grade teacher, helped to update the Appendices. Although Peggy VanLeirsburg Marciniec opted not to be part of the revision team, she provided reaction to some drafts and assisted with permissions.

The *Handbook* has been strengthened by the work of many professionals and their students. Their articles, books, research studies, and conversations have enabled us to write a practical book that is grounded in sound knowledge about reading.

Thanks to all of you.

Jerry and Sue

About the Authors

Jerry L. Johns is a Distinguished Teaching Professor at Northern Illinois University. He directs the Reading Clinic and supervises graduate students who instruct struggling readers. He also teaches undergraduate students in elementary and special education. He has taught students from kindergarten through grade eight and held the position of reading teacher.

Professor Johns is a past president of the Illinois Reading Council, College Reading Association and Northern Illinois Reading Council. He has received recognition for outstanding service to each of these professional organizations and is a member of the Illinois Reading Council Hall of Fame. Dr. Johns has served on numerous committees of the International Reading Association and was a member of the Board of Directors. During 1996-1997, he chaired the committee to select the Outstanding Teacher Educator in Reading.

Dr. Johns has been invited to consult, conduct workshops, and make presentation for teachers and parents throughout the United States and Canada. He has also prepared nearly three hundred publications that have been useful to parents and a diverse group of educators. His *Basic Reading Inventory,* now in a seventh edition, is widely used in undergraduate and graduate classes as well as by practicing teachers. Dr. Johns recently coedited a book on balanced reading instruction. A current project is focused on a reading inventory for students who speak Spanish.

■　■　■

Susan Davis Lenski is an Assistant Professor of Elementary Education at Illinois State University. Before joining the faculty at ISU, Dr. Lenski taught in public schools for 20 years. Her teaching experiences include working with children from kindergarten through high school. Dr. Lenski currently teaches undergraduate and graduate reading and language arts courses.

Professor Lenski has been recognized by several organizations for her commitment to education. Among her numerous awards, Dr. Lenski was presented with the Nila Banton Smith Award from the International Reading Association for her work in integrating content area subjects with reading instruction in secondary school. As an elementary school reading specialist, Dr. Lenski was instrumental in her school receiving an Exemplary Reading Program Award also from the International Reading Association.

Professor Lenski's research interests are in improving reading and writing instruction in elementary and middle schools. She has conducted numerous inservice presentations and has presented at many state and national conferences. Dr. Lenski has written over forty articles for professional journals. This is her third book.

Introduction

This introduction describes the organization of *Improving Reading: A Handbook of Strategies* so that it can be used most effectively. Take a few minutes to get acquainted with the book by reading this introduction and the list of chapters.

General Organization of *Improving Reading*

This book is organized into nine chapters, seven of which focus on major areas where students might struggle with reading. There is also a chapter on writing and a chapter containing ideas for involving parents in the reading program. For each chapter, a brief overview is presented. Within each of the chapters, specific areas of possible need are discussed in separate sections with suggested strategies to help students improve as readers. At the end of each chapter are additional resources that may be helpful in assessment, teaching or sharing with students or parents. These resources are conveniently provided in a size that can be easily reproduced for classroom use. Finally, the appendices contain suggested literature to use with some of the strategies and activities discussed in the book.

Within each chapter, needs that students may have are enumerated as major section headings. For example, Chapter 1, "Encouraging a Love of Reading," contains six sections. The first section of the chapter, Negative Attitude Toward Reading, is numbered as section 1.1; the second area, Lack of Confidence, is section 1.2, and so on. Each of the major headings is followed by a description of the *Behavior Observed* and the *Anticipated Outcome* students may exhibit. These terms are described as follows:

> *Behavior Observed*: Provides a concise statement describing an area with which a student may need assistance.

> *Anticipated Outcome*: States what the possible changed behavior may be after using the suggested strategies.

Sections offer a variety of information that may include *Background, Perspective and Strategies, Teaching Strategy, Practice and Reinforcement Activities*, and *Games*. Each of these subheadings is described as follows:

> *Background*: Presents information and background related to a particular area.

> *Perspective and Strategies*: Presents insights and offers strategies and activities that can help the student who may need that particular assistance or intervention.

> *Teaching Strategy*: Contains one or more ways to help students learn a strategy, skill or technique.

> *Practice and Reinforcement Activities*: Offers numerous ideas for helping students to practice what has been taught.

> *Games*: Describes whole-class, small-group, or individual games that help students practice and refine strategies.

How to Use *Improving Reading*

After a brief survey of this book, you will want to put ideas into practice. Describe a student's need in a phrase or sentence. Then scan the contents for a major heading that is likely to be helpful. An expanded presentation of the contents is located inside the front and back covers. Either of these sources should also help you to locate an appropriate place to begin. You can then read and use those ideas you deem to be most appropriate.

CHAPTER 1

Encouraging a Love of Reading

Overview

One of the primary goals of a reading program is to foster a love of reading in students. Students who want to read and choose to read will become life-long readers. Reading motivation is also important because students who are motivated to read become better readers (Taylor, Frye, & Maruyama, 1990). However, instilling a positive attitude toward reading and stimulating the desire to read are formidable challenges. Teachers often become perplexed and frustrated when they attempt to find techniques and strategies that will encourage students to read books and other types of printed materials.

It may not be possible to turn every student into an avid reader (Harris & Sipay, 1990), but we believe one reason why some students don't choose to read is the way students have been turned or directed toward reading. Many teachers have neglected encouraging a love of reading in the past. Currently, however, teachers believe that creating an interest in reading is a top priority item (O'Flavahan, Gambrell, Guthrie, Stahl, & Alvermann, 1992).

There are many ways that teachers can create an interest in reading in their students (Gambrell, 1996). First, teachers must be an explicit reading model. Teachers need to model for their students a genuine love of reading and a desire to read. They can model their love of reading in many ways. Teachers can discuss books they have read for personal enjoyment; they can discuss their reading habits (e.g., reading before bedtime); and they can tell their students about authors they particularly enjoy. Teachers should also read with their class during silent reading time, however, merely seeing the teacher reading isn't enough. Teachers also need to exhibit a passion for reading.

Another way teachers can create an interest in reading is to have a book-rich reading environment where students can have choices about what they read. Students are more likely to read if books are present in the classroom. When students have many books available, they can find books that interest them among the many selections. Teachers should use all available resources to create a classroom library so that students have easy accessibility of books. For those teachers who already have classroom libraries, Fractor, Woodruff, Martinez, and Teale (1993) recommend several ways to increase student use of libraries:

➤ Make the library a focal area that is private.

➤ Provide comfortable seating for five to ten students.

➤ Secure five to six books per student that represent various reading levels and genres.

➤ Organize the books into categories.

➤ Shelve books by spines and covers.

➤ Provide literature-oriented displays and props.

Finally, teachers should develop appropriate reading-related incentives. When students are eager to read, no special motivational strategies may be needed. The goal of a reading program is for reading to be rewarding rather than rewarded (Davis, 1994); however, using rewards and incentives may not negatively impact intrinsic motivation to read (Camerson & Pierce, 1994). Reading-related incentives should be used only when necessary and should be varied. The overuse of a particular reading incentive may lose its effectiveness. *Celebrate Reading: The Joy of Reading and Writing* (Johns, Davis, Barnhart, Moss, & Wheat, 1992) offers many suggestions that involve students in literacy activities.

For students to become effective, life-long readers, they must have both the *skill* and the *will* to read (Anderson, Heibert, Scott, & Wilkinson, 1985). Therefore, an important role of the teacher is to provide activities and strategies that encourage students to read. This chapter focuses on ways teachers can help students learn to enjoy reading, read more, and gain confidence in themselves as readers.

1.1 Negative Attitude Toward Reading

Behavior Observed	The student does not like to read or exhibits a negative attitude toward reading.
Anticipated Outcome	The student will gain a more positive attitude toward reading.

Perspective and Strategies

A student who does not like to read is usually—but not always—having difficulty with reading. When something is difficult, there seems to be a natural tendency to avoid or shy away from it. You can listen actively and observe to learn possible reasons for such behavior. These clues may provide a means of working *with* the student to explore ways of helping him or her. Although most teachers can readily observe this behavior, there are numerous surveys that may help assess a student's attitude toward reading. The Resources for Chapter 1 contain some attitude surveys for possible use or adaptation. These surveys may be used as pretests and posttests to help you evaluate the student's change in attitude after a plan of action has been implemented. The plan for improving students' attitudes toward reading is deceptively simple:

1. Gather information about the student's interests. Several possible interest surveys are included in Resources for Chapter 1. Once the student's major interests are identified, locate books and other reading materials that are *very easy* for the student to read.

2. Secure books containing jokes and riddles. They are often of interest to students of various ages. Offer such books to students and encourage the reading and sharing of jokes and riddles with other students.

3. Have students write, illustrate, and bind their own books. Good titles for books might be *All About Me* or *An Experience I Would Like to Have*. Write the stories on paper or use a computer. Let students illustrate their stories and share them with one another. Some students may prefer to illustrate their stories before they write or dictate them to help maintain the story line. Also, remember that some students may write more easily when topics are general and abstract. Provide this option.

4. Give positive reinforcement when the student reads. Encourage the student to share what was read.

5. Create a book nook where students can display their favorite books. Encourage students to make murals, pictures, or original book jackets to promote their books. Big pillows, bean-bag chairs, and so on, can help make the book nook inviting. Such activities may help reluctant readers realize that many of their peers enjoy reading.

6. Invite guest speakers to tell students how they use reading in jobs or everyday situations.

7. Model your love of reading to your students. Bring to class copies of books you read for pleasure and read aloud appropriate short sections from the books.

8. Invite a story teller to your classroom. Explain to students that before books were available, people shared stories by telling them to others. Discuss ways books have made stories accessible to more people.

9. Develop a system of individual rewards to help reinforce reading accomplished by the student. Use personal progress charts (see example) to help the student see the number of pages, chapters, stories, or books read. Give special emphasis to charts that permit **small** gains to show visible signs of progress.

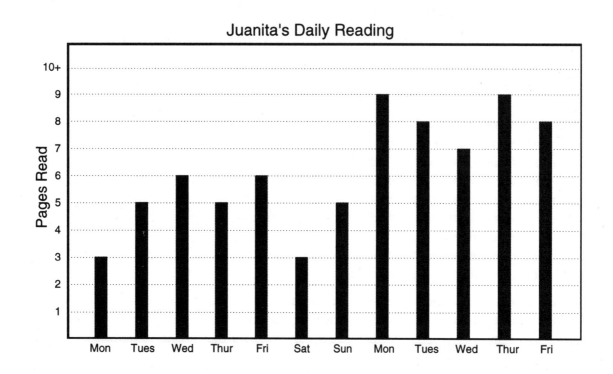

Juanita's Daily Reading

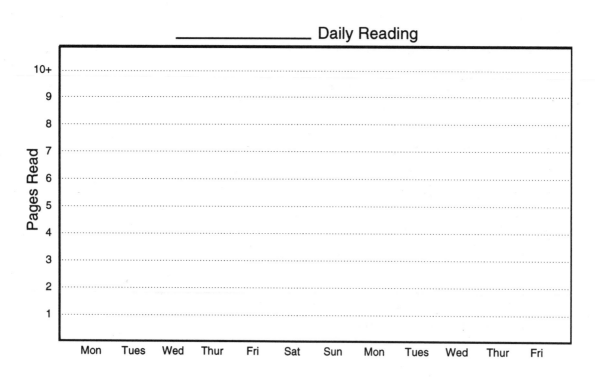

_____ Daily Reading

1.2   Lack of Confidence

Behavior Observed	The student lacks confidence in reading.
Anticipated Outcome	The student will gain greater confidence in reading.

Perspective and Strategies

Younger students may lack confidence in reading because there are many unknown words in their books. Older students, especially those who have experienced difficulty with reading, may have a fear of repeated failure. In both cases, students need to experience success with reading. The following strategies may prove useful.

1. The best way to instill confidence in the student is to ensure that the reading material is at the student's independent level. At this level the student should have no difficulty pronouncing words (1% error rate) or understanding the passage. In short, the independent level is that level at which the student can read fluently without teacher assistance.

2. Praise the student. Use positive reinforcement as much as possible. Encourage the student whenever he or she is reading.

3. Provide opportunities for the student to read and reread materials several times. Rereading material often provides the practice needed to make the reading more fluent. Resources for Chapter 3 contains a description of Structured Repeated Readings.

4. If the student appears to be overwhelmed by books, provide phrases, sentences, or short paragraphs that the student can read prior to attempting full-length passages or books. In addition, some teachers have found that converting basal readers, anthologies, or longer stories into small "books" can help build a student's confidence.

5. Use progress charts or visuals that show the student's gains in areas such as words known, strategies mastered, passages read, or books completed. Construct the charts or visuals in such a way that small gains reveal progress. This approach can be especially motivating if the student is invited to select a theme or format for the activity. For example, Juanita may put a jelly bean cut from construction paper in her drawn jar for each new word she has learned. The words can also be written on the jelly beans. You can also use student-decorated boxes for words learned.

6. Have the student prepare a story or book to be shared with a younger student or a small group of students. Allow time for previewing and practicing the selection to be read.

7. Have the student prepare a story or book to be read to another teacher, the school secretary, volunteers, or the principal. Encourage rereading of stories or books by having the student gather signatures from students, parents, or other adults (the principal, secretary, and so on) who have listened to the book being read.

8. Use pattern books to motivate students to write their own stories. A repeated phrase or theme can help students create stories. For example, a repeated pattern or sentence might be: "Little dog, little dog, why do you dig?" Students write the question and create a response. Students should try to think of several different responses to the questions. Appendix C contains a list of pattern books that may be useful for developing students' stories.

9. Encourage parents to reinforce any reading that is done at home.

10. Use a taped version of a book or story and have the student listen and follow along.

11. Employ choral reading activities to help students gain confidence in sharing a poem with the rest of the class.

12. Permit students to choose what they will read without coercion or encouragement from anyone.

13. Have a small microphone available for students to use to read a book to the class. Have students practice reading a book several times, and then give them the opportunity to go "on stage."

1.3   Self-Concept

Behavior Observed	The student has a poor self-concept.
Anticipated Outcome	The student will acquire a more positive self-concept as a reader.

Perspective and Strategies

Students with positive self-concepts generally have a high motivation to read (Henk & Melnick, 1995). These students are accepted by their peers, and they can adapt to new situations. They also have good feelings about themselves in the physical and cognitive areas. Experiences at home, at school, and with peer groups all influence the student's self-concept. Within the classroom, you may find the following strategies useful.

1. Ensure successful learning experiences in the classroom. Try to avoid experiences that cause excessive anxiety on the part of the student. Provide successful experiences in reading and related areas.

2. Try to capitalize on the student's strengths to improve weaknesses by highlighting abilities during lessons. For example, a lesson on context could integrate the student's phonic abilities in helping to identify unknown words.

3. Separate a student's behavior from the person he or she is. Stress that each student is a unique and valuable person even though some actions or behavior may not be accepted in the classroom.

4. Provide the student with role models for reading by inviting parents, relatives, and community leaders to share the joys reading has given them. Share portions of *Voices of Readers: How We Come to Love Books* (Carlsen & Sherrill, 1988) or *Books I Read When I Was Young* (Cullinan & Weiss, 1980). The latter contains the favorite books of famous people (such as Maya Angelou, Ray Bradbury, Bill Cosby, Bruce Jenner, Jacqueline Onassis, Charles M. Schulz, Neil Simon, Abigail Van Buren [Dear Abby], and Paul Zindel).

5. Display pictures of the students, their names, birthdays, and other interesting information on a bulletin board. Highlight this information whenever possible.

6. Develop a unit titled "All About Me" that includes a class chart of birthdays and ages. Graphs may be made for family members, pets, favorite foods, colors, games, and the like. See section 8.6 for ideas on how to create graphs.

7. Make every day or week someone's "Special Time." The "special" student gets to put a sticker by his or her name, sit in the special rocking chair, be responsible for the calendar, weather chart, attendance slip, and serve as the leader all day. A note is sent home to parents informing them of the event.

8. Begin each day with time for each student to tell about something that has happened to him or her. Complete a sentence such as "I like... ," "I wish... ," "For breakfast I had...." These sentences, if written, can be illustrated and bound into a book for the classroom library.

9. Set up a time when the student can read to younger students.

10. Have a "Student of the Week" bulletin board. Draw a different student's name each week. The student may bring in pictures to put on the bulletin board: family members, vacations, himself or herself as a baby, and pets. Also, help the student write about himself or herself, such as favorite games, important birthdays, or information about family members.

11. Invite an older student to prepare a story for a kindergarten class. Repeat this process several times. Alphabet books make an easy first step. A list of alphabet books that may be useful for this activity is found in Appendix B.

12. Use books with rhyming language, plenty of repetition, and predictable sequences. If the books are used orally, encourage the students to say the familiar lines. Appendix C contains a list of pattern books.

13. Remember the positive influence of the student's friends. "My friends were really the push I had for reading. My best friend read the encyclopedias for fun! She introduced me to many high-brow books and poetry. I imagine we were some of the few seventh graders that had read *Candide* twice" (Carlsen & Sherrill, 1988, p. 72).

14. Decorate a cardboard box as a book box. Put classroom-made books into the book box. Invite students to read these books to a selected audience such as the principal, the students' friends, or their family.

15. Try book stacking with students who have a poor self-concept about reading. Place a stack of five or six books that are very easy to read on each student's desk. When students come into the classroom, ask them to begin reading the stack of books in order. Allow time for students to read all of the books.

1.4   Lack of Motivation

Behavior Observed	The student can read but chooses not to read.
Anticipated Outcome	The student will become more motivated to read and will begin to choose reading as an activity.

Perspective and Strategies

Students who can read but who do so infrequently may be called *reluctant* or *aliterate* readers. Such readers generally comprise two groups. One group is composed of students who are not particularly good readers. They can read but they are reading below grade level; moreover, they do not appear interested in improving their reading. Instead, they prefer to watch television and to participate in activities that do not involve reading.

The second group of reluctant readers comprises students who can read quite well but who choose not to read. These students are reading at or above grade level; however, they are not apt to read in their spare time. Reading does not provide the same satisfaction as nonreading activities. Such students frequently appear to their teachers as bored or apathetic.

To encourage reluctant readers, it may be helpful to consider two types of motivation: natural (intrinsic) and artificial (extrinsic). Reluctant readers, by definition, possess little natural or intrinsic motivation to interact with books and other reading materials. Whatever the causes, these students have become indifferent or antagonistic toward reading. Because many reluctant readers possess little or no intrinsic motivation for reading, one of the central tasks of teachers is to use techniques to bring students and books together.

Extrinsic motivation may be needed because reluctant readers have not, on their own, found much satisfaction in reading. Teachers must, therefore, develop strategies that move these students toward books in order to gain a tangible reward. As reading becomes a more pleasant and satisfying experience, it is hoped that extrinsic motivation will be replaced with natural or intrinsic motivation to read. The teacher who seeks to motivate the reluctant reader is consciously trying to change the student's behavior and attitude toward reading from one of apathy to one of self-satisfaction and involvement. The teacher should also use techniques that will encourage the student to view reading as an activity that merits his or her time and energy. The following strategies should be useful.

1. Conduct individual conferences with students to reveal possible interests that can be used to motivate reading. When students find or are given books that interest them, their apathy can be transformed into delight, self-satisfaction, and eagerness. Several such experiences may help promote self-confidence and an "I can" attitude. Success breeds success.

2. Provide a wide variety of reading materials. Paperback books, magazines, newspapers, and high-interest, low-vocabulary materials often help motivate students to read.

3. Design attractive book displays and bulletin boards with information about books and authors. Students may find something that interests them. Share author talks or audio tapes.

4. Read orally to students. Such reading may pique students' interests and encourage them to read independently. Introduce a new book periodically and read only the beginning to students or highlight interesting chapters. This procedure may entice a reluctant reader to borrow the featured book.

5. Provide reading corners with comfortable cushions, a rug, bean-bag chairs, or a couch. Students can plan and decorate the area. Use cardboard boxes of various sizes or boards and bricks as bookshelves.

6. Bring in thought-provoking objects that will stimulate questions and prompt students' desire to read books about specific topics. Many such objects can be found in closets and other storage areas.

7. Use appropriate popular music to inspire interest in reading by having students write down and examine the lyrics. Use the lyrics for discussions and lessons.

8. Provide periods of time for independent silent reading so students can interact directly with printed material of their own choice. Silent reading has been introduced to students using acronyms. Numerous examples follow:

SSR	Sustained Silent Reading
RIP	Read in Peace
DEAR	Drop Everything and Read
SQUIRT	Sustained Quiet Uninterrupted Independent Reading Time
RABBIT	Read a Book Because It's There
WALTER	We All Like the Extra Reading
SURE	Sustained Uninterrupted Reading Enjoyment
GRAB	Go Read a Book
FRED	Free Reading Every Day
WAR	We All Read
RINGO	Reading Is Now Going On
RIOT	Reading Is Our Thing
OSCAR	Our School Cares About Reading
GRINCH	Good Reading Is Now Coming Here
RIBET	Reading Is Bringing Everyone Together
SUPER	Silent Undisturbed Private Entertainment Reading
FRISBEE	Free Reading in School by Everyone Everywhere
SAFARI	Students and Faculty All Read Independently
ZYLAR	Zip Your Lips and Read

9. Encourage parents to set aside a few minutes each day when everyone in the family reads self-selected material. The program could be called FRED: Family Reading Every Day.

10. A reluctant reader may be motivated to read materials designed to help him or her accomplish a task of interest (for instance, model building or cooking).

11. Emphasize the practical nature of reading. For example, an older student may be motivated to read a driver's manual if he or she hopes to obtain a driver's license. Younger students can be encouraged to read environmental print.

12. Show enthusiasm for reading. Perhaps the most important ingredient in motivating the reluctant reader is your own attitude toward books and reading. Your enthusiasm for reading may naturally be passed on to the students.

13. For a set period of time (six to eight weeks), hold a weekly reading challenge. Brainstorm with your students ideas for topics of reading that are interesting to the students. Topics that work well are sports, animals, fantasy stories, and so on. Have students read books about the class topics. Keep track of the books the students have read for each topic on a bulletin board.

14. Have a reading riot. In the center of the room, place many easy reading books. Have two or three students come to the pile of books and, in 30 seconds, choose one book to read. After each student has a book, give them time to read.

15. Stress the idea that reading is a fun activity.

1.5 Limited Interests

Behavior Observed	The student's reading always seems to focus on a particular topic.
Anticipated Outcome	The student will expand his or her interests in reading.

Perspective and Strategies

Some students seem to go through phases in their reading. One student may read nothing but mysteries; another student may seem to be infatuated with stories about animals. Such students often frustrate teachers who believe that students' interests and tastes should be balanced. Consider the following:

1. Rejoice in the fact that the student is receiving satisfaction from reading. Do your best to help the student find books of interest. Sooner or later, interests will be directed toward related areas or completely new areas. When this occurs, be ready to help the student find books that will satisfy the emerging interest area.

2. To help expand interests, invite community members to share their special interests, hobbies, or experiences. Try to link their sharing to books available in the school or classroom library.

3. Provide plenty of reading material that varies in difficulty, content, and genre.

4. Poll students to determine their major interests and create numerous reading experiences in these areas.

5. Read to students daily. Select a wide variety of material from various genres. Assist students who would like other books similar in nature to the one you have read to them. Perhaps they would like a different book by the same author. Encourage book-sharing ideas among classmates. Introduce a "book of the week" or an "author of the week" (or month).

6. Use movies, filmstrips, photographs, videotapes, and concrete objects to help stimulate an interest in different subjects. Secure books or other reading material that relate to these subjects, and have the material available for the students to read.

7. If available, local authors can be invited to talk about books they have written. Parents can also be invited into the classroom to share the kinds of materials they like to read.

8. Develop a paperback book exchange in the classroom.

9. Encourage students to follow up on their natural curiosity by brainstorming a list of interests that students have. Then conduct a search of books at the students' grade level that would support the students' interest. Staple the lists inside the students' reading folders, and invite students to read at least two books from each list.

10. Have students from other classes or schools at your grade level develop a list of their top 20 books. Share each class's list with other participating classes. Post the lists in a prominent place and encourage your students to read books from each list.

11. Decorate a box to place in your room that you can use as a Suggestion Box. Invite students to think about topics that interest them and have them list the ideas on an index card. Then have them drop the card in the Suggestion Box. Explain that any time students have ideas about books they would like to read, they should write the ideas on a card and drop it in the box. Use the suggestions students submit to guide your choices of read alouds and book talks. See Chapter 6 for ideas on book talks.

12. Guide students in monitoring their reading choices. Ideas for monitoring reading choices can be found in Chapter 6.

1.6   Limited Reading Outside of School

Behavior Observed	The student does little or no reading outside of school.
Anticipated Outcome	The student will do more reading outside the classroom.

Perspective and Strategies

The amount of reading students do out of school is positively related to their reading achievement. "Yet, students report relatively little reading out of school" (Foertsch, 1992, p. 5). By high school, according to national statistics, 29% to 30% of students report that they never read for fun in their spare time (Foertsch, 1992).

A successful approach to encouraging outside reading often begins by helping students become aware of the pleasure and satisfaction that can be attained from reading. Selected classroom activities and strategies listed earlier in this chapter may be a useful beginning. The following ideas may also be helpful:

1. Invite parents, other adults, older students, and possibly published authors to come, read, and share their enthusiasm about books.

2. Maintain a well-stocked classroom library in which the books and other reading materials are rotated regularly. Involve students in setting up the library and developing a system to check out the materials. Encourage students to check out books, brochures, magazines, and related items to be taken home.

3. Send home material to parents that informs them of the importance of modeling reading *and* reading to their children. Personalized lists of possible books for reading can also be sent home to parents. See Chapter 9 for parent letters you can use.

4. Encourage parents to do a project with their children where some directions need to be read in order to complete the project.

5. Maintain dialogue journals with students that focus on reading the student is doing outside of class.

6. Spend time talking with and observing the student in order to determine interests. Then tap into those interests when reading books or recommending possible books for outside reading.

7. Send home, on a rotating basis, a soft quilted bag (or backpack) with a stuffed animal and book of the student's choosing. Make sure parents know in advance about this procedure and why it is being done. The next day the student can conference with you and tell how reading to the stuffed animal went. A home backpack with a book and possible activities can also be circulated among the students.

8. Display, in a place of prominence for several days, books that a particular student enjoys. Encourage other students to interview the chosen student, and make the books available for check out.

9. Encourage students to participate in one of the currently popular book clubs.

10. Secure books with audiotapes and make them available for home use.

11. Encourage reluctant readers to help develop a bulletin board that features topics on subjects they enjoy. These students and others could then try to locate reading materials on these subjects. Provide titles and/or create a display of relevant materials.

12. Encourage students to make their own books and circulate them within the classroom. Students can also check these books out of the classroom library.

13. Have students look in the library for the "ugliest" book cover they can find (at their appropriate level). It will probably be very old, but good (for example, *Homer Price* by McCloskey, 1943). The student then reads the book at home and decides on a "new cover" to spice up the book. The design is the student's. The name of the author of the book must remain the same, but "new cover by _____ _____" can be added. When the cover is completed, have a contest and let the class vote to select the best covers. Put the books in your class library where your students have the first opportunity to check them out. Then place them in your school library again so other students check them out.

14. Initiate a "Family Read Aloud" program. Encourage the family to pick a book at the child's level and set time aside, either at night or on the weekend, when the whole family sits down together and reads the book. Encourage discussion and possible extension activities.

15. Have students list the kinds of reading that their family does. Then have students interview each family member who can read and ask them about types of reading material that they usually read. Reading material may include things like cook books, car manuals, labels on cans, magazines, newspapers, and so on. Have students bring their lists to school and compile a master list of things people read. Post the list in a prominent place in the classroom.

16. Have each student bring three kinds of reading materials to school. These materials may include coffee mugs, T-shirts, cereal boxes and so on. Have students place their reading materials on a large table. Guide students to think about their various reading experiences outside school.

17. Try lots of different things and, when something works, capitalize on it.

Resources for Chapter 1

Interest Inventories

➤ About Me

➤ News About Me

➤ Inventory of Experiences

➤ Sentence Completion Test

Reading Attitude Inventories

➤ Reading Attitude Surveys: Primary and Intermediate Levels

➤ Self-Report Reading Scale

➤ Elementary Reading Attitude Survey

➤ Motivation to Read Profile: Reading Survey

➤ Motivation to Read Profile: Conversational Interview

➤ What Are Some of Your Ideas About Reading?

➤ Rhody Secondary Reading Attitude Assessment

Teacher Resources

➤ Attitudinal Scale for Parents

➤ Checklist for Student's Attitudes and Personal Reading

About Me

1. My name is _____

   _____

2. I like to _____

   _____

3. I feel good when _____

   _____

4. I feel happy when _____

   _____

5. I feel important when _____

   _____

6. I worry when _____

   _____

7. I don't like to _____

   _____

8. I don't like it when _____

   _____

9. I think _____

   _____

10. I would like to be _____

    _____

11. Some of my favorite things are _____

    _____

12. My favorite TV shows are _____

    _____

13. Reading is _____

    _____

News About Me

A News Story About _____
(write your name here)

News About My Family

I have _____ brothers and sisters.

They are _____ years old.

I like to play with _____ .

My mother and I like to _____ .

My father and I like to _____ .

I (like/do not like) to play alone.

I help at home by _____ .

The thing I like to do at home is _____

_____ .

News About My Pets

I have a pet _____ .

I (do/do not) take care of my pet.

I do not have a pet because _____

_____ .

I would like to have a pet _____ .

News About My Books and My Reading

I like to read about _____

_____ .

The best book I ever read was_____

_____ .

I (do get/do not get) books from the library.

I have _____ books of my own at home.

I read aloud to _____ .

My _____ reads to me.

News About My Friends

My best friend is _____ .

I like (him/her) because _____

_____ .

We play _____ .

I would rather play (at my house/at my friend's house) because _____

_____ .

News About Things I Like and Dislike

I do not like _____ .

I like _____ .

I am afraid of _____ .

I am not afraid of _____ .

News About My Wishes

When I grow up, I want to be _____

_____

_____ .

If I could have three wishes I would wish

(1) _____

_____ .

(2) _____

_____ .

(3) _____

_____

_____ .

From Jerry L. Johns and Susan Davis Lenski, *Improving Reading: A Handbook of Strategies* (2nd ed.). Copyright © 1997 Kendall/Hunt Publishing Company (1-800-228-0810). May be reproduced for noncommercial educational purposes.

News About My Travels and Adventures

I have traveled by:

_____ bus	_____ car
_____ airplane	_____ truck
_____ boat	_____ train
_____ bicycle	_____ van

I have visited these interesting places:

_____ circus	_____ zoo
_____ farm	_____ park
_____ hotel	_____ museum
_____ bakery	_____ library
_____ airport	_____ fire station

_____ factory, and_____ .

The best adventure I ever had was __

_____ .

News About My School Subjects

My favorite subject is _____ .

The subject I dislike most is _____ .

I am best at _____ .

I wish I was better in_____ .

News About My Hobbies and Collections

One of my best hobbies is _____

_____ .

I collect _____ .

I want to collect _____ .

My other hobbies are _____

_____ .

Movie, Radio, and Television Favorites

I see _____ movies each week.

I like to listen to _____ on the radio.

I see _____ television programs a day.

My favorite programs are _____

_____ .

Write any other news about yourself below.

_____

_____

_____

_____

_____

_____

Inventory of Experiences

Name_____ Date _____

Special Interests

1. Which outdoor sports do you like?

2. Which indoor games do you like?

3. What types of collections or hobbies do you have?

4. Have you had classes or lessons in music, dancing, or art?

   Describe _____

5. Do you belong to any clubs or groups like 4-H or scouts?

   Describe _____

6. Do you have any pets?

7. What are your favorite TV programs? Movies?

8. What is your favorite subject at school?

9. What do you do with your free time?

10. Who are some of your best friends, and what do you enjoy doing with them?

Your Family

1. What are the names and ages of your brothers and sisters?

2. What are some things you do together?

3. Do you ever go places or play games with your *entire* family?

4. What trips have you taken?

5. Do you receive an allowance or spending money from your parents?

6. Do you have some regular duties or chores to do at home?

You and Books

1. What books and magazines do you have at home?

2. Do you have a library card?

3. What kinds of books or stories do you like?

4. Do you like to have someone read to you?

5. Do you like to read to others?

From Jerry L. Johns and Susan Davis Lenski, *Improving Reading: A Handbook of Strategies* (2nd ed.). Copyright © 1997 Kendall/Hunt Publishing Company (1-800-228-0810). May be reproduced for noncommercial educational purposes.

Sentence Completion Test

> **Directions:**   I am going to begin certain sentences for you. I want you to finish each sentence with the first idea that comes to your mind.

1. My idea of a good time is _____.

2. When I have to read, I _____.

3. I wish my parents knew _____.

4. I can't understand why _____.

5. I wish teachers _____.

6. I wish my mother _____.

7. People think I _____.

8. I especially like to read about _____.

9. To me, homework _____.

10. I hope I'll never _____.

11. I wish people wouldn't _____.

12. When I finish school, _____.

13. When I take my report card home, _____.

14. Most brothers and sisters _____.

15. I feel proud when _____.

16. I wish my father _____.

17. I like to read when _____.

18. I am really interested in _____.

19. I often worry about _____.

20. I wish someone would help me _____.

From Boning, T., & Boning, R. (1975). I'd rather read than… . *The Reading Teacher, 10*(7), 196–200.

Reading Attitude Surveys:
Primary and Intermediate Levels

Jerry L. Johns

Purpose

To acquire a qualitative idea of a student's attitude toward reading.

Administration

1. Select the appropriate attitude survey and reproduce sufficient copies. "Reading and Me" is intended for students through the third grade. "My Ideas About Reading" can be used with students above the third grade.

2. Emphasize that responses will permit students to share their feelings about reading. Encourage students to make each item reflect their genuine or real feelings.

3. Read each of the statements aloud and allow students sufficient time to circle their responses.

Scoring and Interpretation

1. Students are given one point for each item according to the key below.

Reading and Me				*My Ideas about Reading*			
1.	yes	6.	no	1.	yes	6.	yes
2.	yes	7.	yes	2.	no	7.	yes
3.	yes	8.	yes	3.	yes	8.	no
4.	no	9.	no	4.	yes	9.	no
5.	no	10.	yes	5.	no	10.	yes

2. Total the student's points. The higher the total, the more positive the student's attitude.

3. Supplement the student's score with relevant observations.

4. Record scores and observations on the class record sheet.

5. Use of the scale at the beginning and near the end of the school year will provide an opportunity to evaluate a student's changes in attitudes toward reading.

Reading and Me

Jerry L. Johns

Name _____

Date _____

Teacher _____

Directions: The 10 statements that follow will be read to you. After each statement is read, circle either yes or no, depending on what you believe.

Yes   No   1. I can read as fast as good readers.

Yes   No   2. I like to read.

Yes   No   3. I like to read long stories.

Yes   No   4. The books I read in school are too hard.

Yes   No   5. I need more help in reading.

Yes   No   6. I worry quite a bit about my reading in school.

Yes   No   7. I read at home.

Yes   No   8. I would rather read than watch television.

Yes   No   9. I am not a very good reader.

Yes   No   10. I like my parents to read to me.

My Ideas About Reading

Jerry L. Johns

Name _____

Date _____

Teacher _____

| **Directions:** | The 10 statements that follow will be read to you. After each statement is read, circle the response that tells what you feel or believe. |

Agree ? Disagree   1. Reading is a good way to spend spare time.

Agree ? Disagree   2. Most books are too long and dull.

Agree ? Disagree   3. There should be more free reading in school.

Agree ? Disagree   4. Reading is as important as watching television.

Agree ? Disagree   5. Reading is boring.

Agree ? Disagree   6. Reading is rewarding to me.

Agree ? Disagree   7. I think reading is fun.

Agree ? Disagree   8. Teachers ask me to read books that are too hard.

Agree ? Disagree   9. I am not a very good reader.

Agree ? Disagree   10. My parents spend quite a bit of time reading.

Class Summary Sheet for Reading Attitude Survey

Jerry L. Johns

Teacher _____ Grade _____ School _____

| Student | Date Administered _____ | | Date Administered _____ | |
	Score	Comments	Score	Comments

Self-Report Reading Scale

Beatrice Dubnow and Martin H. Jason

Purpose

To help measure elementary students' self-perceptions of their reading abilities.

Administration

1. Reproduce the scale.

2. Explain how students should mark their answers. Because words above the third-grade reading level were not included in the items, most students should be able to complete the scale independently. For younger or less able readers, read the items aloud.

Scoring and Interpretation

1. Students are given one point for each item to which they give an answer representing a positive self-perception. Use the key that follows.

1.	No	12.	Yes
2.	No	13.	Yes
3.	Yes	14.	No
4.	No	15.	Yes
5.	Yes	16.	Yes
6.	No	17.	No
7.	Yes	18.	Yes
8.	No	19.	No
9.	Yes	20.	No
10.	Yes	21.	Yes
11.	No	22.	Yes

2. The student's total score is a qualitative self-perception of his or her reading abilities.

3. Teachers can use the results to help plan intervention strategies.

Self-Report Reading Scale

Please Print

Name _____ Boy ❑ Girl ❑

School _____

Room _____ Grade _____

Today's Date _____
                       Year   Month   Day

Date of Birth _____
                       Year   Month   Day

What to do:
1. These are sentences about reading.
2. Read each sentence and make an ⓧ in the Yes or No box.
3. There are no right or wrong answers. Just mark the way you feel about each one.

---

1. I can do better in my other school work than I can in reading. Yes ❑ No ❑

2. There are too many hard words for me to learn in the stories I read. Yes ❑ No ❑

3. If I took a reading test, I would do all right on it. Yes ❑ No ❑

4. In school I wish I could be a much better reader than I am. Yes ❑ No ❑

5. I can help other pupils in my class to read because I'm a good reader. Yes ❑ No ❑

6. If reading gets too hard for me, I feel like not trying to read anymore. Yes ❑ No ❑

7. Most of the time I can read the same books as well as the good readers. Yes ❑ No ❑

8. When I read in school, I worry a lot about how well I'm doing. Yes ❑ No ❑

9. Most of the time when I see a new word, I can sound it out by myself. Yes ❑ No ❑

10. I can read as well as the best readers. Yes ❑ No ❑

11. Most of the time I feel I need help when I read in school.   Yes ❑   No ❑

12. If my teacher called on me to read to the class, I would do well.   Yes ❑   No ❑

13. I can read as fast as the good readers.   Yes ❑   No ❑

14. Most of the things I read in school are too hard.   Yes ❑   No ❑

15. Pupils in my class think I'm a good reader.   Yes ❑   No ❑

16. Most of the time I can finish my reading work.   Yes ❑   No ❑

17. Most of the time I feel afraid to read to the class.   Yes ❑   No ❑

18. I can read a long story as well as a short one.   Yes ❑   No ❑

19. It's hard for me to answer questions about the main idea of a story.   Yes ❑   No ❑

20. Most of the time I feel I will never be a good reader in school.   Yes ❑   No ❑

21. My teacher thinks I'm a good reader.   Yes ❑   No ❑

22. 1 know what most of the hard words mean when I read them.   Yes ❑   No ❑

For further information see Jason, M.H., & Dubnow, B. (1973). The relationship between self-perceptions of reading abilities and reading achievement. In W.H. MacGinitie (Ed.), *Assessment problems in reading* (pp. 96–101). Newark, DE: International Reading Association.

Elementary Reading Attitude Survey

Michael C. McKenna and Dennis J. Kear

Purpose

To provide a quick indication of student attitudes toward reading.

Administration

1. Reproduce the survey

2. Tell students that you wish to find out how they feel about reading. Emphasize that this is *not* a test and that there are no "right" or "wrong" answers. Encourage sincerity.

3. Distribute the survey forms and, if you wish to monitor the attitudes of specific students, ask them to write their names in the space at the top. Hold up a copy of the survey so that the students can see the first page. Point to the picture of Garfield at the far left of the first item. Ask the students to look at this same picture on their own survey form. Discuss with them the mood Garfield seems to be in (very happy). Then move to the next picture and again discuss Garfield's mood (this time, a little happy). In the same way, move to the third and fourth pictures and talk about Garfield's moods—a little upset and very upset. It is helpful to point out the position of Garfield's *mouth,* especially in the middle two figures.

4. Explain that together you will read some statements about reading and that the students should think about how they feel about each statement. They should then circle the picture of Garfield that is closest to their own feelings. (Emphasize that the students should respond according to their own feelings, not as Garfield might respond!) Read each item aloud slowly and distinctly; then read it a second time while students are thinking. Be sure to read the item *number* and to remind students of page numbers when new pages are reached.

Scoring and Interpretation

1. To score the survey, count four points for each leftmost (happiest) Garfield circle, three for each slightly smiling Garfield, two for each mildly upset Garfield, and one point for each very upset (rightmost) Garfield. Three scores for each student can be obtained: the total for the first 10 items, the total for the second 10, and a composite total. The first half of the survey relates to attitude toward recreational reading; the second half relates to attitude toward academic aspects of reading.

2. You can interpret scores in two ways. One is to note informally where the score falls in regard to the four points of the scale. A total score of 50, for example, would fall about midway on the scale, between the slightly happy and slightly upset figures, therefore indicating a relatively indifferent overall attitude toward reading. The other approach is more formal. It involves converting the raw scores into percentile ranks by means of the table. Be sure to use the norms for the right grade level and to note the column headings (Rec = recreational reading, Aca = academic reading, Tot = total score). If you wish to determine the average percentile rank for your class, average the raw scores first; then use the table to locate the percentile rank corresponding to the raw score mean. Percentile ranks cannot be averaged directly.

McKenna, M.C., & Kear, D.J. (1990). Measuring attitude toward reading: A new tool for teachers. *The Reading Teacher, 43*(9), 626–639. Reprinted with permission of Michael C. McKenna and the International Reading Association.

Elementary Reading Attitude Survey

School _____ Grade _____ Name_____

1. How do you feel when you read a book on a rainy Saturday?

2. How do you feel when you read a book in a school during free time?

3. How do you feel about reading for fun at home?

4. How do you feel about getting a book for a present?

5. How do you feel about spending free time reading?

6. How do you feel about starting a new book?

7. How do you feel about reading during summer?

8. How do you feel about reading instead of playing?

9. How do you feel about going to a bookstore?

10. How do you feel about reading different kinds of books?

11. How do you feel when the teacher asks you questions about what you read?

12. How do you feel about doing reading workbook pages and worksheets?

4

13. How do you feel about reading in school?

14. How do you feel about reading your school books?

15. How do you feel about learning from a book?

16. How do you feel when it's time for reading in class?

17. How do you feel about the stories you read in reading class?

GARFIELD: © 1978 United Feature Syndicate, Inc.

18. How do you feel when you read out loud in class?

19. How do you feel about using a dictionary?

20. How do you feel about taking a reading test?

©Paws, Inc. The GARFIELD character is incorporated in this test with the permission of Paws, Incorporated, and may be reproduced only in connection with the reproduction of the test in its entirety for classroom use prior to December 31, 1999, and any other reproduction or use without the express prior written consent of Paws are prohibited.

34

Elementary Reading Attitude Survey Scoring Sheet

Student Name _____

Teacher _____

Grade _____ Administration Date _____

```
┌────────────────────────────────────────┐
│              Scoring Guide               │
│   4  points    Happiest Garfield         │
│   3  points    Slightly smiling Garfield │
│   2  points    Mildly upset Garfield     │
│   1  point     Very upset Garfield       │
└────────────────────────────────────────┘
```

Recreational reading   Academic reading

1. _____   11. _____

2. _____   12. _____

3. _____   13. _____

4. _____   14. _____

5. _____   15. _____

6. _____   16. _____

7. _____   17. _____

8. _____   18. _____

9. _____   19. _____

10. _____   20. _____

Raw score: _____   Raw score: _____

Total raw score (Recreational + Academic): _____

Percentile Ranks

Recreational ┌──────────┐
              │   │
Academic   ├──────────┤
              │   │
Full scale   └──────────┘

From Jerry L. Johns and Susan Davis Lenski, *Improving Reading: A Handbook of Strategies* (2nd ed.). Copyright © 1997 Kendall/Hunt Publishing Company (1-800-228-0810). May be reproduced for noncommercial educational purposes.

Norms for the Elementary Reading Attitude Survey

To create norms for the interpretation of the Elementary Reading Attitude Survey scores, a large-scale study was conducted in late January, 1989, at which time the survey was administered to 18,138 students in Grades 1–6. Several steps were taken to achieve a sample that was sufficiently stratified (that is, reflective of the American population) to allow confident generalizations. Children were drawn from 95 school districts in 38 U.S. states. The number of girls exceeded by only 5 the number of boys. Ethnic distribution of the sample was also close to that of the U.S. population in 1989. The proportion of Blacks (9.5%) was within 3% of the national proportion, whereas the proportion of Hispanics (6.2%) was within 2%.

Percentile ranks at each grade for both subscales and the full scale are presented in the table. These data can be used to compare individual students' scores with the national sample and they can be interpreted like achievement-test percentile ranks.

Table. Mid-Year Percentile Ranks by Grade and Scale

Raw Score	Grade 1			Grade 2			Grade 3			Grade 4			Grade 5			Grade 6		
	Rec	Aca	Tot	Rec	Aca	Tot	Rec	Ac	Tot	Rec	Aca	Tot	Rec	Aca	Tot	Rec	Aca	Tot
80			99			99			99			99			99			99
79			95			96			98			99			99			99
78			93			95			97			98			99			99
77			92			94			97			98			99			99
76			90			93			96			97			98			99
75			88			92			95			96			98			99
74			86			90			94			95			97			99
73			84			88			92			94			97			98
72			82			86			91			93			96			98
71			80			84			89			91			95			97
70			78			82			86			89			94			96
69			75			79			84			88			92			95
68			72			77			81			86			91			93
67			69			74			79			83			89			92
66			66			71			76			50			87			90
65			62			69			73			78			84			88
64			59			66			70			75			82			86
63			55			63			67			72			79			84
62			52			60			64			69			76			82
61			49			57			61			66			73			79
60			46			54			58			62			70			76
59			43			51			55			59			67			73
58			40			47			51			56			64			69
57			37			45			48			53			61			68
56			34			41			44			48			57			62
55			31			38			41			45			53			58
54			28			35			38			41			50			55
53			25			32			34			38			46			52
52			22			29			31			35			42			48
51			20			26			28			32			39			44
50			18			23			25			28			36			40
49			15			20			23			26			33			37
48			13			18			20			23			29			33
47			12			15			17			20			26			30
46			10			13			15			18			23			27
45			8			11			13			16			20			25
44			7			9			11			13			17			22
43			6			8			9			12			15			20
42			5			7			9			10			13			17
41			5			6			7			9			12			15
40	99	99	4	99	99	5	99	99	6	99	99	7	99	99	10	99	99	13
39	92	91	3	94	94	4	96	97	5	97	98	6	98	99	9	99	99	12
38	89	88	3	92	92	2	94	95	4	95	97	5	96	98	8	97	99	10
37	86	85	2	88	89	2	90	93	3	92	95	4	94	98	7	95	99	8
36	81	79	2	84	85	2	87	91	2	88	93	3	91	96	6	92	98	7
35	77	75	1	79	81	1	81	88	2	84	90	3	87	95	4	88	97	6
34	72	69	1	74	78	1	75	83	2	78	87	2	82	93	4	83	95	5
33	65	63	1	68	73	1	69	79	1	72	83	2	77	90	3	79	93	4
32	58	58	1	62	67	1	63	74	1	66	79	1	71	86	3	74	91	3
31	52	53	1	56	62	1	57	69	0	60	75	1	65	82	2	69	87	2
30	44	49	1	50	57	0	51	63	0	54	70	1	59	77	1	63	82	2
29	38	44	0	44	51	0	45	58	0	47	64	1	53	71	1	58	78	1
28	32	39	0	37	46	0	38	52	0	41	58	1	48	66	1	51	73	1
27	26	34	0	31	41	0	33	47	0	35	52	1	42	60	1	46	67	1
26	21	30	0	25	37	0	26	41	0	29	46	0	36	54	0	39	60	1
25	17	25	0	20	32	0	21	36	0	23	40	0	30	49	0	34	54	0
24	12	21	0	15	27	0	17	31	0	19	35	0	25	42	0	29	49	0
23	9	18	0	11	23	0	13	26	0	14	29	0	20	37	0	24	42	0
22	7	14	0	8	18	0	9	22	0	11	25	0	16	31	0	19	36	0
21	5	11	0	6	15	0	6	18	0	9	20	0	13	26	0	15	30	0
20	4	9	0	4	11	0	5	14	0	6	16	0	10	21	0	12	24	0
19	2	7		2	8		3	11		5	13		7	17		10	20	
18	2	5		2	6		2	8		3	9		6	13		8	15	
17	1	4		1	5		1	5		2	7		4	9		6	11	
16	1	3		1	3		1	4		2	5		3	6		4	8	
15	0	2		0	2		0	3		1	3		2	4		3	6	
14	0	2		0	1		0	1		1	2		1	2		1	3	
13	0	1		0	1		0	1		0	1		1	2		1	2	
12	0	1		0	0		0	0		0	1		0	1		0	1	
11	0	0		0	0		0	0		0	0		0	0		0	0	
10	0	0		0	0		0	0		0	0		0	0		0	0	

Motivation to Read Profile: Reading Survey

Linda B. Gambrell, Barbara Martin Palmer, Rose Marie Codling, and Susan Anders Mazzoni

Purpose

To assess students' self-concepts as readers and the value they place on reading.

Administration

1. Reproduce and distribute copies of the Motivation to Read Profile (MRP).

2. Ask students to write their names in the space provided.

3. Say the following:

    I am going to read some sentences to you. I want to know how you feel about your reading. There are no right or wrong answers, so tell me honestly what you think. I will read each sentence twice. Do not mark your answer until I tell you to. The first time I read the sentence I want you to think about the best answer for you. The second time I read the sentence I want you to fill in the space beside your best answer. Mark only one answer.

Scoring and Interpretation

1. The survey has 20 items based on a 4-point scale. the highest possible score is 80 points. On some items the response options are ordered from least positive to most positive, with the least positive response option having a value of 1 point and the most postiive option have a point value of 4.

2. To assign points for questions 2, 3, 6, 9, 12, 13, 14, 16, 17, and 19, use the scale from 1 to 4 as in the following example:

    > 2. Reading a book is something I like to do.
    > ☐ Never
    > ☐ Not very often
    > ☐ Sometimes
    > ■ Often

If students chose the first answer, give it 1 point.
If students chose the second answer, give it 2 points.
If students chose the third answer, give it 3 points.
If students chose the fourth answer, give it 4 points.

3. On other items, the response options are reversed. These items are 1, 4, 5, 7, 8, 10, 11, 15, 18, 20. For those items recode the responses by reversing the points as in the following example:

> 2. My friends think I am _____.
> ☐ a very good reader
> ■ a good reader
> ☐ an OK reader
> ☐ a poor reader

If students chose the first answer, give it 4 points.
If students chose the second answer, give it 3 points.
If students chose the third answer, give it 2 points.
If students chose the fourth answer, give it 1 point.

4. To calculate the Self-Concept raw score and Value of Reading raw score, add all student responses in the respective columns. The raw score is obtained by combining the column raw scores. To convert the raw scores to percentage socres, divide student raw scores by the total possible score (40 for each subscale, 80 for the full survey).

Motivation to Read Profile: Reading Survey

Name_____ Date _____

Sample 1: I am in _____.
- ❑ Second grade   ❑ Fifth grade
- ❑ Third grade   ❑ Sixth grade
- ❑ Fourth grade

Sample 2: I am a _____.
- ❑ boy
- ❑ girl

1. My friends think I am _____.
   - ❑ a very good reader
   - ❑ a good reader
   - ❑ an OK reader
   - ❑ a poor reader

2. Reading a book is something I like to do.
   - ❑ Never
   - ❑ Not very often
   - ❑ Sometimes
   - ❑ Often

3. I read _____.
   - ❑ not as well as my friends
   - ❑ about the same as my friends
   - ❑ about the same as my friends
   - ❑ a lot better than my friends

4. My best friends think reading is _____.
   - ❑ really fun
   - ❑ fun
   - ❑ OK to do
   - ❑ no fun at all

5. When I come to a word I don't know, I can _____.
   - ❑ almost always figure it out
   - ❑ sometimes figure it out
   - ❑ almost never figure it out
   - ❑ never figure it out

Gambrell, L.B., Palmer, B.M., Codling, R.M., & Mazzoni, S.A. (1996). Assessing reading motivation. *The Reading Teacher,* *49*(7), 518-533.

6. I tell my friends about good books I read.
   ❑ I never do this.
   ❑ I almost never do this.
   ❑ I do this some of the time.
   ❑ I do this a lot.

7. When I am reading by myself, I understand _____.
   ❑ almost everything I read
   ❑ some of what I read
   ❑ almost none of what I read
   ❑ none of what I read

8. People who read a lot are _____.
   ❑ very interesting
   ❑ interesting
   ❑ not very interesting
   ❑ boring

9. I am _____.
   ❑ a poor reader
   ❑ an OK reader
   ❑ a good reader
   ❑ a very good reader

10. I think libraries are _____.
    ❑ a great place to spend time
    ❑ an interesting place to spend time
    ❑ an OK place to spend time
    ❑ a boring place to spend time

11. I worry about what other kids think about my reading _____.
    ❑ every day
    ❑ almost every day
    ❑ once in a while
    ❑ never

12. Knowing how to read well is _____.
    ❑ not very important
    ❑ sort of important
    ❑ important
    ❑ very important

Gambrell, L.B., Palmer, B.M., Codling, R.M., & Mazzoni, S.A. (1996). Assessing reading motivation. *The Reading Teacher,* *49*(7), 518-533.

13. When my teacher asks me a question about what I have read, I _____.
    ❏ can never think of an answer
    ❏ have trouble thinking of an answer
    ❏ sometimes think of an answer
    ❏ always think of an answer

14. I think reading is _____.
    ❏ a boring way to spend time
    ❏ an OK way to spend time
    ❏ an interesting way to spend time
    ❏ a great way to spend time

15. Reading is _____.
    ❏ very easy for me
    ❏ kind of easy for me
    ❏ kind of hard for me
    ❏ very hard for me

16. When I grow up I will spend _____.
    ❏ none of my time reading
    ❏ very little of my time reading
    ❏ some of my time reading
    ❏ a lot of my time reading

17. When I am in a group talking about stories, I _____.
    ❏ almost never talk about my ideas
    ❏ sometimes talk about my ideas
    ❏ almost always talk about my ideas
    ❏ always talk about my ideas

18. I would like for my teacher to read books out loud to the class _____.
    ❏ every day
    ❏ almost every day
    ❏ once in a while
    ❏ never

19. When I read out loud I am a _____.
    ❏ poor reader
    ❏ OK reader
    ❏ good reader
    ❏ very good reader

Gambrell, L.B., Palmer, B.M., Codling, R.M., & Mazzoni, S.A. (1996). Assessing reading motivation. *The Reading Teacher,* *49*(7), 518-533.

20. When someone gives me a book for a present, I feel _____.
- ❏ very happy
- ❏ sort of happy
- ❏ sort of unhappy
- ❏ unhappy

Gambrell, L.B., Palmer, B.M., Codling, R.M., & Mazzoni, S.A. (1996). Assessing reading motivation. *The Reading Teacher, 49*(7), 518-533.

MRP Reading Survey Scoring Sheet

Student Name _____

Grade _____ Teacher _____

Administration Date _____

Recoding Scale
1 = 4
2 = 3
3 = 2
4 = 1

Self-Concept as a Reader		**Value of Reading**	
*recode	1. ____		2. ____
	3. ____	*recode	4. ____
*recode	5. ____		6. ____
*recode	7. ____	*recode	8. ____
	9. ____	*recode	10. ____
*recode	11. ____		12. ____
	13. ____		14. ____
*recode	15. ____		16. ____
	17. ____	*recode	18. ____
	19. ____	*recode	20. ____

SC raw score: ____ /40   **V raw score:** ____ /40

Full survey raw score (Self-Concept & Value): ____ /80

Percentage scores   Self-Concept   [ ]

Value   [ ]

Full Survey   [ ]

Comments: _____

_____

_____

Gambrell, L.B., Palmer, B.M., Codling, R.M., & Mazzoni, S.A. (1996). Assessing reading motivation. *The Reading Teacher,* *49*(7), 518-533.

Motivation to Read Profile: Conversational Interview

Linda B. Gambrell, Barbara Martin Palmer, Rose Marie Codling, and Susan Anders Mazzoni

Purpose

To qualitatively assess students' self-concepts as readers and the value they place on reading.

Administration

1. Reproduce the Conversational Interview so that you have a form for each student.

2. Choose in advance the section(s) or specific questions you want to ask from the conversational Interview. Reviewing the information on students' Reading Surveys may provide information about additional questions that could be added to the interview.

3. Familiarize yourself with the basic questions provided in the interview prior to the interview session in order to establish a more conversational setting.

4. Select a quiet corner of the room and a calm period of the day for the interview.

5. Allow ample time for conducting the Conversational Interview.

6. Follow up on interesting comments and responses to gain a fuller understanding of students' reading experiences.

7. Record students' responses in as much detail as possible. If time and resources permit, you may want to audiotape answer to A1 and B1 to be transcribed after the interview for more in-depth analysis.

8. Enjoy this special time with each student!

Scoring and Interpretation

1. The interview explores three areas: 1) motivational factors related to the reading of narrative text, 2) information about informational reading, and 3) general factors related to reading motivation.

2. Use the students' responses along with the MRP Reading Survey to gain greater depth into students' reading experiences.

Motivation to Read Profile: Conversational Profile

Name_____ Date _____

A. Emphasis: Narrative text

Suggested prompt (designed to engage student in a natural conversation): I have been reading a good book... I was talking with... about it last night. I enjoy talking about good stories and books that I've been reading. Today I'd like to hear about what you have been reading.

1. Tell me about the most interesting story or book you have read this week (or even last week). Take a few minutes to think about it. (Wait time.) Now, tell me about the book or story.

   Probes: What else can you tell me? Is there anything else? _____

   _____

   _____

   _____

   _____

   _____

   _____

2. How did you know or find out about this story? _____

   _____

   _____

   ☐ assigned   ☐ in school
   ☐ chosen   ☐ out of school

3. Why was this story interesting to you? _____

   _____

   _____

   _____

B. Emphasis: Informational text

Suggested prompt (designed to engage student in a natural conversation): Often we read to find out about something or to learn about something. We read for information. For example, I remember a student of mine... who read a lot of books about... to find out as much as he/she could about.... Now, I'd like to hear about some of the informational reading you have been doing.

1. Think about something important that you learned recently, not from your teacher and not from television, but from a book or some other reading material. What did you read about? (Wait time.) Tell me about what you learned.

Gambrell, L.B., Palmer, B.M., Codling, R.M., & Mazzoni, S.A. (1996). Assessing reading motivation. *The Reading Teacher, 49*(7), 518-533.

Probes: What else could you tell me? Is there anything else? _____

_____

_____

_____

2. How did you know or find out about this book/article? _____

_____

_____

    ❑ assigned   ❑ in school

    ❑ chosen   ❑ out of school

3. Why was this book (or article) important to you? _____

_____

_____

C. Emphasis: General reading

1. Did you read anything at home yesterday? _____ What? _____

_____

_____

2. Do you have any books at school (in you desk/storage area/locker/book bag) today that you are reading? _____ Tell me about them. _____

_____

_____

_____

3. Tell me about your favorite author. _____

_____

_____

_____

_____

4. What do you think you have to learn to be a better reader?

_____

_____

_____

Gambrell, L.B., Palmer, B.M., Codling, R.M., & Mazzoni, S.A. (1996). Assessing reading motivation. *The Reading Teacher,* *49*(7), 518-533.

5. Do you know about any books right now that you'd like to read? Tell me about them.

_____

_____

_____

_____

6. How did you find out about these books?

_____

_____

_____

7. What are some things that get you really excited about reading books?

_____

_____

Tell me about...

_____

_____

_____

8. Who gets you really interested and excited about reading books?

_____

_____

Tell me more about what they do.

_____

_____

_____

Gambrell, L.B., Palmer, B.M., Codling, R.M., & Mazzoni, S.A. (1996). Assessing reading motivation. *The Reading Teacher,* *49*(7), 518-533.

What Are Some of Your Ideas About Reading?

Thomas H. Estes

Purpose

To acquire a quantitative idea of a student's attitude toward reading. The scale can be used with students in grades three through twelve.

Administration

1. Reproduce the sheet titled "What Are Some of Your Ideas About Reading?"

2. Assure students that their responses will not affect their grades or standing in the course.

3. Explain how students should mark their answers.

4. Read each of the statements aloud and permit students ample time to circle their responses.

Scoring and Interpretation

1. Assign numerical values to each of the twenty items as follows:

Type and Number of Item	*Numerical Values*				
	SA	A	U	D	SD
Negative: 1, 3, 4, 6, 8, 9, 11, 12, 13, 16, 17, 20	1	2	3	4	5
Positive: 2, 5, 7, 10, 14, 15, 18, 19	5	4	3	2	1

2. Add the numerical values for the positive statements and the negative statements. The student's total score is a quantitative reflection of his or her attitude toward reading. Scores above 60 indicate varying degrees of positive attitudes, and scores below 60 indicate varying degrees of negative attitudes.

3. By administering the scale on a pretest and posttest (September and May) basis, the teacher can note changes in attitude toward reading by subtracting the early score from the later one.

4. Consult the original article for further information on the construction of the attitude scale. Further validation of the scale can be found in Kenneth L. Dulin and Robert D. Chester, "A Validation Study of the Estes Attitude Scale," *Journal of Reading, 18*(1), 1974, 56–59.

Adapted from Estes, T.H. (1971). A scale to measure attitudes toward reading. *Journal of Reading, 15*(2), 135–138.

What Are Some of Your Ideas About Reading?

Name _____ Date_____

SA A U D SD   1. Reading is for learning but not for enjoyment.

SA A U D SD   2. Money spent on books is well spent.

SA A U D SD   3. There is nothing to be gained from reading books.

SA A U D SD   4. Books are a bore.

SA A U D SD   5. Reading is a good way to spend spare time.

SA A U D SD   6. Sharing books in class is a waste of time.

SA A U D SD   7. Reading turns me on.

SA A U D SD   8. Reading is only for students seeking good grades.

SA A U D SD   9. Books aren't usually good enough to finish.

SA A U D SD   10. Reading is rewarding to me.

SA A U D SD   11. Reading becomes boring after about an hour.

SA A U D SD   12. Most books are too long and dull.

SA A U D SD   13. Free reading doesn't teach anything.

SA A U D SD   14. There should be more time for free reading during the school day.

SA A U D SD   15. There are many books that I hope to read.

SA A U D SD   16. Books should not be read except for class requirements.

SA A U D SD   17. Reading is something I can do without.

SA A U D SD   18. A certain amount of summer vacation should be set aside for reading.

SA A U D SD   19. Books make good presents.

SA A U D SD   20. Reading is dull.

Rhody Secondary Reading Attitude Assessment

Regina Tullock-Rhody and J. Estill Alexander

Purpose

To acquire a quantitative idea of students' attitudes toward reading. The assessment can be used with students in grades seven through twelve.

Administration

1. Reproduce the sheet titled "Rhody Secondary Reading Attitude Assessment."

2. Assure students that the score will not affect their grade in any way.

3. Explain how the students should mark their answers. See directions on student copy.

4. Read each of the statements aloud as students read them silently and give students ample time to mark their responses.

Scoring and Interpretation

1. Assign numerical values to each of the 25 items as follows:

Type and Number of Item	*Numerical Values*				
	SD	D	U	A	SA
Positive: 4, 5, 6, 7, 8, 10, 15, 17, 20, 22, 23, 24, 25	1	2	3	4	5
Negative: 1, 2, 3, 9, 11, 12, 13, 14, 16, 18, 19, 21	5	4	3	2	1

2. Add the numerical scores for all the statements. The student's score is a quantitative reflection of his or her attitude toward reading. The possible range of scores is 25 to 125. Interpret the score informally.

3. Items on the scale have been grouped into clusters to help teachers understand students' feelings toward areas of the reading environment. Use the cluster data informally.

Cluster	*Item Number*
Reading in the library	9, 20
Reading in the home	4, 10
Other recreational reading items	5, 17, 22, 24, 25
General reading	1, 2, 3, 6, 7, 8, 12, 13, 14, 15, 16, 19, 21, 23

4. Consult the original article for further information on the development of the attitude assessment.

Adapted from Tullock-Rhody, R., & Alexander, J.E. (1980). A scale for assessing attitudes toward reading in secondary schools. *Journal of Reading, 23*(2), 609–614. Reprinted with permission of Regina Tullock and the International Reading Association.

Rhody Secondary Reading Attitude Assessment

> **Directions:** This is a test to tell how you feel about reading. The score will not affect your grade in any way. You read the statements silently as I read them aloud. Then put an ☒ on the box under the letter or letters that represent how you feel about the statement.
>
> SD = Strongly Disagree   A = Agree
> D = Disagree   SA = Strongly Agree
> U = Undecided

	SD	D	U	A	SA
1. You feel you have better things to do than read.	❏	❏	❏	❏	❏
2. You seldom buy a book.	❏	❏	❏	❏	❏
3. You are willing to tell people that you do not like to read.	❏	❏	❏	❏	❏
4. You have a lot of books in your room at home.	❏	❏	❏	❏	❏
5. You like to read a book whenever you have free time.	❏	❏	❏	❏	❏
6. You get really excited about books you have read.	❏	❏	❏	❏	❏
7. You love to read.	❏	❏	❏	❏	❏
8. You like to read books by well-known authors.	❏	❏	❏	❏	❏
9. You never check out a book from the library.	❏	❏	❏	❏	❏
10. You like to stay at home and read.	❏	❏	❏	❏	❏
11. You seldom read except when you have to do a book report.	❏	❏	❏	❏	❏
12. You think reading is a waste of time.	❏	❏	❏	❏	❏
13. You think reading is boring.	❏	❏	❏	❏	❏
14. You think people are strange when they read a lot.	❏	❏	❏	❏	❏
15. You like to read to escape from problems.	❏	❏	❏	❏	❏
16. You make fun of people who read a lot.	❏	❏	❏	❏	❏
17. You like to share books with your friends.	❏	❏	❏	❏	❏
18. You would rather someone just tell you information so that you won't have to read to get it.	❏	❏	❏	❏	❏
19. You hate reading.	❏	❏	❏	❏	❏
20. You generally check out a book when you go to the library.	❏	❏	❏	❏	❏
21. It takes you a long time to read a book.	❏	❏	❏	❏	❏
22. You like to broaden your interests through reading.	❏	❏	❏	❏	❏
23. You read a lot.	❏	❏	❏	❏	❏
24. You like to improve your vocabulary so you can use more words.	❏	❏	❏	❏	❏
25. You like to get books for gifts.	❏	❏	❏	❏	❏

Attitudinal Scale for Parents

Child's Name: _____ Date: _____

> Please indicate your observation of your child's reading growth since the last report. Feel free to comment where appropriate.
>
> A = Strongly agree   C = Disagree
> B = Agree   D = Strongly disagree

My child:

1. Understands more of what he or she reads.	A	B	C	D
2. Enjoys being read to by family members.	A	B	C	D
3. Finds time for quiet reading at home.	A	B	C	D
4. Sometimes guesses at words, but they usually make sense.	A	B	C	D
5. Can provide a summary of stories read.	A	B	C	D
6. Has a good attitude about reading.	A	B	C	D
7. Enjoys reading to family members.	A	B	C	D
8. Would like to get more books.	A	B	C	D
9. Chooses to write about stories read.	A	B	C	D
10. Is able to complete homework assignments.	A	B	C	D

Strengths I see: _____

_____

_____

Areas that need improvement: _____

_____

_____

Concerns or questions I have: _____

_____

_____

_____

From Fredericks, A.D., & Rasinski, T.V. (1990b). Involving parents in the assessment process. *The Reading Teacher, 44*(4), 346–349.

Checklist for Student's Attitudes and Personal Reading

Student _____ Grade _____ Teacher _____

	Seldom			Sometimes			Often		
	Oct.	Feb.	May	Oct.	Feb.	May	Oct.	Feb.	May
1. Possesses printed materials not assigned									
2. Uses classroom library									
3. Checks out books from school library									
4. Voluntarily shares outside reading									
5. Talks with other students about reading									
6. Seems to have a favorite author									
7. Requests more reading about topics									
8. Uses reading to satisfy personal interests									
9. Reads for recreation									
10. Chooses reading when choices are given									
11. Reading reflects interests in _____									
12. Applies ideas from reading to his/her life									
13. Seems to enjoy reading									
14. Participates in classroom book club									
15. Participates in book exchange club									
16. Parents report reading at home									

From Johns, J.L. (1991). Literacy portfolios: A primer. *Illinois Reading Council Journal, 19*(3), 4–10. May be reproduced for noncommercial educational purposes.

CHAPTER 2

Fostering Emergent Literacy and Beginning Reading

Overview

Many children gain knowledge about print from literacy experiences prior to entering school. Beginning readers may also be helped to unlock print by direct teaching. This chapter offers suggestions to teachers for helping students acquire or refine abilities related to the nature and purpose of reading, concepts about print and words, oral language, phonemic awareness, story schema, auditory and visual discrimination, rhyming, and blending.

Beginning readers often have vague or limited concepts about the purpose and nature of reading. They also may not understand the terms used by teachers such as letters, words, sounds, context, and beginning. In addition, they may not know that reading is a process of constructing meaning from print.

In addition to vague concepts about reading, students frequently exhibit confusion regarding the terms teachers use in instruction. Younger students, for example, often confuse letters with words, or vice versa. They may also show confusion with terms such as beginning, middle, and end. Teachers often assume that students understand these basic, instructional terms. Unfortunately, when this assumption is made, students may be at a great disadvantage for learning. Following are some basic concepts that students should understand. Teachers may choose to assess which concepts students know and which they do not yet understand.

➤ Reading is making sense of print.

➤ Reading is essentially making sense of language that has been written down.

➤ Most words are made up of more than one letter (*I* and *a* are the exceptions).

➤ Words can be different lengths. The number of letters determines whether a word is short, medium, or long.

➤ There are white spaces between words.

➤ Words can be organized into sentences.

➤ With the exception of long vowels, letter names and the sounds associated with words are usually different.

➤ Reading can be done for different reasons or purposes.

➤ There is usually a relationship between the words on a page and pictures or illustrations.

➤ Words are arranged in sentences, sentences into paragraphs, and paragraphs into stories or books.

Consider these concepts and the language that is used during instruction. Be alert for other terms or concepts that your students may not understand. By looking at your instruction through the eyes of your students, you may discover that you take too much for granted when you teach. Plan appropriate instruction to help students develop concepts about print and the specialized terms used in instruction.

One of the most important areas related to emergent literacy and later success in reading (Gillet & Temple, 1990) is phonological awareness. It refers to being able to manipulate phonemes (sounds); this skill enables students to use letter-sound relationships in reading and writing. Activities related to phonemic awareness have been used since Elkonin (1973), a Soviet researcher, developed a method in which students move markers or tokens to show sounds in words. More recently, a similar technique has been used in Reading Recovery (Clay, 1985). Sections 2.3 through 2.8 in this chapter relate directly or indirectly to the area of phonological awareness. We urge you to give careful attention to these sections as you teach emergent or struggling readers.

2.1 Concepts About the Nature and Purpose of Reading

Behavior Observed	The student is unaware of the basic function of print.
Anticipated Outcome	The student will understand that print conveys meaning.

Perspective and Strategies

Students at all ages must realize that reading is the process of making sense from print. They must learn that spoken language—their own and that of others—is made up of words that can also be written down. Later, they will come to understand that these words can be broken down into parts, or syllables, and further into sound units, or phonemes.

1. Introduce a picture book by reading it to an individual or a group of students more than once. Have students join in with the reading as they become more familiar with the story. Give the book to a student and encourage "reading" of the book. Provide all students opportunities for storybook reading on a daily basis. Some useful pattern books can be found in Appendix C.

2. Place a big book (two to three feet high) on a chart stand where it can be readily seen by a group of students. Read a familiar story and have the students read along. Point out features of print: where the text begins on a page, the left-to-right progression of reading, the return sweep, the white spaces between words, and punctuation.

3. Help students create their own books, using their chosen vocabulary. Each page of these short books is student dictated and has one word, phrase, or sentence on it. The student reads the text for a page and then illustrates it. These books can be used to practice the vocabulary associated with directions such as *up*, *down*, *in*, and *out*. Repeated readings to classmates and family members should be encouraged. Building a collection of these books to share within the classroom will help improve sight vocabulary and develop print awareness.

4. Use familiar poems, songs, and text that have been committed to memory. Show the printed form, line by line. Read aloud, pointing to each word. The students then read aloud, pointing to each word, modeling the teacher's behavior. When the student appears to be familiar with the short text and points word by word while reading, the teacher may point to a single word and ask the student to say it. This technique may also be used with short, dictated experience stories as the text.

5. Write *kingcup* on the chalkboard. Ask a student to pronounce the word. Ask other students if they agree. Continue the process until the class agrees that the word is *kingcup*. Ask students whether they can *read* the word. Most students will respond that they can read the word because they view reading as a process of decoding. When this point is reached, ask the students, "How do you know that you can *read* the word?" Many students will respond by saying, "I can read the word because I can pronounce it." Sooner or later, a student is likely to ask what the word means. Lead students to the conclusion that reading involves understanding. Distinguish between being able to say a word and knowing what a word means.

Invite students to suggest ways they might be able to find out what the word *kingcup* means. A common response is to have someone look it up in a dictionary. Have students look up the word and discuss its meaning (a plant with yellow flowers; the marsh marigold). Have students use the word in a sentence. Point out to students that they can now read the word *kingcup*. Tell them that readers are always concerned with meaning. Follow this activity with other words that students can probably pronounce even though the meaning is unknown. Some possible words include yegg, tutu, dingo, truffle, and eyelet.

6. The following example is designed to help students realize that (1) reading is a form of communication, (2) reading can be talk written down, and (3) reading is constructing meaning from print.

Teacher: If you wanted to tell Eric a secret, how would you do it?

Beth: I would just tell him.

Teacher: You mean you would talk to him or whisper to him?

Beth: Yes, that's what I'd do.

Teacher: What would you do if Eric weren't here and you still wanted him to know?

Beth: I might write him a note.

Teacher: OK, and when Eric gets here, what should he do?

Beth: He should read what I wrote down.

Teacher: Good. Have you communicated with Eric?

Beth: Yes.

In this example, Eric has received a note that a student has written. But what did Beth write down? She wrote down what she would have said to Eric if he were here. In other words, her talk has been written down. Each printed word represents only one spoken word, and we can now say that a word is a verbal symbol. The following example demonstrates this concept.

Teacher: Suppose that you were going to tell Eric that you have some new baseball cards. Because you had to write it down, it probably looked like this: I have some new baseball cards. Eric took this note and began to say what you had written. He said to himself: I-have-some-new-baseball-cards. If he were to say that out loud, would that sound like what you were going to say?

Beth: Yes, that's what I would have said.

Teacher: But Eric still has not read what you have written down. He has said the words out loud, but he has not read them. In order to be really reading, Eric must understand what you have said. He must make some meaning from those symbols called words. If he comes to you later and asks to see your hat you wrote about, he has not read anything. You told him about some new baseball cards, not a hat, so he did not read that note. He had not gotten meaning; therefore, no reading has taken place. Reading involves meaning, and if you do not know what something means, you have not read it! Now what are some of the things in daily life that you read—some things you get meaning from?

Beth: We read road signs on the highways like SLOW and STOP. We read cereal boxes that say FREE TOY INSIDE.

7. Use *Hey! I'm Reading!* (Miles, 1995) as a fun and engaging way to help students learn about reading. This book would also be good for parents to share with their children.

Behavior Observed	The student does not know the letters of the alphabet.
Anticipated Outcome	The student will learn the alphabet.

Perspective and Strategies

Although it is not necessary to know the letters of the alphabet to read, letter knowledge can help students learn how the alphabetic system works. Such knowledge can also help with spelling and associating certain sounds with certain letters. To help assess alphabet knowledge, an easy-to-use Assessment of Alphabet Knowledge is found in the Resources for Chapter 2. For students who could benefit from increasing their alphabet knowledge, the following strategies may be useful.

1. Try your best to use meaningful activities within the context of your classroom. As students begin to write their names, their attention is being directed to specific letters. Be direct and tell students that their names are made up of letters. Using students' names is a powerful way to focus on meaningful instruction. Teach students the names of the letters that comprise their names. Make name cards for each student, and invite students to learn or generalize their knowledge by asking questions such as:

   ■ Does anyone have a name that begins with the same letter as Rosanna's name? Invite students to share, and discuss their ideas. Compare the first letters of the names and comment appropriately.

   ■ Does anyone have a letter **in** their name that is the same as the first letter in Rosanna's name? Invite students to hold up their name cards and point to the letter in their name that is the same. Use the opportunity to discuss upper-case letters and lower-case letters.

   ■ Who has a name that begins with *N*?

   ■ Does your name have a lower-case letter that has the same name as the upper-case letter *O* that I'm writing on the chalkboard? If so, hold up your name card, and point to the letter. Does anyone have two *Os*?

2. Because students learn letters by their distinctive features (open or closed, curved or slanted, above or below the line), introduce at least two different letters at a time. Talk about the letters and what makes them similar and/or different. Although you will probably begin with letters that have dissimilar features such as *i* and *b*, you will want to eventually contrast similar letters such as *b* and *d* and verbalize the reasons they are different. It is through such experiences that students will learn what makes the letters different. Dunn-Rankin (1968) noted the following groups of letters that tend to confuse students:

   ■ b, d, p, and o, g, h

   ■ f, l, t, k, i, and h when combined

   ■ e, a, s, c, o

   ■ n, m, u, and h and r

3. Refer to print on signs and posters in the room, and talk about the letters that make up the words.

4. Invite students to bring in objects such as cereal boxes, toothpaste boxes, paper bags, and newspapers. Discuss the words and the letters that make up the words on these items.

5. Be sure a model alphabet is displayed in the room so students can see how the letters are formed. They should also be able to see the corresponding upper-case and lower-case letters.

6. Use a variety of hands-on activities to help students learn the names of the letters and to practice how they are written: alphabet cereal, finger painting, sandpaper letters, playdough letters, and so on.

7. Help students create their personalized alphabet books. Invite students to share them with one another.

8. Make a big book which contains the alphabet song. Have different students point to the letters and words as the students sing along. Take time to discuss the difference between letters and words. Invite students to ask each other questions about the letters and words.

9. Sing or play recordings of songs that spell out words or that use letters as part of the song (e.g., "Bingo," "Old MacDonald Had a Farm").

10. Use the newspaper and invite students to find and circle as many examples (upper case and lower case) of a particular letter as they can within a specific time limit. Use the exercise to also encourage identification of known words.

11. Develop cards for alphabet bingo or dominoes. For bingo, have a student assist in calling the letters. Game cards can include upper-case letters, lower-case letters, or a combination of both.

12. Secure a keyboard and invite students to type and explore the alphabet. If a computer is available with speech capability, there are computer programs that will say the name of the letter when the key is depressed. Other programs have activities that will help students learn the letters.

13. Supply students with magnetic letters and stamp printing sets to stimulate involvement with the alphabet and making words.

14. Take time to point out the differences among the manuscript *a* and the typeset *a*. Do the same for the letter *g*.

15. Provide a print-rich environment in which students are encouraged to explore and talk about their literacy experiences.

16. Develop a writing center where students can compose and draw. Remember that writing is developmental and students may be making letter-like forms as they progress to conventional printing.

17. Have students learn and sing the alphabet song, and point to the letters as they sing. After modeling this process, invite a student to point. Once students are able to sing the song, invite them to be the "alphabet" as they line up to go somewhere (Cunningham, 1995). Laminate a set of alphabet cards and mix them up. Pass them out randomly so each student has one. The teacher keeps any extras. Then have the class sing the alphabet song slowly as each student gets into line.

18. Read alphabet books (see Appendix B) as well as other books that students enjoy. Engage in natural and meaningful sharing about letters, words, and meaning. Some of the books listed in Resources for Chapter 2 will be especially appropriate.

2.3   Concept of a Word

Behavior Observed	The student does not seem to understand what words are.
Anticipated Outcome	The student will develop the concept of a word.

Perspective and Strategies

Words are critical in reading, yet many emergent and struggling readers have difficulty understanding what is meant by a "word." Johns (1980), for example, found that below-average first graders had significantly greater difficulty in locating one or two words than did average and above-average first graders. Even some struggling readers in third grade had difficulty consistently identifying one word or one letter (Johns, 1977). McGee and Richgels (1996) note that emergent readers and writers may use various ways to show words in their writing. One student used a dot between words, another wrote each word in a different color, and a third student circled each word.

Because a concept of word is often a basis for instruction in rhyming, phonological awareness, and phonics, the following concepts may need to be taught explicitly to students:

■ Most words are made up of more than one letter (*I* and *a* are the exceptions).

■ Words can be different lengths. The number of letters determines whether a word is short, medium, or long.

■ There are spaces between words.

■ Words can be organized into sentences.

Consider the following strategies and activities to help students develop the concept for a word and word boundaries. Remember, too, that an awareness of words develops over time with language use and can be enhanced by reading and writing (Roberts, 1992).

1. A student's name is extremely meaningful. Print it on a card, and show it to the student. Point to the student's first name, say it, and then point to the student's last name and say it. Show the student the space that separates the first and last name by pointing to it. Tell the student there are two words on the card, framing each with your hands. In subsequent interactions, you may wish to talk about letters that make the name.

2. Refer to words in the room, and ask students how many words are shown. Have them explain their answer. Provide explanations or clarifications as needed. Help students understand that words (except *I* and *a*) are made up of more than one letter.

3. Encourage students to show you words they can write or read. Have them frame a word with their hands. They can also name and talk about the number of letters that make up the word.

4. Provide ample opportunities for students to talk with each other, write, and read. Although their reading and writing may be in an emergent stage, promoting a risk-taking and supportive environment in the classroom will pay rich dividends in literacy acquisition.

5. Practice counting words (adapted from Cunningham, 1995). Give students ten counters (plastic disks, paper squares, raisins, or anything manipulable) in a paper cup. Start by counting some familiar objects in the room (bulletin boards, doors, plants, pillows, etc.). Have students place one of their counters on their desks as each object is pointed to. Be sure students return their counters to their cup at the end of each count. Then tell students you can also count words by putting down a counter for each word said. Model the process with the sentence, "I am your teacher." First, say the sentence naturally. Then say the sentence slowly, pausing after each word, so students can put down a marker for each word said. Ask students how many words you said. Proceed to other sentences capitalizing on your students (Vinnie is wearing blue today. I saw Clay at the store. Carlos will be seven years old tomorrow). As students begin to understand, invite them to offer sentences. They should say the sentence twice, once in the normal way and then one word at a time. Familiar nursery rhymes may also be used. Later, provide written sentence strips and invite students to count words by placing a counter beneath each. Provide instruction and support as needed (e.g., cutting the sentence strip into individual words). Variations of this activity could include clapping or moving a block forward for each spoken word.

6. Have students point to words as they read experience stories, big books, wall charts, poems, and books. Pointing helps students practice the match between printed words and spoken words.

2.4   Rhyming

Behavior Observed	The student does not understand the concept of rhyming.
Anticipated Outcome	The student will demonstrate the concept of rhyming by supplying words that rhyme.

Perspective and Strategies

Rhyming is a valuable tool in the early stages of reading. Fox (1996) notes that rhyme will benefit reading ability regardless of the age or intelligence of the student. Rhymes help students develop an understanding that phonograms (letter clusters or families) can represent the same sound in different words. Phonograms that can be used to develop the concept of rhyming are given in Resources for Chapter 4.

The following strategies may be useful:

1. Begin with part of a familiar poem (perhaps "Jack and Jill") that contains a rhyming element. Say the line and print it on the chalkboard:

   Jack and Jill

   Went up the hill

   Tell students that two words rhyme: *Jill* and *hill.* Say, "Rhymes are words that sound alike at the ends." Have students inspect the words to find the common element (-ill). Tell them that *Jill* rhymes with *ill* and begins with *jjj.* Ask them what word rhymes with *ill* and begins with *hhh.* Practice other words that fit the same pattern (*pill, mill, bill, dill, kill, till, will*). Use the following format: What word rhymes with *ill* and begins with *ppp*? Model when necessary and give students ample opportunities to respond individually. Have students use the words in sentences. Extend the preceding strategy to nursery rhymes or Dr. Seuss books. Have students listen for and locate rhyming words. They could also underline or circle the rhyming words.

2. Draw or cut out pictures of word pairs that rhyme. Mix the word pairs and have students take turns selecting word pairs that rhyme. Ask students to say the words aloud. Possible word pairs include the following:

nest	box	ten	hat	car	can	green
chest	fox	hen	cat	jar	fan	queen
top	log	pan	late	mice	tree	duck
mop	dog	man	gate	rice	bee	truck
boat	bug	toad	bone	book	corn	growl
coat	rug	road	cone	hook	horn	owl

3. Encourage students to determine a rhyming word when you say: "What word rhymes with (use a phonogram) and begins with (use an initial sound)?" A few examples include

oy: boy, joy, toy, Roy

um: drum, thumb, gum

op: crop, drop, pop, shop, stop, mop

Rhymes have great generalizability. Nearly 500 primary grade words can be derived from a set of only 37 phonograms (Whylie & Durrell, 1970, as cited in Adams, 1990b, pp. 321–322):

-ack	-ail	-ain	-ake	-ale	-ame	-an
-ank	-ap	-ash	-at	-ate	-aw	-ay
-eat	-ell	-est	-ice	-ick	-ide	-ight
-ill	-in	-ine	-ing	-ink	-ip	-ir
-ock	-oke	-op	-ore	-or	-uck	-ug
-ump	-unk					

4. Tell students, "I'm thinking of a word that begins with *b* and rhymes with *cat.*" Have students make up other "I'm thinking of" riddles.

5. Use poetry that contains rhyming words. Help students to identify the words that rhyme. Then read the poem aloud and leave out selected words. Have students supply the rhyming word that was left out.

6. Have students create their own poem using words that rhyme.

7. Have students brainstorm as many rhyming words as they can in 30 seconds. Repeat this activity often to reinforce rhyming skills.

8. Use magnetic letters or letter cards to help the student see how changing the initial letter can make a new word that rhymes with the original word. Help students understand that rhyming words have the same endings. For example:

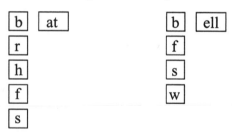

9. Encourage students to write rhyming words and explain how they are able to create the words.

10. Present students with four cards containing illustrations. Three of the cards should rhyme; one of the cards should not rhyme with the other three. Invite students to sort the cards and explain their reasoning. Three sets of sample cads are shown on the following page.

	Set 1	Set 2	Set 3

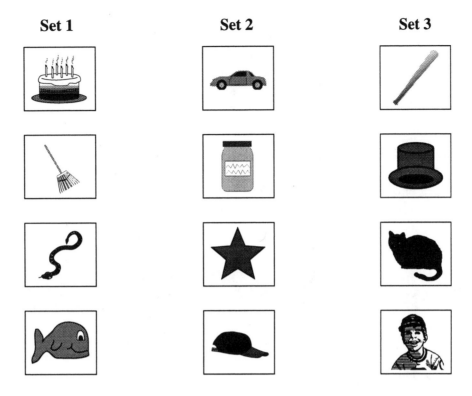

11. Sing songs that have one or more rhyming words. Invite students to identify the rhyming words.

12. Create a rhyming bulletin board. Put blank sheets of paper on the bulletin board where they can be readily reached by students. Invite students to search newspapers or magazines for pictures that rhyme and fasten them to the appropriate piece of paper. Pictures might also be drawn by students.

13. Listen to rhyming books on tape to help solidify the concept of rhyme.

14. Use poems, songs, and chants as ways to encourage students to create their own rhymes.

15. Do riddles with body parts. Fox (1996) offers the following riddles in which all the answers rhyme with *head*.

   ■ What can you toast? (bread)

   ■ What do you call something that's not living anymore? (dead)

   ■ What is the color of blood? (red)

   ■ What do you use to ride down snowy hills? (sled)

   ■ Where do you sleep? (bed)

   Encourage students to make up riddles and questions that rhyme with certain words.

16. Read to students daily from books with rhyming elements.

Games

Remember and Rhyme. For oral practice with rhyming words, students can form small groups and play a game. One student in the group begins with a simple one-syllable word (for example, *nice*, *best*, or *stop*) and says the word aloud. The next player in the group has to say the first student's rhyming word and then add one of his or her own. This process continues until no other rhyming word can be given. Begin again and play with a new word.

Find These Rhyming Words. Try a rhyming word scavenger hunt with a small group of students. Begin with one word that has many others that rhyme with it (for instance, cake, bug, or top). Give the students ten minutes to look for items that rhyme with the given word. Pictures from magazines can be included along with symbols that represent the word. For example, a twig may represent the word nest. Following the ten-minute word-hunting period, form a group and share items found. Write the rhyming words on the chalkboard.

Group Me. Use a deck of cards containing groups of rhyming words. Shuffle the cards and encourage the students to categorize the rhyming words into their appropriate groups after saying each word out loud.

Find a Rhyme. Make a pair of rhyming words for each two students. Put each word on a note card. Each student gets a card. The object of the game is to find the other person who has the word that rhymes. This game can be repeated several times by mixing the cards.

2.5 Auditory Discrimination

Behavior Observed	The student has difficulty distinguishing fine differences in the sounds of spoken words.
Anticipated Outcome	The student will distinguish fine differences in the sounds of spoken words.

Perspective and Strategies

Auditory discrimination is the ability to distinguish between fine sound differences in language. Discriminatory ability is developmental and may not be fully achieved until a student is eight years old. Students who have problems with auditory discrimination may have trouble in beginning reading, especially if intensive phonics instruction is used.

An informal hierarchy of auditory discrimination abilities includes four levels:

Level 1   Environmental sounds that are grossly different, such as a dog barking and a telephone ringing.

Level 2   Words that are grossly different, like *the* and *banana*.

Level 3   Words that are somewhat different, like *father* and *mother*.

Level 4   Words that differ in only one phoneme, such as *big* and *pig*.

An Assessment of Auditory Discrimination can be found in the Resources for Chapter 2. If an auditory discrimination problem is apparent, be sure to investigate possible physical causes through a hearing screening. The school nurse can often conduct the screening. Another physical aspect to check is whether the student has a cold or allergy. Students with allergies, as well as those who swim regularly, may experience temporary hearing difficulties.

Although a physical problem may be present, a more common finding is that the student has not been taught to recognize the fine differences between sounds and words. Also important to remember is that speech sounds may vary from one dialect to another. For example, the difference between standard English and students' everyday language may be great.

Before auditory discrimination instruction can actually begin, the student must be aware of the concepts of same and different. It is best to use actual concrete objects to develop these concepts. Next, progress to sounds. Commercial or teacher-made recordings can be used to practice environmental sounds. A piano can be used to help students differentiate sounds.

It is difficult to isolate auditory discrimination teaching from practice. The following ideas should be useful:

1. If students do not understand the concepts of same and different, begin with environmental sounds and move to words that are obviously different (such as *big–truck*). Some students find it easier to use the words *yes* for *same* and *no* for *different*.

2. Begin with word pairs whose initial sounds differ. Include words that are also the same. Pronounce the two words and have the student indicate whether they are the same or different. Progress to words that differ in ending sounds and then to words that differ in medial

sounds. Possible words for practice are listed here. Additional practice endings can be found in the Resources for Chapter 4.

Beginnings	Middles	Endings
take–make	cat–cut	cat–cap
car–far	sit–sat	fan–fat
dark–bark	log–leg	lad–lap
sod–rod	luck–lick	mom–mop
lit–mitt	pot–pit	rap–rat
dead–bed	Tim–Tom	lip–lit
rock–sock	pet–pat	hot–hop

3. Have students tell whether word pairs are different in the beginning, middle, or end. Be sure the students understand concepts of beginning, middle, and end. Students will also profit from a visual representation of the word pair. They may then develop the concept that words sounding differently usually contain at least one different letter. Homonyms are, of course, the exception.

4. Encourage students to discuss the meanings of words so that they can begin to understand that words that sound different usually do not mean the same thing. Synonyms are the exception.

5. Remember that speech sounds vary from dialect to dialect. For example, *pin* and *pen* may be pronounced the same by some speakers, whereas other speakers use different sounds for the *i* and *e*. See Oral Reading as Performance in Chapter 3 for helpful information on students' dialects.

6. Consult the section on rhyming in this chapter for additional ideas.

Games

Yes-No. Each student has two cards that contain the words *same* and *different* (or *yes* and *no*). The teacher pronounces two words and the students hold up a card that indicates whether the words are the same or different. Points may be given for correct answers.

Picture Pairs. Develop a series of picture pairs whose names differ in only one sound, as shown here:

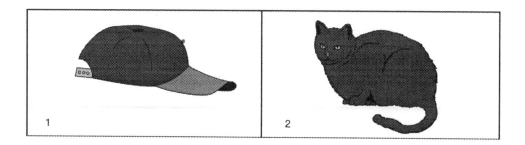

Name both pairs and have students take turns pointing to the picture that was named a second time. A variation is to number the picture pairs and have students hold up cards or fingers to indicate the picture that was named a second time. The following words may make good picture pairs:

chair–hair	mail–snail	cap–map
train–rain	cake–lake	grape–cape
nail–pail	snake–rake	car–star
ball–wall	man–pan	farm–arm
ham–lamb	plane–mane	gate–skate

Additional word pairs can be found in Resources for Chapter 4.

Funny Questions. Ask students questions where the correct answer is one of two words that differ in only one sound. Take turns or allow students to volunteer. Several possible questions are given here:

Would you put your feet in fox or socks?

Would you open a door with a bee or a key?

Would you hit a ball with a bat or a cat?

Would you sit on a mat or a map?

A variation of the game is to have students make up similar questions that could be posed to others in the group.

Pronounce a Word. Have students pronounce the same word after you. Using individual chalkboards or wipe-off cards divided into fourths, have students write each word you pronounce. After all four words are written, ask students to erase words one by one. Observe whether they erase each word as it is pronounced.

2.6   Phonological Awareness

Behavior Observed	The student is unable to segment, manipulate, and match sounds.
Anticipated Outcome	The student will successfully segment, manipulate, and match sounds.

Background

Phonological awareness is the ability to segment and manipulate sounds in words. It is strongly related to success in reading and spelling acquisition and is a powerful predictor of reading achievement (Yopp, 1995). In order to benefit from phonics instruction, students seem to require at least some basic level of phonological awareness. Research reported by Bentin and Leshem (1993) and Tumner, Herriman, and Nesdale (1988) have led some to view phonological awareness as a necessary prerequisite for success in learning to read. "No matter how they are taught, all students must grasp the abstract concepts that words are composed of separate sounds and that individual letters and combinations are used to represent those sounds" (Gunning, 1996).

For a number of students, the ability to segment and manipulate sounds in words does not come naturally; nevertheless, explicit instruction in phonological awareness can be given before and during reading instruction. Some examples (Stanovich, 1993-1994) of questions related to phonological awareness tasks follow:

➤ *Phoneme Deletion:* What would be left if the /h/ sound were taken away from *hat*?

➤ *Word-to-Word Matching:* Do *pen* and *paper* begin with the same sound?

➤ *Blending:* What word would we have if you put these sounds together: /m/, /a/, /t/?

➤ *Phoneme Segmentation:* What sounds do you hear in the word *hot*?

➤ *Phoneme Counting:* How many sounds do you hear in the word *kite*?

➤ *Deleted Phoneme:* What sound do you hear in *seat* that is missing in *eat*?

➤ *Odd Word Out:* Which word starts with a different sound: *bag, nine, beach, bike*?

➤ *Sound to Word Matching:* Is there a /k/ in *Mike*?

To help students gain an awareness that speech consists of a series of sounds or phonemes (e.g., that *mat* is made up of three segments), students need to be able to segment the sounds in words. Instructional and practice activities are offered here and in other sections of this Chapter. See the sections on concept of a word, rhyming, blending, and auditory discrimination. In addition, a test to assess phoneme segmentation can be found in the Resources for Chapter 2. The following strategies are best used when students have developed a concept for words, a concept for rhyme, and the ability to rhyme words. Then proceed to separating words into sounds.

Teaching Strategy 1 (*Syllables*)
(Adapted from Cunningham, 1995)

1. Begin teaching separation of words into components after students are proficient at separating an oral phrase or sentence into words. If students have difficulty with this task, refer to the appropriate section of Chapter 2 for some useful strategies.

2. Use the names of your students for initial activities. Say the first name of one student; then say the name again and clap the syllables. Clap as you say each syllable.

3. Say the first names of other students, and clap the syllables as you say them the second time. Encourage students to clap with you.

4. Continue with other names. As students become proficient, use some of their middle and/or last names. The word *beat* may be a more easily understood term than syllables for young students. By clapping, students should realize that *Bob* is a one-beat word, *Giti* is a two-beat word, *Natalie* is a three-beat word, and so on.

5. When students can clap beats easily, help them see that the length of the word is usually related to the number of claps it gets. Begin with student names that begin with the same letter. Then print the names on different strips of paper so that the short words have short strips and the long words have long strips. For example:

Before showing the words, say *Bob* and *Barbara* and have students decide that *Bob* is a one-beat word and *Barbara* takes more claps and is a three-beat word. Ask them to predict which word is probably longer and has more letters. Then show them the words and develop the understanding that because longer words (like *Barbara*) take several claps, they probably have more letters than shorter words. Use some of the other names of your students to further develop and practice this basic understanding.

6. Then use a similar procedure with word pairs (or triplets). Possible categories and words to use are shown below.

States		Animals	
Maine	Ohio	canary	bobcat
Michigan	Oklahoma	cat	bear
Alabama	Tennessee	chimpanzee	beaver
Alaska	Texas	camel	bear
Maine	Massachusetts	hippopotamus	giraffe
Maryland	Missouri	horse	goat

7. A variation is to show students two words they probably can't read and ask, "Who can figure out which of the two words I'm holding is canary and which is cat?" The goal is to have students recognize that words requiring more claps probably contain more letters.

8. Tapping a pencil or other object could be used instead of clapping syllables. Such variations may help sustain students' attention.

Teaching Strategy 2
(Based on Lundberg, Frost & Peterson, 1988)

1. Begin this strategy by reading "The Three Billy Goats Gruff" to help students gain an understanding of what a troll is. When the troll talks in the story, say the words syllable by syllable.

2. Then pretend to be a troll. Tell students you will say words and students must figure out the word being named. Provide and discuss several examples.

3. Use words like *paper, pencil, candy, marker, erasers, notebook, automobile, airplane, buggy, hamburger,* and *chalkboard.* If possible, have the actual objects so that students can make a visual association **after** they have identified the word.

4. Extend the lesson by having students use tokens (see Teaching Strategy 3) for each syllable heard or hold up a finger for each syllable.

5. Invite students to volunteer for the troll's role. Provide guidance and support as needed.

Teaching Strategy 3 *(Sounds)*
(Based on Elkonin, 1973)

1. Prepare cards with a simple illustration along with a matrix that contains a box for each sound (phoneme) in the word. Note that the boxes represent each sound, not necessarily each letter. The words selected should be familiar to students. Secure sufficient tokens (plastic, pennies, cardboard squares) for each of your students. Additional cards appear in the Resources for Section 2. They can be copied on heavy paper and cut out for use. An example of a sound box with tokens is shown below.

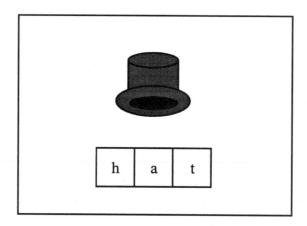

2. Instruct a small group so you can provide assistance as needed. Explain, model, and guide students through the task. Slowly say the word while pushing tokens into the boxes sound by sound. Model the process a second time. Then invite the students to say the word, perhaps stretching the sounds, so they can hear the separate sound while you move the tokens. Invite students to push the tokens into the boxes while you say the word slowly.

3. Then provide another example and begin to transfer the responsibility to the students. Encourage a student to identify the picture and then pronounce the word very carefully and deliberately. The goal is to emphasize each sound without distorting the word and to put a token in each box while saying each sound.

4. Use other examples to help students catch on to the concept of segmenting. Some examples of sound boxes can be found in the Resources for Chapter 2.

5. The following are useful variations that will solidify and expand students' abilities.

   ■ Eliminate the boxes below the pictures and have students just move their tokens to the bottom of the picture.

   ■ Have students simply tell you how many sounds are in the word shown in the picture after they have pronounced it. The pictures used should contain no boxes.

   ■ Say a word aloud and have students repeat it and indicate the number of sounds. Ask, "How many sounds are in the word?" In the beginning, it may be beneficial to stretch out the sounds and repeat the process for each word two or three times.

   ■ Record a word's letters in boxes and have students put tokens on the letters that represent the segmented sounds.

   ■ After students are quite proficient at counting the number of sounds in a word, ask questions about the order of sounds. For example,

   What is the first sound you hear in *duck*?

   What sounds do you hear after /u/ in duck?

   ■ Write a word's letters in the appropriate blocks, and have the students put tokens on the letters that represent the segmented sounds.

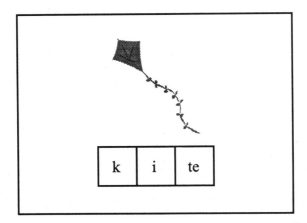

   ■ Invite students to pronounce the word in the picture and then write letters in the boxes instead of using tokens.

Practice and Reinforcement Activities

1. Use nursery rhymes as a natural starting point for helping students develop an understanding of words as units of sound that can be manipulated independently of meaning. Students often enjoy nonsense words, catchy rhymes, and rhythms. Encourage students to experiment with familiar rhymes and words.

2. Have students categorize the names of pictures according to the number of syllables. Some possible pictures to use follow.

3. Use children's literature that playfully deals with sounds in language. In addition to the Dr. Seuss books, other examples include:

   ■ Degan, B. *Jamberry.* New York: Harper and Row, 1983.

   ■ Hutchins, P. *Don't Forget the Bacon!* New York: Morrow, 1976.

   ■ Leedy, L. *Pingo the Plaid Panda.* New York: Holiday House, 1989.

   ■ Pomerantz, C. *How Many Trucks Can a Tow Truck Tow?* New York: Random House, 1987.

   ■ Shaw, N. *Sheep on a Ship.* Boston: Houghton Mifflin, 1989.

   ■ Van Laan, N. *Possum Come-A-Knockin'.* New York: Knopf, 1990.

   Consult Griffith and Olson (1992) for additional titles.

4. Use a variation of the troll activity presented in Teaching Strategy 2. In this case, the troll pronounces individual phonemes of a word instead of syllables, and students must combine the sounds to identify the word.

5. Say a sound and let students whose names begin with that sound line up. A variation would be to invite students to stand or line up if their name contains a particular sound you say anywhere in their name. Be sure students respond to the **sound**. For example, if you say "*kkk,*" Ken, Cathy, and Nikki could all respond.

6. Place three or four familiar pictures on the chalkboard tray, and invite a student to say each word, one sound at a time. Another student is asked to identify the picture. Gradually increase the number of pictures and possibly use some pictures whose sounds are similar.

7. Encourage daily writing, even if it is only single words or short phrases to accompany illustrations. Ideally, students will attempt their own spellings. These approximations will give the teacher a clue as to the development of letter-sound relationships and should be accepted. Writing also helps develop phonemic awareness (McCormick, 1995).

Principles for Encouraging Spelling

1. Some students will feel it necessary to ask the teacher to spell each word for them. Ask the student what sound the word begins with, what sound is heard next, and so on, until the word is spelled. With encouragement and practice, students should become willing to attempt spelling on their own and may need only an occasional sound spelled for them.

2. Spelling provides a clue as to the progress of phonemic segmentation. For example, *gowe* eventually becomes *going* in a student's writing development. The ability to write increasingly conventional spellings is a key to improved reading ability and should be encouraged through writing.

3. The following chart illustrates aspects of the developmental stages of students' spellings (Morris & Perney, 1984). The stages may be thought of as a continuum and, in most cases, are not hard and fast. As students gain knowledge of the English phonological system, they gain control of conventional spelling.

Developmental Spelling Stages

Prephonemic		Phonemic	Transitional	Correct
B	BC	BAC	BACK (c)	back
S	SK	SEK	SINC	sink
M	ML	MAL	MALLE	mail
J	JS	JRAS	DRES	dress
C	CD	SID	SIED	side
F	FT	FET	FEAT	feet
B	BK	BIK	BICKE	bike
S	SK	SEK	STIK	stick

1. Prephonemic spellers perceive and reliably represent the initial consonant, then alter the initial and final consonant in one-syllable words (*b* or *bk* for *bike*).

2. Phonemic (letter name) spellers produce spellings that have short vowels produced as phonologically appropriate substitutions (*sek* for *sink*).

3. Transition spellers begin to represent short vowels correctly, although the vowel markers are often incorrectly placed (*sied* for *side*).

4. Correct spelling is evidenced by spellers who nearly always spell words conventionally.

2.7   Alphabetic Principle

Behavior Observed	The student lacks knowledge of sounds associated with letters of the alphabet.
Anticipated Outcome	The student will gain in awareness of associating letters with their sounds.

Perspective and Strategies

Once beginning readers understand the language and concepts of printed materials, further progress is made by developing the alphabetic principle. The following activities focus on introducing the student to associate selected letters of the alphabet with their sounds.

1. See Chapter 4 for an expanded explanation of letter-sound correspondences.

2. Introduce the concept of beginning sounds by reading aloud alphabet books (see Appendix B) or pattern books (see Appendix C). Draw attention to words that begin with the same sound. *The Little Book of Big Tongue Twisters* by Foley Curtis (New York: Harvey House, 1977) contains alliterative pieces that could be used to introduce most of the beginning sounds.

3. Use graphic displays that combine the letter form with a picture of something that begins with that letter. Draw letters within the picture rather than next to the picture. For example:

Give students lots of practice with the pictures, perhaps drawn on cards, until the letter drawn and its associated object become familiar. Large cards displayed around the classroom are a helpful reminder. Read alphabet books to your class and request that parents do the same at home. Immersion in the alphabetic principle will facilitate sound-symbol association. Appendix B lists some titles of alphabet books.

4. Make alphabet books with your students. At first, simply paste or draw pictures of objects beginning with a given letter on its letter page. For example, the *Ss* page might have a silly smile, a snake, scissors, and spinach. Upon completion of the first step, subsequent alphabet books might carry a theme, such as animals. In this case, the *Ss* page might have pictures of a squirrel, a snake, and a squid. Taken one step further, the alphabet book might include a combination of pictures and written words that begin with *s*.

5. Say a word and have students indicate whether their names begin with the same sound. Remember to stress sounds so names like *Cecil* and *Sam* begin with the same sound as *circus*. Clarify students' responses as necessary.

6. Play the game, "I spy." Tell students that you see or spy something in the room that begins with the same sound as *paper*. As students say words, note words with incorrect sounds ("I'm sorry, *box* does not begin like *paper*") or note that "The word *pen* begins like *paper* but it isn't the word I was thinking of." A more advanced version of the game could involve an ending sound.

7. Model the use of picture sorts of various types. One type (a closed sort) is to sort by pictures whose names have a particular beginning sound. A second type (an open sort) has a number of pictures, and students sort them into different beginning sounds. Have students explain their sorts.

8. Establish mailboxes for each student (hanging file folders in a plastic crate works well), and encourage students to write to each other.

9. Provide plenty of opportunities for students to engage in writing and be supportive of their efforts.

2.8   Blending

Behavior Observed	The student has difficulty blending phonemes into a whole word.
Anticipated Outcome	The student will be able to blend phonemes into whole words.

Background

Students who are able to sound out words successfully are able to blend the sounds associated with letters into a meaningful whole. Although the ultimate goal for the reader is to construct meaning from print, knowledge of phonemic segmentation is an excellent predictor of success in reading (Gillet & Temple, 1990). Providing instruction in blending skills concurrently with segmentation training enhances phonological awareness skills in general. Assuming that students know the sounds associated with letters, the task then becomes one of blending the sounds into a word that is already in the students' listening or meaning vocabulary.

Teaching Strategy 1

1. Begin with a picture that has been cut into several pieces and show how the pieces, when put together properly, make a picture. Simple puzzles can be used. Tell the students that sometimes words can be identified by putting together the sounds associated with the letters or letter combinations.

2. Write several words on the chalkboard that the students may or may not know by sight (such as *sat*, *sit*, or *map*). Students should know, at an automatic level, the letter-sound relationships used in the blending exercises.

3. Have the students watch while you blend the sounds associated with each letter into a whole word. Tell them that you will point to the next letter. Initially, sound the letters in *sat* for about a second (except for the final letter). When done with the sounding procedure, say the word as you would in normal pronunciation.

4. Next, have students sound out the word with you. Touch the letters and sound out the word with the students (for example, *sssaaatt*). Repeat the process until students respond correctly. At the end of the sounding, always ask the students to say the word. Because of the limitations in short-term memory, the longer the pause between sounding and saying the word, the greater the possibility that students will have difficulty saying the word.

5. After students gain confidence with the process, have them sound out words together and individually. Gradually reduce the time during which they sound the individual letter.

6. Note that all vowels and some consonants can be given a continuous sound in blending. Other consonants rely on the following vowel (for example, *ham*, *cat*). To teach blending with such words, have students initially make the sound for the vowel, because they will need to move quickly from the sound associated with the consonant to the sound associated with the vowel.

7. Point out to students that this strategy is not usually the first method of word recognition they will try and that it does not always work. Blending is a useful skill; however, some students tend to have difficulty using it or overuse it even after careful teaching.

8. After numerous blending exercises, help students understand that the goal of blending is to be able to pronounce or say a word that they have already heard.

9. Once parts of a word have been blended into a whole, focus on meaning. For example, if the blended word is *map*, ask students, "What is a map?" or "How could you use map in a sentence?" Keep the focus on meaning, not merely pronunciation.

Teaching Strategy 2
(adapted from Fox, 1996)

1. The basic procedure is for students to imagine the sounds of a word lined up on their shoulder to their hand. This is the blending pathway.

2. Demonstrate the procedure with a word like *kite*. Say the first sound as you place your right hand on your left shoulder, the second sound as you place your hand in the crook of your arm, and the third sound as you place your hand near your wrist. Then slide your right hand down your left arm from your shoulder to your wrist blending the sounds as your arm moves. For left-handed students, use your left hand on your right shoulder.

3. Model the process several times and have students join you.

4. Say the individual sounds in another word, have students place their hands on their arms at the shoulder, and blend the sounds together as they slide their hands down their arms. Then ask students what the word is. Repeat the process with other words.

5. When students are comfortable with the technique, have them blend silently. Then ask a student to say the entire word.

6. One variation is to enlarge the drawing of a slide and place it on the chalkboard tray. Tape or print letters on the slide so they go from the top to the bottom. Pronounce each sound as you slide your hand under each letter. Then ask a student to say the word, and write it at the bottom of the slide. Invite students to do the activity themselves, and provide guidance as necessary.

2.9   Oral Language

Behavior Observed	The student has limited oral expression.
Anticipated Outcome	The student will orally communicate in an effective and appropriate manner.

Perspective and Strategies

Successful readers draw upon what they know about language to interpret fine shades of meaning or to simply understand print. Students who do not have a rich, diverse language background may have difficulty understanding and interpreting text. Oral language, then, may be regarded as the basis for reading. Fostering oral expression provides students with the opportunity to learn language, its structures, and to build vocabulary.

The following suggestions may be helpful for increasing the quantity and quality of oral communication among students. Although these activities may be adapted for work with one student, language learning may be more successful in small groups because it increases interaction and provides more opportunity for oral expression.

1. Be open to what students want to talk about. Make encouraging comments to promote their language use. Listen carefully to what students say, and try to spend 80 percent of your time listening.

2. Provide a concrete experience and have students discuss the event. Opportunities for expression and interaction should be encouraged. During the discussion, list some key terms on the chalkboard. Next, write an experience story incorporating the key terms. Read chorally and take turns so that each student gets a chance to read alone or with a group.

3. Echo reading gives students an opportunity to repeat sentences that use appropriate syntax. Read a line of a story or poem aloud. Students repeat exactly what has been said. Repeat and allow students to echo read line by line. Using the sentence patterns, students may more readily communicate their own material.

4. Provide students with pictures and encourage sharing. Ask questions where appropriate. Invite students to bring in interesting photographs for discussion.

5. Bring in objects and have students discuss what they know about them.

6. Provide care for an animal to help foster a lively interchange of ideas.

7. Read a variety of books to students and discuss them.

8. Encourage students to make up a story that goes along with wordless picture books. A listing of books without words can be found in Appendix A.

9. Use puppets to promote communication among students. Puppets often encourage the shy student to participate in discussions.

10. Plan and take interesting field trips around the school and the community.

11. Introduce concept words such as *same-different*, *in-out*, and *over-under*.

12. Have students speak into a tape recorder one at a time. For the first experience, students may say their name, age, and something that they like to do. Play the tape back after each student has had an opportunity to speak. Exercise caution with students who are hesitant to participate in this activity; do not force the activity upon them. The teacher may also participate in this activity and serve as a role model. Later, students can tape record a story that they have made up or one to accompany a wordless picture book. Students will sometimes tell more elaborate stories when they speak into a tape recorder. The teacher or classroom volunteer may then make a copy of the individual story and have students illustrate it.

13. Expand the student's utterances. For example, if the student says, "The cat is black," the teacher may comment, "Yes, the cat is black except for the white markings on its paws."

14. Provide parents or caregivers with a list of suggestions for promoting rich oral language in the home. For example:

   ■ Read stories and books. Ask questions about the content, talk about the illustrations, and discuss points of interest.

   ■ Listen to your children. Provide many opportunities to use language. Don't become frustrated or impatient if they have difficulty expressing themselves clearly.

   ■ Take walks or excursions in the neighborhood or community. Talk about what you see. Point out things that children might miss. Give labels to these things and explain them in words appropriate for the child's level of maturity.

   ■ Talk to your children. Encourage them to talk about friends, interests, and special events at school.

   ■ Play card and board games that provide an opportunity for conversations about the game and other topics.

   ■ Help children expand their statements.

   Chapter 8 contains additional suggestions for working with families.

15. Encourage conversation by asking questions that require more than a "yes-or-no" answer.

16. Classify objects in various ways: by color, by shape, or by purpose. For example, have students list things that are green. Also, discuss an object in as much detail as possible.

17. Invite adults or older students into the classroom to listen to small groups of students share. Topics could include favorite play activities, television, or animals.

18. Create a picture file so students can take a picture and talk about it with a partner or small group of classmates.

19. Provide play or real telephones so students can have conversations with each other.

20. Encourage small-group and one-on-one discussions. Some of the best conversations may be the natural, language-rich activities that are part of daily classroom routines.

2.10   Visual Discrimination

Behavior Observed	The student has trouble discriminating differences among letters and words.
Anticipated Outcome	The student will discriminate differences among letters and words.

Background

Reading is more than a visual process; nevertheless, being able to discriminate letters and words accurately is crucial for efficient reading. In order to informally assess a student's visual discrimination, a hierarchy of five levels follows.

Level 1   Concrete objects

Level 2   Pictures

Level 3   Geometric shapes

Level 4   Letters

Level 5   Words and phrases

A student experiencing difficulty in the visual discrimination of letters or words may need to begin by differentiating similarities and differences in concrete objects, pictures, or geometric shapes. The emphasis should then move to exercises related to letters, words, and phrases, because these areas have the closest relationship to reading.

Prior to visual discrimination training, ensure that any visual problems are checked through visual screening or testing. Sometimes, especially in the early stages of reading instruction, there may be a visual cause that is responsible for discrimination problems. Once the visual problem has been corrected by lenses or treatment, specific teaching and practice strategies may be undertaken.

Before beginning instruction in visual discrimination, be sure the student understands the concepts of same and different. Beginning readers, and some older students experiencing difficulty in reading, fail to understand the "same-different" concepts. Usually, with the aid of concrete objects, these concepts can be established.

Teaching Strategy 1 *(Letters)*

1. For students who are having difficulty discriminating between letters, begin with unlike pairs that are grossly different (for example, *x–o*, *n–p*) and move to pairs that require finer discrimination (such as *c–o*, *r–n*, *m–n*, *p–q*, *b–d*).

2. Encourage students to verbalize reasons why the letter pairs are different. Let the students know that some letter pairs are particularly difficult to tell apart and model appropriate types of comments (for example, the *m* and the *n* are different because one letter has two humps and the other has one hump).

Teaching Strategy 2 *(Words)*

1. If students demonstrate the ability to discriminate between concrete objects, pictures, and geometric forms, proceed with words. On the chalkboard, write words that have gross structural or physical differences (such as *house*, *elephant*) and also words that are the same (for example, *run*, *run*). Discuss the similarities and differences in the word pairs.

2. Encourage students to express their thoughts on why the words are the same or different. Use questions such as:

   Are these words the same or different?

   How do you know?

   Are you sure that the different words have a different number of letters? Count them.

   Are you sure that the two words have exactly the same number of letters and kinds of letters?

   Are the letters in exactly the same position?

3. As these and other questions are asked, it is often useful to place one word of a pair under the other to aid discussion and promote a clearer grasp of the concept. For example, the first word pair is different because the first letter in each word is different; the other word pair is the same because all the letters are identical and occur in the same position.

house	run
	↕↕↕
elephant	run

4. Use a similar procedure when a certain part of the word is different from that of another word. For example:

[h]o p e	p[e]n	h o[t]
[r]o p e	p[i]n	h o[p]

5. Use a variety of words and encourage students to discuss why the words are the same or different. Some possible word pairs include these:

grandfather	bang	boy	went
grandmother	banging	boys	want

6. Prepare a short passage, display a particular word (such as *cat*), and have students circle the word each time it occurs in the passage.

Practice and Reinforcement Activities

1. Most practice activities are variations of matching games. A common activity is to ask students to draw a circle around a letter or word that is the same as the example. The choices vary in difficulty. A variation of this activity is to have students put a line through the letter or word that does not match the sample.

2. Use two columns of words (or letters) and have students draw lines from words in the left column to the same words (or letters) in the right column.

3. Give students a set of cards containing words (or letters) and have them hold up the word (or letter) that matches your sample.

4. Prepare a page with a letter or word at the top of the page and have students circle the letter or word each time it appears.

Games

Wordo. Word or Letter Bingo. Prepare cards containing words or letters. Hold up a stimulus card and have students place a marker on the square that is the same as the stimulus. The first student who gets Wordo wins.

W	O	R	D	O
big	if	was	it	on
no	get	to	then	when
saw	where	got	too	there

W	O	R	D	O
no	where	to	too	there
saw	get	was	then	on
big	if	got	it	when

Match. Prepare two cards for each letter or word that tends to cause confusion. Students take turns matching the letters or words. The student who gets the most pairs wins. One variation of the game involves the use of a stopwatch or timer. Each student attempts to better his or her previous time.

Letters and Names. Prepare a large set of cards containing the letters of the alphabet (capital and lowercase letters). Give students their names on individual letter cards. Hold up one large card at a time. Students who have the same letter(s) turn over the appropriate card(s) in their names. Play the game until the number of students designated have turned over all the letters in their names. The games can be played with first names, last names, or entire names. One variation is to have students exchange names with a friend. Favorite words can also be used.

Behavior Observed	The student reverses letters or words.
Anticipated Outcome	The student will reduce the number of reversals.

Perspective and Strategies

It is not unusual for some beginning readers and for older students experiencing difficulty in reading to reverse letters or words. To succeed in reading, students must learn that reading is a left-to-right activity.

Researchers have hypothesized many causes to explain reversals. Among them are visual problems and mixed dominance as well as an unfamiliarity with directionality as it relates to letter and word discrimination. The recommended procedure is to provide direct instruction with letters or words that are causing the student difficulty. If the student is a beginning reader, some reversals may be developmental in nature; however, if they persist, referral for more intensive study may be warranted. The following strategies may be helpful.

1. Teach students the concepts of left and right by showing them the difference between their left hand and right hand. Give oral directions where students must use their left hand or right hand to touch a book, pick up a pencil, open the door, and so on. Other body parts may also be used.

2. Transfer the concepts of left and right to reading by demonstrating how names are read from left to right.

3. Develop brief stories that can be placed on the chalkboard. Choose one student to point to the words as they are read to the class. Stress that reading goes from left to right. The hand or pointer indicates the required direction in reading. A sample is shown here.

   Today is December 17.

   The weather is cold and snowy.

   Christmas vacation begins after school today.

   Christmas will soon be here.

4. Provide exercises where students draw lines to connect dots horizontally and obliquely and relate the activity to lines of print. An example follows:

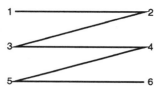

5. Have students draw an arrow, pointing to the right, under the first letter of a word or sentence.

6. Provide exercises to help eliminate common reversals (such as *was* and *saw, no* and *on*) by practicing on paper where the student is directed to trace over a word whenever it appears. An example follows:

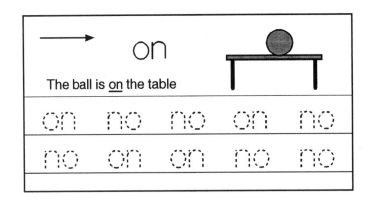

7. Provide sentences in which a reversal will result in a sentence that doesn't make sense. When students read each sentence ask, "Does it make sense?" Ask this question, even when sentences are read correctly, to promote thinking while reading. Several sample sentences follow:

Was–Saw Confusion	**There–Three confusion**
I *saw* my dad.	We have *three* cats.
She *was* eating an apple.	*There* is his dog.
We *saw* the book.	Put the book over *there.*
It *was* in the box.	The *three* boys are playing.

8. Place commonly reversed words so they can be closely compared. Discuss similarities and differences. An example follows:

   w a s   Both have three letters.

             Both have the same three letters but in different positions.

   s a w   Both have an *a* in the middle.

9. Use a sentence that the student can read (or a word he or she can spell); make an elongated picture (snake, dragon, alligator); and write the sentence over the picture. Cut out the sentence and ask the student to put the sentence back together from left to right. Then have the student write the sentence. Words or stories can be substituted for sentences in this activity.

10. Provide lots of practice using a multisensory approach that involves forming the letter or word in sand, finger paint, or shaving cream. Pipe cleaners, Play Doh, or sandpaper can also be used to make letters or words.

11. Use the word *bed* to help the student learn *b* and *d*. Teach the student to spell *bed*, and draw attention to the two "posts" on the bed to help with letter formation. Find and share a good illustration of a poster bed with the student or use the illustration on the following page.

12. Use the word *pig* to help the student learn *p* and *g*. Teach the spelling and use the following graphic to help the student see that the *p* and *g* can help form the lines of a circle.

13. Provide letter or word activities where the student is asked to circle a particular letter or word. For example, circle every *n*.

```
n   x   o   m   n   u   m   u   n
w   h   n   n   v   m   n   v   h
```

Games

Fish. On paper fish write words that students frequently confuse. Attach a paper clip to each fish. Using a fishing pole made of a yardstick, string, and magnet, have the student fish for words. If the word can be pronounced correctly, the student keeps it; if not, he or she throws it back. Students having difficulty should play this game with students who already recognize the words. The words can also be used in sentences.

Tricky Words. Students who have some reading ability should be encouraged to read troublesome words or phrases in short sentences. Prepare a gameboard with phrases or sentences containing frequently confused words (for example, I *saw* the bear. He *was* here.). Students roll dice and proceed to the appropriate space. If the student can read the phrase, he or she can stay there. If the phrase or word is not read correctly, the student returns to his or her previous position. The student who first crosses the finish line wins.

Behavior Observed	The student does not understand the parts that make up a story and may be unable to retell story events successfully.
Anticipated Outcome	The student will understand the parts of a story and will retell story events accurately.

Background

Good readers possess background for text structure that allows them to anticipate and understand how the details relate to the main theme of a written piece of discourse. For beginning readers, this sense of story must be developed sufficiently for comprehension to occur.

Simple stories include characters, a sequence of events, conflict, and resolution. In reading, a sense of what composes stories influences the student's prediction, comprehension, and recall of stories. In writing, students often create stories around their internal concept or understanding of those elements that compose a story.

Texts contain a variety of elements, or story structures, that relate characters and occur in a certain sequence. Most story structures include:

setting

initiating event

internal response

attempt

outcome   These elements make up episodes.
                    There may be one or more per story.
consequence

reaction

Teaching Strategy 1 *(For Younger Students)*

1. Encourage students to predict what the material or story will be about using clues such as title and cover illustrations. Read a little of the text, perhaps one or two pages. Discuss the accuracy of the predictions. Predict what will happen next by asking open-ended questions. Check out that prediction by asking students to defend their answers from material specific to the story or text. Continue the prediction-confirmation pattern until the passage has been completed. Daily practice with predictions will enhance story structure and improve comprehension.

2. Begin with a well-known story such as *Goldilocks and the Three Bears* or *Little Red Riding Hood.* Encourage students to share what they remember about the story. Write their responses on the chalkboard. For example:

There was a little girl named Goldilocks.

There were three bears.

Goldilocks went into the bears' house when they were gone.

3. After students have shared their responses, ask them to name some of the parts that make up a story. Responses might include where it takes place, people, animals, and things happening. Use words offered by the students and begin to develop the concept that stories are made up of places (settings), people and/or animals (characters), and things happening (actions or episodes). Also, tell students that stories have a beginning, middle, and end.

4. Write three major story elements on the chalkboard and have students that have previously shared information classify their responses under the proper elements. For example:

Goldilocks and the Three Bears

Places	People and Animals	Things that Happen
in the woods	Goldilocks	She went into the
house	Papa Bear	bears' house.

5. Then read the story to the class and encourage them to listen carefully so they can confirm or enlarge upon their earlier contributions. After the story has been read, have students share story elements. Write them on the chalkboard. Encourage a discussion that emphasizes and expands major story elements.

Goldilocks and the Three Bears

Places	People and Animals	Things That Happen
a house in the woods	Goldilocks	The bears went for a walk in the woods.
kitchen	three bears	Goldilocks went into their house while they were away.
living room	Papa Bear	She found three bowls of porridge.
bedroom	Mama Bear	She ate Baby Bear's porridge.
	Baby Bear	She sat in the three bears' chairs.
		She broke Baby Bear's chair.
		She went into the bedroom and tried out the beds.
		She fell asleep in Baby Bear's bed.
		The three bears returned.

6. Repeat this basic procedure with other stories. Emphasize how students can use their knowledge of story structure to better understand or remember a story. Knowledge of story structure may also aid in predicting what might happen next in new stories.

Teaching Strategy 2 *(For Older Students)*

1. Consider the approach used with younger students. It is possible to develop the elements of story structure in greater depth through character analysis, details of the setting, and a discussion of theme and plot. Also, some variations of well-known stories can be anlayzed. For example, five versions of Cinderella include:

- Climo, S. *The Egyptian Cinderella*. New York: HarperCollins, 1989.

- Huck, C. *Princess Furball*. New York: Greenwillow, 1989.

- Martin, R. *The Rough-Face Girl*. New York: Putnam, 1992.

- Steel, F.A. *Tattercoats*, New York: Bradbury, 1976.

- Steptoe, J. *Mufaro's Beautiful Daughters*. New York: Lathrop, Lee & Shepárdi, 1993.

2. Use a visual representation of story structure to help students understand major story elements. Discuss them. Students should understand that the setting is the place or location of the story and the time (present, past, or future) when the story takes place. The characters are the people or animals that the story focuses on. There can be major or minor characters. The plot is the general plan of the story, which is composed of actions or episodes. The episodes lead to a climax, which is the high point of the story.

3. After the story elements have been presented and discussed, read a well-known story (for example, *The City Mouse and the Country Mouse* or *The Three Billy Goats Gruff*) and have students form small groups to construct a visual representation of the story. Have the various groups discuss their representations. Encourage the use of proper terminology (setting, character, episodes) presented earlier. Repeat this basic procedure with other stories. The use of key questions can be used to help students uncover the major story elements, for example:

Setting	Where does the story take place?
	When does the story take place?
	Does the action of this story occur in different places? If so, where?
Characters	Who are the people or animals in this story?
	Are some people more important than others? If so, which ones?
	What words does the author use to describe the characters or animals?
	What other words can also be used to describe the character?
Plot	What happens in this story?
	What problems or difficulties are there?
	How are the problems or difficulties solved?
	In what order do the major events happen?
	Who or what started the events in the story?

Practice and Reinforcement Activities

1. Encourage parents to read to their children. Reading aloud often helps the listener to internalize the story structure. Discussions with the child can also help in developing a sense of story structure.

2. Provide many opportunities for students to hear and read many different kinds of literature. Discuss the major story elements with them. Storytelling can also be used.

3. When appropriate, have students role play or dramatize stories. If an entire story does not lend itself to dramatization, select one or more episodes and have several groups of students present scenes to the class.

4. Have students make drawings or illustrations of the major events in a story. These drawings can serve as a basis for retelling the story.

5. Retell a familiar story by changing certain key elements (setting, character, and events). Then, have students correct the retelling. Depending on the students involved, you may want to change "obvious" characters, events, or settings. Later, brief written summaries of stories can be used. After students read the summaries, they correct the erroneous information. An excellent story of this type is *The True Story of the 3 Pigs by A. Wolf* (Scieszka, 1989).

6. Help students learn to use semantic webbing. According to Freeman and Reynolds (1980), semantic webbing contains the following: (1) a core question—focus of the web, which is initially chosen by the teacher; (2) web strands—answers that students give to the core questions; (3) strand supports—facts, inferences, and generalizations that students give to differentiate one strand from another; and (4) strand ties—the relationships that strands have with one another. As students become more comfortable with semantic webbing, they can show relationships among characters and events (adapted from Freeman & Reynolds, 1980) as shown here:

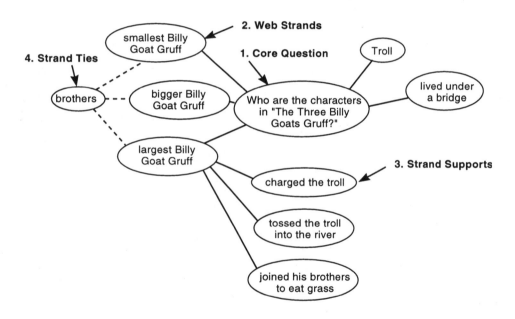

7. Semantic webbing is especially useful for helping students to identify story elements related to characters and events. Possible core questions of a generic nature include these:

Who are the characters?

What words describe the characters?

What are the major events?

What happens in each major event?

8. The example below, based on "Little Miss Muffet," may be used to help students visualize the major elements in the story. The terminology can be changed to match the words used in lessons. Acting out nursery rhymes with logical sequences can help students identify story elements. Change the order of events so students will see how the new order destroys the story line.

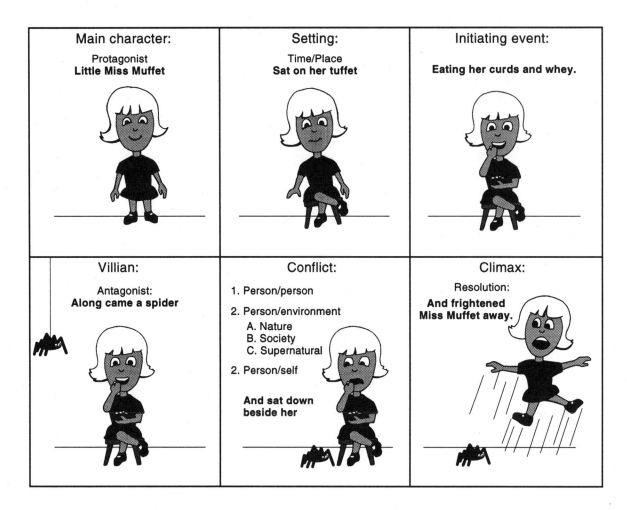

9. Have older students begin a story by writing the setting. Then have students exchange papers and write about characters. Repeat the process with problem/conflict, and solution/resolution. Then return the story to the student who began it. After giving time for independent reading, invite students to share in small groups.

10. Write or dictate stories based on wordless picture books. A list of such books can be found in Appendix A.

Resources for Chapter 2

Informal Tests

➤ Assessment of Alphabet Knowledge

➤ Phoneme Segmentation

➤ Assessment of Auditory Discrimination

Teacher Resources

➤ Phonemic Awareness: Books To Read Aloud

➤ Sound Boxes (for 2.6 Teaching Strategy 3)

Assessment of Alphabet Knowledge

Jerry L. Johns

Purpose

Alphabet Knowledge contains upper-case and lower-case letters of the alphabet in non-sequential order to help assess letter-identification ability.

Administration

1. Duplicate the Record Sheet and get two 3" × 5" cards.

2. Place the alphabet page before the student and ask him or her to identify any known letters. Say, **"Here are some letters. I want to see how many you know."** Encourage the student to say "pass" or "skip it" if a particular letter is not known.

3. Use the 3" × 5" cards to block off everything but the lines being read. If necessary, point to each letter with a finger.

4. As the student responds, use the Record Booklet to note correct (+) and incorrect responses. When responses are incorrect, record the actual response or dk (student doesn't know) above the stimulus letter. If the student self-corrects, write OK; self-corrections can be made at any time.

Letter	Meaning of Recording
+	
O	Identified correctly
D.K.	
H	Don't know
C	
S	Said C for S
B o.k.	
E	Said B for E but self-corrected

Scoring and Interpretation

Count the correct number of responses for the upper-case letters and the lower-case letters. Based on the number of correct responses, make a judgment of the student's alphabet knowledge. Unknown letters or incorrect responses may help form the basis for instructional interventions.

Assessment of Alphabet Knowledge Record Sheet

Jerry L. Johns

> **Directions:** Present the alphabet sheet. Use 3" × 5" cards to block off everything but the lines being read. If necessary, point to each letter with a finger. Then say, **"Here are some letters. I want to see how many you know."** Place + above correctly identified letters. Record the student's responses for incorrect letters. Total correct responses, and record the score in the box.

```
O   H   S   E   G   P

X   V   I   M   J   D   K

B   T   R   Z   F   N

Y   Q   W   C   U   A   L
```

```
b   x   e   c   j   m

l   u   r   t   q   h   y

s   d   o   a   k   w

i   p   v   f   n   z   q
```

Phoneme Segmentation

Hallie Kay Yopp

Purpose

Phonemic awareness refers to the student's knowledge of phonemes or sounds in speech. This ability is strongly related to success in reading and spelling acquisition. This assessment was designed for use with English speaking kindergartners. It may also be used with older students experiencing difficulty in literacy acquisition.

Administration

1. Duplicate the Record Sheet.

2. With the student, say **"Today we're going to play a word game. I'm going to say a word and I want you to break the word apart. You are going to tell me each sound in the word in order. For example, if I say 'old,' you should say '/o/-/l/-/d/.'"** (Administrator: *Be sure to say the sounds, not the letters, in the word.*)

3. Then say, **"Let's try a few together."** The practice items are *ride*, *go*, and *man*. If necessary, help the student by segmenting the word for the student. Encourage the student to repeat the segmented sounds.

4. During the test, feedback is provided to the student. You could nod or say "Right" or "That's right." If the student is incorrect, correct him or her. You should also provide the appropriate response.

5. Proceed through all 22 items. Circle those items that the student correctly segments. Incorrect responses may be recorded on the blank line following the item.

Scoring and Interpretation

The student's score is the number of items he or she correctly segments into all constituent phonemes. No partial credit is given. For example, *she* (item 5) contains two phonemes /sh/-/e/; *grew* (item 7) contains three phonemes /g/-/r/-/ew/; and *three* (item 15) contains three phonemes /th/-/r/-/ee/. If the student notes letter names instead of sounds, the response is coded as incorrect, and the type of error is noted in the record sheet. Such notes are helpful in understanding the student. Some students may partially segment, simply repeat the stimulus item, provide nonsense responses, or give letter names. For further information on this test, see Hallie Kay Yopp, "A Test for Assessing Phonemic Awareness in Young Children," *The Reading Teacher*, 49(1) (September 1995), 20-29. A wide range of scores is likely. Yopp (1995) reported that two samples of kindergartners achieved mean scores of 11.78 and 11.39.

Phoneme Segmentation

Hallie Kay Yopp

> ***Directions:*** Today we're going to play a word game. I'm going to say a word and I want you to break the word apart. You are going to tell me each sound in the word in order. For example, if I say "old," you should say "/o/-/l/-/d/." (*Administrator: Be sure to say the sounds, not the letters, in the word.*) Let's try a few together.

Practice items: (*Assist the child in segmenting these items as necessary.*)   ride,   go,   man

Test items: (*Circle those items that the student correctly segments; incorrect responses may be recorded on the blank line following the item.*)   The correct number of phonemes is indicated in parentheses.

1. dog (3) _____
2. keep (3) _____
3. fine (3) _____
4. no (2) _____
5. she (2) _____
6. wave (3) _____
7. grew (3) _____
8. that (3) _____
9. red (3) _____
10. me (2) _____
11. sat (3) _____

12. lay (2) _____
13. race (3) _____
14. zoo (2) _____
15. three (3) _____
16. job (3) _____
17. in (2) _____
18. ice (2) _____
19. at (2) _____
20. top (2) _____
21. by (2) _____
22. do (2) _____

Total Correct [ ]

The author, Hallie Kay Yopp, California State University, Fullerton, grants permission for this test to be reproduced. The author acknowledges the contribution of the late Harry Singer to the development of this test. Adapted from Yopp, H.K. (1995). A test for assessing phonemic awareness in young children. *The Reading Teacher, 49*(1), 20-29.

Assessment of Auditory Discrimination

Jerry L. Johns

Purpose

To informally evaluate the student's ability to distinguish between words that differ in one phoneme (sound) by listening.

Administration

1. Practice the words on the list, saying them clearly in a normal voice.

2. Do not rush the student during the testing. Darken the Same or Different box if the student responds correctly. Draw a line through the square if the student makes an incorrect response.

3. If the student misses a pair or asks for one to be repeated, move on to the next and return to it at the conclusion of the test.

4. Facing the student, say:

   "Listen to the two words I am about to say: *FAIR–FAR*."

   "Do they sound exactly the same or are they different?" (For young children, the examiner may prefer the words "alike" and "not alike" in place of the words "same" and "different.")

   "Yes, they are different."

   "Listen to these two words: *CAP–CAP*."

   "Are they the same or different?"

   "Now I am going to read you pairs of words. I want you to tell me if they are the same or different. Do you understand what you are to do? Please turn your back to me and listen very carefully."

5. Say all the words distinctly but in a normal voice.

Scoring and Interpretation

1. Add up the incorrect Same and Different responses and enter the number in the error score boxes. The following error score would indicate inadequate auditory ability:

   > 5-year-olds – errors in Different box greater than 6
   > 6-year-olds – errors in Different box greater than 5
   > 7-year-olds – errors in Different box greater than 4
   > 8-year-olds – errors in Different box greater than 3

2. More than three errors in the Same box indicates an invalid test. The alternate form of the test should be used.

Assessment of Auditory Discrimination: Forms A and B

Jerry L. Johns

Form A		Same	Different		Form B		Same	Different
1. though	– show		☐		1. breathe	– brief		☐
2. bad	– dad		☐		2. grove	– growth		☐
3. sit	– sick		☐		3. fuss	– thus		☐
4. jump	– jump	☐			4. mall	– mall	☐	
5. buff	– bus		☐		5. fame	– feign		☐
6. mat	– gnat		☐		6. mast	– mask		☐
7. dub	– dug		☐		7. thing	– thing	☐	
8. oath	– oaf		☐		8. disk	– desk		☐
9. lag	– lad		☐		9. duck	– dock		☐
10. judge	– judge	☐			10. suit	– soup		☐
11. set	– sit		☐		11. crab	– crag		☐
12. watch	– watch	☐			12. zig	– zig	☐	
13. ball	– bowl		☐		13. brash	– brass		☐
14. sink	– think		☐		14. sad	– said		☐
15. luck	– lock		☐		15. van	– than		☐
16. tot	– top		☐		16. thin	– shin		☐
17. duck	– duck	☐			17. mud	– mug		☐
18. foam	– phone		☐		18. save	– shave		☐
19. mauve	– moth		☐		19. bask	– bath		☐
20. seek	– sheik		☐		20. age	– age	☐	
21. fought	– thought		☐		21. froze	– froze	☐	
22. done	– gun		☐		22. sew	– saw		☐
23. chop	– chop	☐			23. bib	– bid		☐
24. can	– tan		☐		24. came	– tame		☐
25. boat	– goat		☐		25. cat	– pat		☐
26. lab	– lad		☐		26. busy	– dizzy		☐
27. light	– sight		☐		27. debt	– get		☐
28. zinc	– zinc	☐			28. tank	– thank		☐
29. sing	– sing	☐			29. fought	– sought		☐
30. bed	– bad		☐		30. guessed	– best		☐
31. moss	– moth		☐		31. touch	– touch	☐	
32. till	– pill		☐		32. tick	– tip		☐
33. fall	– fall	☐			33. tail	– pail		☐
34. mass	– mash		☐		34. jury	– jury	☐	
35. vine	– thine		☐		35. champ	– champ	☐	
36. rode	– rode	☐			36. lass	– laugh		☐
37. cot	– pot		☐		37. maze	– maze	☐	
38. rap	– rack		☐		38. math	– mass		☐
39. mash	– math		☐		39. star	– star	☐	
40. mar	– mar	☐			40. nice	– mice		☐

Error Score: Same [ ] Different [ ] Error Score: Same [ ] Different [ ]

Inadequate auditory discrimination is indicated by more than:

6 errors in Different box for 5-year-olds 4 errors in Different box for 7-year-olds
5 errors in Different box for 6-year-olds 3 errors in Different box for 8-year-olds

An invalid test is indicated by more than 3 errors in same box.

From Jerry L. Johns and Susan Davis Lenski, *Improving Reading: A Handbook of Strategies* (2nd ed.). Copyright © 1997 Kendall/Hunt Publishing Company (1-800-228-0810). May be reproduced for noncommercial educational purposes.

Phonemic Awareness: Books to Read Aloud

Brown, M.W. *Four Fur Feet.* New York: Doubleday, 1993.
In this book, the student is drawn to the /f/ sound as the phrase "four fur feet" is repeated in every sentence as a furry animal walks around the world. The same pattern is used throughout the story.

Carter, D. *More Bugs in Boxes.* New York: Simon and Schuster, 1990.
This pop-up book contains a series of questions and answers about make-believe bugs who are found inside a variety of boxes. Both the questions and answers make use of alliteration: "What kind of bug is in the rosy red rectangle box? A bright blue big mouth bug."

Deming, A.G. *Who is Tapping at My Window?* New York: Penguin, 1994.
A young girl hears a tapping at her window and asks, "Who is there?" The farm animals each respond, "It's not I," and she discovers that it is the rain. The book is predictable in that each pair of animals rhymes (e.g., dog/frog).

Geraghty, P. *Stop That Noise!* New York: Crown, 1992.
A mouse is annoyed with the many sounds of the forest. The animal and machine sounds make the book useful in drawing students' attention to the sounds in language.

Gordon, J. *Six Sleepy Sheep.* New York: Puffin Books, 1991.
The use of the /s/ sound throughout the book is useful for developing a letter-sound association.

Kuskin, K. *Roar and More.* New York: HarperTrophy, 1990.
This book contains many poems and pictures that portray the sounds that animals make. Both the use of rhyme and presentation of animal sounds draw students' attention to sounds.

Lewison, W. *Buzz Said the Bee.* New York: Scholastic, 1992.
A series of animals sit on top of one another in this story. Before each animal climbs on top of the next, it does something that rhymes with the animal it approaches. For example, "the pig takes a bow before sitting on the cow."

Otto, C. *Dinosaur Chase.* New York: HarperTrophy, 1991.
Both alliteration and rhyme are present in this simple, colorful book.

Parry, C. *Zoomerang-a-Boomerang: Poems to Make Your Belly Laugh.* New York: Puffin Books, 1991.
Practically all of the poems in this collection play with language, particularly through the use of predictable and humorous rhyme patterns.

Pomerantz, C. *If I Had a Paka.* New York: Mulberry, 1993.
Eleven languages are represented among the 12 poems included in this book. Attention is drawn to phonemes (sounds) when languages other than English are introduced. Rhyme and repetition are also included.

Sendak, M. *Alligators All Around: An Alphabet.* New York: HarperTrophy, 1990.
This book uses alliteration for each letter of the alphabet.

Adapted from Yopp, H.K. (1995). Read-aloud books for developing phonemic awareness: An annotated bibliography. *The Reading Teacher, 48*(6), 538-542.

Sound Boxes

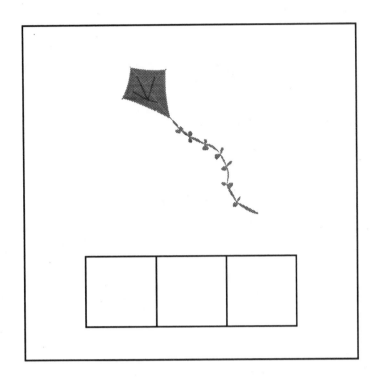

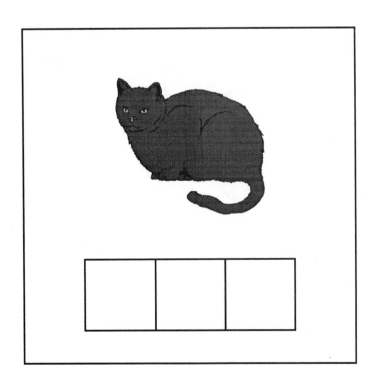

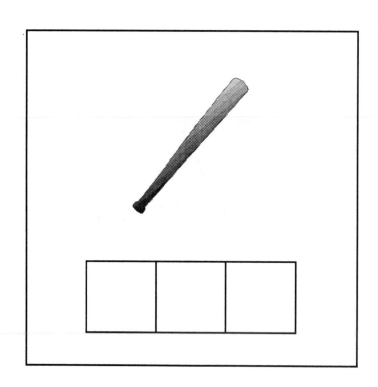

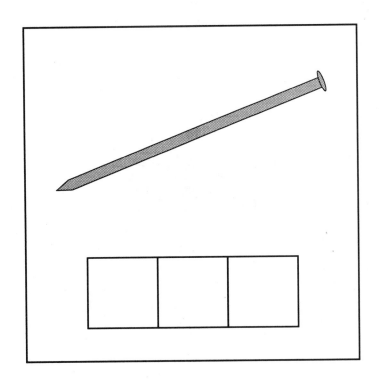

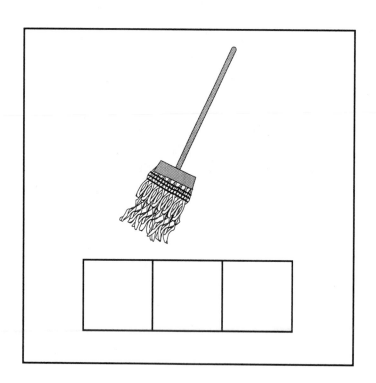

CHAPTER 3

Developing Fluency and Successful Oral Reading Behaviors

Overview

Reading fluency is the ability to read text in a normal speaking voice with appropriate intonation and inflection. Students who read fluently have developed automaticity (Samuels, 1994). Automaticity means that students do not have to devote their attention to the task of decoding words; they can focus on constructing the meaning of what they are reading. Suppose Maria is able to read each of the words in a passage correctly, but pauses after each word. She may have difficulty understanding the passage because of her lack of fluency. Good readers read fluently without much thought about how they are reading. Struggling readers, on the other hand, may read word by word in a monotone or spend so much time trying to pronounce words that they have little or no attention focused on constructing meaning.

Related to fluency are a variety of oral reading behaviors. Although oral reading has traditionally been misused, good teachers understand that both silent reading and oral reading are valuable tools for instructional decisions. Just as silent reading tends to be a better method for assessing reading comprehension, oral reading provides important information about the reader's proficiency in applying reading strategies.

Oral reading can serve two primary purposes: assessment and performance. When used as an assessment tool, oral reading should be private. Teachers should listen to students individually to assess reading miscues or to identify problems with reading fluency. On the other hand, oral reading can be an end in itself, a public performance. If students are reading aloud for the purpose of performing, they should read for an appropriate audience.

This chapter is divided into two parts. The first part examines oral reading as assessment. It begins with a rationale for using oral reading as a diagnostic tool and then considers fluency and common difficulties students may have when reading aloud. The second part discusses reading as performance. Again, it begins with a rationale for oral reading as performance and then provides suggestions for using oral reading in the classroom.

Oral Reading as Assessment

Oral reading can provide teachers with useful diagnostic information about the strategies students employ as they read. Imagine a second-grade student, Maria, who has just silently read a grade-appropriate book. Maria is unable to retell any part of the story. Is Maria's comprehension problem the result of insufficient background knowledge, a weak understanding of story structure, or could it be the result of too many miscues? Of course, the answer is impossible to determine without listening to Maria read aloud.

Say that you ask Maria to read her favorite part of the story. Using picture clues, Maria turns to her chosen chapter, but as she reads, you notice she makes several miscues per page. These miscues, or deviations from the text, signal to you that Maria's lack of comprehension may be attributed, at least in part, to oral reading difficulties. You can then pinpoint Maria's problems and use some of the recommendations in this chapter to create mini-lessons for Maria and other students with the same problem.

You may have students who read all of the words in a passage correctly but still do not understand what the words are saying because they are not reading them in natural phrases. Word by word reading can hinder comprehension. If you have students who are not fluent readers, refer to sections 3.1 and 3.2 for strategies to help build reading fluency.

You should not attempt oral reading as a diagnostic tool, as in the case of miscues, in a public setting or in the traditional round-robin reading situation. Round-robin reading is asking one student to read aloud while a group of students listen. Think back to your own days in school. Most likely you had at least one teacher who used round-robin reading. Were you uncomfortable when it was your turn to read? Many students who are asked to read aloud in front of a group are acutely embarrassed. What did you do when other students were reading? Students often read ahead, lose their place, yell out corrections, or simply tune out. None of these behaviors promote good reading or a stimulating reading discussion, yet some teachers persist in round-robin reading in their classes. Round-robin reading is not a good use of class time. See Resources for Chapter 3 for Oral Reading Alternatives to Round-Robin Reading.

How, then, should you listen to students read aloud if you don't have them read in front of the class? Remember, listening to oral reading is a private performance between you and your student. Instead of wasting time with round-robin reading, make a commitment to listen to each student read every two or three weeks. That means you should listen to two or three students read every day.

Reading with individual students should take only ten minutes out of your daily schedule. While the class is completing reading-writing activities, simply ask one student at a time to read with you. Make this a personal time between you and your student. Don't sit at your desk, but move to the student's desk or to another table. During the session, alternate between choosing the selection for the student and letting the student make the decision about what to read. The passage you select may be from a reading book, trade book, or graded reading passage. When you select material for oral reading, choose a passage the student has not yet read. Remember, your purpose is to listen for the reading strategies your student uses while reading rather than to hear a practiced piece of prose.

When the student reads to you, note the kinds of miscues he or she makes. You may jot down the miscues while you are tape recording the student and record them on a chart (see Resources for Chapter 3). As the student reads, you can also assess the use of comprehension strategies by asking the student to retell the story.

At the end of two or three weeks, you should have information about the oral reading strategies of each student. You can group the students for instruction by their reading needs. For example, students who are word-by-word readers can meet with you for a lesson on reading fluency. Students who tend to omit words can be grouped together for that lesson. It's important to remember that one of the purposes of listening to your students read aloud is to make instructional decisions. Listening to oral reading can be the basis for much of what you teach.

Listening to oral reading can also be the basis for retrospective miscue analysis. Retrospective miscue analysis invites and engages students to reflect upon and evaluate the reading process by analyzing their oral reading miscues (Goodman & Marek, 1996). In essence, students can use retrospective miscue analysis to realize the predicting, confirming, and correcting behaviors that characterize good readers; moreover, such analysis "can help them come to revalue themselves as readers" (Goodman & Marek, 1996, p. ix). Whenever available and appropriate, we urge you to use students' reading miscues for instructional purposes in the various situations we describe. For each situation, the behaviors are listed with the outcome you should anticipate after you have designed appropriate intervention. Please remember that you need not use every strategy listed in each part. Use only the ones that best complement the needs of your students.

3.1 Lack of Fluency

Behavior Observed	The student's oral reading lacks fluency.
Anticipated Outcome	The student will read more fluently.

Perspective and Strategies

Many emergent readers lack fluency as they begin reading. They may be *choppy readers,* reading with many stops, starts, and hesitations. They may be *monotonous readers* and read with little or no expression, or they may be inappropriately *hasty readers* and race through the passage ignoring phrasing and punctuation (Wilson, 1988). The cause of fluency problems for beginning readers is that they are processing many new things at the same time. They are just beginning to expand their sight vocabulary and are learning word-identification strategies. For beginning readers, fluency may be considered a developmental process. As they learn more reading strategies, they become more fluent. Such is the case for most beginning readers, whatever their age.

Older readers may also have difficulty reading fluently. These students probably lack a basic sight vocabulary and effective word-identification strategies. They may also be reading books that are too difficult for them.

Clay (1967) has noted that average readers typically move through the four stages of reading described below. Teachers who see students *remaining* at the second or third stage have cause for concern and may need to use intervention strategies.

Stage	Characteristics/Behaviors
1	Reading sounds fluent, but students make many miscues. Students are unaware or unconcerned that their reading does not accurately represent the passage or text.
2	Students are conscious of matching their speech to words in the passage or text. Students may point to individual words. Students may read in a staccato fashion.
3	Students continue reading word by word, but finger-pointing disappears. Students are still conscious of matching their oral responses to each word.
4	Students no longer read word by word. Meaningful phrase units characterize reading.

Numerous strategies for developing sight vocabulary and word identification are presented in Chapter 4, and they should be considered in tandem with the following strategies. Note that there are two major classifications of strategies—one for younger, emergent readers and another for older, struggling readers.

For Younger, Emergent Readers

1. Recognize that reading is a developmental process and fluency will develop as students increase their sight vocabularies and acquire a repertoire of word-identification strategies. A lack of fluency may be expected at this level.

2. Encourage the repeated readings of pattern books. See Appendix C for a listing of pattern books and related activities. Plenty of practice will help students learn sight words automatically and will build their confidence. Students can read to each other, to their favorite stuffed animal, to parents and relatives, and so on.

3. Use daily class experience stories and guide students in the reading. A story could be as simple as the following:

   Today is _____.

   The date is _____, November _____.

   The weather is _____.

   Begin by inviting volunteers to supply missing words. Then read the story to the class. Encourage students to join you. Point to words and phrases. Use your hand to indicate phrases and have individuals and the whole class read and reread the story. Comment positively on the smoothness of the reading.

4. Provide opportunities for students to listen to talking books on audio tapes or computer programs. Capitalize on their interests when a particularly popular audio tape or computer program is identified by staying out of the way while students enjoy the same experience over and over.

5. Fasten a sheet of paper in the front of books that students can read to others at home or school. The sheet is signed by the person who has listened to the book.

6. Use echo reading where you read a phrase or sentence and the student repeats it after you and tries to "echo" your phrasing and expression.

7. Identify songs and rhymes that are enjoyed by students. Print the words on chart paper, the overhead projector, or the chalkboard. Engage in repeated readings or singings.

8. Read a passage for students explaining that you are reading with expression. Tell students to pay attention to *how* you read the passage. Then ask students to read the passage with you. Ask students to try to read with the same expression that you use. Reread the passage together until students seem comfortable with the text. Next, fade out of the reading by lowering your voice or stopping reading while students continue. Finally, ask a student to read the passage alone and give praise for appropriate expression.

9. Make a videotape of yourself reading an easy book. Send the book and videotape home with the student to practice reading at home.

For Older, Struggling Readers

1. Be sure students are not asked to read books that are too difficult. A student who makes ten or more miscues in 100 words is probably being asked to read material that is too difficult. Seek easier materials where the student will make fewer than seven miscues in every 100 words. Remember that word recognition must be accurate before it can become automatic.

2. The method of structured repeated readings found in the Resources for Chapter 3 is an excellent strategy. It motivates struggling readers and provides a visible means for them to see their progress.

3. Encourage wide reading and rereading of easy books.

4. Invite students to prepare a story to read orally to younger readers. Have the student practice with a tape recorder and also share the story with you before it is shared with the group of younger students. Ensure that the experience will be a positive one.

5. Have students practice so-called "easy" books that can be enjoyed by younger students. The books can be recorded on video and/or audio tape and shared with younger students.

6. Try the neurological impress method. The basic procedure is listed in the box.

PROCEDURE FOR THE NEUROLOGICAL IMPRESS METHOD (NIM)
(Adapted from Heckelman, 1969)

1. The student sits slightly in front of the teacher so that the teacher's voice is close to the student's ear.

2. The student is told not to think about reading; you are helping him or her to slide the eyes across the paper. Another explanation is that just as we practice swimming in order to become good swimmers, we need to practice reading to become good readers.

3. The teacher and student read the same material out loud *together*; the teacher reads a *little* louder and faster than the student.

4. *Re-read* the initial lines or paragraph several times together before going on to new material (that is, wait until you feel the student is confident in reading that section). Drop your voice back behind the student's if you think he or she is gaining fluency.

5. In the *initial* sessions, 2-3 minutes of reading lines is sufficient. The aim is to establish a fluent reading pattern in the reader; appropriate *intonation* and *expression* in reading the lines are vital.

6. At *no* time correct the student or test the student in any way. The major concern is with the style of reading rather than with reading accuracy.

7. The teacher runs his or her finger under the words *simultaneously* with the words being read. The student should take over this function when he or she is confident enough. The teacher can help the student by placing his or her hand over the student's and guiding it smoothly. *Make sure finger and voice* are operating together.

8. *Echoing* is used as a supplementary technique to NIM if a student has extreme difficulty with saying a phrase or word. The student must repeat the phrase *after* the teacher several times and when he or she has satisfactorily repeated the phrase, the teacher then goes back to the *written* version.

9. Periodically, the pace *must* be speeded up just for a few minutes.

10. Start with reading material *lower* than the student is presently able to handle.

11. Do 15 minutes a day to a total period of time of 8-12 hours over several weeks.

---

7. Remember that lack of fluency may be a symptom of an inadequate sight vocabulary and/or word identification strategies. Refer to Chapter 4 for strategies to strengthen these areas.

3.2 Lack of Fluency: Incorrect Phrasing

Behavior Observed	The student ignores punctuation, adds punctuation, or uses inappropriate intonation.
Anticipated Outcome	The student will read text more fluently.

Perspective and Strategies

Incorrect phrasing may be the result of poor reading habits, a lack of fluency, or an overreliance on phonics. It may also be related to failure to follow the author's flow of ideas. You need to determine why the student is using incorrect phrasing and try to remedy the situation. The following strategies may help:

1. The student should be shown examples where punctuation is ignored or substituted. Discuss whether the student should have paid closer attention to the punctuation. Be sure to consider possible impact on meaning. Invite students to hypothesize the predicting behaviors that may help explain the miscue. The following examples may be useful:

   Sharon Kay is my best friend.   Sharon, Kay is my best friend.

   Jake, my puppy is sick.   Jake, my puppy, is sick.

   John Allen and Mark Wayne are friends.   John, Allen, and Mark Wayne are friends.

2. Write experience stories with the student. Ask the student to read the story back to you, paying close attention to the natural phrasing of the words.

3. Read pattern books with the student. (See Appendix C for a list of pattern books.) Each time the pattern is repeated, ask the student to read it. Stress that the pattern should sound like speech.

4. List common phrases on cards and place them in a pocket chart. Ask the student to read the phrases as they would sound naturally. Some possible phrases include the following:

on the road	out of sight
over the hill	on the table
in my room	in the closet
on the playground	by the river

   Words for phrase building can be found in the Resources for Chapter 4.

5. On a page of copied text, place slash marks at each natural break. Have the student try to read fluently to each slash mark before pausing.

   My friend and I / decided to / ride our bikes / to school today.

   Tomorrow / our class / will go / on a field trip.

6. Give the student ample opportunities to read with correct phrasing and punctuation by reading along with him or her. First, read an easy text to the student. Then, ask the student to read along with you. Finally, ask the student to read the story independently as you support the effort by softly reading in the background.

7. Use echo reading to encourage reading fluency. Chose an easy text, read one line, and ask the student to read the same line with the same intonation that you used.

8. Often, students experiencing difficulty with reading hear only other novice readers reading aloud. Model good reading fluency in front of the entire class by reading to the class each day. Also, model good reading with the student having difficulty with inappropriate phrasing. Alternate reading pages or paragraphs with the student.

9. Use repeated readings with partners as a technique to build fluency. Ask two students to choose short selections and read them until they know them well. Have each student read the selection to the other.

10. Have students mark or note places in their reading where they have ignored punctuation, added unnecessary punctuation, or used inappropriate intonation. Then invite students to talk about these instances with you. Later, small groups of students could share with each other. The goal is for students to learn from their miscues. Some guiding questions could include:

    ■ Why did I read the sentence that way?

    ■ What was I thinking about as I read?

    ■ Did I decide something didn't make sense? Why?

    ■ If it didn't make sense, what did I do (if anything)?

    ■ Did I repeat to confirm or correct what I was reading?

    ■ What have I learned about my reading from these examples?

11. Model phrasing by first reading a sentence word for word and asking the student to comment. Then use different phrasing to help the student grasp the idea that certain words go together. For example,

    The/little/puppy/began/to/bark.

    The little/puppy/began/to bark.

    The little puppy/began to bark.

12. Use the Oral Reading Opportunities that follow Section 3.10 to select natural, meaningful ways for students to share their reading using appropriate phrasing.

3.3 Failure to Attempt Unknown Words

Behavior Observed	The student waits to be told unknown words and does not attempt them independently.
Anticipated Outcome	The student will use appropriate strategies to decode unknown words.

Perspective and Strategies

The failure of some students to attempt unknown words may be due to several factors. First, students may not have been taught a functional strategy for word identification, and they do not have a variety of strategies to use when confronted with an unknown word in reading. Although students may have been taught phonics and the use of context, they do not realize that these strategies may be used during reading. Second, the teacher may tell students unknown words, thereby reducing their need to acquire internal strategies for word identification. Third, students who are struggling readers may be reluctant to take risks. Instead, they manipulate the teacher or other students to tell them words they don't know. The following strategies may be useful.

1. When the student hesitates at an unknown word, wait ten seconds before saying anything. If there is no response, ask the student to try the word using the known sounds. Praise the student for any attempt at the word.

2. Discuss what the student thinks should be done when confronted with an unknown word.

   For example, ask the student to think about a time when he or she was reading and came to an unknown word. Ask the student what strategies were used to figure out the word. If the student is unable to suggest any strategies, guide the student in expressing strategies that emphasize the sound-symbol correspondence of the word (see sections 4.1 and 4.2 in Chapter 4), strategies that use the meaning of the sentence, and strategies that use knowledge about the English language (see section 4.7 in Chapter 4).

3. Have the student give the word some sounds and take a guess at the word. Then have the student read on to the end of the phrase or sentence and decide whether the word made sense.

4. Ask the student to go back a line and see if the preceding sentence and the words around the unknown word suggest a possibility. Read the sentence aloud for the student, skipping the unknown word, and ask what word would make sense in the blank.

5. Ask the student to reread the sentence and try to guess a word that begins with the initial sound of the unknown word and makes sense in the sentence.

6. Provide oral examples where the student uses context to anticipate the missing word.

   I really like to watch _____.

   I would like to see the _____ game.

   It's time to go to _____.

   I found _____ in my backpack.

7. Use easy cloze exercises where the student is asked to predict a word that makes sense. Discuss various choices offered by the students, and invite them to share how and why they made their specific predictions. Gradually include graphic information about the exact word the author used. Use examples like the following:

I like _____.

I like to go to _____.

I like to go to s_ _ _ _ l.

8. If the student encounters several unknown words in a line of print, the reading material is probably too difficult. Provide reading material that is easy for the student to read.

9. Invite other students to share their experiences with unknown words using a chart like the following:

Page	Difficult Word/Phrase	What I Did	How It Worked

Have students complete the chart during a reading assignment by filling in the various categories. Then have students share their strategies by focusing on predicting, confirming, and correcting strategies. Be sure to reinforce the strategies that are especially good—even if they did not result in success.

10. Be alert for instances in your reading where you encounter a difficult word. Bring in the passage and model for students what you did to deal with the word. Thinking aloud is especially helpful.

3.4   Meaning-Changing Substitutions

Behavior Observed	The student substitutes a word or words, and the text does not make sense.
Anticipated Outcome	The student will read the text with fewer substitutions.

Perspective and Strategies

Remind the student that reading is a process of constructing meaning from print. Ask, "Does this make sense?" The student should be taught to use semantic (meaning) cues in reading. Try the following strategies:

1. Remind the student to think while reading and encourage the student to stop and reread the material if it does not make sense. The student may be viewing reading as "saying words" rather than reading for meaning.

2. Give the student oral exercises to identify words that do not make sense in the context of the sentence. For example:

   The mail carrier delivered the groceries.

   Helen set her calendar so it would ring at seven o'clock.

   Bill went to the store to buy some candy for her sister.

   Have the student explain why a particular word does not make sense and invite a substitute word or phrase. For example, if the student identifies *groceries* in the first sentence, have the student explain why the word doesn't make sense and offer a word that would make sense. The student might say, "Mail carriers do not deliver groceries, but they do deliver mail, letters, and packages. Any of those words would make sense." You might also ask the student what word or words wouldn't make sense if *groceries* was the correct word (i.e., *mail carrier*) and what word or words might be substituted for mail carrier (e.g., store, man, boy).

3. Give the student oral and written exercises containing cloze tasks and instruct the student to anticipate omitted words that make sense. Develop the idea that language dictates that only certain types of words can be placed after certain language structures.

   After playing, the children _____ inside.

   I will see you after _____.

   He was reading a _____.

   "I lost my money," _____ Carlos.

For example, in the sentence, "I saw an _____ in the tree," the word *an* signals that a word beginning with a vowel (e.g., apple) would be required. Provide another example where the preceding part of the sentence may signal an adjective or noun (e.g., The _____ frog jumped in the pond; The little _____ began to bark).

4. Use small-group activities in which certain key words in a story are covered. Ask for responses from the group and have students evaluate the response. The ultimate criterion is: "Does the word make sense?" Invite students to explain how the words in the story help the reader to predict other words.

5. Keep track of substitutions to see whether certain words are habitually associated with other words. Write selections where the grammatical structures make it highly unlikely for the habitual associations to occur. For example:

    was and *saw*

    Once upon a time there *was* a girl named Jennifer. Her hair *was* long and brown. Jennifer liked to wear headbands in her hair. One day, while she *was* walking downtown, she *saw* some headbands in a store window. She *saw* blue, yellow, and pink headbands. The blue headband *was* the prettiest, so she bought it.

    in and *on*

    Vanessa liked to collect insects. She kept the spiders *in* a jar *on* top of her dresser. One Friday, her mother invited some friends to come over for coffee. They were talking *in* the kitchen. Vanessa took her jar of spiders *in* the kitchen and set it *on* the table. When one lady reached for a cup *on* the table, she bumped the jar. It landed *on* the floor. What do you think happened next?

    when and *then*

    Adam and his mother had some errands to do. His mother said, "I will get my coat; *then* I will be ready to go. *When* you find your jacket, come out to the car. First, we will go to the supermarket; *then* we can go to the pet shop to find out *when* the puppy will be ready to come home. *When* we bring the puppy home, you will get the basket out of the closet. *Then* the puppy will have a nice place to sleep."

6. Provide sentences that contain a substituted word written above the text. Have students discuss whether the substituted word makes sense. For example:

    they
    They went to the zoo because there were many things to see.

    hat
    He hit the ball out of the park.

    saw
    She was the first one to finish the race.

7. Provide exercises that contain substitutions two different readers made in the same sentence. Discuss which substitution appears to be closer to the author's meaning. For example:

    the
    Michael decided to ride along a little road.

    walk
    Michael decided to ride along a little road.

8. Tape-record the student's reading. Have the student listen to the reading and note the substitutions that occur. Ask the student what word would make sense in the sentence. Then check the letters in the word to determine which word the author had written.

9. If there are many substitutions that distort the author's intended meaning, the book may be too difficult. Choose materials that are easy for the student to read.

10. Have students keep track of their reading and report instances where a word that did not make sense was substituted for a word in the text. Invite students to share how they dealt with the substitution. Help them realize the predicting, confirming, and correcting behaviors that they may have used.

3.5   Nonmeaning-Changing Substitutions

Behavior Observed	The student substitutes a word or words, and the phrase or sentence still makes sense.
Anticipated Outcome	The student will read the text with fewer substitutions.

Perspective and Strategies

Substitutions in reading may occur for several reasons. First, the student may be ignoring graphophonic cues in reading. Second, the student may be relying too heavily on context clues to predict words that make sense in the sentence. Third, the student's oral language may be different from the author's written language, and the student produces a response that makes sense. For example, the student may say "can't" for "cannot."

Because the basic meaning of the text is not adversely affected, there may be no need for the teacher to take any action. A student who continues to substitute words that are unlike the text, however, may not be willing to take the time to identify unknown words. For students who habitually make these kinds of substitutions, you may want to try one of the following strategies:

1. After the student has completed the passage, point out the words that are unlike the text. Ask the student to reread the sentence paying close attention to these words. If the student rereads the word correctly, mention the change. Tell the student that although the first attempt may not have changed the author's meaning, it is more likely that the text's meaning will not be changed by reading the printed words. If the student repeats the miscue, draw attention to the sounds in the word. Ask the student to think of another word that uses the sounds represented by the letters in the word.

2. Some students make substitutions in reading because they are not given enough time to decode unknown words. As the student is reading, encourage all attempts at identifying unfamiliar words. Be patient and use wait time.

3. For students who make many substitutions, tape record the student reading an easy passage. Give the student a copy of the text and play back the audiotape. Ask the student to underline any words from the audiotape that do not match the printed text. Ask the student to use the sounds of the letters to help figure out the underlined word. If the student is unable to correct the miscue, tell the student the word.

4. Students who make many miscues in reading may be reading from a passage that is too difficult. Give the student easier reading material and stress the point that reading means understanding the printed text.

3.6 Nonword Substitutions

Behavior Observed	The student produces a nonword instead of a real word.
Anticipated Outcome	The student will say words that make sense in the text.

Perspective and Strategies

The student must be helped to realize that reading is a meaningful process and words pronounced should make sense. Reading should sound like oral language.

1. Ask the student what the nonword means. It is possible that the student knows the meaning but has mispronounced the word.

2. Provide oral and written examples in which the student attempts to predict the appropriate word that has been omitted. Stress that some words can be predicted from context.

    After school, we went to play _____.

    I will mail the _____.

    The horse _____ over the fence.

3. Provide examples that contain a nonword and ask the student to tell what real word could replace the nonword. Have the student explain why he or she was able to give a real word. Praise the student for saying that the other words in the sentence provided cues. For example:

    He drank a glass of fex.

    The zop bought some candy.

4. Place removable opaque tape over certain words in the student's reading materials that can be easily predicted. Encourage the student to supply a real word that makes sense. Help the student to transfer this same strategy to identifying unknown words.

5. Five or more nonwords per 100 words probably means that the reading material is too difficult. Provide materials that are easy for the student to read aloud.

6. Tape record the student reading. Play back the audiotape pausing at each nonword. Ask the student, "Does this make sense? What word would make sense in that spot?" To avoid the student forming a mental set, ask the same question from time to time when the student's reading does make sense.

7. Model how you can use context and phonic knowledge to pronounce a word. For example, you could read *mansion* as *mīnsīn* in the sentence, "The big old *mansion* in the neighborhood had several broken windows." Then you might say, "I know *mīnsīn* doesn't make sense. Let me take another look at the word and think of words that could have broken windows. A *house, garage,* and *car* can have broken windows, but none of those words begins with the same beginning sound as mansion. Let me try the word again. I see the word *man* but *mansin* doesn't sound like a word I know. Perhaps it's *mānsin.* No, that doesn't make sense. Let me try again: *mānshun, mănshun.* I've heard of a mansion. Let me try that word in the sentence to see if it makes sense. Yes, the word *mansion* makes sense. It is another name for a house that is big. I think that's it." Be sure students realize the predicting, correcting, and confirming behaviors that characterized your reading.

3.7 Repetitions of Words or Phrases

Behavior Observed	The student repeats words, phrases, or sentences.
Anticipated Outcome	The student will be able to read the text with fewer repetitions.

Perspective and Strategies

Repetition may help the student understand what he or she has read. The teacher must decide whether the student is analyzing the repeated word, anticipating a difficult word, making a legitimate effort to have the reading make sense, or merely repeating from habit. Consider the following.

1. If the student's repetitions are frequent, it is possible that the reading material is too difficult. If this is the case, provide the student with reading material at a level that is easy to read.

2. Repetitions that serve as "stalls" provide the student with extra time to try to figure out an unknown word. This may be a normal part of the reading process. Excessive use of the stall technique, however, may indicate that the reading material is too difficult and/or effective reading strategies are needed. It may also indicate a need to teach how the flow of language can be used to anticipate words.

3. Praise the student when a word, phrase, or sentence is repeated to preserve ongoing meaning. Tell the student that this behavior is fully acceptable in order to make sense of what is read.

4. If repetitions are merely a habit, it may be helpful to have the student record a passage on audiotape and discuss it with the teacher. The student should be guided to note which repetitions are habitual, resulting in less efficient reading.

5. Sometimes a student repeatedly overcorrects to ensure word-for-word accuracy. The student should be encouraged not to break the meaning flow of the text when the miscue does not significantly alter the meaning.

6. Invite students to share and discuss instances when they repeated words, phrases, or sentences in their reading. Help them see how their repetitions may contribute or detract from efficient reading. For example, repeating to confirm meaning would be an effective use. Many repetitions may make reading less efficient because it is not done to correct a miscue or to help make sense of the passage.

3.8 Meaning-Changing Omissions

Behavior Observed	The student omits one or more words, and the text does not make sense or distorts the author's intended meaning.
Anticipated Outcome	The student will read text with fewer omissions.

Perspective and Strategies

Because this type of omission changes the meaning or does not make sense of the text, the student needs to understand that reading is the process of constructing meaning from print. Suggested strategies follow:

1. Frequent omissions may mean that the reading material is too difficult. Supply reading material at a lower level.

2. Provide exercises that contain omissions made by a reader. In a pocket chart, make sentences from word cards that have a word that can be omitted without losing the grammatical sense of the sentence. Have students discuss whether the omission changes the author's intended meaning and how they arrived at that conclusion. Use sentences like the following:

   Jeff walked to the toy store. (toy)

   I have twenty-five dollars. (five)

3. Remind the student that reading is supposed to make sense and convey the author's meaning. Ask the student, "Did that make sense?" Use this same question from time to time when the omission also makes sense. Help students reflect on their reading so they come to realize that some miscues may change the meaning and not be corrected—especially if they make sense in the context of the passage. At other times, students will correct miscues that do not make sense. Encourage students to explain their various behaviors so they gain greater insight into their reading.

4. Ask the student to follow the line of print with his or her finger or a marker. Often students who omit text are reading too fast. Following text with a marker or finger may slow the reading down and increase concentration on the text.

5. Place the student in a group for choral reading. Choral reading is reading text aloud in a group. By reading in a group, the student may pay closer attention to the text.

6. Have the student tape record his or her reading. With a printed copy of the selection, help the student mark the omissions. Then discuss the omissions with the student, seeking the student's insights about the omissions and their impact meaning. Help the student realize the importance of monitoring his or her reading to construct meaning.

Behavior Observed	The student omits a word or words, and the text still makes sense.
Anticipated Outcome	The student will read text with fewer omissions.

Perspective and Strategies

Omissions that result in little or no change in meaning should not require any direct action from the teacher unless the student habitually omits words. If the omissions occur frequently, try the following strategies:

1. Ask the student to slow down when reading aloud. Younger students may wish to follow the line of print with a marker or their finger to make sure they do not omit text. Even expert readers occasionally use this strategy with challenging text, so do not discourage its use with young children.

2. Give the student several opportunities to read with a taped story. Make it a challenge for the student to keep up with the reader without omitting words.

3. Older students develop an eye-voice span where their eyes are "ahead" of their voice. Omissions may occur when the student's eyes are reading faster than his or her voice. When this type of behavior is observed, discuss it with the student to gain insight.

4. Tape record the student's reading and have him or her listen to the tape while following with the selection, paying particular attention to omissions. Then ask the student to evaluate the quality of the omissions and offer reasons why they occurred. During the discussion, help the student realize that although the overall meaning is retained, some omitted words probably would have provided greater detail or a richer meaning.

Behavior Observed	The student habitually tries to sound out words when confronted with an unknown word in text.
Anticipated Outcome	The student will use both phonics and context to determine unknown words.

Perspective and Strategies

Some students may have been taught that the appropriate strategy to figure out unknown words is to sound them out. These students may not have been taught other strategies that can be used with unknown words. In either case, teachers must instruct students to use their knowledge of language (syntax) and context (meaning) cues. The following strategies may be useful:

1. Ask the student why he or she uses phonics frequently. Use the student's response to make instructional decisions. For example, if phonics is the student's basic or first word-identification strategy, see sections 4.6, 4.7, and 4.9 in Chapter 4.

2. Show students that they can sometimes correctly predict a word in oral language before hearing it. Help them transfer this same knowledge in reading. For example:

   He gave the kitten some _____.

   Put a stamp on the _____.

   Ten dimes make a _____.

3. Provide examples where two readers made different miscues on the same unknown word. Discuss the responses of the two readers in an attempt to decide which reader has been most effective and the reasons for the effectiveness. Be sure students give reasons for their decisions.

   Text   The car went down the old street.

   Reader 1 The car went down the old road.

   Reader 2 The car went down the old stream.

4. Provide words that students are unable to pronounce. The difficult words can then be placed in a context that builds meaning for the words. Through these exercises, the student should realize that he or she can understand without always sounding out words, for example:

   guerdon.

   After finding a purse, Jason returned it to the owner. The owner of the purse gave a *guerdon* to Jeff, who bought a model with it.

engrossed

Dana was *engrossed* in an adventure story. Her mom and dad both had to call her for dinner. Finally, she put the book down and came to the table.

5. Help students build fluency by using Structured Repeated Readings in Resources for Chapter 3.

6. Consult Chapter 4 for ways to help develop a variety of word-identification strategies and how to use them.

Oral Reading as Performance

Because of the importance of speaking to an audience, teachers should give their students a wide range of opportunities to practice oral language. Students who read aloud for an audience are subtly learning several things. They are learning how language is used in written text; they are learning how to communicate to an audience; and they are learning how to interpret text. Students reading aloud can also stimulate interest in stories and encourage other students to read. Oral reading, therefore, is a beneficial practice when students have adequately prepared and are sharing their reading with an appropriate audience.

Teachers can provide different kinds of experiences with reading aloud. Some may be time-consuming and rather formal, such as reader's theater and storytelling. Others may be more spontaneous, such as reading an exciting part of a story. With both types of reading, however, students should always have the opportunity to read the passage silently before performing and should rehearse their part before reading before their audience. The following are examples of ways to use oral reading as performance.

Reader's Theater

Ask students to:

1. Choose a piece of literature with a strong story line or a chapter from a content area book that could be read in parts.

2. Read the piece silently. Discuss the contents of the story and ask the students to read it again.

3. Develop a script from the literature. Students may use the entire story, or they may decide to create a scene from the story.

4. Assign parts and rehearse the play.

5. Present the play to an appropriate audience.

Storytelling

Ask students to:

1. Choose a favorite piece of literature.

2. Read the story several times, thinking about the sequence of action in the plot.

3. Think or write the entire story without the text. Include the story line and the main point of the story.

4. Retell the story to a friend, a group, or for a tape recording.

Functional Situations for Oral Reading

- Poetry and rhymes
- Student-written advertisements
- Announcements from the office
- Riddles and jokes
- Letters from pen pals

Oral Reading Opportunities

- Read what a certain character said.

- Read the most exciting part of the story.

- Read a funny part of the story.

- Read the part you like best.

- Read the part that tells you the most about a character.

- Read the part that makes you see the setting most clearly.

- Read the most surprising part of the story.

- Read the part that explains the goal or problem of the main character.

- Read the part that explains the outcome or solution of the story.

- Read the part that you think your best friend would like.

Taking Account of Dialects

Changes of sounds and endings in some words may be a result of the student's dialect (adapted from Rubin, 1993). A dialect of English is a variation of standard English, which is the language most widely used in print and by the media. When students read aloud, they may pronounce standard written English with their own dialect and may even change grammatical structures. Because reading in dialect rarely affects comprehension, you should not consider dialect differences to be significant miscues.

Spanish

A student with a Spanish-language background might exhibit the following dialect differences when he or she reads standard English.

➤ The vowel sounds in the following words may be difficult for the Spanish-speaking child to pronounce: *i* in *bit, a* in *bat,* schwa sound in *but,* and *u* in *full.*

➤ There are several sounds in English that are not found in Spanish: *v* in *vote, th* in *then, z* in *zoo, zh* in *measure,* and *j* in *jump.* The Spanish-speaking child will probably replace these sounds with similar sounds from the Spanish language.

➤ English words that end in *r* plus the final consonants *d, t, l, p,* or *s* are usually pronounced without the consonant (*car* for *card, car* for *cart*).

➤ English has many words that blend an *s* with a consonant, which does not occur in Spanish. Spanish-speaking children may have difficulty with words that end with an *s*-consonant blend: *wasp, last, disk.*

➤ In Spanish, no words begin with an *s*-consonant blend; a vowel always precedes the consonant. Spanish-speaking students may have difficulty beginning a word with an *s* sound and may even pronounce a vowel before the *s* (*es-tar* for *star*).

➤ There are also several grammatical differences between Spanish and English. Spanish-speaking children may have the following difficulties with standard English:

Subject-verb agreement: The cars runs.

Verb tense: I need help yesterday.

Use of negatives: He no go to school.

Omission of noun determiners: He is farmer.

Omission of pronouns: Is farmer?

Word order of adjectives: The hat red is pretty.

Comparative forms: My car is more big.

African-American English

African-American students who speak with a nonstandard English dialect may read aloud using their dialect. Unless the changes interfere with meaning, they should not be considered significant miscues. The following differences exist between the African-American dialect and standard English.

➤ In African-American English, the *r* sound becomes a schwa or is not pronounced before vowels or consonants: *pass* for *Paris, cat* for *carrot.*

- The *l* sound is also dropped and may be replaced by a *u* sound: *hep* for *help*, *too* for *tool*, *awe* for *all*, *fought* for *fault*.

- Consonant clusters at the ends of words are often simplified to single consonants: *pass* for *past*, *men* for *meant*, *wine* for *wind*, *hole* for *hold*, *sick* for *six*.

- Endings of words may be dropped or changed: *boo* for *boot*, *row* for *road*, *feet* for *feed*, *see* for *seed*.

- The possessive forms of words may be deleted: *John cousin* for *John's cousin*, *they book* for *their book*, *you* or *you-all* for *your*.

- Speakers of the African-American dialect may make changes in verb forms as they read: *I be happy* for *I am happy*. *He goin'* for *He is going*.

- In African-American English, there is no third person singular marker. Students may read: *He don't* for *He doesn't*, *He do* for *He does*, or *He have* for *He has*.

- The past tense for regular verbs may be dropped, such as *miss* for *missed*, *fine* for *fined*, *raise* for *raised*.

- In African-American English, the word *ain't* is used as a past negative as in *I ain't neither*.

- African-American speakers may also use negatives differently than do standard American speakers: *Nobody had no bloody nose. She didn't play with none of us. Nobody don't know about no club.*

Chinese

Among the many Chinese dialects, Mandarin is spoken by the majority of the people in China, but most of the Chinese students in schools speak the Cantonese dialect. There are several difficulties speakers of Cantonese may have as they read standard English.

- English has many more vowel sounds than Chinese, so students may have difficulty with the vowel sounds in *buy, bough, bought, beat,* and *bait.*

- English also has consonant sounds not found in Chinese: *th* in *that, s* in *she, n* in *need,* and *r* in *rice.*

- In Chinese, many consonants are not used to end words as they are in English. Students may add an extra syllable to a final sound, such as *day offu* for *day off.*

- Because consonant clusters do not exist in Cantonese, students may have difficulty with words such as the following: *wished, dogs, laughed.*

- In Chinese, most grammatical relationships are indicated by word order rather than by changes in form as in English. The Chinese student may say *Yesterday he give I two book* for *Yesterday he gave me two books.*

- The Chinese-speaking student may not use the plural form of nouns, because plurality is indicated by the word preceding the noun in their language. The student may read *three book* for *three books.*

- The word order for questions is not inverted in Chinese as it is in English. The Chinese-speaking student may have difficulty reading questions because of that difference.

Resources for Chapter 3

➤ A Suggested Method for Recording a Student's Oral Reading Miscues

➤ Qualitative Summary of Miscues

➤ Structured Repeated Readings

➤ Oral Reading Alternatives to Round-Robin Reading

A Suggested Method for Recording a Student's Oral Reading Miscues

Substitutions

    a
Jim saw the boy.

Omissions

Poor little ~~Baby~~ Bear could not move from the tall tree.

Insertions

    he
He strolled along the path and soon ^ was deep in the forest

Reversals

Are they twins?

Repetitions

  A. Correcting a miscue

       ⓒ   *see*
    Baby Bear|did not know where he was.

  B. Abandoning a correct form

       ⓐⓒ *along*
    He stayed|alone in the pine tree all night

  C. Unsuccessfully attempting to correct an initial miscue

          2. ha-
      ⓤⓒ *1. heavy*
    He had slept|hard all night.

  D. Plain repetition
    Jim saw <u>a bear</u>.

Additional Markings

  A. Partial Words

      res-
    The hunters rescued the boys.

  B. Non word substitutions

      $ frontmer
    People on the frontier had shooting contests.

  C. Punctuation ignored

    . . . from same maple and oak trees/As Bill

  D. Intonation

    He played a record' that was his favorite.

  E. Word pronounced by examiner

        P
    Men on the frontier often had shooting contests.

  F. Dialect

      ⓓ *goed*
    He went home

  G. Lip movement
    place LM in margin

  H. Finger pointing
    place FP above word

  I. Vocalization
    place V in text

From Johns, J.L. (1997). *Basic reading inventory* (7th ed.). Dubuque, IA: Kendall/Hunt Publishing Company (1-800-228-0810). May be reproduced for noncommercial educational purposes.

Qualitative Summary of Miscues

Jerry L. Johns

MISCUE	TEXT	GRAPHIC SIMILARITY			CONTEXT		Self-Correction of Unacceptable Miscues
		Beginning	Middle	End	Acceptable	Unacceptable	
	Column Total						
	Number of Miscues Analyzed						
	Percentage						

PREDICTION STRATEGY

Graphic Similarity

	B	M	E
100%			
90			
80			
70			
60			
50			
40			
30			
20			
10			

__% __% __%

Miscues Acceptable in Context

100%	
90	
80	
70	
60	
50	
40	
30	
20	
10	

__%

CORRECTION STRATEGY

Unacceptable Miscues Self-Corrected

100%	
90	
80	
70	
60	
50	
40	
30	
20	
10	

__%

From Johns, J.L. (1997). *Basic reading inventory* (7th ed.). Dubuque, IA: Kendall/Hunt Publishing Company (1-800-228-0810). May be reproduced for noncommercial educational purposes.

Structured Repeated Readings

The repeated readings strategy is useful with students who:

- read word by word.
- experience little success in reading. .
- lack motivation.
- read very slowly.
- lack conversational qualities in oral reading.
- show little confidence in reading.

Using Structured Repeated Readings

Follow these steps to apply the strategy:

1. Select a passage or story of 50 to 200 words at an appropriate level of difficulty for the student.

2. Have the student read the selection orally. Keep track of the time and miscues.

3. Record the time in seconds and number of miscues on a chart.

4. Ask the student to reread the same material silently.

5. Then have the student reread the selection orally to the teacher. Chart time and miscues again.

6. Continue the procedure over a period of time until a rate of about 85 words per minute is achieved.

7. Repeat the strategy with a new selection.

Alternate Procedure

1. The student reads the selection along with a tape-recorded narration using earphones. (Caution: The rate of reading on the tape must match the student's ability to follow along.)

2. The student repeats Step 1 until audio support is no longer needed.

3. The student begins the process outlined in the original procedure.

Example

This is how structured repeated readings worked with Tracy, a student experiencing difficulty in reading. The following six steps correspond to those in the original explanation:

1. The teacher chose a selection for Tracy to read. The selection contained 132 words.

2. Tracy read the selection orally to the teacher. She made 6 miscues and it took her 124 seconds. To convert seconds into rate, multiply the number of words in the selection by 60 and then divide by the time (in seconds) it takes the student to read the passage. For Tracy, the rate is 64 words per minute (wpm).

number of words in selection		constant	seconds required for reading		rate
(132	×	60)	÷	124 =	64 wpm

3. The teacher, with Tracy's help, recorded the scores (6 miscues and 124 seconds) on the accompanying Reading Progress Chart.

4. Tracy practiced the same selection silently several times by herself.

5. Later, Tracy read the same selection to her teacher a second time. On this reading she made 5 miscues and took 100 seconds—quite an improvement over her first reading.

6. The procedure was repeated over a period of several days. By the third reading, Tracy achieved a rate of about 88 words per minute:

$$(132 \times 60) \div 90 = 88$$

$$7{,}920 \div 90 = 88$$

At this point, the teacher could have introduced a new passage, but Tracy wanted to try to improve her reading of the first passage even more. The result, after three more readings and some independent practice, was a rate of 132 wpm ($7{,}920 \div 60 = 132$) with no miscues. Then Tracy felt she was ready to move on to a new passage.

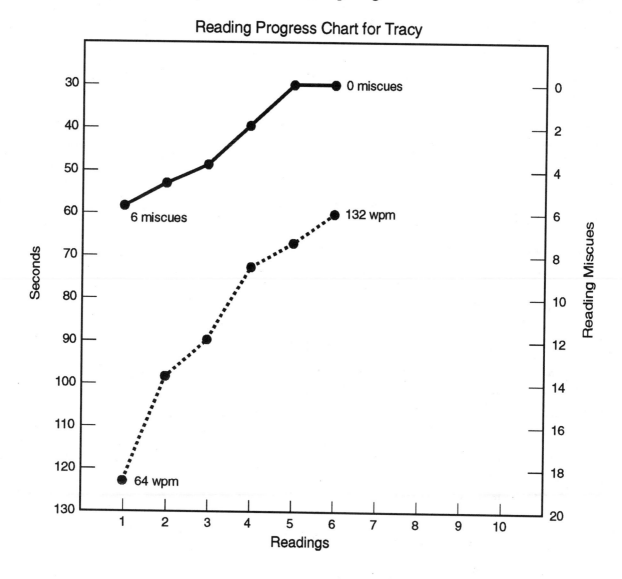

Reading Progress Chart for Tracy

Additional Comments

Notice that the Reading Progress Chart was set up to show visible evidence of gain. A blank chart is provided for teachers to duplicate and use with appropriate students. The chart is a real motivational tool for most students. They enjoy watching their progress. The chart, however, should not be posted in the classroom without students' permission. Some students are private about their reading and may not wish for others to see their chart.

Comprehension is not the main focus of this strategy. However, comprehension questions can be asked or retellings completed after the initial and final readings to help assess improvement, or a different comprehension question can be posed after each rereading. As less attention is needed for decoding, more attention becomes available for comprehension. With greater fluency, the student can concentrate on the meaning of the selection.

Often the question of counting miscues arises. Should all miscues be recorded or only those significant ones that change meaning? Some teachers begin by counting all miscues and then moving to discussing miscues with the student to determine those that are significant.

Remember:

➤ Repeated readings are a supplement to reading instruction.

➤ Some students respond more readily than others.

➤ The 85 wpm criterion isn't an absolute; use your judgment.

➤ Repeated readings focuses on fluency and rate of reading.

➤ With increased fluency, students make fewer miscues and can focus more on comprehension.

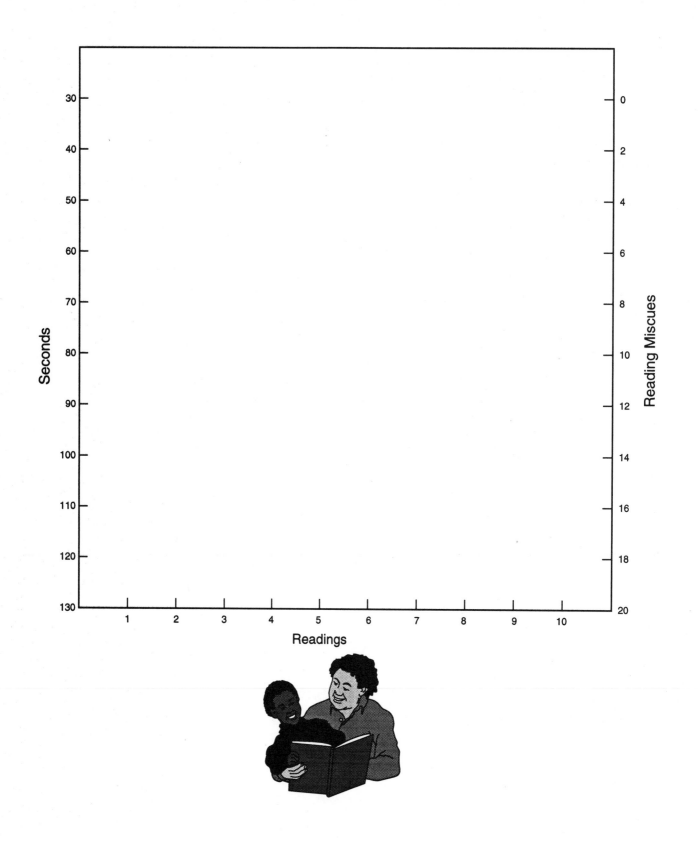

Seconds

Reading Miscues

Readings

Oral Reading Alternatives to Round-Robin Reading

1. *Choral Reading.* All students read text aloud together.

2. *Glossing.* The teacher models reading fluency by reading a selection slowly with expression. The teacher "glosses" by stopping to explain a word or phrase. Students listen, or listen and follow along with the printed text.

3. *Official Announcer.* Give each student the opportunity to be the official announcer by assigning a student each day to read announcements, student writing, and memos. Students may ask the teacher for assistance with the text before reading to the class.

4. *Radio Program.* A small group of students reads a play or radio script into a tape recorder for class presentations.

5. *Overviewer.* A student reads aloud titles, subheads, and vocabulary words before the class reads a selection.

6. *Flash Cards.* Using sight words or vocabulary words on cards, students try to read the group of cards as rapidly and accurately as possible. Phrases can also be used.

7. *Play Reading.* Students read plays for class presentations.

8. *Singing.* Students read lyrics of a song before singing it.

9. *Games.* Many board games require students to read text as they play.

10. *Formal Speech.* Students write and read a persuasive speech for the class.

11. *Find the Answer.* The teacher asks a question about a text. Students read the part of the text that includes the answer.

12. *Joke of the Day.* Students read aloud a joke or riddle for the class.

Fry, E.B., Kress, J.E., & Fountoukidis, D.L. (1993). *The reading teacher's book of lists* (3rd ed.). Englewood Cliffs, NJ: Prentice-Hall.

CHAPTER 4

Identifying and Understanding Words

Overview

The ability to identify and understand words is a foundation of the reading process (Stanovich, 1991). Although we realize that the meaning of text is much larger than the sum of the definitions of each word (Brozo & Simpson, 1991), it is important for students to have strategies to identify words and to understand the concepts behind those words.

There are several strategies readers use as they encounter words. One strategy is to read words by sight. That means that you see the word and pronounce it correctly. There are many words you read by sight—probably all of the words in this paragraph, in fact. You don't need to try to figure out the words because they belong to your lexicon of *sight words*. All proficient readers have a large number or words they can read by sight.

Not all words are known by sight for any reader. As far as we know, no one knows all 600,000 words in the English language. When readers come to words they don't know by sight, they can figure out the words by one or more of these ways: by phonological recoding (decoding), by analogy to known spelling patterns, and by using context clues.

When you come to a word you can't pronounce, you could try to figure it out initially by using the sounds symbolized by the letters or letter combinations and then blending those sounds together. For example, if you don't know the word *enigmatic,* you can give each letter one or more sounds from the variety of sounds the letters symbolize to phonologically recode the word, trying various pronunciations in an effort to have the word sound like one you have heard before.

Because English is not a highly phonetic language, not all words can be read using their letter sounds. The word *tough,* for example, cannot be read by its letter sounds. Many words that do not have phonetic spelling have syllables that can be read by analogy to a known spelling pattern. For example, students who have never seen the word *tough* can use what they know about the word part *ough* sound in the known word *rough* to figure out the word. Many words in text have at least one part that can be read by analogy.

Phonological recoding and analogy can give readers a good sense of an unfamiliar word; however, students need to test the words within the context of the text to see whether they make sense. If students use what they know about letter sounds and spelling patterns and the word makes sense in the context of the text, it is probably correct. Context can help students test words and it is also useful to assist students in identifying unknown words. Context clues, therefore, can be an additional way for students to identify words.

As you know, identifying words is only part of reading. We all have encountered students who can identify words without understanding. That's because words are actually symbols for concepts. Words don't have a single meaning. They have a range of meanings that are unique to each individual. All of us, for example, have had experience with the word *picnic.* When you see that word, you may have a different picture in your mind than we do. You may picture an idyllic scene by a lake; someone else may picture eating fried chicken on a stoop of an apartment building. No one has the exact same concept of any word because all people's experiences are different.

When students read, teachers want them to have well-developed concepts for words they encounter. If students can't visualize a picnic on a city street, for example, they may have difficulty comprehending a text set in an urban environment. Therefore, teachers need to help students develop their own conception of words. To foster independent readers, teachers also need to teach students strategies that will help them become independent word learners. Independent word learners have one of the tools necessary for proficient reading.

This chapter about identifying and understanding words is divided into two main parts. The first part addresses identifying words using phonics, word patterns, structural analysis, sight, and context. Many sections in Chapter 2 contain ideas that will be helpful in developing or strengthening students' word identification (see 2.2, 2.3, 2.4, 2.5, 2.6, 2.7, and 2.8). The second part is devoted to helping students develop concepts and meanings for words.

4.1 Phonics: Consonants

Behavior Observed	The student has difficulty associating the sounds that consonants symbolize.
Anticipated Outcome	The student will be able to use the sounds of consonants to phonologically recode unknown words.

Background

The whole idea of phonics is to give students a means to associate sounds with letters and letter combinations so students can pronounce a word that is not known at sight. If the pronounciation can be related to a word in the student's experience, there is a connection with meaning. Phonics only helps students read (understand) words for which they already have meaning. For example, if the student sounds *yyy-eeeg* and says *yegg*, but has no meaning for the word, phonics is of little value. Fortunately, however, students have meanings for many words, and if they can decode a word, they are often able to associate meaning with the word, especially in the first few years of school.

"It would be irresponsible and inexcusable not to teach phonics" (Routman, 1996, p. 91). Using phonics, or the sounds people assign to letters, is one way students can pronounce unfamiliar words. The value of phonics should not be underestimated. Phonics is one of the cueing systems readers use for words that are not in their sight vocabulary. Unfortunately, the teaching of phonics has been the topic of controversy for decades. It is our belief that phonics should be an important foundation of a balanced reading program, and it should be taught as one of the strategies readers can use when they want to identify an unfamiliar word. In short, phonics is a vital component (along with context, and structural analysis) of balanced word identification.

Although there are 26 letters (graphemes) in the English alphabet, there are (depending on the dialect) forty or more sounds (phonemes). Because the consonants are more regular than the vowels, they are often introduced first. For the 25 consonant sounds listed in the box (adapted from Gunning, 1996 and Mazurkiewicz, 1976), begin teaching sounds that occur with the highest frequency and that are quite easy for students to say (e.g., sounds for *m*, *r*, and *s*).

The basic teaching strategies and practice and reinforcement activities used for initial consonants can be used with final consonants, consonant diagraphs (e.g., *ch, gh, kn, ph, sc, si, th, ti, wh, wr*), consonant blends in the initial position (e.g., *bl, cl, fl, gl, pl, sl, br, cr, dr, fr, sch, sm, sl*), and blends in the final position (e.g., *ld, lf, lk, nce, nk, nt*).

Letter-Sound Correspondences for Consonants

Sound (Phoneme)	Letter (Grapheme)	Initial	Final	Key Words
/b/	b, bb	barn	ebb, cab, robe	bell, ball
/d/	d, dd, ed	deer	bad	dog
/f/	f, ff, ph, lf	fun, photo	laugh	fish
/g/	g, gg, gh	gate, ghost, guide	rag	goat
/h/	h, wh	house, who		horse, hat
/hw/	wh	whale		whale
/j/	g, j, dg	jug, gym, soldier	age, judge	jar
/k/	k, lk, ck, q	can, kite, quick, chaos	back, ache	cat, key
/l/	l, ll	lion	mail	leaf
/m/	m, mm	me	him, comb, autumn	monkey, man
/n/	n, nn, kn, gn	now, know, gnu, pneumonia	pan	nest, nail
/p/	p, pp	pot	top	pencil, pen
/r/	r, rr, wr	ride, write		rabbit, ring
/s/	s, c, ss	sight, city	bus, miss, face	sun, Santa
/t/	t, tt, ed	time	rat, watt, jumped	table
/v/	v [f in of]	vase	love	valentine, vest
/w/	w	we, wheel		wagon
/y/	y, i	yacht, onion		yo-yo
/z/	z, zz	zipper	has, buzz	zebra
/ch/	ch	chip, cello, question	match	chair
/zh/	z, si	azure, version	beige, garage	garage
/th/	th	thin	breath	thumb
/th/	th	this	breathe	the
/sh/	sh, ti, ssi, s, si, sci	ship, sure, chef, action	push, special, mission	sheep
/ŋ/	n, ng		sing	ring

Teaching Strategy 1 (*Exemplified by Teaching the Sound for the Letter D*)

1. Younger students may need to be told that letters have a name and that a sound can also be associated with the letter. Sometimes teachers say that letters make sounds, but that is not correct. Letters do not say anything; however, sounds can be associated with the letters. Begin by teaching letter-sound correspondences in the initial position of the word.

2. Print an uppercase and a lowercase *d* on the chalkboard and ask students to name words that begin with a *d*. Encourage students to think of names of children in the class or friends whose names begin with a *d*. Pictures and concrete objects can also be used.

3. Record the students' responses on the chalkboard as in this example:

D	d
Don	dad
Dave	duck
Donna	dog
Debbi	door
Dan	down
Dion	deer

4. Ask the students to examine each list and note similarities and differences between the words. As the discussion continues, develop the concept that the *d* represents the same sound at the beginning of each word listed on the chalkboard.

5. Say each word on the list while you move your hand under the word. Emphasize the *d* sound distinctly so the students can hear it. Have students pronounce each word after you. Help students see that all the words begin with the same letter and that the letter *d* stands for the sound *ddd* heard at the beginning of each word.

6. Ask the students to think of other words that begin with the sound associated with *d*. Add these words to the list.

7. Conclude the lesson by asking students to listen while you say some words. If a word begins with the sound associated with *d*, have them raise their hand. If the word begins with a different sound, they should not raise their hand. Use words from the list on the chalkboard as well as new words (for instance, *Dave, Tom, door, Marie, zoo, down*).

8. Refer to the Practice and Reinforcement Activities for additional ideas.

Teaching Strategy 2 *(Exemplified by Teaching the Sound for the Letter B)*

1. Say five or six words and have students listen carefully to hear how each word begins. When you say the sounds, elongate but do not separate the sound associated with the initial consonant, for example, *bbball, bbbat,* and *bbboy*.

2. Ask the students what they noticed about the beginning sounds of all the words that you pronounced. The expected response is that they all begin with the same sound.

3. Encourage students to give other words with the same sound that is heard at the beginning of *ball, bat,* and *boy*.

4. To provide auditory training, say three words (two that have the same beginning sound and one that is different) and have students say the word that does not begin like the other two. Elongate the initial consonant sound in each word. Repeat this procedure several times. Pictures and concrete objects can also be used (box, bear, badge, banana, balloon, beaver).

5. Place the letter *b* on the chalkboard and make a list of words that begin with *b*. Encourage students to suggest additional words. Explore what all the words have in common. Guide students to realize that words all begin alike when you see them and sound alike at the beginning when you hear them.

6. Use a picture or concrete object to help students associate the sound with the letter. Sometimes the pictures can be put together or arranged to make the shape of the letter that is associated with a particular sound being learned. For example:

Teaching Strategy 3 (Using Alphabet Books)

1. Secure an alphabet book. Appendix B contains a listing of alphabet books that may be useful. Choose the page dealing with the consonant being taught (for example, *t*).

2. Read the *T* page aloud: "Tiny Tom told Tim to take a toy." Tell students that many of the words begin the same way. Then read the page again pointing to each word that begins with *t*.

3. Help students realize that *t* spells the sound heard at the beginning of almost all the words.

4. Secure another alphabet book and read the sentence. Invite students to help identify the *t* words. Relate the words in the two books by writing them on the chalkboard or a poster. Then show students that the words begin with *t* and have the *ttt* sound.

5. Invite students to practice by providing cards with words from the alphabet books as well as new words (for example *tag*). Show the word, cover the *t*, point to the remaining part of the word, and say, "This part of the word says *ag*. Now I'll uncover the *t*. What is the word? Guide students as needed, and provide additional practice using words such as:

tail	tall	take	talk
tape	tank	team	ten
tent	tooth	tongue	toot

Refer to the pictures in the alphabet books whenever possible to keep the focus on the word's meaning. In addition, use students' names to help practice the letter-sound relationship.

Teaching Strategy 4 (Using Whole Text)

1. Read a story to the class that has words with the consonant sound you wish to emphasize.

2. Write several sentences from the story on sentence strips.

3. Read the sentences to the class and have students echo read each sentence after you.

4. Point to the target words and ask the students to read them after you.

146

5. Ask students to identify the letters in the target words. Then ask them which sound is the same in each word. Have the students make the sound with you.

6. Reread the sentences emphasizing the targeted sound.

7. Encourage the students to read the sentences and to use the letter sound in their writing.

Practice and Reinforcement Activities

The following activities are exemplified with the letter *d* but can be adapted to other consonants.

1. Have students look through magazines and stories to find pictures that can be associated with the sound *d*. The pictures can be arranged on a bulletin board or on individual letter sheets. Include the capital and lowercase letters on the display.

2. Use oral sentences where the missing word begins with the letter-sound association being learned. After students share responses that might make sense, have them choose the words that make sense and begin with the correct sound. For *d*, possible sentences might include

   My _____ loves me. (dad)

   I gave my _____ a bone. (dog)

   I saw a _____ at the farm. (duck, dog)

   The toy cost me a _____. (dime, dollar)

3. Provide a group of pictures and have students take turns sorting those whose names begin with the sound being studied. Pictures can also be sorted according to whether the sound at the beginning, middle, or end of the words is different or the same.

4. Have students bring in objects whose names begin with the sound being studied.

5. Place pictures and/or objects in a box. Some of the items should begin with the sound being studied; a few should not. Have a student reach into the box, take out an item, name it, and indicate whether the initial sound of the object is the same as or different from the sound being studied. Then have the student use the word in a sentence.

6. List words on the chalkboard that begin with consonants not being studied which can be erased and replaced with the consonant that is being practiced. Have a student pronounce the word. Then erase the first letter of the word and put a *d* in its place to make a new word. Have students use their knowledge of the letter-sound association for *d* to pronounce the new word. Repeat this procedure with each of the other words listed here. Have students use the new words in sentences. Resources for Chapter 4 include a list of pattern words that should be helpful for this activity.

hot	dot
tip	dip
tog	dog
sent	dent
pig	dig
kid	did
him	dim

7. When students are reading and come across an unfamiliar word that contains the letter being studied, encourage them to use the context along with their knowledge of the letter sound to pronounce the word.

8. Orally read sentences where students give a word beginning with the sound being learned. The word must make sense in the sentence. Examples include:

    Jim's pet is a _____. (dog)

    Another name for a plate is a _____. (dish)

    At night it is _____. (dark)

    It's about time to eat _____. (dinner)

9. Have students name objects in the classroom that begin with the sound associated with the letter being learned. A variation is to have students find objects in the classroom with the same beginning sound as their names.

10. Read words that begin with different sounds on a tape recorder. Play the tape for the students asking them to stand up if they hear a word that begins with the letter *d*.

11. Place 10 or more word cards in a pocket chart each beginning with a different sound. Ask a student to think of another word that begins with one of the beginning sounds of the words. For example, if one of the word cards contained *little*, the student might say the word *like*. Play until all ten sounds are used. The meanings of the words in the pocket chart should be known to students.

12. Use the sounds of consonants during your regular school routine. For example, when the class is dismissed for the day, ask students whose last names begin with *D* to leave first.

13. Have teams of students create tongue twisters with the letter *d*. For example, a sample sentence might be: Dan drove to the downtown Dairy Dream for diet drinks.

14. Have students think of words beginning with the letter *d*. Students take turns saying a new word without repeating any words. When a student is unable to add a new word, ask another student to suggest one.

15. Place pictures in an envelope and have students sort the pictures according to initial, medial, or final sound.

16. Prepare a list of sentences that have a missing word. Sketch or cut out pictures that complete each sentence. Put them on cards, and ask students to select the appropriate card to complete each sentence that begins with a particular sound.

17. Connect an action with each consonant sound. For example, when you teach the sound *d*, ask the students to dance. You can make a game of this activity after you have taught several of the letter sounds. Make a card with each letter. Show one letter to the class and call on a student to show the class the action you learned for that letter. Examples of actions for consonants, digraphs, and blends follow (Cunningham, 1993):

b	bounce	t	talk	fl	fly
c	catch	v	vacuum	fr	frown
d	dance	w	wiggle	gr	grab
f	fall	y	yawn	pl	plant
g	gallop	z	zip	sw	swim
h	hop	ch	cheer	sk	skip
j	jump	sh	shiver	sl	sleep
k	kick	th	think	sm	smile
l	laugh	wh	whistle	sp	spin
m	march	br	breathe	st	stand
n	nod	bl	blink	tr	track
p	paint	cr	crawl	tw	twist
r	run	cl	climb		
s	sit	dr	drive		

18. When students have learned several consonant sounds, provide sentences or stories with a word missing and invite students to use the context and their knowledge of certain sounds to predict the word. For example, We ran _____ the stairs. Remind students that the word begins with the sound that begins like *dog*. If a word is given that makes sense but does not begin with *d* (for example, up) discuss why it is not the right answer. Invite students to share their thinking about particular responses and guide them as necessary.

Games

Pick Up. Give the student ten cards with a different consonant on each card. Lay out ten cards on the table. As you read a list of words, ask the student to pick up the card corresponding to the initial, medial, or final sound of the word.

Consonant Rummy. Use a deck of cards with a consonant on each one. Each player is dealt eight cards. The first player asks another player for the consonant that begins a certain word. For example, "I'd like Jen to give me a letter that begins the word down." If the player does not have the letter *d*, the caller picks a card from the deck and the next student takes a turn. The first student to have four cards of the same letter is the winner.

4.2 Phonics: Vowels

Behavior Observed	The student has difficulty associating the sounds that vowels symbolize.
Anticipated Outcome	The student will be able to use the sounds of vowels to help decode unknown words.

Background

Vowels are much more difficult for students to learn than consonants. Unlike most consonants, vowels can represent more than one sound. Most vowels have two or three common sounds, but there are also many exceptions for certain vowels. For example, the long *e* sound can be spelled seventeen different ways: *see, team, equal, he, key, Caesar, deceive, receipt, people, demesne, machine, field, debris, amoeba, quay,* and *pity* (May, 1990). Although it is not necessary to teach students rules for each of these vowel sounds, there are some vowel generalizations that can help students as they learn to phonologically recode words.

Beginning readers need to begin to learn the sounds for long and short vowels, and as students progress in reading, they can also learn about some of the less frequently occurring vowel sounds in the English language. As you teach your students vowel sounds, however, you need to remember that having students learn the sounds of vowels is not useful in itself. The purpose of teaching vowel sounds is for students to be able to make better predictions about unfamiliar words. If you find that you are spending more time in teaching the sounds associated with the letters than your students spend reading text, you should probably balance the proportion of time you are spending teaching phonics with opportunities for students to read printed materials.

The following are some of the sounds associated with vowels (adapted from Baer, 1991):

		Vowel Digraphs	
a as in *age*	*oi* as in *oil*		
a as in *an*	*ou* as in *out*	ee, ea	*e* as in *ease*
e as in *ease*	*oo* as in *too*	ai, ay	*a* as in *age*
e as in *end*	*oo* as in *good*	oa, ow	*o* as in *old*
i as in *ice*	*a* as in *dare*	oo	*oo* as in *too*
i as in *inch*	*u* as in *her*	oo	*oo* as in *good*
o as in *old*	*e* as in *about*	ou, ow	*ou* as in *out*
o as in *odd*	*a* as in *father*	oi	*oi* as in *oil*
u as in *use*	*o* as in *off*	au	*o* as in *off*
u as in *up*			

Teaching the various sounds of the vowels will probably span at least two grade levels. Generally, "short" vowels are taught first because they have fewer spellings. Some "long" vowels, however, are quite easy to learn, especially when they are the final letter in two-letter words (e.g., *me, he, we*). Even though vowels can be taught in a manner similar to consonants (see 4.1), we have provided teaching strategies for two different vowels.

Teaching Strategy 1 *(Exemplified by Teaching Short I)*

1. Students may need to be reminded that there are vowels and consonants and that sounds can be associated with both vowels and consonants.

2. Write the vowels on the chalkboard and circle the vowel that will be the focus of the lesson. Tell the students that there are two common sounds (long and short) associated with *i* and that they will be taught to associate the short sound with *i*.

3. If possible, select some objects and pictures whose names exemplify the short sound associated with *i* (for example, baseball *mitt,* fish's *fin,* jar *lid*). Appropriate names of class members may also be used (for example, *Bill, Jill*). Say the words and have students listen for the sound of the vowel.

4. Place the words on the chalkboard in a single column. Point to each word and pronounce it, emphasizing the sound associated with *i*. Have the students say each word as you move your hand from left to right under the word.

5. Ask the students to inspect the words and note their similarities and differences. When students note that all the words have an *i*, emphasize that the sound associated with this letter is called the short sound of *i*.

6. Then pronounce pairs of words orally (one containing the short sound of *i*), and have students identify the word containing the short *i*. By using some words with the long sound of *i*, students should be able to note how this sound differs from the short sound of *i*. An alternative is to pronounce a word and have students show a card with a short *i* if the word contains that sound. Possible words include:

fit–fat	ham–him
line–lit	dig–dog
rid–ride	mitt–met
rim–ram	jam–Jim

7. Encourage students to think of additional words with the short *i* vowel sound. List those words on the chalkboard. Have students use the words in sentences.

8. If desired, help students understand the generalization that the vowel *i* in the middle of a word surrounded by consonants usually has a short sound. This generalization can also be applied to other vowels in a similar position.

9. After the student has learned the vowel sounds, develop word wheels where the various words can be made by turning the wheel. Possible words for this activity can be found in Resources for Chapter 4.

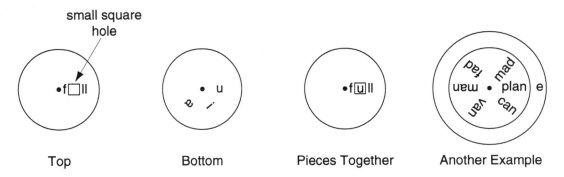

| Top | Bottom | Pieces Together | Another Example |

Teaching Strategy 2 (Exemplified by Teaching Long *E*)

1. Tell students that you will help them learn the long sound for *e*. Print *e* on the chalkboard and ask students to tell you the name of the letter.

2. Help students realize that the name of the letter and the long sound are the same. You might say, "Notice that the name of the letter and the long sound of the vowel are the same." Have the students say the sound together.

3. Then say, "Watch as I put a letter in front of the e and make a word." Print a *m* and say, "I know the sound *mmm* and when I put it with the *ē* it makes *me*." Have the students repeat the sounds and make the word by blending the sounds.

4. Guide students in creating other words that end with *ē* (*be, he, we*).

Practice and Reinforcement Activities

1. Provide cards with the vowel, a key word for that vowel, and a picture for that word. For example, you may want to remember the sound for *i* with the word *twins*. The card should have a picture of twins with the word and the letter.

2. Place a column of words on the chalkboard that contain the short vowel sounds. Show students that adding a final *e* to the words often changes the vowel sound from short to long. Begin a second column where an *e* is added to each word. Have a student pronounce these words and use each of them in a sentence. Emphasize the change in vowel sound when the final *e* is added. Sample words are shown here:

can	cane	bit	bite
man	mane	hop	hope
tub	tube	cut	cute
hid	hide	not	note
rid	ride	mad	made
rob	robe	kit	kite

3. Have students read a short passage and circle words with long vowel sounds. Then copy the words on a separate sheet of paper in an attempt to categorize them. Each category should then be labeled with a description of what the long-vowel words have in common.

152

4. Create cards that have long vowel sounds, short vowel sounds, and r-controlled vowel sounds. Have students sort each card into the categories by vowel sounds.

5. Teach students the importance of vowels by placing the cards with the consonants on a table. Ask a volunteer to make a word with the letter cards. The students should quickly see that it is impossible to write words without vowels. Then include vowel cards and ask the students to make words (DeGenaro, 1993).

6. Write basic sight words using two colors of crayons—one color for vowels and another color for consonants.

7. Provide students with letter tiles and have them engage in word-building activities. Fox (1996) provides many helpful suggestions for word building.

8. Use Venn diagrams to help students explore letters that represent more than one sound in words. For example:

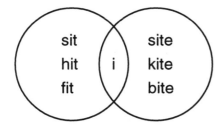 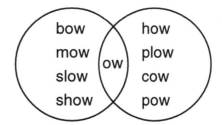

9. Help students experience printed materials that contain phonic elements. If some of the books are too difficult for independent reading, they can be shared aloud and discussed. Among the books compiled by Gunning (1996) are the following:

Oppenheim, J. (1990). *Wake, Up Baby!* New York: Bantam. (long *a*)
Ziefert, H. (1990). *Follow Me!* New York: Puffin. (long *e*)
Hoff, S. (1988). *Mrs. Brice's Mice.* New York: Harper. (long *i*)
Schade, S. (1992). *Toad on the Road.* New York: Random House. (long *o*)

Game

Tic-Tac-Toe. Prepare cards that have the vowel sounds you have taught. For example, perhaps you have taught long *i,* long *a,* long *e,* and short *i.* Each student should select a card. On the tic-tac-toe board, students should write a word with the vowel on the card that was selected.

Practice and Reinforcement Activities

1. Provide letter tiles and encourage students to build words with onsets and rimes. Letters can be written on bathroom tiles (1") with a permanent marker. Velcro can be attached to a small plywood board. After using the letter tiles, they can be secured on the plywood board for easy storage.

2. Encourage students to write sentences with rhymes being learned.

3. Use books that contain patterns being studied. In addition, some of the older linguistic readers (The cat sat on a mat, etc.) could be used for practice with certain onsets and rimes.

4. Use pocket charts so students can manipulate various letters to create words.

Behavior Observed	The student is unable to use knowledge about word patterns to identify unfamiliar words.
Anticipated Outcome	The student will be able to identify unfamiliar words by using common word patterns.

Background

Proficient readers rarely sound out words letter by letter. Instead, they use what they know about common spelling patterns to figure out the word. This means that readers will make the connection between spelling patterns they know to unfamiliar words. For example, if students encounter the word *hobbit* in reading, they may know that the word pattern *ob* may sound like *rob* or *mob* and that the pattern *it* may sound like *mit* or *bit*. Using what they know about consonant sounds, then, students can figure out a word that they do not know by sight.

Using word patterns is another strategy that students should use as they read. Like phonics and context clues, using word patterns is not a panacea; not all unfamiliar words will have familiar word patterns in them. For instructional purposes, however, you should help your students use this strategy as one more way to read unfamiliar words.

A word pattern has two components: an onset and a rime (Adams, 1990a). The onset is the initial part of a word that precedes a vowel (for example, the *h* in *hat* or the *sh* in *ship*). The rime is the part of the word that rhymes (for example, the *at* in *hat* or the *ip* in *ship*). Rimes are also known as word families or phonograms. A list of word patterns is included in the Resources for Chapter 4. The list will be helpful for teaching.

An innovative developmental approach that helps students explore letter patterns, letter-sound correspondences, and words has been developed by Cunningham and Cunningham (1992). The approach involves students in making words, and over 300 lessons have been developed for students in the elementary school (Cunningham & Hall, 1994a, 1994b). The steps for making word lessons are shown in the box (adapted from Cunningham and Cunningham, 1992) on the following page.

Planning Lessons to Make Words

1. Choose the word that will be made last in the lesson (for example, *stand*). Consider your students' interests and word knowledge when selecting words.

2. Make a list of other words that can be made from *stand* (*at, sat, Stan, Dan, tan, an, and, sand*). From these words, arrange the words in order from the shortest to the longest.

3. Decide on the words you will use based on patterns, words of various size, words that can be made by rearranging the letters (for example, *and, Dan*), and proper names to show the use of capital letters. When making your final selections, keep in mind that most students should have *heard* the words and know what they mean.

4. Make big letter cards to use in a pocket chart or on the ledge of the chalkboard. Then prepare an envelope that contains the order of the words and the patterns that will be stressed. Finally, print the words on cards.

Teaching Strategy 1 (Making Words)

1. Use the above box to plan the lesson or consult Cunningham and Hall (1994a, 1994b) for ready-made lessons. Distribute the necessary letters to each student. Keep the letters in reclosable bags and have individual students pass out the different letters. Each card should contain an upper-case letter on one side and a lower-case letter on the other. At the end of the lesson, the same students pick up the letters they originally distributed. Finally, you should have large letter cards that you can use with a pocket chart on the chalkboard ledge to model as necessary. Below is a sample lesson.

2. Have the letters distributed (a, d, n, s, t). If necessary, hold up the large letter cards, and have students hold up their small letter cards that match your card.

3. Say, "Use two letters to make *at*." Use the word in a sentence.

4. Invite a student to assemble the correct response using the large letter cards in the pocket chart or on the chalkboard ledge. Have the student read the word, and have students correct their individual responses as necessary. Students should be able to fix their word by comparing their word to the large letter cards.

5. Continue steps 3 and 4 with other word-making directions such as:

   ■ Add a letter to make *sat*.

   ■ Remove a letter to make *at*.

   ■ Change a letter to make *an*.

   ■ Add a letter to make *tan*.

   ■ Add a letter to make *Stan*.

   ■ See what word you can make with all the letters (*stand*).

6. When all the words have been made, take words you previously printed on index cards and put them in the pocket chart or on the ledge of the chalkboard. Keep these guidelines in mind:

    ■ Do one word at a time.

    ■ Present the words in the order they were made.

    ■ Have students say and spell the words with you.

    ■ Use the words for sorting and pointing out patterns (for example, find the word that has the same pattern as *tan*). Align the words so students can see the pattern.

    ■ Transfer word learning to writing by asking students to spell a few of the words you say.

7. Remember that word building can be used with upper-grade students and students at all ages who are struggling with reading (Cunningham & Hall, 1994a).

Teaching Strategy 2 (*Exemplified with -ay*)

1. Write the word *day* on the chalkboard or on a sentence strip.

2. Read the word to the students drawing attention to the *-ay* sound.

3. Substitute a different initial consonant such as *m* for *may*. Say, if d-a-y spells *day,* what do you think m-a-y spells? Repeat this activity with three or four different consonants. Write each word on the chalkboard or a sentence strip.

4. Ask the students to say each of the words. Although this may seem like an easy activity, many young students have difficulty reading rhyming words.

5. Write a sentence for each word or have students write sentences for the words. Ask students to read the sentences aloud paying close attention to the word pattern that is being studied.

6. For students who are able to progress to the next step, write an unfamiliar word on the chalkboard that contains the word pattern. An example for *-ay* may be to*day* or *may*be.

Teaching Strategy 3 (Exemplified with *-ill*)

1. Write *-ill* on the chalkboard and ask students what letter would need to be added to *ill* to make the word *hill.*

2. Add the *h* to *ill*, pronounce the sounds, and then blend the sounds as you say the whole word. Have students repeat the blending.

3. Then write *ill* underneath *hill* and ask students what letter should be added to *ill* to make the word *Bill.* Ask a student to blend the sounds to form the word.

4. Invite students to examine the two words and note how they are the same and how they are different. Guide students to understand that the words end with the letters *i, l, l* which make the sounds heard in *ill*; the words are different in the initial sounds and that accounts for the two different words.

5. Continue with other examples and model words like *Jill* and *fill*. Invite students to suggest other onsets that could be used to make a new word.

6. Use the words in oral sentences, written sentences, and possibly create stories. For example:

> Jill climbed a hill.
> She looked for Bill.
> She saw Bill fill a bucket.

Behavior Observed	The student does not use knowledge about word parts to read new words.
Anticipated Outcome	The student will use knowledge about word parts to read new words.

Background

When students come to an unknown word that is made up of more than one syllable, they can use structural analysis skills to divide that word into pronounceable units. Structural analysis skills can allow students to focus on the larger units of letter patterns within words. Such skills typically include inflectional endings, prefixes, suffixes, contractions, compound words, and syllabication. Teaching structural analysis does not mean that you rely on workbooks. You can teach students how to figure out longer words by using background knowledge students have about words and word parts, focusing on that knowledge, applying what students know to a new reading situation, and extending what students already know by imparting additional knowledge about words.

Teaching Strategy 1 (Inflectional Endings)

1. Tell students that inflectional endings are the endings that can form a plural noun (dogs, quizzes), show the present tense of a verb (barks, wishes), are the present participle of a verb (walking), show past tense (talked), show possession (Jerry's), and show comparisons in adjectives and adverbs (bigger, biggest).

2. Present a root word that your students know from previous lessons. Write the word on a sentence strip or on the chalkboard. Have the students pronounce the word and use it in a sentence.

3. Then have the students watch carefully while you add an ending to the word. Have different students pronounce each derived word. If a student makes an error, cover the ending and have the student pronounce the root word. Then have the student try the changed word again.

4. Once the words are pronounced correctly, have students use each new word in a sentence. Discuss the change in meaning that occurred when the ending was added. Students should understand that adding an ending to words changes the way the word is used in a sentence.

5. Conclude the lesson by helping students realize that some long words are really root words with inflected endings added. Encourage them to look for such endings when they are unable to pronounce a word at sight.

Teaching Strategy 2 (*Affixes*)

1. Affixes are prefixes and suffixes that are attached to a base word. Resources for Chapter 4 contain prefixes and suffixes that can be used for teaching and practice.

2. Explain to students that prefixes and suffixes form syllables because they are a pronunciation unit. They can be added to root words to change their meanings or part of speech. Provide examples.

    reread   *re* is a prefix; *read* is a root word

    painless   *pain* is a root word; *less* is a suffix

3. Have students supply some words that contain affixes. Write them on the chalkboard. Then ask students how they think knowing prefixes and suffixes can help them in reading. Through discussion, lead students to the following conclusions about prefixes and suffixes:

   ■ Knowing them can help me recognize words more rapidly; I don't have to sound out an unknown word letter by letter.

   ■ They can help me figure out some of the longer words in reading.

   ■ Sometimes I can use affixes to help determine the meaning of the word.

4. Model how to figure out unfamiliar words with prefixes and suffixes. Think aloud as you read. For example, if the word is *unicycle*, the following might be shared. "I can't recognize the word immediately, so I look for the root word. It is *cycle,* and I know what a cycle is. I can see that the prefix is *uni-*. I know that the word is *unicycle*, but what does it mean? Because I know that *uni-* often means one, I have a pretty good idea that unicycle means a one-wheeled cycle. I may need to look up the word in a dictionary to be sure of its meaning, but I now have an idea of the word and can ask myself whether the meaning makes sense in the sentence."

Teaching Strategy 3 *(Contractions)*

1. Tell students that some words in our language, called contractions, are really two words joined together so that not all of the sounds are heard. Give students an example of a contraction such as *didn't*. Explain that *didn't* is a contraction for *did not*.

2. Show students how to write the contraction *didn't* by writing both *did* and *not* on the chalkboard. Explain that when forming a contraction, the letters which are not written are replaced by an apostrophe. Show the students how to write an apostrophe in the word *didn't*.

3. Have the students write a sentence that uses *did not*. Then ask them to replace *did not* with the contraction *didn't*.

4. Repeat these steps with other contractions that are found in the Resources for Chapter 4.

Teaching Strategy 4 *(Compound Words)*

1. Explain to students that two words are sometimes put together to make a longer word. These words are called *compound words* when they retain some meaning from the two words. Stress that some meaning from each of the two words should be retained so words like *father* are not considered compound words.

2. Write several compound words on sentence strips. Ask students to pronounce the words and to use each one in a sentence. Write the sentences on strips and find the two words that make up each compound word.

3. Stress that looking for compound words in longer words may help students pronounce such words. Make it clear that some seemingly difficult words are actually compound words.

4. Provide sentences and help students identify the compound word and the two words that compose it. Sample sentences include:

> I saw a footprint in the snow.
>
> There was an earthquake in California.
>
> Please put the dishes in the dishwasher.

5. Conclude the lesson by helping students realize that they can sometimes recognize a longer word by identifying the two words that compose it.

6. Repeat these steps with other compound words that are found in the Resources for Chapter 4.

Teaching Strategy 5 (Syllabication)

1. Tell students that long words can be divided into smaller sections or syllables. By knowing how to divide words into syllables, students can have another strategy to figure out words as they read.

2. Say a multisyllabic word such as *bicycle*. Have the students say *bicycle* several times.

3. Tell students that you will clap your hands one time for each syllable in the word *bicycle*. As you say the word, clapping for each syllable, stretch out the word such as *bi—cy—cle*.

4. Say several more words that have more than one syllable, clapping one time for each syllable. Have students clap with you.

5. Explain that there are generalizations for the ways words are divided into syllables. Spend time teaching the syllables in words that follow the syllable generalizations.

Syllable Generalizations
(Adapted from McCormick, 1995)

1. When there are two like consonants, divide between them as in *pup/py*.

2. When there are two unlike consonants, divide between them as in *wal/rus*.

3. When a consonant is between two vowels, divide after the first vowel as in *si/lent*.

4. Prefixes, suffixes, and inflectional endings are their own syllable as in *pre/heat*.

5. When a syllable ends in a vowel, the vowel is long as in *o/pen*.

6. When a syllable ends in a consonant, the vowel is short as in *cab/in*.

Practice and Reinforcement Activities

1. Provide sentences containing root words that have the inflected ending omitted. Students read each sentence and add the appropriate ending. For example:

> Bill was look _____ for his mother.
>
> The cat jump_____ over the branch.
>
> I miss_____ the bus for school.

2. Prepare one set of cards that has root words and another set that contains different inflected endings (such as *s, ed, ing, er, est*). The root words for this activity should be the type that remain unchanged when an inflected ending is added. Students draw a card from each set and try to match the root-word card with an inflected-ending card to make a new word. Have students write the new words formed and use them in a sentence. Possible root words for this activity include the following:

ask	play	warm
call	thank	deep
help	new	hard
jump	small	

3. Ask the students to circle the inflected endings in one of their pieces of writing. After finding endings in their own writing, they may want to read a story written by a classmate and find endings in a classmate's writing.

4. Write two columns of root words on the chalkboard, one that requires no change in spelling before adding an *ed*, and the other that requires doubling the final consonant before the *ed* is added. Try to use words that are in the students' sight vocabularies. Pronounce the words in the first group and then add *ed* to the words and have the students pronounce the new word. If students have difficulty, cover the ending, have them pronounce the root word, and then try the word with the *ed*. Ask students to use the words in sentences before and after adding *ed*.

5. Invite students to bring personal possessions to the front of the classroom. Tell students that they will be learning different ways of saying the same thing. For example, take Annette's barrette and say the following sentences:

    This is the barrette of Annette.

    The barrette belongs to Annette.

    This is Annette's barrette.

Emphasize that each of the sentences means the same thing. Then write the sentences on sentence strips and direct the attention of the students to the last sentence. Identify the apostrophe and say that the *'s* on the end of the word Annette shows that the noun following her name belongs to her. Encourage the class to suggest phrases or sentences in which *'s* is used to show possession. Write the sentences on sentence strips.

6. Print prefixes and suffixes on tag board or file cards. Pass out the cards to students. Write root words on sentence strips. Hold one root word card in front of the class. A student who has a prefix or suffix that would make a new word comes up to the front of the class and places the card in front of or behind the root word card. The student pronounces the word, and if correct, the student may take the root word. Invite students to use the word in a sentence and, if necessary, discuss the meaning of the word.

7. As you introduce a new suffix, prepare several flip strips. To create a flip strip, print root words on the front left-hand side of colored strips of construction paper. On the back, print suffixes so that when the paper is folded a new word appears. Give the flip strips to students to practice making words with suffixes.

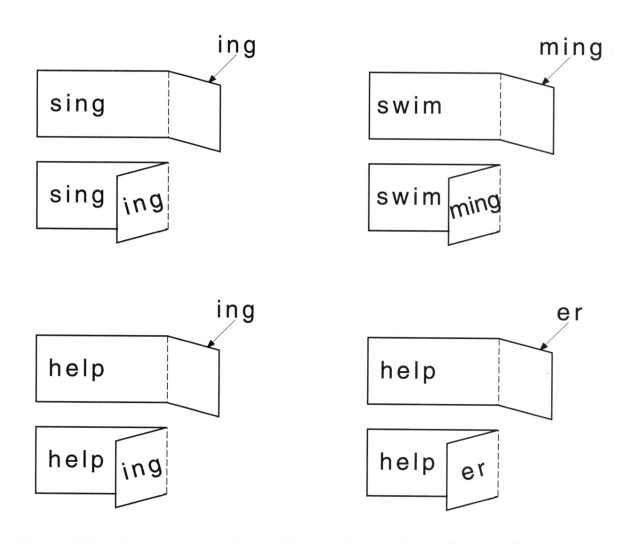

Games

Group Ball Toss. Draw a target on a piece of felt with a marker and write in root words. Glue a strip of velcro around a lightweight ball. Mount the target on the chalkboard and beside the target write word endings. Divide students into teams and let them take turns throwing the ball at the target. When the ball hits the target, the student reads the word closest to the ball, then writes the word on the chalkboard with one of the inflectional endings. If the word is correct, the team scores one point. The students can play until one team gets 20 points (McCormick, 1995).

Compound Word Dominoes. Write two compound words on tag board or index cards cut in half. Write the words facing the short sides and draw a line down the center. Distribute the cards to four students. Have students take turns making compound words by matching the words with two different cards. The Resources in Chapter 4 have a list of compound words that might be useful.

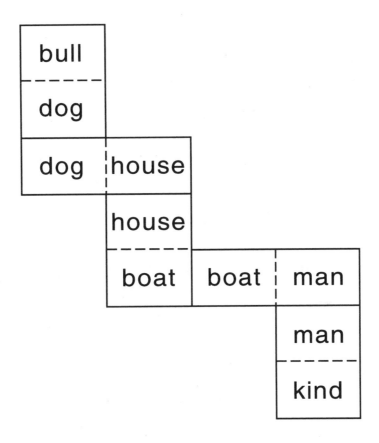

Twister. Draw 20 large circles on a 6' x 4' oilcloth and attach words written on cards in the center of these circles. Using two teams, have students from Team 1 put a hand on one word and a foot on a second word of a compound word. Then the student places a second hand on a word and a second foot on another word which would make sense as a compound word. If the words are correct, a student from Team 2 tries the same activity. The Team 2 student, however, needs to manipulate around the student from Team 1. Then another student from Team 1 joins the two students on the Twister board and so on until no more words can be formed.

4.5   Basic Sight Words

Behavior Observed	The student cannot identify basic sight words automatically.
Anticipated Outcome	The student will be able to identify basic sight words without hesitation.

Background

There are certain words in the English language that occur regularly in text. Look at these thirteen words:

a   and   for   he   in   is   it   of   that   the   to   was   you

These words account for approximately 25% of all of the words in school texts. Because they occur so frequently, they are called *basic sight words* or *high-frequency words*. You probably noticed that the words are difficult to define or describe. That's because they are *function words*, or words that are used to connect other words. They have little meaning themselves. Obviously, students who can read basic sight words automatically will have a much easier time reading text, but because basic sight words are abstract, they are difficult to teach.

The thirteen words listed here are not the only high-frequency words in the English language. In fact, 109 words make up over 50% of the words used in school texts, and only 5,000 words make up 90% of the words in texts (Adams, 1990b). Although that may seem like a lot of words, remember that a typical high school senior will have a vocabulary of approximately 40,000 words and that students generally learn 3,000 words per year. Knowing how quickly students learn words makes the task of teaching sight words much more manageable. You may be wondering what words make up the high frequency list of words. There are four word lists in the Resources for Chapter 4 for you to use in selecting sight words to teach.

You may want to teach basic sight vocabulary through direct instruction or indirect instruction. A combination of both approaches can also be effective.

Teaching Strategy 1 *(Direct Instruction)*

1. Select a word that the students want to learn to read by sight. The word may be one that is in a story the class is reading or it may be one that students need for writing.

2. Write the word on the chalkboard and ask the students to write the word on a card. If a student is unable to copy the word correctly, you may want to write it for him or her.

3. Locate a story or create a language experience story that uses the word several times.

4. Read the story to the class. Each time you say the sight word, ask students to raise their card.

5. Ask the students to read the word on their card, saying the word and then each letter.

6. Cut the word into letters and ask the students to arrange them to make up the word. Place the letters in envelopes so that the students can practice arranging the letters at other times during the day.

7. Write several sentences on the chalkboard with a blank space for the word. Ask the student to write the word in the blank and then read the sentences out loud.

8. Give the students text in which the word under study occurs frequently. Ask the students to carefully notice the word while reading.

Teaching Strategy 2 (*Indirect Instruction*)

1. Select a pattern book that emphasizes the word you want the students to learn. A list of pattern books can be found in Appendix C.

2. Read the book aloud to the students. If possible, secure a big book version so students can follow along.

3. Read the book again, asking the students to join in whenever they can. Point to each word as it is being read.

4. Ask the students to take turns reading the book with you and to each other.

5. Write the text of the book on sentence strips or ask the students to write it for you. Then ask the students to read the text from sentence strips.

6. Write the word being studied on word cards. Ask students to match the word to the sentence strips.

7. Cut the sentence strips into words. Mix up the words and ask the students to arrange them in order.

8. Take out the word being studied from the sentence, and ask students to write the word from memory.

9. Ask the students to create a sentence using the targeted word.

10. Create a rebus story using the word under study. Draw pictures for the nouns so that the student must read the high frequency words.

Practice and Reinforcement Activities

Even though students have had many exposures to a particular sight word during the previous teaching strategies, the words need to be practiced many more times before they become automatic. The following activities are designed to reinforce sight words.

1. Place the sight words on a "Word Wall."

2. Have the students put the sight word cards in alphabetical order.

3. Have students sort the words by categories. They may make up imaginative categories for the words, because most of them have little concrete meaning. Sample categories for some of the words on the Revised Dolch List (see Resources for Chapter 4) are shown in the box.

Category	Examples
Numbers	one, two, three
Other People	he, her, him, she, them
Talk Words	call, say, tell, ask
Action Words	run, leave, put, walk
Question Words	who, what, when, would
Size Words	big, little, long, round
Color Words	black, blue, white, red
Temperature Words	cold, hot, warm

4. Ask the students to find the words in texts around the room. For example, the word *and* may be on a "Friends and Neighbors" bulletin board.

5. Use words games such as Bingo, Hangman, Word Dominoes, Word Checkers, or Go Fish.

6. Have students use the buddy system to practice word cards.

7. Place word cards in a file box to use as a word bank of known words for writing.

8. Prepare cards that contain an illustrated sentence with the basic sight word underlined. Cards containing words and phrases may also be used.

9. Develop line searches. Be sure that the words only go from left to right. Ask students to circle the hidden word among each line of letters. Students can also be asked to use the word in an oral or a written sentence. The following is an example of line searches.

m f d (b i g) k   d d s a (b l u e) d s   d e (t h a t) d s   d e s d (w h e n) d s

10. Use familiar rhymes to help students learn basic sight words in a meaningful context. Write a rhyme on the chalkboard or on sentence strips. Write the basic sight words in a contrasting color from the rest of the rhyme. In the following example, the basic sight words are in italics.

> Humpty Dumpty
> Sat *on a* wall.
> Humpty Dumpty
> *Had a* great fall.

11. Chant the spelling of words.

12. Have students write words. Writing provides a kinesthetic mode to help students learn and remember words.

13. Have students unscramble words they are learning:

tge	flul	mrfo	egno	tgo	og	dogo
<u>get</u>	<u>full</u>	____	____	____	____	____

14. Use a tachistoscope (a quick-exposure device) or cards to briefly expose a word, phrase, or sentence. Give students repeated practice over several days.

15. Provide sentences where the student writes the correct word in the blank. Provide choices for the answer.

I like _____*that*_____ one.
     not   that   came

He _____ do his work.
   any   didn't   about

The night seemed _____ long.
        must   very   no

He _____ many nice things.
  such   when   does

16. Have students locate the most common basic sight words (a, and, for, he, in, is, it, of, that, the, to, was, you) in newspapers or magazines. This activity will help students realize how frequently such words occur. Use a selection about one hundred words in length.

17. Create "flexible" sentences using words from the Revised Dolch List and the list of high frequency nouns. Students can read the many different sentences with a partner.

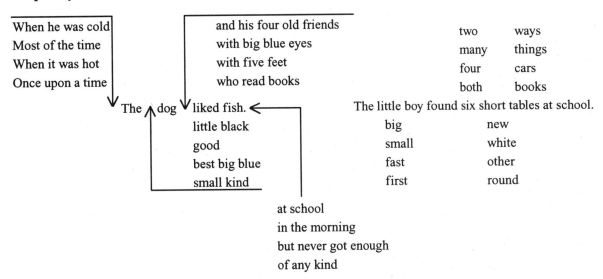

18. To aid in the practice of words such as *in, on, under, over, behind*, get a cup and straw. Place the straw in various positions and ask students to use a word that answers the question, "Where is the straw?" Alternative ideas include a stuffed animal and a cardboard box.

19. Provide lots of easy reading materials.

4.6   Sight Vocabulary

Behavior Observed	The student's sight vocabulary is so limited that it interferes with reading fluency.
Anticipated Outcome	The student will increase his or her sight vocabulary.

Background

Students who know words by sight are able to pronounce them automatically. A large sight vocabulary enables students to read fluently and to focus their attention on making sense of the passage. It also helps students use other reading strategies such as context clues more effectively.

A student's sight vocabulary, then, is composed of all of the words recognized in an instant. Some words recognized at sight occur very frequently in printed materials and are often referred to as basic sight words (for example, *when, then, the*). Basic sight words are a vital part of the student's sight vocabulary but are a subset of the total number of sight words a student may have. The following list shows the basic sight vocabulary in relation to the student's entire sight vocabulary.

Total Sight Vocabulary		
when*	elephant	K-Mart
big	Illinois	Bryan
there	Ms. Grant	grandma
so	Garfield	library
was	baseball	chocolate

* Basic sight vocabulary is in bold print.

Basic sight words tend to be abstract words. The other words that compose sight vocabulary usually refer to real things. This difference generally permits greater variety in teaching and practicing words that are not basic sight words.

When selecting words to teach as sight words, remember that many repetitions of the word may be necessary before the word becomes part of the student's sight vocabulary. The crucial variable is often the meaningfulness of the word to the student. The word *sled*, for example, might become a sight word quickly for a student who uses a sled frequently. A student who has never used a sled may have greater difficulty learning the word.

Teaching Strategy

1. When possible, use the actual object or a picture of the word being taught. Have a student identify the object. If you have no access to a visual representation of the word, begin with the next step.

2. Pronounce the word and write it on the chalkboard. Have students pronounce it. If necessary, discuss the meaning of the word with the students. Have students try to think of synonyms for the word. Students should also be encouraged to relate the word to their experience.

3. Encourage students to use the word in different sentences. Write some of these sentences on the chalkboard and underline the word being taught. If a word has more than one meaning, be sure sentences are provided that exemplify these meanings.

4. If students are confusing two or more words (for example, *chair* and *chew*), compare the words by having students point out similarities and differences between the words. Students might also close their eyes and picture the word that is being taught.

Practice and Reinforcement Activities

1. See 4.1 for additional activities.

2. Students should read many books that are easy for them. There are many books appropriate for students who have limited sight vocabularies. See Appendix C for a list of pattern books.

3. For words that can be represented by a picture, print the word on the front of a card under the picture. The back of the card should contain the printed word. You can use logos from stores and businesses for some sight words.

A list of leveled books for students in the early stages of reading has been provided by Brooks (1996). Several titles recommended for emerging to beginning readers include:

Cocca-Leffler, M. (1994). *What a Pest!* New York: Grosset and Dunlap.
dePaola, T. (1994). *Kit and Kat.* New York: Grosset and Dunlap.
Ziefert, H. (1995). *Nicky, 1-2-3.* New York: Puffin.

4. Provide many varied opportunities for students to interact with print. Some techniques include the following:

- sustained silent reading

- read-along stories and books

- repeated readings

- shared reading

- poems, songs, and rhymes

Games

How Many? Have students write the words on cards. Each word should have at least four cards. The students can then play the card game "How Many?" The word cards are shuffled and the deck is placed face down. Students take turns rolling a die to determine how many words are drawn from the deck. Each word is pronounced, placed on the table, and used in a sentence. Any words pronounced incorrectly are returned to the bottom of the deck. The student with the most words wins.

Word Sort. Prepare ten word cards relating to each of the categories appropriate for the words. Shuffle the cards and deal them to each of the players. Players take turns rolling a die and placing one or two words under the correct category.

Around the World. Using sight word flash cards, show a card to a pair of students. The student who responds correctly first can move on to another student. The object is for a student to make it around the class, or around the world. The winning student can then hold the cards for you while the class resumes play.

Word Hunt. Place several sight word cards around the room. Ask the students to hunt for the cards, reading them aloud when they find one. The student with the most cards wins.

Concentration. Place several pairs of sight word cards face down on a table. Have students take turns uncovering and pronouncing two cards, looking for pairs. When a student finds a pair, he or she pronounces the word and takes the cards. The student with the most pairs wins the game.

4.7 Using Context to Predict Known Words

Behavior Observed	The student has difficulty using context clues to anticipate a familiar word.
Anticipated Outcome	The student will use context as one reading strategy to anticipate known words.

Background

The context of a word is the words surrounding it. One of the ways to identify words is to use the other words in the sentence and to make a prediction about what word would make sense. Using context clues to anticipate known words can make reading a more efficient process.

To make a good prediction about a word, the student's knowledge and experiences play an important role. For example, consider these sentences:

The dog was chewing on a _____.

Peaches grow on _____.

The baby began to _____.

Students with prior knowledge about dogs, peaches, and babies should have little difficulty supplying a word that would make sense in the sentences. The students are able to draw upon their existing knowledge to make a prediction about the missing words.

Unfortunately, some students' reading comes to an abrupt halt when they come across a word they don't recognize at sight, even if only one word would make sense in the sentence. For example, peaches only grow on trees. No other response would make sense in the sentence. For the other sentences, however, the student would also need to consider at least the initial sound in the unknown word. For example, the baby began to *sm-*, or the baby began to *cr-*, would elicit two different responses, each correct in the context. Context clues, therefore, are helpful but should not be considered the only strategy to use when students try to read unfamiliar words.

Teaching Strategies

1. Select a text that the students will need to read. Preview the text and determine which words might give the students difficulty. Model how you would use the context to help figure it out. Think aloud so the students can hear your strategies.

2. List some common topics that students might be asked to read about and encourage them to list words that are likely to appear in the stories. Develop the notion that certain words might be expected to be associated with a particular topic.

3. Present incomplete sentences orally and have students suggest words that would make sense. Begin with sentences in which a large number of meaningful responses are possible and conclude with a sentence in which only a few choices make sense. Help students understand that if they listen to a sentence, they can usually think of a word that makes sense. Possible sentences include:

I like to eat _____.

One day of the week is _____.

There is no school on _____.

4. Write sentences with a missing word on the chalkboard and have students suggest words that make sense. Supply additional words, including some that do not make sense, and ask students why a particular word is or is not appropriate. Discuss clues within the sentence that may help students make decisions. Underline such clues. For example, in "I like to eat _____," the words *like* and *eat* are important clues; *eat* is probably the most important clue.

Practice and Reinforcement Activities

1. Daily routine activities will help students use oral context skills to predict words. Examples include:

    Today is _____.

    The two students absent are _____ and _____.

2. Read familiar pattern books to the students, pausing at appropriate places so students can predict the missing word. A list of pattern books can be found in Appendix C.

3. Make tape recordings of books omitting several words. Give the student a copy of the text to underline the words omitted on the tape.

4. Use a book at the student's independent level and mask selected words with tape (Post-it Notes work well). Have the student make predictions for the words before the tape is removed. Then remove the tape to see what the author has written. Discuss different responses to determine overall appropriateness.

5. Provide a passage from a text in which selected words have been replaced with lines. Instruct students to read the passage and write in their choices of words. Stress that their words should make sense. Later, discuss their choices in conjunction with the words used by the author.

6. Using a text the students will be reading, read several sentences omitting several words, and have students predict the words that have been omitted. Then tell students the words used by the author and develop the idea that it is sometimes possible to predict a word the author will use.

4.8 Using Context Clues to Predict Meanings for Unknown Words

Behavior Observed	The student has difficulty using context clues to predict meanings for unknown words.
Anticipated Outcome	The student will use context as one reading strategy to predict meanings for unknown words.

Background

The words surrounding an unknown word can sometimes be used by the student to predict its meaning. When this process occurs, the student is using context clues. Such clues help students associate meaning with words that they may not be able to pronounce and can aid students in constructing the meaning of a sentence or passage.

For example, suppose a student comes across the word *yegg* in a passage. It is probable that the student will be able to pronounce the word but will not know what it means. Depending on the context, the student may or may not be able to make a reasonable guess at the meaning of the word. If the only context is "Two people saw the *yegg*," it is unlikely that the student could use the context to figure out the meaning of *yegg*. The student could determine that a *yegg* is something that can be seen, but such information is not very helpful in determining the meaning, because millions of things can be seen.

A different context might be more helpful. For example, "The *yegg*, a burglar, was seen by two people." In this sentence, the meaning is given in an appositive phrase, and the student may be able to associate the meaning with the word.

Many teachers encourage students to use context to figure out meanings for unfamiliar words. Unfortunately, such advice often has two limitations. First, little direct instruction is given. Second, teachers need to be aware that not many words are actually defined by their context. Some words, however, can be determined solely by their context. These words will probably be found in one of the following types of sentences (two examples of each type follow the description):

➤ Definition or Description: Words are directly defined by the sentence.

A *kingcup* is a yellow flower.

The *commencement* or beginning of the journey was exciting.

➤ Appositive Phrase: The definition of the unknown word or the word itself is in a phrase set off by commas.

The *kithara*, a musical instrument, was played in ancient Greece.

The *kinglet*, a tiny bird, eats insects.

➤ Linked Synonyms: The unknown word is in a series of known words.

His *barbarous*, cruel actions were unexpected.

Her *aim*, goal, and inclination was to finish the book.

➤ Comparisons and Contrasts: The word can be defined by its opposite in the sentence.

Rather than his usual lively self, today William appeared to be *ponderous*.

Unlike the *dowdy* customer, the salesperson was neat and clean.

➤ Examples: The word can be defined by examples in the sentence.

My family is very *musical*. My sister plays the violin; my father plays the piano; and my mother sings.

His *machinations* to get a promotion were obvious. He bragged about his accomplishments, and told his boss his colleagues were inept.

➤ Classification: The word can be defined by its relationship to known words.

The water *molecule* is comprised of two parts hydrogen and one part oxygen.

Mike was an important player on the *offensive* football team. His skills at passing the ball to any player within reach were stunning.

➤ Experience: The word can be defined by applying previous experience to the unknown word.

As I stepped onto the diving platform, I felt *paralyzing* fear. The water surface appeared unforgiving. If I landed any way other than vertical, I could end up with a serious injury.

He looked *deliriously* happy. As he held his new son in his arms, his eyes glowed with emotion, and his lips slowly spread into the widest grin of his life.

Teaching Strategy 1

1. Develop a series of passages in which context can be used easily to help reveal the meaning of an unfamiliar word. Use a hierarchy in which context clues can be ranked informally from easy to hard.

2. Write a word on the chalkboard that the students may or may not be able to pronounce. Ask whether anyone knows the meaning of the word. If words are carefully selected, few, if any, students should know their meaning. Suppose the word is *kingcup* and a few students think they know what it means. Those students could be asked to remain quiet while the lesson continues.

3. Ask students how they might make a good prediction for the meaning of *kingcup*. Common responses include looking in the dictionary, asking someone, and seeing the word in a sentence. Stress that seeing a word in a sentence is using context.

4. Now write the unfamiliar word in a sentence where the meaning is made clear by definition or description.

A kingcup is a yellow flower.

5. Have the students read the sentence and then identify the word or words that reveal the meaning for the unfamiliar word. Circle or underline these words.

6. Repeat this procedure with additional words. In subsequent lessons, teach other types of context clues in a similar manner. Occasionally, use an unfamiliar word in a context in which the meaning is not clear. These instances will help students realize that there are limitations to using context to determine word meanings.

Teaching Strategy 2
(Adapted from Gunning, 1996)

1. Explain to the students that context clues can be important in understanding the meaning of unknown words. From a passage the students are reading, select four or five words that can be defined by their context. Write the words on the chalkboard.

2. For each word, have students apply the following questions (Sternberg & Powell, 1983):

   - What information in the passage will help me figure out the meaning of the word?

   - When I put together all the information that I know about the word, what word makes sense in the sentence?

   - What do I know that will help me figure out this word?

3. Write down the student guesses for each word on the chalkboard. Explain that if a word does not make sense, a different word should be tried. Try several words in the passage until students read the unknown words correctly. Discuss the meaning of the word.

4. Reflect on the strategies students used as they applied context clues to their reading. Discuss the strategies they used, and suggest other strategies students could use as they try to understand the meaning of unknown words.

Practice and Reinforcement Activities

1. Watch for examples in instructional materials in which context can be used to build meaning for an unfamiliar word, and use these examples to help reinforce students' use of context.

2. Encourage students to consult dictionaries to find words whose meanings are likely to be unfamiliar to other students in the class. Then have students write a sentence or brief passage that could be shared with other students who would attempt to identify the meaning of the word.

3. Provide brief passages that contain unfamiliar words and have students select or write the meaning of the underlined word based on the context.

4. To encourage students to use self-monitoring strategies as they read, print the following questions on a brightly-colored bookmark:

   - Did what I just read make sense to me?

   - Can I retell this passage in my own words?

   - Are there any words I don't understand?

   - Are there any sentences that confuse me?

Remind the students to ask themselves these questions as they read (Richek, Caldwell, Jennings, & Lerner, 1996).

4.9   Lack of Flexible Word-Identification Strategies

Behavior Observed	The student does not use a variety of word-identification strategies.
Anticipated Outcome	The student will use various strategies for identifying unknown words.

Background

Students with difficulty in reading often do not apply all of the word-identification strategies they have learned. They may, for example, use decoding, but rarely use the context of the sentence when they encounter an unknown word. Good readers, however, recognize that the most efficient method of figuring out unknown words varies with the reading situation. Therefore, teachers need to emphasize that students use reading strategies most appropriate for the situation.

The following ideas (Ruddell, 1993) are meant to help teachers begin to refine the process of teaching students to develop a set of flexible word-identification strategies.

Teaching Strategy (CSSR)

1. *Context.* Tell students that when they come to a word they don't know, they should read to the end of the sentence to see whether the rest of the sentence defines the word. Students needing practice in figuring out unfamiliar words from context should be taught the strategies in 4.8.

2. *Structure.* If the word cannot be identified by the context, students should look at the parts of the words. They should look for any familiar word parts that can help them understand the new word. For teaching strategies using the structure of words, see sections 4.3 and 4.4.

3. *Sound.* If the word has familiar word parts, students should try to pronounce the word using their knowledge of the sounds of consonants and vowels. After trying to give some of the letters the sounds they represent, the students should reread the sentence, thinking about the way the word is used. Often students will be able to read the word using these three steps. For teaching strategies using the sounds associated with letters, see sections 4.1 and 4.2.

4. *Reference.* If students are unable to identify the word, they may use reference materials such as a glossary or a dictionary. After finding a word in the dictionary, however, the students still need to determine how it is used in the context of the sentence.

5. You may want to model this procedure with your students. For example, consider the unknown word *amicable* in the sentence, "The family came to an amicable agreement about vacation plans." You might say: "I don't know the word a-m-i-c-a-b-l-e, so I would first read to the end of the sentence. I know that the word describes agreement, but nothing in the sentence tells me what kind of agreement they had. It might have been friendly, but it might not have been. After reading to the end of the sentence, I look for word parts that I know. The word has parts I can pronounce, but it doesn't have a base word or affixes that will help me understand the word. Next, I try to read the word by giving the letters the sounds that I know

(sound out word). I know the sounds in the word, so I can pronounce it. After pronouncing *amicable*, I reread the sentence. Yes, I've heard the word before, and it makes sense in the sentence. Just to be sure, however, I check the dictionary and find that *amicable* means 'friendly or peaceable.' I think I'll remember the word the next time I see it."

Behavior Observed	The student's knowledge of word meanings is limited.
Anticipated Outcome	The student will increase the number of known words and expand the range of meanings for words encountered in text.

Background

Helping students expand and enrich their meaning vocabulary is not easily accomplished. You need to do far more than provide your students with a list of vocabulary words to study for a test on Friday. Students learn new vocabulary words in four ways (Manzo & Manzo, 1993). The first way is incidentally, through their own reading and conversation. Children come to school knowing approximately 5,000 words, and during their twelve years at school, they learn another 36,000. Many of these words are learned without teacher intervention; they are learned through students' exposure to language.

The second way students learn new vocabulary is through direct instruction. Teachers can have an impact on students' learning vocabulary through well-thought out vocabulary instruction. Giving students the definitions for new words, however, usually does not ensure that those words will become part of their students' vocabulary. That is because giving definitions for words merely provides students with the denotation, or general meaning, of a word. Each word, however, also has a connotation. The connotation of a word is the range of meanings it has and the specific context in which it occurs (Readence, Bean, & Baldwin, 1992).

The third way students learn new vocabulary is through self-instruction. As students read, they can consciously try to learn new words. Teachers can help instill in students a desire to learn words, and they can provide students with strategies that help them make the new words part of their expressive vocabulary.

Finally, students learn vocabulary through mental manipulation of words while thinking, speaking, and writing. Students are constantly exposed to new words in school, at home, and in books. As they use these new words, they begin to extend their knowledge of the word's meaning. Students learn new words to different degrees. With every word, students may be anywhere on a continuum from not knowing the word at all, having heard the word but being unsure about its meaning, having a general sense of the meaning of the word, to having the word in their expressive vocabulary (Beck & McKeown, 1991). Even if they know more meanings for a word, they often initially lack the understanding of a word's richness.

Teaching the various meanings of a word, however, is not sufficient. Word knowledge should be constantly changing as new information is added to students' existing schemata (background knowledge) and as new schemata are developed. That means teachers need to encourage students to continue to expand their meanings of words on their own as well as to provide instruction on new words. Gunning (1996) suggests that to assist students in enriching their meaning vocabulary, teachers need to provide students with experiences that will build their background knowledge, help them relate new words to that background, assist them in building relationships between words, help them develop depth of meaning of new words, present several exposures to each word to students, help students become interested in words, and help students transfer words to their own vocabulary. The following strategies will help students enrich their meaning vocabularies.

Teaching Strategy 1 (Knowledge Rating Guide)

A Knowledge Rating Guide (Blachowicz, 1986) can help students understand to what degree they initially know a specific word and can provide a vehicle for a class discussion which allows students to expand their background knowledge of the words. To prepare and use a Knowledge Rating Guide, use the following steps:

1. Prepare a list of words that you want the students to learn.

2. Next to each word, draw three columns similar to the example.

	Can define	Have seen/heard	Unknown
glacier	_____	_____	_____
avalanche	_____	_____	_____

3. Ask students to place a check in the column that best describes what they know about the new word. If they are unclear about the directions, model the procedure for them. For example, you could say, "The first word on this list is glacier. I know that a glacier is made of ice, and I have heard the word many times, but I'm not exactly sure if I could define the word. I think I'll place a check under the column *Have seen/heard*. On the other hand, I do know what an avalanche is. It's falling rock or snow. I'll check *Can define* for that word."

4. After students have filled out the Knowledge Rating Guide, discuss the words with them. Ask which words were difficult, which were easy, which most of the students knew, and which words few students knew. As you discuss the words, ask students to share their background knowledge and experience with the words.

5. From the class discussion, ask students to make predictions about further meanings of the words and how they would be used in a text.

Teaching Strategy 2 (Possible Sentences)

Possible Sentences (Moore & Moore, 1986) is a vocabulary strategy where students predict the meanings of words in a passage to be read. This strategy helps students learn how to make predictions of unknown words as well as heightening motivation to read.

1. List 5-10 vocabulary words that are crucial to the meaning of the passage. Write these words on the chalkboard and read them to the class.

2. Ask students individually or in small groups to select at least two words from the list to write in one sentence that might occur in a reading passage. Ask the students to read their sentences aloud and write them on the chalkboard underlining the vocabulary words. Continue writing sentences until all of the words have been used.

3. Ask the students to read the passage silently looking for the vocabulary words and checking the accuracy of the "possible" sentences.

4. After all of the students have read the passage, lead a class discussion evaluating the sentences that the students created. Discuss to what extent the vocabulary was accurately used in the "possible" sentences.

5. Once students feel they know the meanings of the new words, ask them to create new sentences using the vocabulary words once more. These new sentences can be a check to determine whether or not the students have learned the meanings of the new words.

Teaching Strategy 3 (Vocabulary Self-Collection)

Vocabulary Self-Collection (VSC) is a strategy that encourages students to find words from their environment to learn (Haggard, 1982). VSC helps students understand that learning new words needs to be a consciously active process that should be part of their lives.

1. Ask students to look for unknown words in their reading, conversations, and their environment. As they find words, ask students to write them down on a note card.

2. Each day, up to five students who have found a new word should write the word on the chalkboard.

3. At an appropriate time, ask the students who submitted the words to define them.

4. After each definition, ask the class to try to add to the word's definition or to further clarify its meaning.

5. All students should record the words with their meanings in a vocabulary notebook for reference as students read and write.

Teaching Strategy 4 *(Contextual Redefinition)*

Contextual redefinition (Cunningham, Cunningham, & Arthur, 1981) can give students a better understanding of how to learn words in the context of text as well as helping them discover the meanings of new words on their own.

1. Select unfamiliar words from the students' text that could be considered key to understanding the text.

2. Write sentences for the words that give the meaning in context.

3. Then ask the students to define the new words aloud. Discuss how the context helped the students understand the definitions.

4. You might then ask the students to verify their definition by checking a dictionary. The dictionary can also help them learn other ways the words are used.

   For example, try to define the following words using your background knowledge:

   jejune _____

   convivial _____

   Now read the following sentences that contain the words *jejune* and *convivial*:

   The teacher was surprised by his *jejune,* immature answer to the problem.

   Her *convivial* personality was appealing to friends who enjoyed parties.

If you didn't know the words before, you probably know now that one of the definitions for *jejune* is immature and one of the definitions for *convivial* is sociable. Remember that words are symbols for concepts, so you can't understand the connotations for either word by reading one sentence. You do, however, get a sense of the meaning for each word, and if you would read either word in a text, you would probably know enough about the word to comprehend the phrase it was in.

Contextual redefinition is a useful strategy for a variety of reasons. First, the strategy illustrates how difficult it is to identify definitions of words in isolation. Second, students tap into their background knowledge by making a prediction about the word. Some students may have a tentative knowledge of the word before you teach its definition. This strategy helps them bring what they know to the teaching situation. Third, contextual redefinition helps students become engaged in the lesson rather than listing sterile definitions, and finally, the strategy encourages students to use the dictionary to confirm predictions rather than being used as the first strategy they use when they come to an unknown word (Readence, Bean, & Baldwin, 1992).

Teaching Strategy 5 (*Preview in Context*)

This strategy (Readence, Bean, & Baldwin, 1992) asks students to look for words in the context of their text to give them a better understanding of which definition of the word will be used. Discussing key words before reading also helps students begin to develop *schemata* (background knowledge) for the topic of the text selection.

1. Select words from text that you think will be unfamiliar to your students. Make sure you choose words that are key to the understanding of the text and don't make your list too long. It's better to have an effective lesson with four or five words than to have a lesson of ten words that the students forget.

2. Show students where the words are in the text and read the context surrounding the new word. You may read the passage aloud or have the students read it silently. If you are using a content area text, you might also want to spend some time explaining the concepts in the text.

3. Help students learn the word meaning by discussing it in its context. You might want to ask the students questions leading them to the definition, as in the following example:

   The protective coloring of the horned viper helps *camouflage* him by hiding him from his enemies and by helping him blend into his background.

   Teacher: What do you know about the word *camouflage* from this sentence?

   Student: The horned viper is hiding from his enemies.

   Teacher: How does being camouflaged help him?

   Student: He blends into his background.

   Teacher: What else does the sentence tell us about being camouflaged?

   Student: I think the part where it says *protective coloring* is another way of saying *camouflage*.

4. Expand word meanings. After students learn the initial meaning of the word, provide additional contexts for the same word. That way students who come across the word in different contexts will make predictions about what they know about the word's meaning to another situation.

   Teacher: How many of you have seen *camouflage* shirts or pants?

   Student: I have some on my GI Joe.

   Teacher: What are they like?

   Student: They're all different colors, but mostly brown and green.

Teacher: Why do you think they are those particular colors?

Student: So he can hide from the bad guys.

Teacher: How are the GI Joe camouflage clothes similar to the snake's skin?

Student: Both the clothes and the skin help them blend into the background.

Teaching Strategy 6 (*List-Group-Label*)

One of the ways students develop the concepts for words is to learn the relationship of that word to other words. Classification strategies such as list-group-label (Tierney, Readence, & Dishner, 1990) help students learn how words fit in relation to other words. These strategies also engage students in the content of the text they are reading.

1. Select one or more related topics about a passage the students have read. Make sure there are several subtopics for the topic you have chosen. For example, if the students read a chapter about animals, you might think of the subtopics farm animals, pets, wild animals, and characteristics of animals.

2. Write the name of the topic on the chalkboard. Ask students to think of all of the terms that are associated with the topic. List them on the chalkboard. The following list is an example of possible terms students might give for the topic animals:

dog	cat	lion	elephant
cow	hen	gerbils	warm-blooded
horse	hamster	giraffe	breathing
born alive	white mice	cheetah	goat

3. Ask students to organize the list into groups and give each group a label. Students can work in small groups or alone. Be prepared for a variety of answers. Because the object of the lesson is for students to interact with the concepts, you can allow them to differ on some decisions about where an item would fit in a list. For example, white mice in this list would probably be considered a pet, but some students may argue that the term would belong in a different category.

Teaching Strategy 7 (*Feature Analysis*)

Using feature analysis (Pittelman, Heimlich, Berglund, & French, 1991) helps students realize that several words may have certain features in common. It also helps them learn the distinguishing concepts behind different words.

1. Select a general category and list some words within the category. One example is the term *transportation*. Of that general category, car, bicycle, and airplane are all examples of modes of transportation.

2. List some features common to each word and one or more unique features for each word. For transportation, some of the features include two wheels, wings, uses fuel, has an engine, and carries passengers. You may suggest a feature or two and ask the students to think of other features. Students may not be able to think of features unless the teacher first provides some examples.

3. Ask students to determine which features fit with which words. Have them make an x or +
for features that fit, or an x if it fits and a - if the features don't describe the word. The
following is an example for the category transportation:

Transportation	two wheels	wings	uses fuel	engine	passengers
car	–	–	x	x	x
bicycle	x	–	–	–	x
airplane	–	x	x	x	x

4. Ask students to explain their rationale for each word. Then ask students how the terms are
similar and how they are different.

5. Another way to introduce feature analysis is to ask students to use their own names as terms
to describe. For features, they might use such ideas as "has a brother," "owns a pet," or "has
freckles." Students can have fun using feature analysis and can get to know each other as
well. A blank form for the feature analysis is included here.

Feature Chart

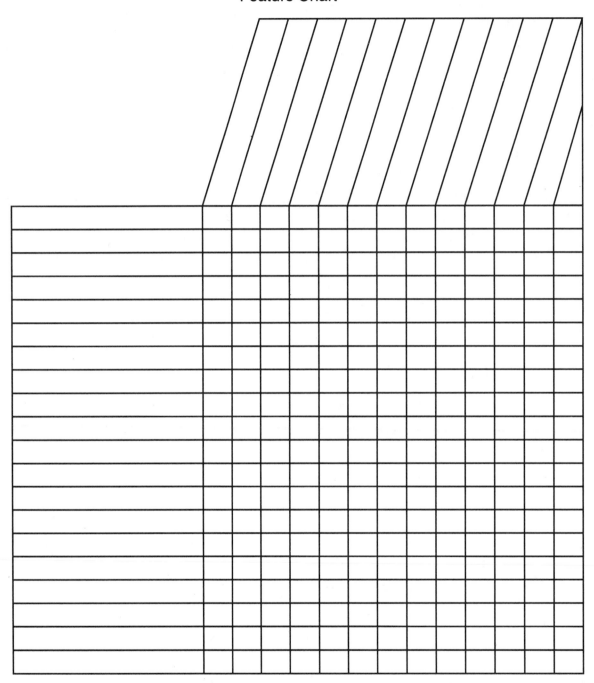

Teaching Strategy 8 *(Semantic Mapping)*

A semantic map (Heimlich & Pittelman, 1986) is a graphic representation of related concepts. Semantic mapping is another way students can learn the relationships of words to other words.

1. Select a topic from the text you have been reading. For example, if students were reading text about band music, the key word might be musical instruments.

2. Write the word on the chalkboard.

3. Ask students to brainstorm as many related words as they can. Examples for musical instruments might be *cornet, clarinet, snare drum, cymbol, xylophone, oboe, flute, trumpet, French horn, saxophone.*

4. Organize the words into a diagram similar to the example.

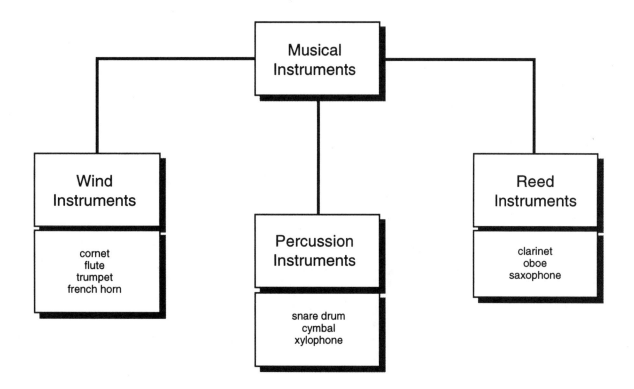

5. Students can add words to the diagram as they think of them.

6. Ask students to give names to the categories represented on the diagram. In this example, the category names are in larger type.

7. Discuss why the words fit into the categories. Ask the students to give the salient features that separate the categories.

Teaching Strategy 9 *(Word Map)*

A word map (Readence, Bean, & Baldwin, 1992) helps students develop a framework for a word. A word map gives the category of the word, the ways it's different from other similar words, and examples.

1. Discuss the word map with the students, explaining how it helps students think about a variety of aspects of a concept.

2. Model an example such as the one that follows. "The term we have been studying is an emu. (Write emu in the middle box.) Let's think about what an emu is. We've learned that an emu is a bird, so that goes in the top box that represents the class or category of the term. On the right we will write properties or characteristics of the emu. We know that the emu is an Australian bird, that it is tall, and that it can't fly. At the bottom of the word map, we write examples or illustrations of the emu. In this case, we'll write that it is smaller than the ostrich and that it is like the rhea. That completes our word map."

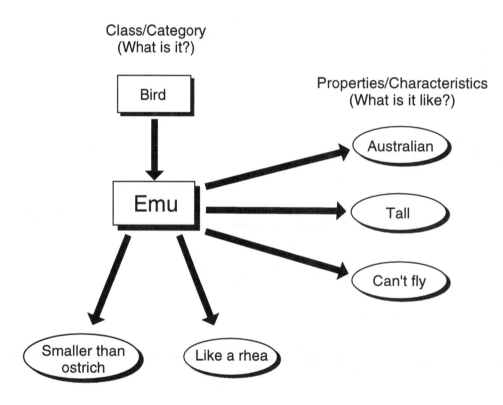

3. After the students have listened to you complete a word map, give them a blank map and suggest a term to describe. You might suggest that students work in small groups.

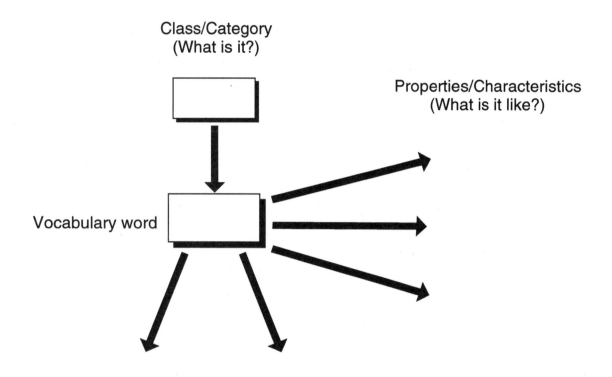

Class/Category
(What is it?)

Properties/Characteristics
(What is it like?)

Vocabulary word

Examples/Illustrations

Teaching Strategy 10 *(Graphic Organizers)*

Graphic organizers are pictorial representations of how words are related. They can assist students in understanding the relationship between words and ideas.

1. To create a graphic organizer, first make a list of key terms from the text you are using.

2. Then cluster the terms by groups.

3. Finally, determine which kind of diagram fits the material best.

There are many types of graphic organizers, including the following:

Chain of Command

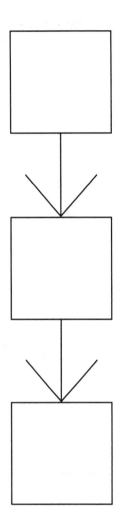

Continuums

Cycle

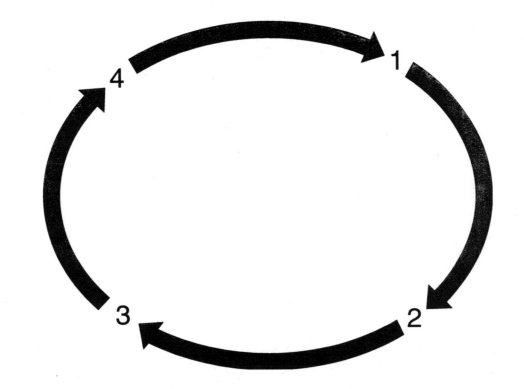

Venn Diagrams

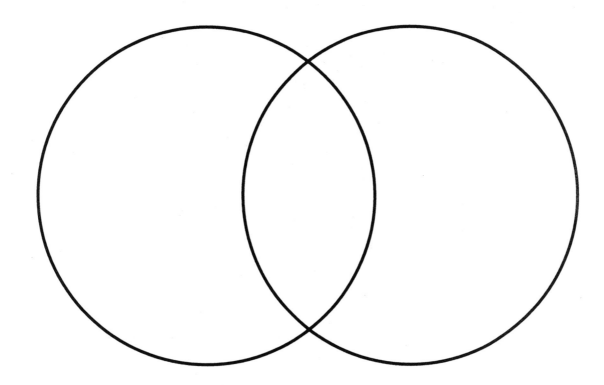

Hierarchy

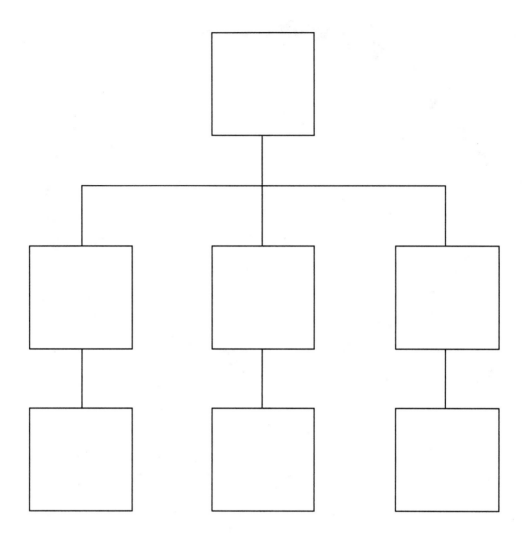

Time Lines

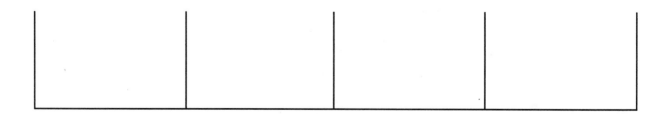

Overlapping Concepts

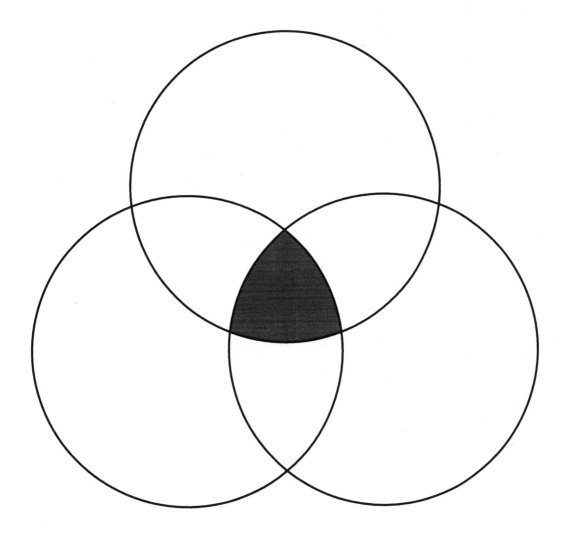

Cause-Effect

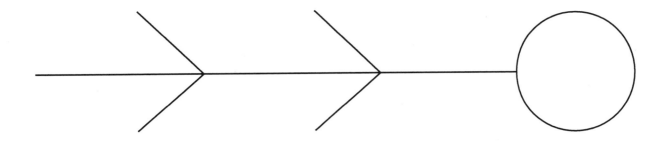

Parts of a Concept

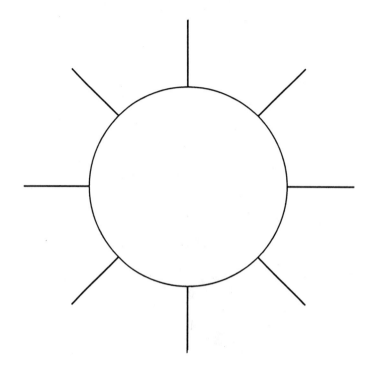

Parts of a Whole

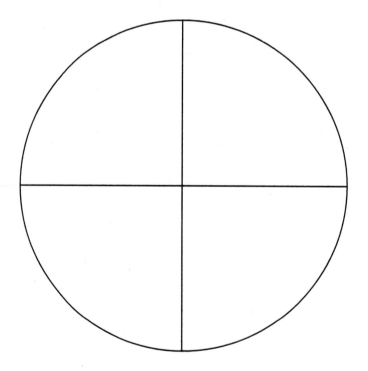

Priorities in Descending Order

_____

_____

_____

_____

Relationships

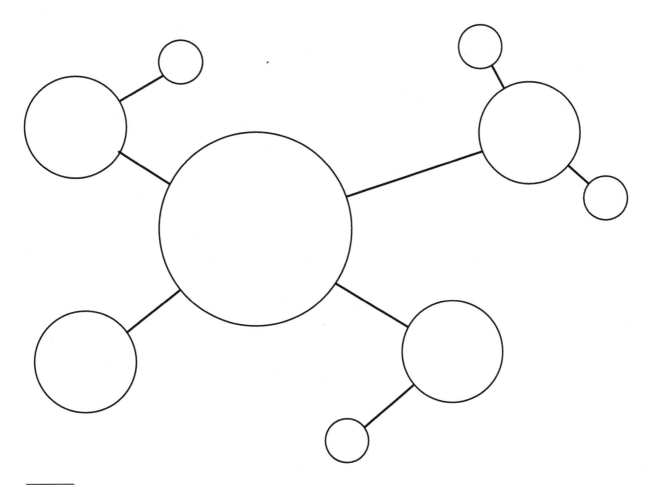

Practice and Reinforcement Activities

1. Students should be encouraged to develop a keen interest in words and the meanings of words. Through independent word study, students can enlarge their vocabularies. One way for students to develop their word awareness is by keeping a list of words in a journal. They may want to write down where they found the word, how the word was used, and an explanation of the word's definition.

2. After students have read a story in class, ask them to discuss what words they thought were interesting and what they think the words mean. They may want to look up the definitions in a dictionary to confirm their predictions.

3. Students should try to use new vocabulary words in their personal writing. Even though they may use a word incorrectly, they should continue to experiment with language by using words they have learned.

4. Provide several common words and have students try to use each word in a few sentences where it has a different meaning each time. Have students share their sentences and discuss the various meanings of the words. Possible words for such exercises include:

tip	part
run	cast
center	dress
circle	fly
slip	

5. Select a group of words from a content area. Divide the students into groups and ask them to find pictures of the words or objects that are associated with the words.

6. Help students learn words through their own reading by providing them with time to read. You might use one of the independent silent reading strategies found in Chapter 1. When you give students silent reading time, try to do some reading of your own. This might be a good time to catch up on reading professional journals or that mystery that you've been trying to finish. Your students will learn that you too like to read. That positive reading model will encourage them to read for pleasure themselves.

7. Develop a portion of your classroom library for books and games that use words in fun ways. Have a group of books that describe figures of speech and books that have riddles, jokes, and puns. These types of books show students that words can be fun. Some examples of books that you might consider follow:

   Clark, E.C. (1991). *I Never Saw a Purple Cow and Other Nonsense Rhymes*. Boston: Little, Brown.

   Cole, J. (1989). *Anna Banana: 101 Jump-Rope Rhymes*. New York: Morrow.

   Rosenbloom, J. (1988). *The World's Best Sports Riddles and Jokes*. New York: Sterling.

   Terban. M. (1989). *Superdupers: Really Funny Real Words*. New York: Clarion.

8. Ask students to keep and pencil and paper handy when they read. As they come to a word they don't know, ask them to write down the word to look up at a later date or ask someone for the word's meaning. Then they can add the word to a Word Wall or a bulletin board.

9. Read to your students, no matter what their age. Reading interesting novels, short stories, or poems helps students expand their listening vocabulary. As you read, ask students to write

on an index card any word that they hear that they do not know. After you have finished reading, collect the index cards. At a time convenient for you, look through the words and determine which ones you want to review with the class. The best time to review these new words is right after you have finished reading the selection. As you describe the meaning of the new word, find it in the context from which you read it. Explain the meaning of the word, read the word in its context, then explain the meaning of the word again. Finally, have students use the new word in another sentence. After you have provided the students with this range of meanings, ask them if they can share any other meanings for the word or sentences using the word. Then add the word to a compilation of new words in a class book.

10. Once a week, write a new word on the chalkboard. Without telling the students the meaning of the word, use the word in your discussions, in directions, in conversations, and in handouts. Use the word as often as possible. Ask students to try to guess the word's meaning by your use of the word. At the end of the day, ask students to write down what they think the new word means. You may decide to tell them the meaning of the word at this point, or you might decide to keep the students in suspense by waiting until the next day to tell them the word. After spending so much time on one word, however, make sure the students continue hearing and reading it. Place the word on the Word Wall and encourage students to use the word in their speaking and writing.

11. If one of the words that you want your students to learn can be dramatized, ask students to create brief scenes that use the word either in conversation or in action. For example, when asked to dramatize the word *amiable*, some sixth-grade students developed this scenario:

> Diana: Jean, I would like you to meet my good friend, Carmel. Carmel is one of the most good-natured, kindest girls I know.
>
> Jean: It's good to meet you, Carmel.
>
> Carmel: Thank you, Diana, for describing me as *amiable*. That's one of the nicest compliments I've ever received.

Games

Tom Swifties. Older elementary students love writing Tom Swifties. Tom Swift was a character in a series of books written in the 1930s. With every utterance, Tom seemed to express himself in an unusual way. From the character came the game, Tom Swifties. To play, ask students to write a sentence that has a quotation and a pun that matches what Tom says. The following are examples of Tom Swifties.

> "I'm from Texas," Tom *stated*.
>
> "I'll never pet that lion again," Tom said *offhandedly*.
>
> "I'm sick of stamping on these grapes," Tom *whined*.
>
> "I didn't know we derailed," Tom said *distractedly*.

You might need to begin by explaining that a pun is a word that can mean more than one thing. After students understand the meaning of a pun, try to create a list of words that could be used instead of the word *said*. Then develop a pun for each word. Some examples of words that could work as Tom Swifties follow. You can finish the sentences.

Tom snarled.

Tom moaned.

Tom sputtered.

Tom blubbered.

Palindromes. Students are fascinated with palindromes—words that can be read forwards and backwards. Words such as *mom, dad, mum,* and *did* are all palindromes. Ask students to think of as many words as they can that can be read forwards and backwards. If they are unable to think of many, ask them to use the dictionary for ideas. After they understand what a palindrome is, have students to work in groups to create phrases or sentences that are palindromes. Phrases and sentences are more difficult to create since they are not made of word palindromes but groups of words that can be read forwards and backwards, disregarding spaces. The following are examples of palindrome phrases and sentences.

Madam, I'm Adam.

A Toyota

Was it a car or a cat I saw?

Step on no pets.

Able was I ere I saw Elba.

Clues and Questions. This strategy helps students practice words that they have learned in class. Write the vocabulary word on a file card. Ask students to select several of the cards and write questions for the words. Then place the cards back in the file and divide the class into teams. One team chooses a card and asks the questions or gives clues. The opposing team tries to guess the vocabulary word.

Four Square. Students can learn the meanings of words from this strategy. Draw a square with four quadrants. In the top left quadrant, write the vocabulary word. On its right, write a personal association with the word. In the bottom left-hand square, write the word's meaning. In the bottom right, write what the word does not mean. An example follows:

Triathlete	Ironman
3 sport event	couch potato

Resources for Chapter 4

➤ Words for Use in Teaching Vowels Sounds

➤ Rank Order of the 300 Most Common Words

➤ Revised Dolch List

➤ Revised Dolch List (Organized by Reader Level)

➤ High-Frequency Nouns

➤ Word Patterns

➤ Commonly Occurring Contractions

➤ A List of Compound Words

➤ Fifteen Frequently Occurring Prefixes

➤ Affixes with Invariant Meanings

➤ Twenty-Four Useful Suffixes

Words for Use in Teaching Vowel Sounds

Short Sounds

a		e		i		o		u	
and	fat	bell	beg	is	it	sock	clock	rug	us
can	apple	red	slept	twin	dig	frog	stop	run	up
add	last	rest	sled	slid	hip	hog	pop	dug	dust
at	mad	pet	met	hill	tin	odd	hot	rut	rub
cat	fast	bed	help	brick	hit	mop	log	must	but
hand	glad	step	sell	his	big	hop	cot	sun	bus
dad	am	men	hen	did	will	pond	not	fun	bum
flag	bad	send	wet	milk	in	fog	dot	drum	duck
bag	had	pen	egg	rib	trip	pot	doll	tug	bug
fact	tan	bet	chest	drill	ill	lot	ox	struck	mud

Long Sounds

a		e		i		o		u	
fade	may	Pete	east	Mike	like	hose	note	use	flute
say	bake	three	see	hide	time	hope	poke	music	plume
tape	pay	eat	eve	bike	ripe	rose	open	cue	cute
same	rain	peep	free	pike	pile	note	over	mule	rule
pain	Jane	feed	jeep	dime	mice	boat	slope	tube	blue
take	tame	be	team	die	fine	robe	rode	fuel	rude
way	save	mean	beet	dine	light	home	row	clue	unit
wave	age	green	bean	five	ride	joke	nose	fuse	cube
ate	day	weed	she	side	pine	bone	rope	suit	brute
take	make	keep	seat	nice	pie	cone	stove	dual	tune

198

Rank Order of the 300 Most Common Words

the	up	make	right	food	body	money
of	said	now	should	under	end	become
and	out	way	small	always	hand	group
to	if	each	old	however	head	government
a	some	called	think	man	read	later
in	would	did	take	air	others	living
is	so	just	still	asked	year	change
that	people	after	place	both	since	days
it	them	water	find	being	against	animals
was	other	through	off	does	young	word
for	more	get	different	going	give	let
you	will	because	part	big	set	wanted
he	into	back	found	without	kind	across
on	your	where	us	looked	room	American
as	which	know	world	say	eyes	early
are	do	little	away	left	number	though
they	then	such	life	began	far	four
with	many	even	three	mother	person	face
be	these	much	went	during	city	best
his	no	our	those	tell	better	became
at	time	must	own	land	white	seen
or	been	before	help	next	side	himself
from	who	good	every	once	family	sure
had	like	too	here	need	night	energy
I	could	long	house	high	didn't	sun
not	has	me	might	last	country	second
have	him	years	between	until	name	feet
this	how	day	never	children	it's	really
but	than	used	home	along	ever	certain
by	two	work	thought	took	form	turned
were	may	any	put	together	usually	toward
one	only	go	again	sometimes	hard	parts
all	most	use	important	saw	knew	black
she	its	things	while	enough	today	ways
when	made	well	something	light	times	show
an	over	look	states	got	soon	means
their	see	another	don't	example	told	door
there	first	around	why	words	several	special
her	new	man	large	united	system	course
can	very	great	want	almost	state	known
we	my	same	few	father	upon	move
what	also	came	school	live	thing	yet
about	down	come	often	keep	earth	

Revised Dolch List

a	could	he	might	same	told
about	cut	heard	more	saw	too
across	did	help	most	say	took
after	didn't	her	much	see	toward
again	do	here	must	she	try
all	does	high	my	short	turn
always	done	him	near	should	two
am	don't	his	need	show	under
an	down	hold	never	six	up
and	draw	hot	next	small	upon
another	eat	how	new	so	us
any	enough	I	no	some	use
are	even	I'm	not	soon	very
around	every	if	now	start	walk
as	far	in	of	still	want
ask	fast	into	off	stop	warm
at	find	is	oh	take	was
away	first	it	old	tell	we
be	five	its	on	ten	well
because	for	just	once	than	went
been	found	keep	one	that	were
before	four	kind	only	the	what
began	from	know	open	their	when
best	full	last	or	them	where
better	gave	leave	other	then	which
big	get	left	our	there	while
black	give	let	out	these	white
blue	go	light	over	they	who
both	going	like	own	think	why
bring	gone	little	play	this	will
but	good	long	put	those	with
by	got	look	ran	thought	work
call	green	made	read	three	would
came	grow	make	red	through	yes
can	had	many	right	to	yet
close	hard	may	round	today	you
cold	has	me	run	together	your
come	have	mean	said		

The rationale and research for this list is described in Johns, J.L. (1981). The development of the revised Dolch list. *Illinois School Research and Development, 17(3),* 15–24.

Revised Dolch List
(Organized by Reader Level)

Jerry L. Johns

Preprimer		Primer		Grade 1		Grade 2	
a	look	about	on	after	long	across	near
and	make	all	one	again	made	always	need
are	me	around	out	am	many	because	once
at	my	ask	put	an	more	been	only
big	no	away	run	another	much	best	open
blue	not	but	saw	any	must	both	round
call	play	eat	say	as	never	close	same
can	ran	fast	she	be	next	done	short
come	red	from	show	before	off	draw	six
did	said	good	so	began	oh	enough	small
do	see	has	some	better	old	even	start
down	stop	him	soon	black	or	every	ten
for	that	his	take	bring	other	full	thought
get	the	into	then	by	our	grow	through
go	this	know	they	came	over	heard	today
green	to	let	too	cold	own	high	together
have	up	like	two	could	read	hot	toward
he	want	may	us	cut	right	I'm	turn
help	we	new	went	didn't	should	keep	upon
here	what	now	yes	does	still	leave	use
I	who	of	your	don't	tell	left	warm
in	will			far	than	mean	well
is	with			find	their	might	while
it	work			first	them	most	yet
little	you			five	there		
				found	these		
				four	think		
				gave	those		
				give	three		
				going	told		
				gone	took		
				got	try		
				had	under		
				hard	very		
				her	walk		
				hold	was		
				how	were		
				if	when		
				its	where		
				just	which		
				kind	white		
				last	why		
				light	would		

From Jerry L. Johns and Susan Davis Lenski, *Improving Reading: A Handbook of Strategies* (2nd ed.). Copyright © 1997 Kendall/Hunt Publishing Company (1-800-228-0810). May be reproduced for noncommercial educational purposes.

High-Frequency Nouns

Jerry L. Johns

air	girl	nothing
back	group	people
book	hand	place
boy	head	road
car	home	room
children	house	school
city	man	side
day	men	table
dog	money	thing
door	morning	time
eye	mother	top
face	Mr.	town
father	Mrs.	tree
feet	name	water
friend	night	way
		year

The development of this list is described in Johns, J.L. (1975). Dolch list of common nouns—A comparison. *The Reading Teacher, 28*(7), 338–340.

Word Patterns

Short *a* Sounds

-ab	-ack	-ad	-ag	-am	-amp	-an
cab	back	ad	bag	am	camp	an
dab	hack	bad	gag	dam	damp	ban
gab	jack	cad	hag	ham	lamp	can
jab	pack	dad	tag	jam	champ	fan
lab	rack	fad	nag	lamb	clamp	man
nab	sack	had	rag	clam	cramp	pan
tab	tack	lad	sag	cram	stamp	ran
blab	black	mad	tag	slam	tramp	tan
tab	slack	pad	wag	swam		van
slab	crack	sad	brag			clan
crab	track	clad	drag			plan
drab	shack	glad	flag			scan
grab	whack	shad	shag			span
scab	smack		snag			than
stab	snack		stag			
	stack					

-and	-ang	-ank	-ap	-ash	-ast	-at
and	bang	bank	cap	ash	cast	at
band	fang	rank	gap	bash	fast	bat
hand	gang	sank	lap	cash	last	cat
land	hang	tank	map	dash	mast	fat
sand	rang	yank	nap	gash	past	hat
gland	sang	blank	rap	hash	vast	mat
grand	tang	clank	sap	lash	blast	pat
stand	clang	plank	tap	mash		sat
	slang	crank	chap	rash		vat
		drank	clap	sash		brat
		frank	flap	clash		chat
		spank	slap	crash		flat
		thank	snap	smash		slat
			trap	stash		scat
				trash		that

-atch

catch
hatch
latch
match
patch
thatch

Short *e* Sounds

-eck	-ed	-eg	-ell	-en	-end	-ent
deck	bed	beg	bell	den	end	bent
heck	fed	egg	dell	hen	bend	dent
neck	led	keg	fell	men	lend	lent
peck	red	leg	sell	pen	mend	rent
check	wed	peg	tell	ten	send	sent
speck	bled		well	glen	blend	tent
	fled		yell	then	spend	went
	sled		quell	when	trend	spent
	shed		shell			
	sped		smell			
			spell			
			swell			

-ess	-est	-et
less	best	bet
mess	nest	get
bless	pest	jet
chess	rest	let
dress	test	met
	vest	net
	west	pet
	chest	set
	crest	wet
	quest	vet
		fret

Short *i* Sounds

-ib	-ick	-id	-ift	-ig	-ill	-im
bib	kick	bid	gift	big	bill	dim
fib	lick	did	lift	dig	fill	him
rib	nick	hid	rift	fig	gill	rim
crib	pick	kid	sift	jig	hill	skim
	sick	lid	drift	pig	kill	slim
	tick	rid	shift	rig	mill	swim
	wick	grid	swift	wig	pill	trim
	brick	skid		brig	rill	whim
	trick	slid		swig	sill	
	chick				till	
	thick				will	
	click				chill	
	flick				drill	
	slick				grill	
	quick				quill	
	stick				spill	

From Jerry L. Johns and Susan Davis Lenski, *Improving Reading: A Handbook of Strategies* (2nd ed.). Copyright © 1997 Kendall/Hunt Publishing Company (1-800-228-0810). May be reproduced for noncommercial educational purposes.

-in	-ing	-ink	-ip	-ish	-it	-itch
in	bing	ink	dip	dish	it	itch
bin	ring	pink	hip	fish	bit	ditch
din	sing	sink	lip	wish	fit	pitch
fin	wing	wink	nip	swish	hit	witch
kin	bring	blink	rip		kit	stitch
pin	fling	slink	sip		lit	switch
sin	sting	stink	tip		pit	
tin	sting	think	zip		sit	
win	swing		yip		wit	
chin	thing		chip		grit	
shin			ship		mitt	
thin			whip		quit	
grin			flip		slit	
skin			slip		skit	
spin			grip		spit	
twin			trip		twit	
			quip			
			skip			
			snip			

Short *o* Sounds

-ob	-ock	-od	-og	-ong	-ot
cob	cock	cod	bog	bong	cot
fob	dock	hod	cog	gong	dot
gob	hock	nod	dog	long	got
job	lock	pod	fog	song	hot
rob	mock	rod	hog	tong	not
mob	pock	sod	jog	wrong	pot
sob	rock	clod	log	strong	rot
blob	sock	plod	clog		blot
slob	tock	shod	frog		clot
snob	clock		smog		plot
	flock				slot
	crock				shot
	frock				spot
	shock				trot
	smock				
	stock				

Short *u* Sounds

-ub	-uck	-ud	-uff	-ug	-ull	-um
cub	buck	bud	buff	bug	cull	bum
dub	duck	cud	cuff	dug	dull	gum
hub	luck	mud	huff	hug	gull	hum
nub	muck	stud	muff	jug	hull	mum
pub	puck	thud	puff	lug	lull	rum
rub	suck		bluff	mug	mull	sum
sub	tuck		gruff	pug	null	glum
tub	chuck		stuff	rug	skull	slum
club	shuck			tug		drum
grub	cluck			chug		scum
stub	pluck			thug		chum
	stuck			plug		
				slug		
				smug		

-ump	-un	-unch	-ung	-unk	-up	-ush
bump	bun	bunch	dung	bunk	up	gush
dump	fun	lunch	hung	dunk	cup	hush
hump	gun	punch	lung	hunk	pup	lush
jump	nun	brunch	rung	junk	sup	mush
lump	pun	crunch	sung	sunk		rush
pump	run		clung	chunk		blush
clump	sun		flung	drunk		flush
plump	shun		stung	flunk		plush
slump	spun		swung	skunk		slush
stump	stun					brush
thump						crush
						shush

-ust	-ut
bust	but
dust	cut
just	gut
lust	hut
must	jut
rust	nut
crust	rut
	shut

Long *a* Sounds

-ace	-ade	-age	-aid	-ail	-ain	-ale
ace	fade	age	aid	ail	gain	ale
face	jade	cage	laid	bail	main	dale
lace	lade	page	maid	fail	pain	hale
mace	made	rage	paid	hail	rain	hale
pace	wade	sage	raid	jail	vain	kale
race	blade	wage	braid	mail	brain	male
brace	glade	stage		nail	drain	pale
place	grade			pail	grain	sale
space	trade			rail	train	tale
	shade			sail	chain	vale
	spade			tail	plain	scale
				vail	slain	shale
				wail	stain	stale
				frail		whale
				quail		
				snail		
				trail		

-ame	-ane	-ape	-aste	-ate	-ave	-ay
came	cane	ape	baste	ate	cave	bay
dame	lane	cape	haste	date	gave	day
fame	mane	gape	paste	fate	nave	gay
game	pane	nape	taste	gate	pave	hay
lame	sane	rape	chaste	hate	rave	jay
name	vane	tape		late	save	lay
same	wane	drape		rate	brave	nay
tame	crane	grape		sate	crave	pay
blame		shape		crate	grave	ray
flame				grate	shave	say
frame				plate	slave	way
shame				skate		clay
				slate		play
				state		fray
						tray
						stay
						sway

-aze

daze
gaze
haze
maze
blaze
glaze
graze

Long *e* Sounds

-e	-ea	-each	-ead	-eak	-eal	-eam
be	pea	each	bead	beak	deal	beam
he	sea	beach	lead	leak	heal	ream
me	tea	peach	read	peak	meal	seam
we	flea	reach	plead	weak	peal	team
she	plea	teach		bleak	real	cream
		bleach		freak	seal	dream
				speak	veal	gleam
					zeal	
					steal	

-ean	-eat	-ee	-eed	-eek	-eel	-een
bean	eat	bee	deed	leek	eel	keen
dean	beat	fee	feed	meek	feel	seen
lean	feat	see	heed	peek	heel	teen
mean	heat	tee	need	reek	keel	green
wean	meat	wee	seed	seek	peel	queen
clean	neat	free	weed	week	reel	sheen
glean	peat	tree	bleed	cheek		
	seat	glee	breed	creek		
	cheat	thee	creed	sleek		
	cleat	three	freed			
	pleat		greed			
	treat		speed			
	wheat		steed			
			tweed			

-eep	-eet
beep	beet
deep	feet
jeep	meet
keep	fleet
peep	greet
seep	sheet
weep	sleet
creep	sweet
sheep	tweet
steep	
sweep	

Long *o* Sounds

-o	-oad	-oam	-oan	-oast	-oat	-obe
go	goad	foam	loan	boast	oat	lobe
no	load	loam	moan	coast	boat	robe
so	road	roam	roan	roast	coat	globe
	toad		groan	toast	goat	
					moat	
					bloat	
					float	
					gloat	

-ode	-oe	-oke	-old	-ole	-olt	-ome
ode	doe	coke	old	dole	bolt	dome
bode	foe	joke	bold	hole	colt	home
code	hoe	poke	cold	mole	dolt	Nome
mode	toe	woke	gold	pole	jolt	
rode	woe	yoke	hold	role	volt	
		bloke	mold	stole		
		choke	sold			
		smoke	told			
		spoke				

-one	-ope	-ose	-ost	-ote	-ow
bone	cope	hose	ghost	note	bow
cone	dope	nose	host	rote	low
lone	hope	pose	most	tote	mow
pone	mope	rose	post	vote	row
tone	rope	chose		quote	sow
zone	scope	those			tow
shone	slope	close			blow
stone					flow
					glow
					slow
					crow
					grow
					show
					snow

Long *u* Sounds

-use	-ute
use	cute
fuse	mute
muse	flute

Long *i* Sounds

-ice	-ide	-ie	-ife	-igh	-ight	-ike
lice	bide	die	knife	high	bright	bike
mice	hide	lie	life	nigh	fight	dike
nice	ride	pie	rife	sigh	flight	hike
rice	side	tie	wife	thigh	fright	like
vice	tide	vie			light	mike
slice	wide				might	pike
spice	bride				night	spike
twice	glide				plight	
	slide				right	
					sight	
					slight	
					tight	

-ild	-ile	-ime	-ind	-ine	-ipe	-ire
mild	file	dime	bind	dine	pipe	ire
wild	mile	lime	find	fine	ripe	dire
child	pile	time	hind	line	wipe	fire
	rile	chime	kind	mine	gripe	hire
	tile	crime	mind	nine	swipe	mire
	vile	grime	rind	pine		sire
	smile	slime	wind	tine		tire
	while		blind	vine		wire
			grind	shine		
				spine		
				swine		
				thine		
				twine		
				whine		

-ite	-ive
bite	dive
kite	five
mite	hive
site	live
quite	chive
spite	drive
white	

Commonly Occurring Contractions

1. let's	17. aren't	33. she'd
2. didn't	18. I'm	34. weren't
3. it's	19. he's	35. I'd
4. won't	20. we're	36. you've
5. that's	21. you're	37. you'd
6. can't	22. what's	38. we'd
7. wasn't	23. there's	39. anybody'd
8. isn't	24. she's	40. they'll
9. hadn't	25. wouldn't	41. we've
10. don't	26. she'll	42. who'll
11. I'll	27. here's	43. he'd
12. we'll	28. ain't	44. who'd
13. I've	29. couldn't	45. doesn't
14. he'll	30. they're	46. where's
15. hasn't	31. they'd	47. they've
16. haven't	32. you'll	

A List of Compound Words

afternoon	everyone	peanut
airplane	everything	pinball
anyone	eyebrows	playground
backbone	farmland	playhouse
barefoot	firecracker	quarterback
barnyard	firefly	quicksand
baseball	firehouse	railroad
basketball	fireplace	rainbow
bathtub	fishhook	raincoat
bedroom	flashlight	rowboat
beehive	football	sailboat
billboard	fullback	sandpaper
birthplace	goldfish	skyscraper
bookcase	hallway	snowball
bookmark	headlight	snowflake
campfire	highchair	sometimes
chalkboard	highway	sunrise
checkerboard	homesick	sunset
classroom	horseshoe	sunshine
cookbook	jellybean	teenager
copyright	mailbox	thunderstorm
cowboy	mailman	toothbrush
cupcake	maybe	underline
daydream	motorcycle	uphill
deadline	necktie	volleyball
doghouse	neighborhood	waterfall
downhill	newspaper	watermelon
downtown	notebook	whirlpool
downstairs	oatmeal	wildlife
dragonfly	outlaw	without
driveway	outside	wristwatch
drugstore	overboard	
earthquake	pancake	

Fifteen Frequently Occurring Prefixes

Prefix	Meaning(s)
ab-	away, from, off
ad-	at, to, toward
be-	make, against, to a great degree
com-	with, together, in association
de-	separation, away, opposite of, reduce, from
dis-	opposite of, apart, away, not
en-	cause to be, put in or on
ex-	from, out of, former, apart, away
in-	into, in, within
in-	not
pre-	before in place, time, rank, order
pro-	before, forward, for, in favor of
re-	again, back
sub	under, beneath, subordinate
in-	not, the opposite of, reversal

These fifteen prefixes accounted for 82 percent of the 61 basic forms of prefixes as reported in Stauffer, R.G. (1969b). *Teaching reading as a thinking process.* New York: Harper & Row.

Affixes with Invariant Meanings

Combining Forms	Prefixes	Noun Suffixes	
anthropo-	apo-	-acity	-ism
auto-	circum-	-ana	-ist
biblio-	equi-	-ance	-itis
bio-	extra-	-archy	-kin
centro- (centri-)	intra-	-ard (-art)	-latry
cosmo-	intro-	-aster	-let
heter- (hetero-)	mal-	-ation (-tion, -ion)	-ment
homo-	mis-	-bility	-meter
hydro-	non-	-chrome	-metry
iso-	syn-	-cide	-mony
lith-	**Adjective Endings**	-cle	-ness
micro-	-able (-ible, -ble)	-cule	-ock
mono-	-acious	-dom	-ology
neuro-	-est	-ee	-phobia
omni-	-ferous	-eer	-phore
pan-	-fic	-ence	-ric
penta-	-fold	-ery	-scope
phil- (philo-)	-form	-ess	-scopy
phono-	-ful	-far	-ship
photo-	-genous	-fication	-ster
pneumo-	-less	-gram	-stress
poly-	-like	-graph	-trix
proto-	-most	-grapher	-tude
pseudo-	-ous	-graphy	-ty
tele	-ose	-hood	-ule
uni-	-scopic	-ics	
	-wards	-ier	
	-wise		

From Deighton, L.C. (1959). *Vocabulary development in the classroom.* New York: Teachers College.

Twenty-Four Useful Suffixes

Suffix	Meaning(s)	Example
-able	capable of being	allowable
-age	act of	marriage
-al	have the nature of	causal
-an (-n, -ian)	one/who, relating to	librarian
-ance	state of being	brilliance
-ant	person or thing that acts	claimant
-ary	of or pertaining to	alimentary
-ate	cause to be	activate
-ence	state or quality of being	congruence
-ent	one who	recipient
-er	relating to	beater
-ful	having much, tending to	colorful
-ic (-etic)	pertaining to, resembling	heroic
-ical	of, like, pertaining to	monarchical
-ion (-tion, -ation)	act of, state, or condition	affirmation
-ish	having the nature of	dragonish
-ity (-ty)	quality, state, or condition of being	adaptability
-ive	tending or disposed to	meditative
-less	without, having no	aimless
-ment	state of being, act of	admonishment
-ness	quality, state, or condition of being	fairness
-or	person or thing that does	conqueror
-ous	having, abounding in	delirious
-y	pertaining to, causing	loamy

These suffixes occur with sufficient frequency and in enough words to be considered useful knowledge for high school students. From Thorndike, E.L. (1941). *The teaching of English suffixes.* New York: Teachers College.

CHAPTER 5

Promoting Comprehension

Overview

Reading is the process of making sense from print, and comprehension is the goal of all reading. Comprehension, or an understanding of the text, varies with every reader. Just think how different each of your students is. Each one has a unique set of life experiences, different experiences with print, and different abilities to process text. Since all of your students are different from each other, and they are all different from you, each one of you will understand a piece of text in a slightly different way.

Comprehension of text, or what a reader understands, is constructed by the individual reader. No two readers will produce the exact same meaning from a text, and no reader's understanding of a text will exactly match what the author had in mind while writing (Goodman, 1996). Your students, therefore, will construct different meanings from the text, some with a rich understanding of what the text could mean and some with a more superficial understanding of the text. How readers apply various strategies as they process text, however, will influence the depth of their understanding.

Readers who achieve a deep comprehension of text apply a variety of strategies as they construct meaning. First, active readers use their prior knowledge as they read. Using prior knowledge allows readers to seek and select relevant ideas from the text and make predictions about the text's meaning (Vacca & Vacca, 1996). Second, active readers also use text structures to construct meaning. Students can use narrative text structures, such as the events in a plot, to help them understand a passage. They can use the organization of expository text, such as the structure of a comparison-contrast passage, to understand how ideas relate to one another. Knowing how a text is organized can enhance comprehension. Third, active readers monitor their comprehension while they read. As students read, they must consciously think about whether or not they are making sense of the text. Finally, active readers process text after reading (Brozo & Simpson, 1995). In order to have a deep understanding of text, readers must think about the text in a variety of ways so that their understanding increases after they have finished reading.

Students who use few comprehension strategies while reading need instruction on how to comprehend text. For example, students may not be using their prior knowledge as they read, or they may have difficulty discerning the main idea of a passage. As teachers, we want our students to be able to use a variety of strategies as they read so they can construct meaning beyond the literal level. We can help them construct meaning by teaching them comprehension strategies to use during the entire reading process.

Behavior Observed	The student has difficulty identifying or stating the main idea of a reading selection.
Anticipated Outcome	The student will identify or state the main idea of a reading selection.

Background

The identification of the main idea or central thought in what is read usually involves several processes. Students must distinguish between essential elements, make inferences, and make judgments—all higher-level thinking skills. Although the main idea may be stated somewhere in a passage (text explicit), it is also likely that the main idea may not be explicitly expressed, and students will need to infer it (text implicit).

Years ago, the identification of main ideas was "taught" with workbooks and skill sheets. Educators know now that there are limitations with these materials. Workbook exercises rarely teach main ideas or transfer to other reading materials. Such exercises may only provide practice in the task of identifying main ideas. In order for students to learn how to select or infer the main idea, the teacher should use the following teaching ideas.

Teaching Strategy 1 (*For Younger Students*)

1. Tell students that this lesson will help them learn how to figure out the main idea of a passage. Begin by presenting lists of words (without headings) on the chalkboard. Ask students to think of a word or phrase that could be used to describe what the words are mostly about. Several lists are shown here. Be sure to select words that are appropriate for your students.

Animals	Clothes	Cars	Places to Stay
dog	shirt	Firebird	house
cat	pants	Mustang	apartment
hamster	dress	Corvette	duplex
guinea pig	shoes	RX7	trailer
horse	jeans	Ferrari	hotel

2. Discuss the words or phrases offered by the students. Stress that the words or phrases describe the topic; they tell what the words are mostly about. Relate the discussion to reading. Ask students to think of favorite books or stories and tell what the topics are. Indicate that the main idea is the most important idea given about a topic. Other pieces of information that support the main idea are called details.

3. Draw a wheel with spokes on the chalkboard and tell students that the center of the wheel represents the main idea and the spokes represent the supporting details.

219

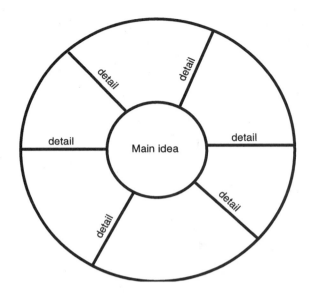

Then present a short passage and help students model how to go about finding the main idea, for example:

> Did you know it takes the planet Pluto over 200 years to go around the sun? Our planet, Earth, takes 365 days. Mercury, the smallest planet, only takes 88 days to go around the sun. All of the nine planets in our solar system take a different number of days or years to go around the sun.

After reading the paragraph aloud with students, think aloud to determine the main idea. "At first I thought the paragraph was going to be about Pluto, but then other planets were mentioned. In fact, one sentence says something about all nine planets … so, I think the paragraph is about planets, but what about planets? Each sentence gives some information about how long it takes planets to go around the sun … so I'm sure the paragraph is mostly about how long it takes planets to go around the sun."

4. Then use another passage. Think aloud and explain why certain details are eliminated as the main idea. Encourage students to share their thoughts and also to think aloud as they process information in making their decision to find the main idea. Choose a sample passage like the following one for this activity. Guide students as needed.

> Owls are one of the only kinds of birds that you can see at night. That's because owls are nocturnal. They hunt at night, usually looking for small animals to eat. Owls can hunt at night because they have large eyes that can see in the dark. Their eyes are 50 times more powerful than are the eyes of humans. Owls also have extremely sensitive hearing and can hear the rustling of a mouse from high in a tree.

5. Make the point that in some passages the main idea is directly stated. In others, it is not. Also, some paragraphs may not contain a main idea, because they may be transitional paragraphs.

6. Use additional paragraphs or passages to help students learn how to figure out the main idea. Perhaps you could develop a wall chart that contains the following reminders:

1. What is the paragraph mostly about?

2. What is the most important idea given about the topic?

3. Look for details that tell about the main idea. If you can't locate any details, you probably don't have the main idea.

4. Remember that the main idea is sometimes right in the passage. Other times you have to use the details to figure out the main idea.

Teaching Strategy 2 *(For Older Students)*

1. Look for the topic.

   ■ Read the passage.

   ■ Ask yourself: What is this entire paragraph, or passage about, or to what does most of this paragraph, or passage seem to refer? The answer to these questions will give you the topic.

2. Next, find the main idea or central theme.

   ■ Ask yourself: What is the most general statement made about the topic?

   ■ Go back and examine each sentence.

   ■ What seems to be repeated, hinted at, or emphasized in most sentences?

   ■ Is there one general idea in the passage which is repeated, hinted at, or emphasized in each sentence?

   ■ If so, that is probably the main idea.

   ■ If not, then you have to infer what the main idea is, because it is not stated.

3. If the strategies in step 2 didn't work, try these:

   ■ Think of each sentence in the passage as a factor in an addition problem in math. For example, try to figure out what each of the specific statements made in the passage add up to, or where they lead: (A specific statement) + (A specific statement) + (A specific statement) = Total: The main idea (A general statement).

   ■ All of the sentences in a passage might not add up to the main idea. Only add up those that are connected by the same idea.

   ■ Ask yourself: In what direction does each of these specific points seem to lead? The answer gives you the main idea.

   ■ Ask yourself: Is there a general statement that applies to most of these ideas? The answer gives you the main idea.

4. If the material is really difficult and the strategies in steps 2 and 3 did not work, try these:

   Draw a large letter T (see illustration).

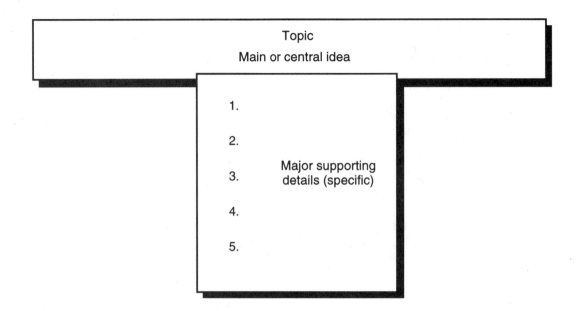

- Divide the top part in half horizontally.

- Ask yourself: What is most of this passage about?

- The answer will be the topic of the passage.

- Fill in the top part of the *T* with the topic.

- Get your answers to that question by writing, in the stem of the *T*, the sentences that seem to be connected by the same idea and seem to be specific.

- Then ask yourself: What general idea do these sentences seem to support or to what general idea do these ideas seem to point?

- The answer will be the main idea.

Practice and Reinforcement Activities

1. Pictures may be used to help students develop the notion of topic and to answer the question: What is this picture mostly about? Discussions can be used to develop an understanding of main idea and important supporting details.

2. Have students read a short passage and select the best title from several given. Students could also create their own title or write a phrase or sentence that best describes the main idea of the passage.

3. Provide several passages, each followed by four sentences. One sentence states the main idea of the passage, another is too broad, one is too detailed, and the last contains information not stated in the paragraph. After students have selected their main idea for each passage, discuss their choices as well as why other statements were not appropriate for the main idea. Guided discussion is particularly important, because it will help students clarify their thinking.

4. Read a short passage to students and have them relate, in one sentence, the main idea. Write some of their sentences on the board as a basis for discussion.

5. Cut out passages from old books or articles that are at a variety of reading levels. Fasten the passages to five-by-eight note cards. On the back of each card write several possible phrases or sentences that describe the main idea. Students read the passage, write their answers on a separate sheet of paper, and then compare them with the answers on the back of the cards.

6. Use newspaper articles and have students underline the main idea if stated, or write it if an inference is necessary. In a different colored pencil, marker, or pen, the student can underline the supporting details.

7. To help develop the inclusive nature of a main idea, provide lists where students can practice understanding the difference between general and specific ideas. Be sure to relate the lists to the study of main ideas and discuss reasons for the best answer. Several exercises are shown here:

Pennies, nickels, and dimes are all _____.

Robins, sparrows, and hawks are all _____.

Circle the word that includes the others:

snow	stamps	Earth	games
rain	coins	Saturn	bingo
weather	stickers	planets	checkers
fog	collections	Jupiter	Hopscotch

8. Use students' knowledge of familiar stories (such as *The Three Little Pigs*, *Hansel and Gretel*, and *The Gingerbread Boy*) and have them discuss their perceptions of the major thought in the stories.

9. Have students look through various types of reading materials to find examples of the main idea or topic sentence. Typical examples include:

main idea

details

details

main idea

Students can also write their own paragraphs using these two different types of paragraph structures.

10. Have students read a selection and draw the outline of their hand on a sheet of paper. The main idea can be written on the hand and the supporting details on the fingers.

11. List and number a series of statements on cards. Have students read the sentences and select the one that best describes the main idea. Place the number and the main idea on the back of the card so the activity is self-correcting.

FRONT OF CARD   BACK OF CARD

1. Bats can fly.	
2. Bats are found in caves.	
3. Bats are unusual animals.	The main idea is 3:
4. Bats are clumsy on the ground.	Bats are unusual animals.
5. Bats can scare people.	

12. Use illustrations from a story or have students draw pictures to help them understand main ideas. Begin with familiar stories. Discuss the illustrations or pictures.

13. Practice naming lists of things that are arranged in categories. Students or the teacher lists four or five items, such as paper, pencils, notebooks, pens, journal. Then invite a student to offer the title of the category—how these things fit together. Give several students a chance to offer the category title. Sometimes more than one answer is acceptable.

Games

Match. Provide students with sets of six pictures and a title for them on individual strips of tagboard. Include a few additional titles that do not match the picture with the appropriate title. By writing the same number on the back of the title strip and picture, students can check their work.

Where? On five-by-eight note cards, provide reading passages in which the main idea or topic sentence is found at the beginning or the end. Also, have passages where the main idea or topic sentence is not included. Provide cards to match the passages like the following.

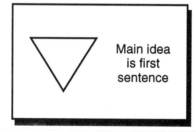 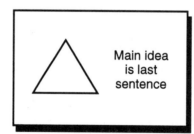 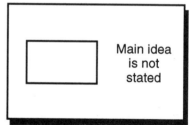

Have students match the appropriate cards with the passages. Place the appropriate geometric shape on the back of each passage to provide a means of self-checking.

Categories. Use pictures or objects from five categories (such as farm, jobs, food, colors, outdoors). Mix up the pictures or objects from the categories and have students sort them according to a logical scheme or attribute. Discuss the resulting categories and have students provide reasons for each category. Possible categories may include:

animals	clothing	energy
foods	energy	musical instruments
flowers	fruits	tools
school supplies	shapes	vehicles
games	drinks	books

5.2 Facts or Details

Behavior Observed	The student has difficulty recalling important facts or details in a passage.
Anticipated Outcome	The student will recall important facts or details from a passage.

Background

Important facts or details can often be taught along with main ideas. Facts and details are frequently at the factual level of comprehension (text explicit) but can also be interpretive or applicative (text implicit). For example, consider the following passage and question:

Jerry saw Beth. She was wearing a red dress.

What color was her dress?

Most teachers would consider the question to be at the factual or literal level. The correct answer (red) is certainly explicitly contained in the passage. However, to get the answer, the student has to do a bit of inferencing and infer that the word *her* in the question refers to Beth. Although such an inference might be considered to be lower level, it is, nevertheless, an inference that is text implicit. When teachers work with facts and details, they should be alert for the higher-level comprehension thinking strategies (interpretive and applicative) that are sometimes demanded of the student.

Teaching Strategy 1

1. List several different topics on the chalkboard (for example, birds, animals, airplanes, or colors). Select one that seems to be of interest to most students.

2. Write the topic on the chalkboard and have students share information they know about the topic. As students share, write sentences containing their thoughts. For example:

Airplanes

- Airplanes can fly.

- Pilots fly airplanes.

- There are many different kinds of airplanes.

- Airplanes can carry people.

3. Tell students that you will ask them questions that can be answered by understanding the sentences. For example, What can airplanes carry? As the questions are answered, have students indicate which sentence provided the answer to the question. If students give correct answers that are not contained in the sentences, acknowledge the response as correct. Then ask the student to try finding the answer that is given in a sentence that is written on the chalkboard. For example, if you ask, "What can airplanes carry?" and the student says,

"Cargo," indicate that the response is correct. Then ask whether the student can also provide an answer that is contained in one of the sentences written on the chalkboard.

4. After several similar exercises, tell students they are learning how to answer questions that ask them to locate facts and details.

5. Develop another topic with sentences and encourage students to ask questions that other students who read the sentences can answer. Discuss various answers as appropriate.

6. Indicate that such questions can also be asked about the information and ideas contained in their reading. On the chalkboard, write a brief passage from a literature selection or content textbook and ask factual questions. Use a procedure similar to the one already described. A sample passage follows:

> It was the sweetest, most mysterious place anyone could imagine. The high walls which shut it in were covered with the leafless stems of climbing roses which were so thick that they were matted together. Mary Lennox knew they were roses because she had seen a great many roses in India. All the ground was covered with grass of a wintry brown and out of it grew clumps of bushes which were surely roses if they were alive. There were numbers of standard roses which had so spread their branches that they were like little trees (Burnett, 1911/1990, p. 80).

Teaching Strategy 2

1. Write a sentence on the chalkboard. Have students read it silently and then have someone read it out loud. For example:

   Early that morning, Brittany packed her lunch in the kitchen.

2. Tell students to use the information in the sentence to answer the questions you ask. Ask several questions (who, what, when, where) and remind students to use the information in the sentence for their answers. Tell students that the questions are checking the students' ability to identify facts and details. Remind students to ask who, what, when, and where as they read.

3. Continue this procedure with another sentence and then move to several sentences and brief passages. Encourage discussion and think aloud as necessary.

4. Use concrete objects and have students demonstrate the meaning of a sentence. For example, use several plastic animals and a small box. Have students read a sentence and manipulate or arrange objects to answer the question. Sample questions may include:

Sentence: The cat and dog are near the box.

Question: Where are the cat and dog? (Show me.)

Sentence: The horse is near the box and the cat is in the box.

Question: Where are the cat and the horse? (Show me.)

Practice and Reinforcement Activities

1. During regular instructional periods ask students factual questions about the materials they are reading. Have students locate the sentence or phrase in the passage that supports their answer.

2. Take a brief passage at an appropriate instructional level for the students being taught and number each sentence. Write it on the chalkboard, use it on an overhead projector, or reproduce it so each student has a copy. Then have each student make individual response cards with a number that corresponds to each numbered sentence in the passage. Ask factual questions and have students hold up that card that corresponds to the sentence containing the correct answer. Discuss answers where appropriate. A sample passage with questions appears here:

Passage	Possible Questions
[1]Dennis helped his father load the mini-van. [2]It took quite a while. [3]They put in sleeping bags, a small tent, fishing rods, a pocket radio, and sacks of food, so there was enough for several days. [4]They were going camping.	1. Who is this story about? (1) 2. Where are they going? (4) 3. How much food did they take? (3) 4. What did they load? (3) 5. How long did it take? (2)

3. Provide sentences for students to read that will enable them to answer who, what, when, and where questions. Here is an example:

   Last evening, Michael left his book at the library.

   Who? _____

   What? _____

   When? _____

   Where? _____

4. Encourage students to write brief passages along with questions that can be answered by using information in the passage. Have students exchange their papers and answer the questions.

Game

Get the Facts. Use a world almanac, book of facts, *Guinness Book of World Records,* or another source to develop a series of sentences or short passages. Put this information on the front of a note card and put one question (with the answer) on the back of the card. Place the cards sentence-side up in front of the students.

After one student reads the sentence silently, the card is given to another student who reads the question. If it is answered correctly, the student who answered the question gets the card. Incorrectly answered questions are placed at the bottom of the pile. The correct answer should not be revealed. Questions can be developed around various themes: sports, people, movies, silly facts, celebrities, cars, TV shows, and so on. A possible list of sentences and questions related to silly facts (Sobol, 1981) follows.

Sentences	Questions
Green-yellow is the safest color for a car.	What is the safest color for a car?
The hair and skin that is seen on your body is dead.	What is dead?
Your heart weighs less than a pound, but it pumps 2,000 gallons of blood every day.	How much blood does your heart pump every day?
Cats and gorillas need fourteen hours of sleep out of every twenty-four.	How many hours a day do most cats and gorillas sleep?
An elephant generally drinks about fifty gallons of water a day.	What drinks fifty gallons of water a day?
A mole can tunnel through nearly three hundred feet of earth each day.	How far can a mole tunnel each day?
A bee has 5,000 nostrils and can smell an apple tree two miles away.	How many nostrils does a bee have?
The eyes of a giant squid are as large as a basketball.	How large are a giant squid's eyes?
A pig has forty-four teeth.	What animal has forty-four teeth?

5.3   Sequence

Behavior Observed	The student has difficulty sequencing events.
Anticipated Outcome	The student will sequence events correctly.

Background

Students who have difficulty retelling the events from a story in the proper order may be experiencing problems with understanding sequence. The same is true for students who have trouble following multistep directions.

Students who possess the ability to recognize or recall the sequence in a passage are often able to imply what occurred between two stated events or incidents. They can also make predictions about what might happen next in a passage based on the previous sequence of events. Sequencing demands that students use at least the literal level of comprehension. More often, however, the interpretive level as well as the applicative level must be used. In order to correctly sequence events, the students must interpret a passage of print or a series of pictures and then anticipate which event must come next (and also which cannot).

To teach sequence of events, begin with concrete experiences and then move to printed materials. In addition, consider the importance of sequence relative to the particular type of reading material and the student's purpose(s) for reading. Following are strategies that are helpful in teaching sequence.

Teaching Strategy 1

1. Gather a series of objects that can be put in order. Some examples are

pencils of varying lengths	paper of different sizes
straws of different lengths	books of differing sizes
balls of various sizes	chalk of varying lengths

2. Use a series of objects (such as three pencils of varying lengths) and have students arrange them from shortest to longest. Tell students that they are arranging the pencils in a particular order or sequence. Repeat this process with other objects (nested dolls or other toys also work well). Have students give directions for ordering or arranging the objects in a particular sequence.

3. Transfer the notion of sequence by using a series of three pictures. Have a student arrange the pictures in sequence and then discuss the reasons for a particular sequence. Have students make up a brief story that explains the sequence and have them share it aloud. Two possible sets of pictures are given here:

4. Help students become aware of sequences in their daily activities by discussing the order of the letters in their names, how a book is read (left to right and top to bottom), eating (breakfast, lunch, and dinner), getting dressed (socks before shoes, shirt before coat), and coming to school. Stress that the sequence or order observed in these activities also occurs in reading.

5. Use an activity like brushing teeth and have students list the major steps in the sequence. Write these steps on the chalkboard and encourage discussion.

6. To begin the transfer to reading, present sentence strips that relate to a particular sequence and have a student arrange them in proper order. Vary the number and complexity of the sentences for the group being taught. Think aloud and discuss the arrangement. Tell the students that during reading there is often a sequence or order to the story. For example:

_____ Mario and Mike raked the leaves.

_____ Dad asked if the two boys wanted to earn some money.

_____ They put the piles into large brown bags.

_____ Dad looked out the window and saw the lawn covered with leaves.

_____ The boys counted the money they had earned.

Read the sentences with students and demonstrate how to choose the correct sequence by thinking aloud. "I wonder which thing happened first. Well, Mario and Mike didn't rake the leaves first because I think someone asked them to do that job. It was dad who asked the boys to rake the leaves so the boys could earn some money. That's right, but something came before that… Oh, Dad must have seen a lot of leaves first and maybe he didn't have time to rake. So, the fourth sentence down is the first thing that happened. Next, Dad must have asked the two boys if they wanted to earn some money. That's the second one down. Then the boys raked and put the leaves into the brown recyclable bags. Then they got paid for their work and counted their money… so, the sentences are numbered 3, 2, 4, 1, 5." Read the sentences in order with the students and ask them whether they agree. Encourage suggestions.

7. Retell several familiar stories (such as *The Three Little Pigs*, *Snow White*, *Peter Pan*) and ask students questions about the sequence of the events. Use words that help signal sequence (*first, then, later, next, finally*), and highlight these words through discussion.

8. Give students a brief passage at their instructional level that contains several events and a list of the major events in scrambled order. After students have read the passage, have them number the events in the order in which they happened. Discuss their answers.

Teaching Strategy 2

1. Tell students that in stories they read, events usually happen in a particular order or sequence. Invite their sharing based on books they have read or TV programs or movies they have seen. Stress that a series of events can often show the progression of time.

2. Ask students to think about events in their daily lives like getting up, dressing, eating, going to school, going home, playing, doing homework, and going to bed.

   Encourage discussion and then provide a chart on which the day's activities in school can be listed, for example:

Time	Events/Activities
8:40	Arrive at school
8:50	School begins
8:50–9:00	Attendance, lunch count
9:00–9:30	Science

3. After activities at school have been listed, encourage students to share events that take place before and after school. Distribute the following chart that they can complete with events in their daily routines.

231

When	Time	Events/Activities
Before school		
At school		
After school		
At bedtime		

4. After students have completed their charts, help them to get a sense of events over a twenty-four hour period. A circle should help students see the sequence and repeated events in their daily routines.

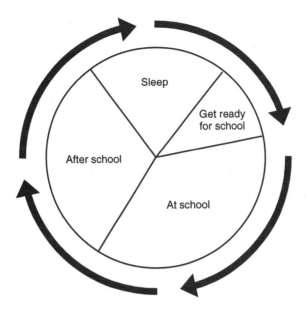

5. Stress that stories have a sequence of events. Relate important events in history or in the lives of famous people. Have students think about their own lives and construct a time line of their lives.

6. Conclude the lesson by reading aloud a short story with a clear sequence. Folk and fairy tales often are short stories with obvious sequences. Then discuss and list the important events on the chalkboard.

Practice and Reinforcement Activities

1. Students who need practice in acquiring the concept of sequence should be given various concrete objects and instructed to order them according to size, length, shape, and so forth.

2. Provide comic strips or stories told through pictures that are presented in a mixed-up order. Have students arrange the pictures in the order in which they happened and retell the story. For example:

233

3. Give students three or four letters of the alphabet and have them place the letters in correct sequence.

4. Provide an oral set of directions for the student to carry out several specific actions. Use words to help signal sequence (*first, then, last*). Other signal words include *yesterday, today,* and *tomorrow.*

5. After students have read a selection, ask them questions about the order of events.

6. List the major events of a selection in a scrambled order on the chalkboard. Instruct students to rewrite the list in the correct order or number the events in the order in which they happened. Have students discuss their answers.

7. After a selection has been read, students can draw pictures to illustrate the order of major events or write sentences that describe them.

8. Scrambled sentences can be arranged in proper order and discussed, for example:

   _____ Thomas Edison worked hard and invented electric lights.

   _____ Once there were no electric lights.

   _____ Today we have electric lights in our homes.

9. Have students arrange sentence strips that go with pictures to tell the story in the proper sequence.

10. Prepare paragraphs that have a sentence missing and provide two to four alternative sentences that could be the missing sentence. Ask students to select the sentence that best fits within the sequence of the paragraph. Discuss why the other sentences are less likely choices.

    _____. Use strong twine, sticks, and paper for the kite. Tie rags together for the tail. Wait for a windy day to try to fly your kite.

    1. You can buy a kite at the store.
    2. You need several things to make a kite.
    3. Flying a kite is not easy.

11. Provide activities where students can practice the correct sequence of events. For example:

1. noon	1. fruit	1. get dressed
2. sunrise	2. flower	2. get up
3. sunset	3. bud	3. go to school
123 132 [213]	312 123 [321]	231 [213] 312

12. Prepare sentences or brief passages that have a sequence of events or activities. Have students answer the questions posed and then discuss how they arrived at their answers.

    Bill took out the garbage after he cleaned his room.

    What did Bill do first? _____

    What did Bill do next? _____

    What helped you decide on the sequence?

    Jessica left home before Katie.

    Who left last? _____

    What helped you decide on the sequence?

13. Have students develop lists of words that may give clues to sequence (such as *later, soon, tomorrow, yesterday, in the future, in the evening*). Discuss these words and have students write short selections that include some of them. Students can also write or ask questions that focus on sequence.

14. Have students list important times or events in their lives. Then help them arrange the events in order by years. Stress the notion that the events have been placed in a time sequence.

15. Have students list step-by-step instructions for cooking, making something, doing a magic trick, and so on. Other students can follow the directions as written in sequence.

16. Read stories to your students that have a clear sequence of events. Create story cards of the events and place them in random order on the table. Ask students to place the event in the order of the story. An example of story cards from *If You Give A Moose A Muffin* (Numeroff, 1991) appears on the following page.

Games

Scramble. Prepare several sets of the same five sentence strips that can be formed into a paragraph. Divide the group into several teams and give each an envelope containing the sentence strips. The first team that arranges the sentence strips into a logical paragraph wins. One variation of the game uses a sentence that has been cut into words or phrases. A sequence of pictures can also be used.

How Is It Ordered? Develop a series of paragraphs that vary in how the reading is sequenced, such as time, events, directions, actions of the main character, or which ingredient comes next. Make note cards with the various sequences as headings. Place the paragraphs on note cards and have students draw a card, read it, and place it under the correct heading.

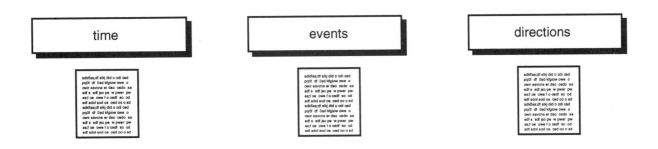

Going to New York. The first student says "I went to New York and took my _____." The next student repeats the object named and adds another. Subsequent students do the same, naming the objects in the proper order. The game can be played by a single group of students or by several students taking alternate turns. Help transfer the game to reading by telling students that there is a sequence in reading selections that needs to be remembered. Alternate names for the game can be used (I went for a walk and saw a (an) _____).

a muffin	blackberry bush	carboard and paints
jam	needle and thread	a sweater
socks	a sheet	soap
jam	Muffin Mix	

5.4 Predicting Outcomes

Behavior Observed	The student has difficulty drawing conclusions or making inferences about a passage.
Anticipated Outcome	The student will draw conclusions and make inferences about text.

Background

Drawing conclusions and making inferences may be thought of as predicting outcomes and involves using material that is implicit or not directly stated in the text. This level of comprehension—interpretive—requires more reasoning skill than factual recall on the part of the reader. When a student draws a conclusion, the main idea, supporting details, and sequence of events in a passage are often used as the basis for the conclusion. A conclusion can be regarded as a reasoned deduction or inference. Although fine distinctions can be made between the two terms, teachers may assume that the terms describe students' attempts to infer a reasonable prediction of outcomes or conclusions based on the available information. There are generally ten types of inferences that compose the bulk of students' reading (Johnson & Johnson, 1986). They are explained with examples that follow.

➤ Location

> While we raced along the freeway, we could feel the wind in our hair.

➤ Agent (Occupation or Pastime)

> Eric viewed the overgrown lawn and started the mower.

➤ Time

> When the electricity failed, the darkness was total.

➤ Action

> Alex ran down the field with the ball, eluding blockers and scoring a touchdown.

➤ Instrument (Tool or Device)

> With effort and determination, Lisa held the tool and readied to pound the nail.

➤ Cause-Effect

> In the morning, we noticed drifts as high as our car.

➤ Object

> The surface was finely sanded oak, and the legs were sturdy enough to handle our huge Thanksgiving feast.

➤ Category

The Corvette and Ferrari held the waving candidate and his family, while the Cougar carried city politicians.

➤ Problem-Solution

She bumped her head, so she grabbed for her icepack.

➤ Feeling-Attitude

When I stepped up to receive my diploma, my parents cheered as tears filled their eyes.

Teachers can help students who have difficulty in reading by being aware of the types of inferences and the demands placed on the reader as part of predicting outcomes. Teachers can guide students' learning through the following strategies.

Teaching Strategy

1. Explain to students that in much of their reading they are able to use the information presented to predict conclusions or make inferences. Tell students that conclusions and inferences are based on what is stated in the story or text as well as what they already know.

2. Give students an opportunity to predict a conclusion or make an inference after several facts are given, for example:

Fact 1:   The sun did not shine on Saturday.

Fact 2:   There were many clouds in the sky.

Fact 3:   The grass, houses, roads, and sidewalks were wet.

Fact 4:   Our picnic was canceled.

Then ask students to predict a conclusion or make an inference. Discuss the basis on which the conclusion or inference is made.

3. Present a series of events and several possible conclusions, for example:

Event: It snowed all night, and by Friday morning there was more than a foot of snow on the ground.

Possible Outcomes: We went swimming in our outdoor pool.

We shoveled the sidewalk and driveway.

We didn't have school.

We put the top down on our convertible.

Be sure to discuss the reasons why some conclusions are more probable than others.

4. Give students part of a selection to read. At the end of the reading, have students consider the facts and events that have been presented in order to infer what will happen next. After listing the students' predictions on the chalkboard, read students the remainder of the selection and then discuss whether any of their predictions were right.

5. Help students realize that they make inferences based on the information they have gained by reading and from their own personal experiences which may relate to the passage they are reading.

Practice and Reinforcement Activities

1. Students who have difficulty seeing relationships may also have trouble drawing conclusions, making inferences, and predicting outcomes. These students can often be helped to see relationships through classification exercises. Present objects (concrete objects, pictures, or words) and have students identify the one that does not belong as well as explain why the others do belong. Examples include these columns:

bed	mountain	cow	black	book
table	river	robin	blue	pencil
apple	lake	horse	green	magazine
chair	ocean	pig	one	pamphlet

2. Provide reading materials at the student's instructional level and ask questions that encourage the student to use information in the passage to draw conclusions. Take time to discuss the basis for the conclusions that were drawn.

3. Provide statements in which students are asked to give logical conclusions. For example:

   What would happen if you

   … didn't sleep for two days?

   … had to stay in bed for a week?

   … had a birthday every month?

   … ate a pound of candy?

   … crashed into a tree on your bicycle?

4. Give students brief passages where a conclusion must be drawn. For example:

   Bill was reading about the sun, the moon, and Mars.

   It was a book about the _____ (planets, solar system).

5. Provide pictures or illustrations and have students classify them under one or more of the following:

Animals		Sports			Seasons			
Large	Small	Football	Golf	Soccer	Summer	Fall	Winter	Spring

6. When students are reading a selection that lends itself to inference-making, stop them at the appropriate point and ask them to write their predictions about what will happen next or how they think the story will end. Discuss their predictions, the basis for their judgment, and the supporting evidence in the story. Then let students read to the end of the story to see whether their predictions were right.

7. Provide students with pictures, illustrations, or verbal descriptions of events. Encourage them to list possible causes of the event and then select those that seem most appropriate. Sample events include:

   ■ a soccer player being congratulated near the opponent's goal

   ■ a child who has just blown out the candles on a cake

■ a boy and girl with sad expressions on their faces looking out their front window and seeing that it's raining

■ a patient sitting in a doctor's office

8. Provide sentences where students use the information given to answer a question. Stress that the answer isn't stated so students must reason it out or infer it. Discuss students' answers.

At recess the students got their gloves, bats, and balls. What were they likely to do?

During a very severe storm, the electricity went off. Dad lit a match. What did he probably want to find?

Maria had a day off school. She looked in the newspaper to find the best sales. Then she left the house. Where did she probably go?

A variation of this activity is to provide possible answers and have students select the best one, for example:

Jesse and his father went walking on a warm spring day. There was a nice breeze in the air. What might Jesse and his father do to have fun?

_____ rake leaves _____ fly a kite _____ watch TV

Be sure to discuss students' answers and their reasons for choosing them.

Behavior Observed	The student has difficulty judging, analyzing, and evaluating written material.
Anticipated Outcome	The student will use information from text to judge, analyze, and evaluate written material.

Background

The ability to read between and beyond the lines is regarded as higher-level comprehension and is often referred to as critical reading or problem solving. It involves the ability to judge, analyze, or evaluate what is read. Implicit task demands of the reader at this level include distinguishing fact from opinion, recognizing propaganda techniques, evaluating the author's bias, competence, accuracy, and viewpoint, and reacting to what has been written on the basis of one's background and experience.

Reading instruction and classroom questions have focused on the lower levels of comprehension. This emphasis is short-sighted and prohibits readers from reaching their full potential. However, there are actions teachers can take to help students evaluate and react to what is read. Several strategies are presented here.

Teaching Strategy 1 *(Distinguishing Fact from Opinion)*

1. Ask students whether they believe everything they read. Encourage students to share their reasons and look for the opportunity during this discussion to use the words *fact* and *opinion.*

2. Discuss the differences between facts and opinions. You may look up the words in the dictionary and discuss their meanings. List attributes of facts and opinions that are derived from each word's meaning:

Facts	Opinions
something known to exist	a belief
real or true	judgment
an actual event	a personal attitude
you can prove it	what someone thinks about something

3. Write the following sentence on the chalkboard: *Greg looks outside and sees that it is raining.* Have students decide whether *it is raining* is fact or opinion. Help them decide that it is a fact because Greg can see it raining.

4. Now have students assume that they asked three different people, "What's the weather?" and the following responses are given:

Tiffany: Rainy

Roman: Great

Esther: Terrible

Ask students to identify each response as fact or opinion and to offer possible explanations for the two opinions. For example, Roman said the weather was "great" and may be a farmer who knows a recent planting needs rain. Esther said the weather was "terrible" because she may have planned a picnic and is disappointed.

5. Take time to stress that a person's background, feelings, attitudes, and beliefs can influence how events, actions, and even facts are interpreted. Relate these factors to the reading done by students.

6. Provide a brief passage and have students decide which statements are facts and which are opinions:

> Pennsylvania is the best state. Its capital is Harrisburg. Pennsylvania became a state on December 12, 1787. It is one of the oldest states. Almost everyone likes Pennsylvania.

Be sure to allow ample time for students to share reasons why they identify a sentence as fact or opinion. Stress that some writers state their opinions as if they were facts.

Teaching Strategy 2 (*Reacting to What Is Read*)

1. Tell students that there are many ways they can react to what an author has written. Invite their responses and list them on the chalkboard. Some possible responses include:

   ■ Agree or disagree with some or all of the reading.

   ■ Evaluate the author's attitudes or point of view.

   ■ Relate what the author has said to my background and experiences.

   ■ Evaluate the validity of the author's arguments.

2. Take each response and develop the idea that in order to react, students must combine their knowledge, attitudes, or beliefs along with the information or point of view presented by the author.

3. Present students with sentences and model the thinking you use to agree, disagree, or evaluate. Consider the following statement and example:

   > Fall is the best of all the seasons.

   > "I like fall the best because the weather is often crisp and clear. Clear blue sky and changing leaves offer a colorful backdrop for long walks in nature. I'm not sure that everyone feels that way. Allergy sufferers seem to sneeze a lot before the first frost. There are many rainy, windy days that may make some people miserable. So, I guess that statement is not true for all people."

   Ask students their opinion and then discuss other seasons or issues. Guide students as needed.

Teaching Strategy 3 *(Evaluating Propaganda Techniques)*

1. Discuss common propaganda techniques and give examples as you list them. Allow students to also give examples of each technique. Some common propaganda techniques (Fry, Kress, & Fountoukidis, 1993) follow:

   - *Bandwagon*—Using the argument that everyone is doing something, and you should, too. *Example*—"Last year 30 million people switched to FLY High athletic shoes. Isn't it time you did, too?"

   - *Card Stacking*—Telling only one side of the story as though there were no opposing view. *Example*—"This tape is designed to give the best video performance money can buy."

   - *Flag Waving*—Connecting a product or service to patriotism. *Example*—"Buy the Wolf Van—American all the way!"

   - *Glittering Generality*—Using idealistic terms based on detail to create an association in the reader's mind between the person or object and something that is good, valued, and desired. *Example*—"Jamaica has been on the student council for three years. You couldn't find a more honest young woman."

   - *Name Calling*—Using negative or derogatory words to create an association in the reader's mind to something that is bad, feared, or distasteful. *Example*—"Do you really want to elect Tom, who is a gang member?"

   - *Plain Folks*—Using a person who represents the "typical" target of the ad to communicate to the audience the message that because we are alike and I would use/buy this, you should, too. *Example*—"Change to Drip for your sinus problems. It helped me. It'll help you, too."

   - *Prestige Identification*—Showing a celebrity with the object, person, or cause in order to increase the audience's impression of prestige of the object, person, or cause. *Example*—"We treat our restaurant patrons like stars."

   - *Testimonial*—Using the words or testimony of someone to persuade you to think or act like he or she does. *Example*—"I'm a teacher and I use this program to teach reading."

2. Provide students with newspaper, magazine, or videotaped TV advertisements or campaign materials. Tell them that they are to be critical readers of this material and that which is said is often opinion that attempts to sway their point of view.

3. Have students find examples of the propaganda techniques as they go through the advertisements and campaign literature you have given them. Examples should be shared and discussed with the class.

Practice and Reinforcement Activities

1. Provide sentences and have students identify them as fact or opinion. Some sentences may require research. Take time to discuss students' responses and reasons for their decisions, for example:

    _F_ Charles Lindbergh made the first solo flight across the Atlantic.

    _O_ Lindbergh's plane is nice.

    _F_ Amelia Earhart was the first woman to fly solo across the Atlantic Ocean.

    _F_ Earhart wrote a book called *Soaring Wings.*

    _O_ I read her book and liked it.

    _O_ Generally, airplanes are the best way to travel.

2. Prepare questions for a selection and have students decide whether they are facts or opinions. Have students discuss their responses.

3. Present a problem and have students suggest as many solutions to the problem as possible. Then evaluate the proposed solutions and select the ones that appear to be the most workable. Use this same technique with problems in stories.

4. Additional resources for the fact-and-opinion exercises can be found in newspaper articles, advertising, editorials, columns, and cartoons.

5. Challenge students to write their own persuasive paragraph or advertisements using one of the persuasive propaganda techniques discussed. Volunteers can share them with the class.

5.6   Using Prior Knowledge

Behavior Observed	The student does not use prior knowledge before reading.
Anticipated Outcome	The student will use prior knowledge before reading to enhance comprehension of text.

Perspective and Strategies

The ability to access what you know about a subject before reading can help you understand the text with richer comprehension. Using what you know to help you connect your existing knowledge with the new knowledge from the text is called accessing prior knowledge. What students know is structured in their minds in schema, or abstract frameworks around which memory is stored. If students have knowledge about frogs and toads, for example, they will better understand the Frog and Toad stories by Arnold Lobel.

Since all of our students have limited background knowledge to a certain extent, because of the number of years they have lived and the experience they have had, teachers need to help students both access their prior knowledge and develop their knowledge before they read.

This section contains several strategies that can help students access their prior knowledge before reading. Try several of them to find which ones work for you. They include:

- Brainstorming

- Exclusion Brainstorming

- Feature Analysis

- K-W-L

- Predict-O-Gram

- Semantic Webbing

- Story Impressions

Before Reading Strategies

Brainstorming

Prior knowledge, what students already know about a topic, is a major determinant of whether they will understand what they read. Prior knowledge must be activated or developed by prereading activities. One of the simplest activities is to brainstorm by asking: What do you think of when I say _____?

Before reading *Owl Babies* (Waddell, 1975), ask students to brainstorm what they know about owls. An example of a brainstorming web before reading the book could be the following:

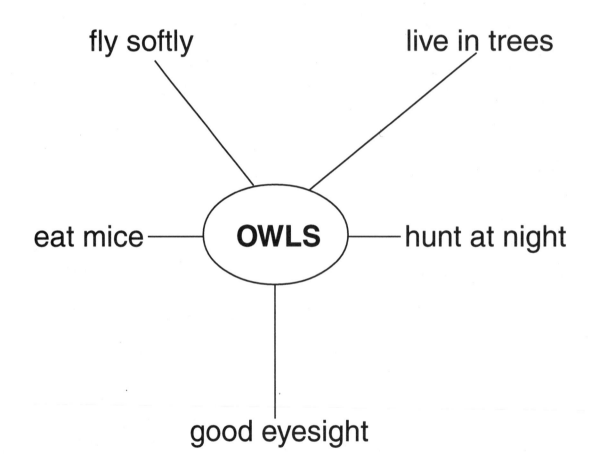

Exclusion Brainstorming

Use exclusion brainstorming by placing the title of a selection on the chalkboard along with a few well-chosen words. Some of the words should fit the topic; others should not; some should be ambiguous. Students choose which words they feel will be likely to occur in the selection and which will not. Students should give reasons for their choices. Following the reading of the selection, the students can return to the exclusion brainstorming list to see how their choices compared to the actual text. Exclusion brainstorming prior to reading for *Sam's Sandwich* (Pelham, 1990) might look like this:

Sam's Sandwich

horse	lettuce	ants	fly	brother
cake	cucumber	worm	swim	snail
picnic	salami	rain	plate	ketchup

Feature Analysis

This strategy serves to activate prior knowledge and compare vocabulary terms prior to reading a selection. Along with vocabulary development, feature analysis is a good strategy for relational concept building. Students compare what the words mean and how they relate to one another. This type of discussion can help lay the basis for rich and detailed comprehension.

Students fill in the chart and compare how things are different and how they are alike. A feature analysis about pets follows:

Kinds	Features			
	fur?	tail?	number of legs?	land or water?
cat	yes	yes	4	land
goldfish	no	yes	0	water
dog	yes	yes	4	land
snake	no	no	0	both
turtle	no	yes	4	both

Feature analysis can be used at all age levels and difficulty of text. It is especially helpful in comparing science and social studies concepts. A feature analysis (Johnson & Pearson, 1984) chart that you may adapt for your use follows.

Feature Analysis

Kinds	Features				

K-W-L

This strategy is begun with students prior to reading a selection. Students are asked what they already **K**now about a topic, what they **W**ant to learn about the topic, and what they have **L**earned as a result of their reading (Ogle, 1989). Not only does K-W-L help students activate prior knowledge as they fill in the chart, but it also gives them a chance to reflect on and organize what they have learned from reading about a topic from one or several sources. A K-W-L chart about planets may look something like this for a particular student or class just after the **K** part of the chart has been discussed:

	Planets	
K	W	L
(what I already know)	(what I want to find out)	(what I have learned)
Earth is a planet. *There are 9 planets.* *Planets are in space.* *Moons go around them.* *The sun is not one.*		

Next, the students will share what they wonder about the topic—what they want to know. Then, students read to find the answers to their questions using various resources. Finally, the last cell—what I have learned—is completed. Students can actively monitor their learning through all phases of reading using this strategy. We have found that some teachers add a fourth column labeled what I still want to learn. Use the blank K-W-L chart or adapt it for your classroom needs.

K-W-L Chart

Donna Ogle

(title)		
K	W	L
(what I already know)	(what I want to find out)	(what I have learned)

From Ogle, D.M. (1989). The know, want to know, learn strategy. In K.D. Muth (Ed.), *Children's Comprehension of Text* (pp. 205–223). Newark, DE: International Reading Association.

Predict-O-Gram

Students focus on vocabulary and chart whether words from a teacher-generated list will tell about setting, plot, characters, and so on. After students have charted the words, the selection is read. Following reading, students check to see how their chart, or the class chart, compares with the text. Students may move words to their proper places in the chart, if necessary, after reading. For this reason, vocabulary words placed on Post-It Notes are effective. A Predict-O-Gram (Blachowicz, 1986) prior to reading *Clean Your Room, Harvey Moon* (Cummings, 1991) might look like this:

Directions: What do you think these words will be used to tell about? Write them on a square on the Predict-O-Gram. You may have more than one word on a square.

Saturday Harvey doom clean broom marched
dirty lunch creature dripping found sticky

Setting	Characters	Goal or Problem
Saturday	*creature* *Harvey*	*clean*
Action	**Resolution**	**Other Things**

Use the accompanying blank Predict-O-Gram or adapt it for your students.

Predict-O-Gram

Camille L.Z. Blachowicz

Directions: What do you think these words will be used to tell about? Write them on a square on the Predict-O-Gram. You may have more than one word on a square.

_____

_____

_____

_____

Predict-O-Gram for _____

Setting	Characters	Goal or Problem
Action	**Resolution**	**Other Things**

From Blachowicz, C.L.Z. (1986). Making Connections: Alternatives to the vocabulary notebook. *Journal of Reading, 29(7),* 643–649.

Semantic Webbing

This strategy not only activates prior knowledge but also helps students organize the information they know. Semantic maps graphically display words, concepts, and ideas in categories and indicate how they relate to one another. New knowledge can be added to the web during or after reading, helping students to link existing knowledge and new concepts. A semantic web about friends might look like this:

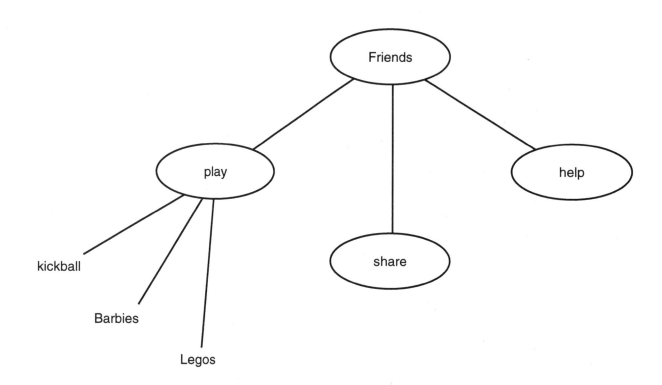

Semantic maps often look like an octopus with irregular legs. They grow in shape and direction as the discussion about concepts progresses. There is no one correct shape or linear form. You must create your own as you and your students discuss words and how they relate to one another.

Story Impressions

Story Impressions (McGinley & Denner, 1987) begin with the teacher supplying a list of words from an unfamiliar story or selection. The students look at the order of this list and read the words aloud. Then, individually or in groups, students attempt to make up a story using the list of words in order. Seeing relationships and connecting concepts is a good way to get students prepared to read a story by activating the knowledge that they already have about the topic. Story impressions are difficult for young or inexperienced readers. It is fine to have a short word list or to work as a group. These adaptations are helpful to those students having difficulty. A story impression for the first chapter of *Little House in the Big Woods* (Wilder, 1932) could be:

girl
↓
Wisconsin
↓
deer
↓
moon
↓
Pa
↓
swift
↓
hinges
↓
chopping
↓
smoke
↓
coming
↓
venison
↓
middle
↓
pigpen
↓
bounced
↓
watched
↓
banked

Students read the word list in order as indicated by the arrows. Then, students write a story that uses the words in order. It's a good idea to have students share their stories aloud; some can be humorous! As you create the word list for a story impression, choose words that seemingly do not relate to one another. Remember, young readers and students experiencing difficulty with reading could benefit by adapting this strategy by using a shorter word list or doing the story impression as a group. You may also find modeling the procedure to be helpful to your students.

5.7   Monitoring Comprehension While Reading

Behavior Observed	The student does not monitor comprehension while reading.
Anticipated Outcome	The student will use strategies to monitor comprehension while reading.

Perspective and Strategies

As students read, they need to decide whether or not they are understanding what they have read. (For more information on Strategic Reading, see Chapter 6.) Students who fail to monitor their comprehension while reading frequently read to the end of the page or the passage and have little or no understanding of the text. You can introduce strategies that will foster comprehension monitoring as students read.

This section contains several strategies that can help students monitor their comprehension while reading. Try several of them to find which ones work for you. They include:

■ DR-TA

■ QAR

■ Reciprocal Teaching

■ ReQuest

■ Say Something

■ Questioning

DR-TA

The Directed Reading-Thinking Activity (Stauffer, 1969a) is a strategy that can be applied to both fiction and nonfiction materials. The technique encourages students to make predictions about what will happen next as they pause at designated points in reading a selection. Prior knowledge is activated and students are encouraged to monitor their comprehension.

1. Students consider the title of a selection and the teacher asks, "What do you think this book (selection) will be about?" Students draw upon their background knowledge and make predictions that are written on the chalkboard.

2. The selection is read silently or aloud, and at a preselected point the teacher asks students to review their predictions and see whether they were correct. Discussion includes the reasons predictions are correct or incorrect. At this point, new predictions might be made that reflect additional information and inferences from the selection. Three or four preselected points to review predictions are generally appropriate for a short selection. The last one should be just at the climax of the selection.

3. While using the DR-TA procedure, teachers must ensure that their questioning of students is open-ended, calling for predictions. For example, "Why do you think that way?" or "What in the passage makes you believe that?" Upon completion of the selection, students should discuss the accuracy of their predictions, what was helpful information, and what was confusing. DR-TA can enable students to make personal predictions that are written down at their desks instead of at the chalkboard. In this way, students can become more involved in their reading. The ultimate goal is for students to integrate the predict-read-confirm-predict strategy in their daily reading.

QARs (*Question/Answer/Relationships*)

The strategy, Question-Answer Relationships (QAR) (Raphael,1984), is an example of a self-questioning exercise that can facilitate a student's understanding of text. By using a QAR, students identify different types of questions they can ask themselves while reading.

Typically, QAR proceeds in this way:

1. The teacher explains that there are two kinds of information: in the book (text explicit) and in the head (text implicit). The first question-answering strategy, RIGHT THERE, is to find the words used to create the question and look at the other words in that sentence to find the answer. The answer is within a single sentence.

2. The second QAR, THINK AND SEARCH, also involves a question that has an answer in the story, but this answer requires information from more than one sentence or paragraph.

3. The third QAR, ON MY OWN, represents a question for which the answer must result from the student's own background knowledge.

4. The fourth QAR, WRITER AND ME, represents a slightly different interpretive question. The answer might be found in the student's own background knowledge, but would not make sense unless the student had read the text.

5. There are four principles of instruction when using QARs:

   ■ Give immediate feedback.

   ■ Progress from shorter to longer text.

   ■ Build independence by guiding students from group to independent activities.

   ■ Provide transitions from the easier task to the more difficult.

6. Students should be taught the four QARs and how to tell the difference. Understanding question/answer relationships increases comprehension, and thus, student achievement. Following is a diagram that depicts the four major sources of QARs and may be helpful to share with students.

An example of a QAR using *The Magic School Bus Lost in the Solar System* (Cole, 1990) follows:

Right There

1. What were the students in Ms. Fizzles's class going to see at the planetarium? *(a sky show about the solar system)*

2. What are meteorites? *(falling chunks of rock and metal)*

Think and Search

1. What amazing thing happened at the red light? *(The bus started tilting back and the roar of rockets was heard. The bus was blasting off.)*

2. What had changed when the roar of the rocket stopped? *(The bus had turned into a spaceship. Everyone was dressed in spacesuits. Everyone was lighter than feathers and floated above their seats.)*

Author and You

1. What do you think Ms. Fizzles's class was studying in science class?*(The solar system, space, and/or the planets)*

2. Had the children been on the bus before? How do you know? *(Yes, the text says, "as usual, it took a while to get the old bus started.")*

On my Own

1. What do you know about the solar system?

2. Have you ever been to a planetarium? If so, what did you see there?

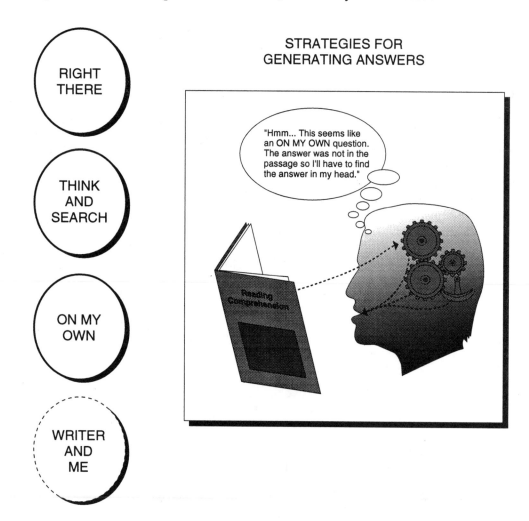

Adapted from Raphael, T.E. (1984). Teaching learners about sources of information for answering comprehension questions. *Journal of Reading, 27*(4), 303–311.

Reciprocal Teaching

This a method for modeling and approaching a reading passage in a systematic way developed by Palinscar and Brown (1986). The teacher demonstrates the strategy by modeling a sequence of comprehension processes: summarizing, questioning, clarifying, and predicting. Following teacher demonstration, students take turns following the same process. Reciprocal teaching is effective with most types of text but is generally most helpful for nonfiction that contains new facts and information. Briefly, the steps are:

1. The teacher divides a selection into shorter parts or paragraphs. Then everyone reads a passage silently.

2. After silent reading is completed, the teacher models the procedure.

   ■ *Summarize* the selection in one (or a few) sentences.

   ■ *Question* the group (usually a small group) with open-ended questions that avoid trivial details.

   ■ *Clarify* hard parts by explaining, giving examples, or drawing analogies.

   ■ *Predict* what the next section might be about based on the material just read and discussed.

3. Eventually release responsibility to students.

ReQuest

ReQuest (Manzo, 1969) is designed to improve students' comprehension by developing questioning behavior. The teacher encourages students to set their own purpose for reading and to ask questions about the material by modeling questioning behavior. During the questioning, much information is learned and the teacher can see exactly what part of the text is causing difficulty. ReQuest may be used with individual students or adapted for a small group. The process goes like this:

1. The teacher and students read the first sentence of the passage. After the sentence is read silently, a student asks as many questions as he or she can. The teacher then answers all of the questions as clearly and completely as possible.

2. Next, the teacher takes a turn to ask questions about the same sentence and a student answers as fully as possible. In this way, the teacher can model both good questioning strategies and appropriate, complete answers.

3. The process continues to the next sentence; the students ask questions, and the teacher answers. Then the teacher asks, and the student answers.

4. Gradually, as students begin to use the strategy effectively, larger sections of text can be read silently prior to the questioning.

Say Something

To promote student understanding during reading, use the Say Something strategy (Harste & Short, 1988). Two or more students read the same passage of a text, either silently or in chorus. After the students have read a meaningful chunk of text, ask them to stop and "say something" to their group members, one at a time. The students can respond in any way to the text when they offer their ideas to the group. They can "say something" about the plot; they can tell the group how they feel about the story; they can predict what will come next; or they can relate the story to their lives. After each of the students has responded in the group, they return to read more text and repeat the process of responding to each other about the text. This strategy can help students stop during their reading and construct some portion of meaning from the text.

Questioning

Effective questioning can both guide and extend student comprehension. The kinds of questions teachers ask can help students focus on the important aspects of text and literature. Studies have shown that the bulk of teacher questioning requires students to look primarily at the factual (text explicit) level of comprehension, but this practice has been improving and has been replaced by inferential questions and questions that call for paraphrasing different portions of the text that are text implicit (O'Flahaven, Hartman, & Pearson, 1988). This text implicit questioning leads to higher-level comprehension because it requires the use of factual information.

Better readers are most frequently asked text implicit questions because it is felt they are the better thinkers. However, students having difficulty with reading should also be asked text implicit questions. Teachers should avoid too many low-level, single-correct-answer questions. Students need to be guided through the process by teacher modeling and thinking aloud, so students can learn how interpretive and applicative questions are answered. Speculative and predictive questions (Hammond, 1983) that can be asked following reading include:

Did you find the answers to your questions?

Are any questions still unanswered? Which ones?

What did you learn that was unexpected?

What did the writer do to make you think or feel a certain way?

How did the author use language to get across ideas?

Did you identify with the main character? What characteristics were like/unlike you?

How might this story have been different if _____?

If you were the author, how would you have changed the ending?

Behavior Observed	The student does not use text structure as a guide while reading.
Anticipated Outcome	The student will use text structure to assist in understanding the text.

Perspective and Strategies

The majority of the stories or passages you ask your students to read will be one of two kinds of text: narrative text or expository text. Narrative text is a story or events in a sequence. Narrative texts include story elements such as plot, setting, characters, and theme. Expository texts are organized differently. Expository texts "explain" or tell about a subject. Their ideas may be organized by sequence, listing or description, comparison-contrast, cause-effect, and problem-solution. When students understand the structure of texts and use them to guide their understanding, they can comprehend text more readily.

This section contains several strategies that can help students use text structure to improve their comprehension. Try several of them to find which ones work for you. They include:

■ Story Maps

■ Character Map

■ Story Frames

■ Idea Mapping

■ Probable Passages

Story Maps

Story maps can help students understand how a story is organized. While students read or after they have read a story, ask them to fill in each of the sections. Try the different kinds of maps with different stories.

(See attached for examples of story maps.)

Story Map Using Story Grammar

Title

Setting

Characters

Problem

Events

▼

▼

▼

▼

Solution

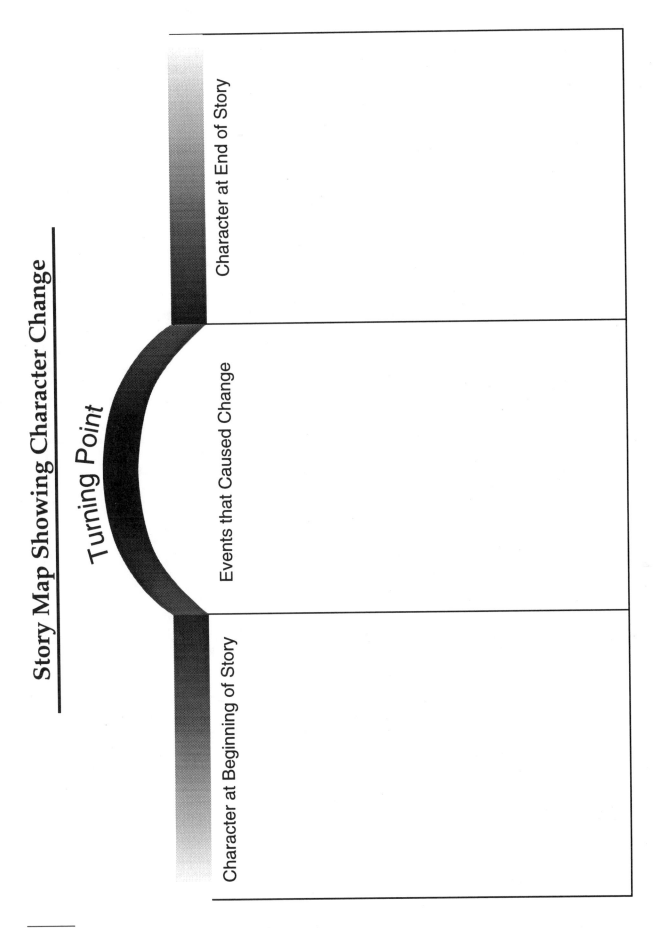

Story Map Showing Character Change

Turning Point

Character at End of Story

Events that Caused Change

Character at Beginning of Story

Story Map Using Events

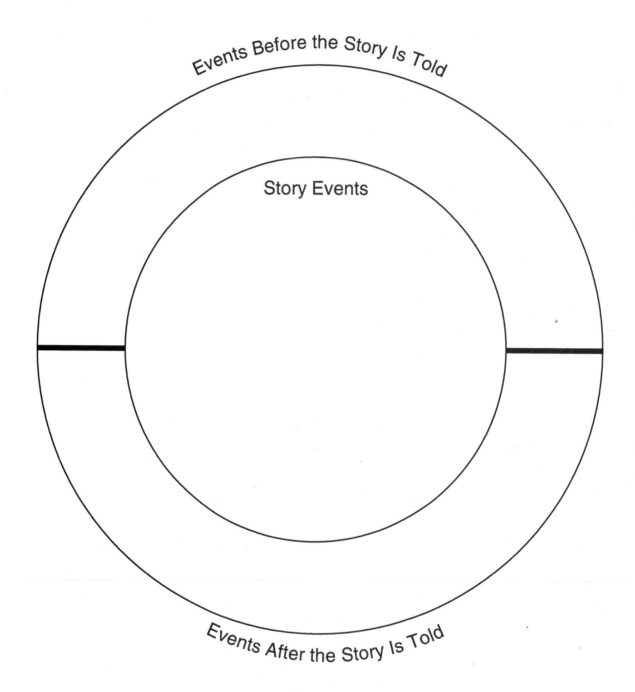

Events Before the Story Is Told

Story Events

Events After the Story Is Told

Story Map Showing Attempts and Outcomes

Title

Setting

Characters

Goal

Problem

Attempts	Outcomes

Solution

Story Map Using Chronological Events

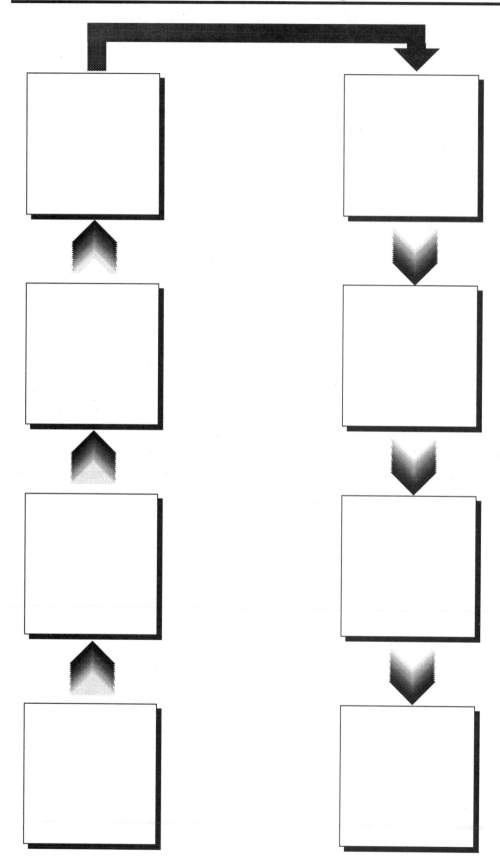

Story Map Showing Events

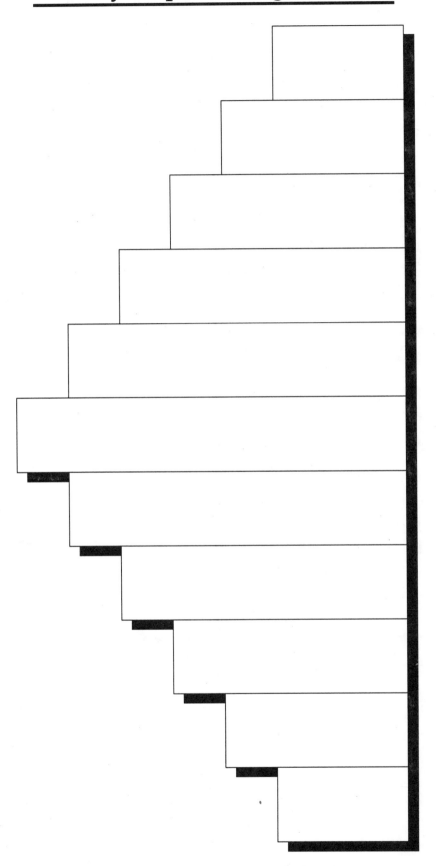

Story Map Showing Story Elements

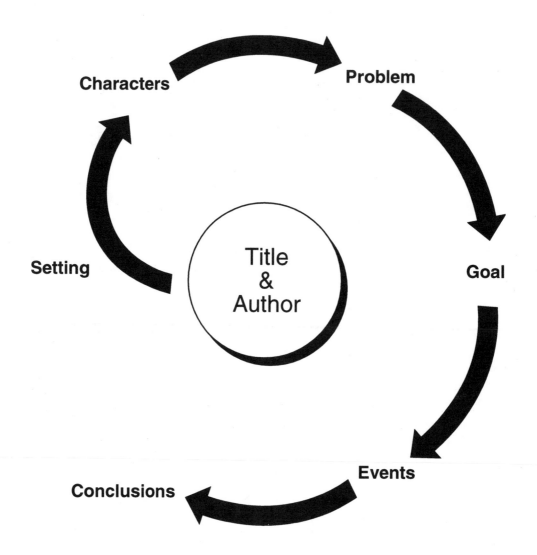

Character Map

The character map strategy helps students gain insight about qualities that characters in both fiction and nonfiction may possess. This activity provides an excellent basis for classroom discussion because it requires students to form and support opinions. A general character map and directions follow:

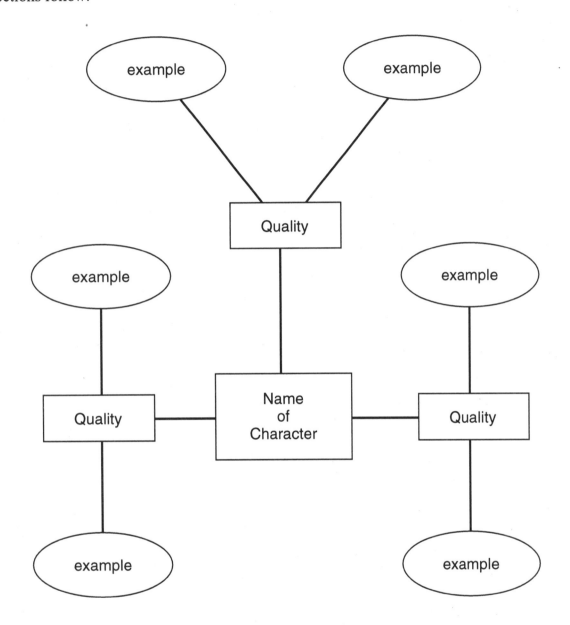

Directions

1. Students write or draw a character they wish to study in the central square.

2. In the rectangles, students list adjectives or qualities that describe that character.

3. In the ovals, students write examples that support the adjectives or qualities.

4. Through discussions students may confirm, add to, refine, or change their initial responses. Use the accompanying blank character map or adapt it to your students.

Character Map

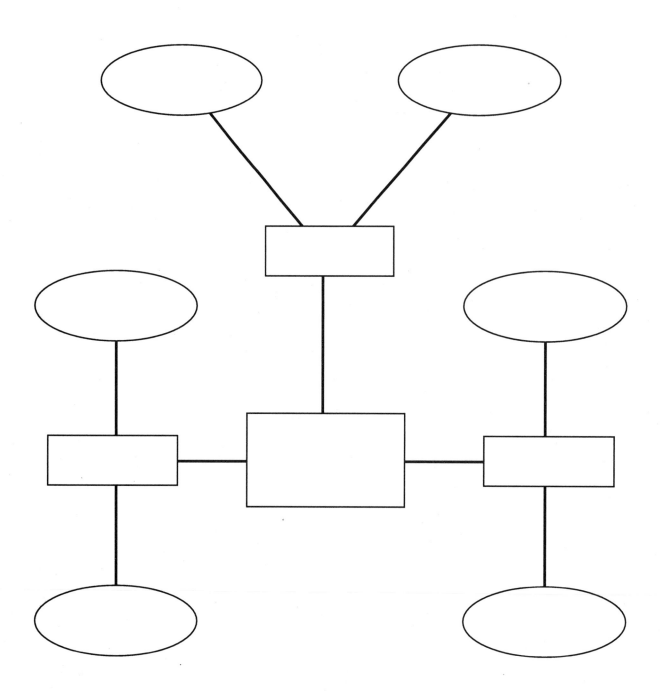

Directions

1. Write or draw in the central square a character you wish to study.

2. In the rectangles, list adjectives or qualities that describe that character.

3. In the ovals, write examples that support the adjectives or qualities.

Story Frames

Story frames can help students improve their comprehension ability by enabling them to monitor their comprehension. Fowler (1982) offers five types of story frames, but suggests using only one in the beginning.

1. Display a story frame on an overhead transparency following the reading of a literature selection.

2. Model filling in the blanks in the story frame, then have students continue to fill them in.

3. After students have had some experience with this strategy, more than one story frame can be worked on simultaneously. Not all frames are suitable for all stories.

Following are the five types of story frames.

Story Summary with One Character Included

Our story is about _____

_____ .

_____ is an important character in the story.

_____ tried to _____

_____ .

The story ends when _____

_____ .

Important Idea or Plot

In this story the problem starts when _____

_____ .

After that, _____ .

Next, _____ .

Then, _____ .

The problem is finally solved when _____

_____ .

The story ends_____

_____ .

Setting

This story takes place _____ .

I know this because the author uses the words " _____

_____ ."

Other clues that show when the story takes place are _____

_____ .

Character Analysis

_____ is an important character in our story.

_____ is important because _____

_____ .

Once he or she _____ .

Another time, _____ .

I think that_____
(character's name)

is _____
(character trait)

because _____ .

Character Comparison

_____ and _____
                                        (characters' names)

are two characters in our story. _____ is
                                        (character's name)

_____ .
        (character's trait)

While _____ is
        (character's name)

_____ .
        (character's trait)

For instance, _____ tries to

_____

and _____ tries to

_____ learns a lesson when

_____ .

Idea-Mapping

Idea-Mapping (Armbruster, 1986) is a visual demonstration of how information in a text is organized. An Idea-Map helps students as they process expository text and also helps them to recall the text as they elaborate on the meaning of the passage. Each Idea-Map is based on the type of text structure that the student is reading. Expository texts may be organized by sequence, listing or description, comparison-contrast, cause-effect, or problem-solution. You may need to identify the text structure for your students initially and provide them with the appropriate Idea-Map to use as they read. As they read, ask the students to fill in the sections with information from the text. After they have used the Idea-Maps for a while, they should be able to identify the structure of each text themselves.

An example of a description Idea-Map follows:

Topic: **Moving Ice Changes the Land**
Details: Glaciers are snow piles that melt and refreeze.
Glaciers become mounds of ice.
Rocks become frozen to the bottom of the ice.
Weight of ice makes glaciers move.
Rocks on the bottom of the glacier cut into rocks.
Glaciers can pick up rocks and carry them away.
Main Idea: **A glacier is a sheet of moving ice.**

Blank Idea-Maps can be found on following pages.

Main Idea-Map

Topic

Details

Main Idea Sentence

Compare-Contrast Idea-Map

Topic:		Topic:
	=	
	=	
	=	
	≠	
	≠	
	≠	

Description Idea-Map

Topic:

Sequence Idea-Map

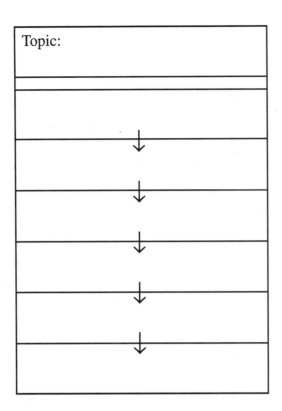

Problem–Solution Idea-Map

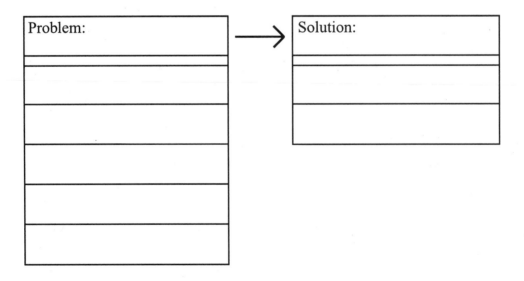

Cause–Effect Idea-Map

Cause:

→

Effect:

Probable Passages

Probable passages (Wood, 1984) is a strategy that is especially helpful for students using the text patterns cause-effect, compare-contrast, and problem-solution. Before students begin reading, identify the text structure. Then find words in the passage that are important for text comprehension. Write the words on the chalkboard under their text categories. An example using a problem-solution text follows:

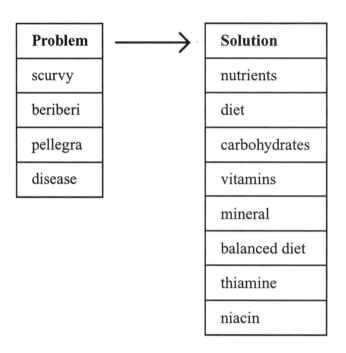

Problem	Solution
scurvy	nutrients
beriberi	diet
pellegra	carbohydrates
disease	vitamins
	mineral
	balanced diet
	thiamine
	niacin

Explain how the terms on the list are used and what problem and solution mean in this situation. Then ask the students to write a Probable Passage, or a passage that makes sense, that contains the text structure and the identified words. After students have completed their Probable Passage, ask them to read the original text. Finally, they should edit their own passage to reflect missing or contradictory information they learned from the passage.

5.9 Processing Text

Behavior Observed	The student does not process text after reading.
Anticipated Outcome	The student will use text-processing strategies to enhance comprehension.

Perspective and Strategies

In order for students to have a rich comprehension of text, they need to process the information in the text in an elaborative fashion. After students have finished reading, they need to think about the text, talk about the text, manipulate the ideas, and make connections to their existing knowledge. As they work with the text, students can continue learning more about the story or passage and improve their comprehension.

This section contains several strategies that can help students process text after reading. Try several of them to find which ones work for you. They include:

■ Herringbone

■ Retelling

■ Story Pyramid

■ Summarizing

■ Venn Diagrams

■ Discussion Web

■ Using Multiple Intelligences

Herringbone

The Herringbone strategy helps students organize information, especially that from expository or narrative selections. The Herringbone shape is presented on the chalkboard, an overhead projector, or copies may be made for each student. After reading a selection, students are instructed to find the answers to the questions on the Herringbone form. Students may then record them on clean forms or make their own Herringbone and answer the questions. Modeling this strategy on an overhead or the chalkboard first is advised. For a modification of this strategy, students can fill out the Herringbone questions as they read. The Herringbone shape and questions look like this:

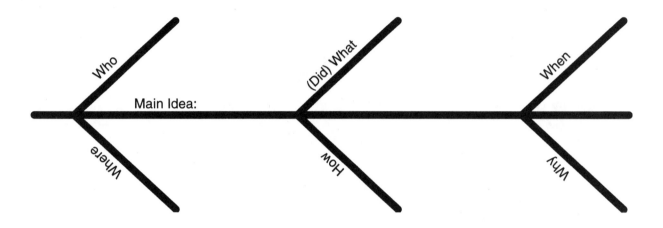

A blank copy of the Herringbone is provided on the next page. Copy and use it to help your students organize information from expository or narrative text.

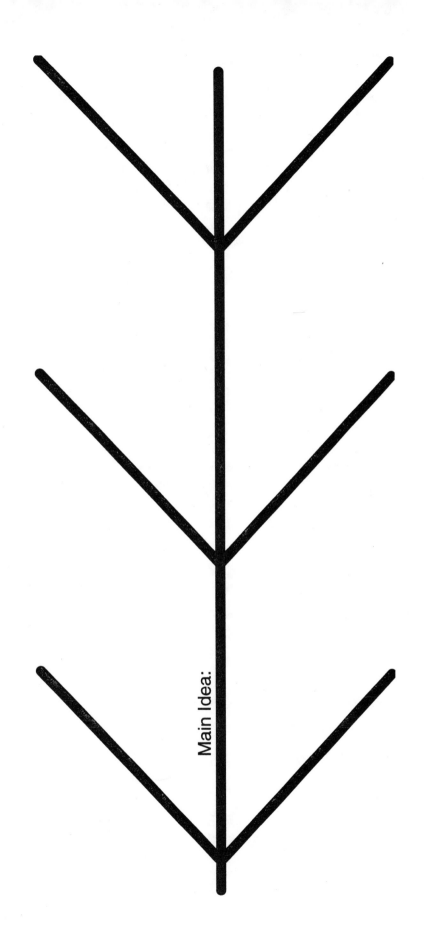

Main Idea:

Retelling

Retelling is a strategy to help students summarize, organize, and recognize elements in all types of printed materials. However, retellings are generally applied to literature selections and often used in the lower grades. Students having difficulty in reading can be helped to remember story sequence and character elements in the story by using words such as *first, next, last, then,* and *finally.* Although retellings can be written, they are most often thought of as an oral activity.

Refer to the following procedures and guidelines for helpful suggestions for retelling narrative and expository text. Additional retelling suggestions can be found in Johns (1997).

Retelling Procedure for Narrative Passages

1. Ask the student to retell the passage by saying, "Tell me about (name or title of passage) as if you were telling it to someone who has never heard it before."

2. Use the following prompts only when necessary:

   ■ What comes next?

   ■ Then what happened?

   If the student stops retelling and does not continue with the prompts, ask a question about the passage that is based on that point in the passage at which the student has paused. For example, "What did the boys do after raking the leaves?"

3. When a student is unable to retell the story, or if the retelling lacks sequence and detail, prompt the retelling step by step. The following questions may help you:

   ■ Who was the passage about?

   ■ When did the story happen?

   ■ Where did the story happen?

   ■ What was the main character's problem?

   ■ How did he (or she) try to solve the problem? What was done first/next?

   ■ How was the problem solved?

   ■ How did the story end?

Retelling Expectations for Expository Passages

Independent level retelling will generally reflect:

■ the text structure

■ organization of how the material was presented

■ main ideas and details contained in the text

Instructional level retelling will generally reflect:

■ less content than at the independent level

■ some minor misrepresentations and inaccuracies

■ organization that differs from the actual text

Frustration level retelling will generally be:

- haphazard
- incomplete
- characterized by bits of information not related logically or sequentially

Story Pyramid

Brenda Waldo

This activity can help students reflect on and organize their responses to literature. Students think of words that describe characters, setting, and events from a selection that has been read. Although it can be adapted to most groups, younger students and beginning readers may need extra help or additional modeling from the teacher to complete the story pyramid. The story pyramid and directions follow.

1 _____

2 _____ _____

3 _____ _____ _____

4 _____ _____ _____ _____

5 _____ _____ _____ _____ _____

Directions

1. Insert 1 word that names a character.
2. Insert 2 words that describe the setting.
3. Insert 3 words that describe a character.
4. Insert 4 words in a sentence that describe one event.
5. Insert 5 words in a sentence that describe another event.

You can also adapt the story pyramid by adding more lines such as the resolution or conclusion.

Summarizing

Summarizing is a postreading strategy that increases understanding and fosters memory of text and literature selections. Summaries can be simple or sophisticated, written or oral. Encouraging students to remember using words like *first, then, next,* and *last* can help the students organize what they remember in order to summarize.

Stanfill (1978) helps students organize good summaries by having them state the thing being summarized, telling what it begins with, what's in the middle, and what it ends with. This procedure is called the one-sentence summary. Teachers need to model how to write good summaries before students can be expected to correctly use this strategy. Chapter 8 contains additional information on summary writing.

Venn Diagram

The Venn diagram is used to compare and contrast information (for example, characters, settings, themes of two stories, or types of government) and can be used with most types of literature selections and text at all levels. The teacher models this strategy using class input to determine what is the same about two things and also what is unique to each of the two things. Two overlapping circles are drawn; characteristics that are shared by the two things are written on the shared area. On each of the circle areas outside the shared space, characteristics that are unique to each item are recorded. After sufficient modeling, students should be able to complete Venn diagrams on their own or in small groups. A Venn diagram comparing and contrasting trees might look like this:

Trees

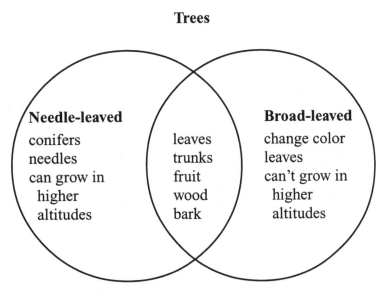

It is possible and more complex to compare three things by having a triple Venn Diagram. Students must find those attributes that one thing has, that two things share, and that three things share. A triple Venn is drawn like this:

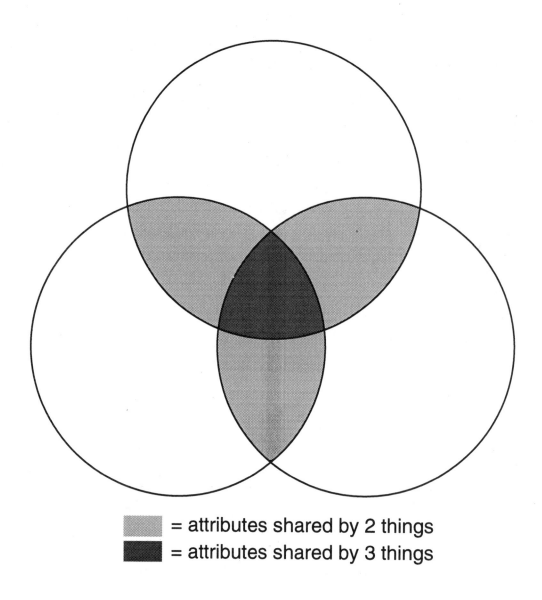

= attributes shared by 2 things
= attributes shared by 3 things

You may copy the accompanying blank Venn diagrams to use with your students.

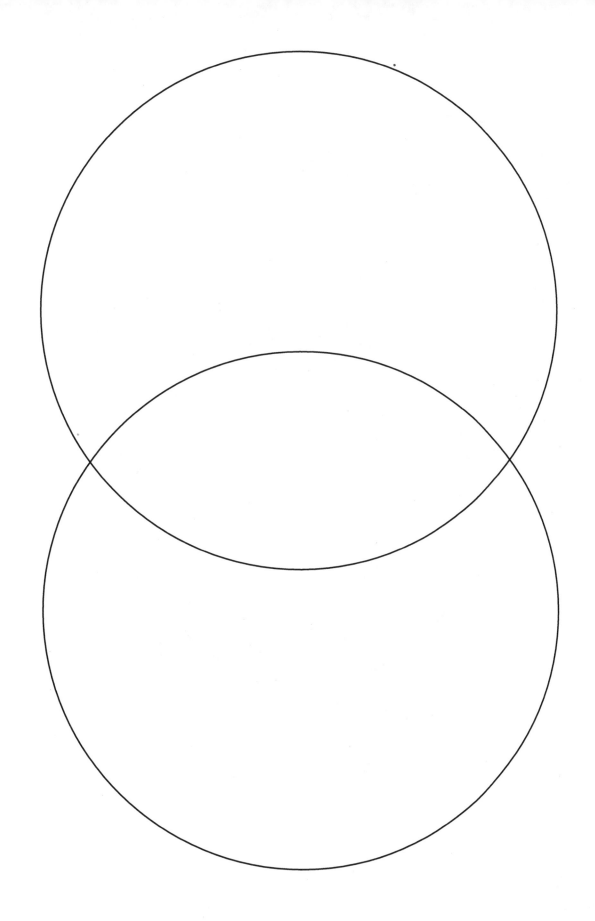

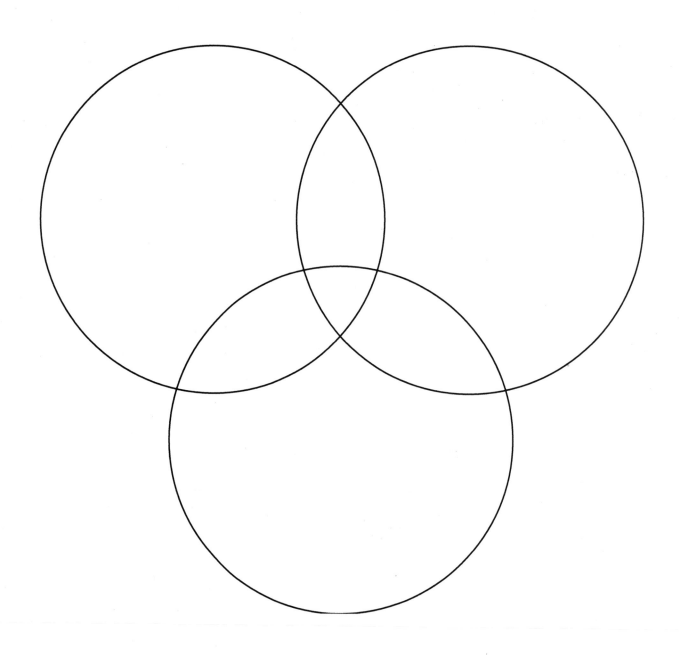

Discussion Web

A Discussion Web (Alvermann, 1991) is a strategy that can be used to help students process text deeply after they have read a passage by asking them to think of two sides to a question. Begin by thinking of a question that could have answers that could be supported from the text both with the answer of "yes" and with the answer of "no." Write the question in the box in the center of the Discussion Web. Then ask students either alone or in small groups to generate reasons that would support the answer of "yes" and also the answer "no." After they have competed the Discussion Web, discuss their answers as a whole group. Finally, ask each individual student to come to a conclusion and write the conclusion on the lines at the bottom of the Web.

An example for a Discussion Web (from Vacca & Vacca, 1996) for *Where the Red Fern Grows* (Rawls, 1961) follows:

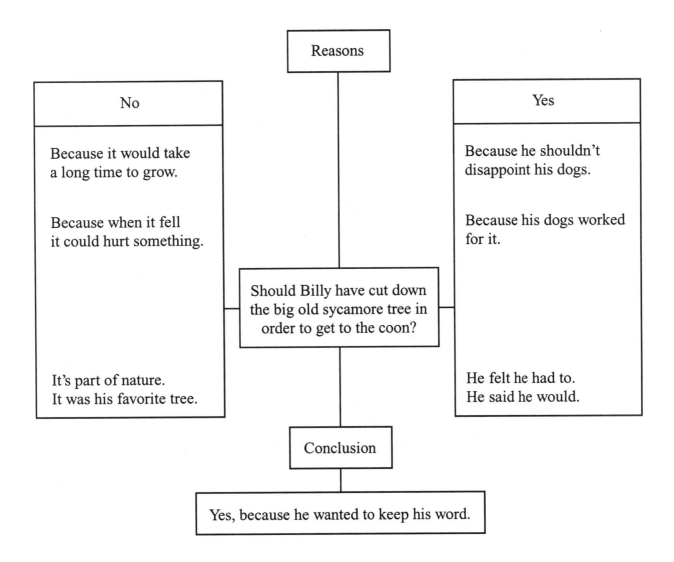

A sample of a blank Discussion Web is on next page.

Discussion Web

Donna Alvermann

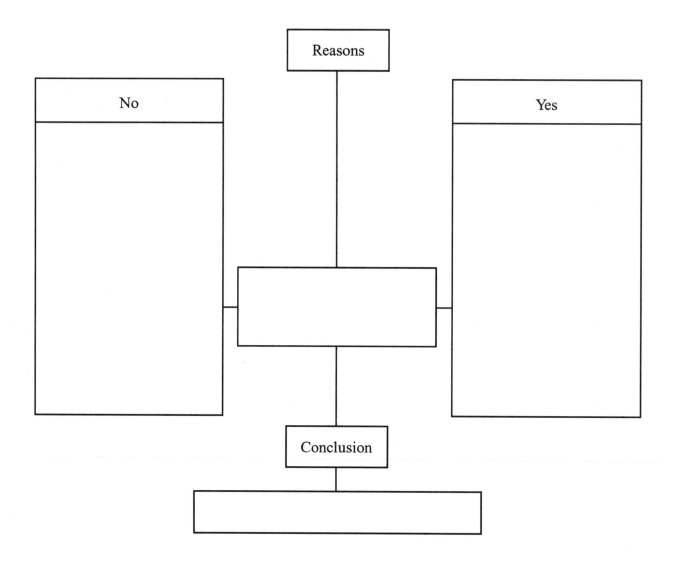

Using Multiple Intelligences

As you provide students with strategies to elaborate on text, you need to keep in mind that not all students think in the same ways. Each of us has preferred ways of thinking. Gardner (1993) has identified seven types of thinking which he calls intelligences. As you ask students to process text, try to give them a variety of options. You may have a strong verbal/linguistic intelligence and give assignments that fit that strength; your students may have other strengths. It is important, therefore, that you vary the types of activities you ask your students to accomplish. A general description for the intelligences follows (Eanes, 1997):

Learners with strong **verbal/linguistic** intelligence often:

- Enjoy reading, writing, and speaking.
- Enjoy research and report writing.
- Recall names, places, dates, and details.
- Prefer typing to writing.
- Like books, periodicals, and recording.
- Enjoy storytelling and oral reading to share stories.
- Enjoy creative writing, poetry, and joke telling.

Learners with strong **logical/mathematical** intelligence often:

- Have good problem-solving and reasoning skills.
- Like to formulate and answer logical questions.
- Enjoy sorting, categorizing, and classifying.
- Like to explore and analyze.
- Like puzzles, mysteries, and riddles.
- Like technology.
- Are strong in math.

Learners with strong **visual/spatial** intelligence often:

- Need visuals to understand new concepts.
- Use a great deal of mental imagery.
- Like to make and read maps, charts, and diagrams.
- Enjoy mazes and puzzles.
- Have a strong imagination.
- Are good at designing, drawing, creating, and constructing.
- Enjoy videos, photographs, slides, and multimedia.
- Enjoy giving media presentations.

Learners with strong **body/kinesthetic** intelligence often:

■ Are good at physical activities.

■ Like to move around.

■ Like to touch things.

■ Use lots of gestures for communicating.

■ Enjoy hands-on learning.

■ Like to communicate through drama, dance, and movement.

Learners with strong **musical/rhythmic** intelligence often:

■ Enjoy listening and responding to music.

■ Recall melodies easily.

■ Notice things like pitch and rhythm.

■ Are highly aware of sounds in the environment.

■ Are fascinated by computerized sound systems.

■ Learn better while listening to certain types of music.

■ Love stories about music.

Learners with strong **interpersonal** intelligence often:

■ Have strong leadership skills.

■ Are very sociable and have good interpersonal skills.

■ Are good at organizing people.

■ Are good communicators.

■ Are good mediators and listeners.

■ Solve problems by talking through them.

■ Like discussion.

■ Enjoy interviewing and debating.

■ Learn best by talking to others.

■ Enjoy cooperative learning.

Learners with strong **intrapersonal** intelligence often:

- Have a strong sense of self.
- Are very self-confident.
- Prefer working alone.
- Have good instincts about strengths and abilities.
- Pursue interests, dreams, and goals.
- Seek help to pursue or achieve goals.
- Like independent research projects.
- Like cumulative writing projects.
- Like to sit quietly.

Elaborative Strategies Using the Multiple Intelligences

As you prepare reading instruction for your students, try to provide a variety of strategies that will appeal to students who have different strengths. You might want to vary your assignments over several weeks, or give students a choice of assignments. The following ideas would be appropriate for each of the seven different intelligences.

Verbal/Linguistic Intelligence

1. Tell or retell the story.
2. Respond to the story by drawing or writing.
3. Read related stories.
4. Write a story to go with a wordless picture book.
5. Model a new story on the one just read.
6. Create a comparison/contrast chart with another story by the same author.
7. Write a script for Readers' Theater.

Logical/Mathematical Intelligence

1. Sort objects related to the story.
2. Measure or graph distances related to the story.
3. Make a matrix using the characters in the story.
4. Create a map showing the setting.
5. Discuss the character's motivations and decide whether they are reasonable.
6. Plan an itinerary for places a character visited.

Visual/Spatial Intelligence

1. Visualize your favorite part of the story, and draw it.
2. Design a cover for the book.
3. Recreate several illustrations.
4. Make a newspaper, magazine, or video ad for the story.
5. Imagine you are part of the plot and draw an image that portrays how you are feeling.

Body/Kinesthetic Intelligence

1. Role play the story.
2. Create a puppet show for the story.
3. Have a special day relating to the book. Dress like the characters.
4. Act out a sequence of events from the plot.
5. Invent a game from the story.

Musical/Rhythmic Intelligence

1. Write a jingle or rap having to do with something in the story.

2. During a shared reading, create actions to fit the plot.

3. Sing a song related to the story, and add verses that fit the plot.

4. Put words relating to the story to an existing tune.

5. March in a parade singing a song related to the story.

Interpersonal Intelligence

1. In groups, design something relating to a character in the story.

2. Work with a partner and write a different version of the story.

3. In literature groups, discuss the plot, setting, character, and problem for the story.

4. Discuss the problem of the story and decide in groups how to solve the problem in ways the character did not use.

5. Discuss a character in the story and try to convince group members that they would or would not be a good friend to have.

Intrapersonal Intelligence

1. Have students write down all they want to know about the topic relating to the story.

2. Designate a day for students to wear or bring something related to the story.

3. Ask students to tell about something similar that happened to them.

4. Write about how students would feel and what they would do if they were a character in the story.

5. Ask students to write their memories of an event from the story as a diary entry.

CHAPTER 6

Developing Strategic Readers

Overview

As teachers, we want our students to become self-directed readers. Our goal is for students to be able to apply reading strategies independently in all of the various reading situations in which they find themselves. To become a strategic reader, students must be able to plan, monitor, analyze, and regulate their reading (Paris, Lipson, & Wixson, 1983). They need to know which strategies to use in a reading situation, how to activate their background knowledge to increase comprehension, how to set purposes for reading, how to vary their reading rate, and how to monitor their comprehension while reading. Our role as teachers is to instruct students, both directly and indirectly, about which strategies are appropriate for a reading task, how to use the strategy, and how to determine the effectiveness of the strategy.

Teachers whose goal is to teach strategic reading should think in terms of the entire reading process: preparing to read, constructing meaning while reading, and reflecting after reading (Paris, Wasik, & Turner, 1991). When teaching prereading strategies, teachers should help students activate their background knowledge and set purposes for reading. During reading, teachers need to assist students in monitoring their comprehension and in drawing inferences about the meaning of the text. After reading, teachers should instruct students in ways to reflect on their reading about both the meaning of the passage and how they felt about what the author had to say.

Ultimately, however, students should become responsible for their own understanding of text by using a variety of metacognitive strategies. The role of the teacher, then, is to provide instruction in strategic reading and to monitor their teaching of strategies. As students become adept at applying strategies, teachers need to gradually step back and let their students make decisions about how to apply the reading strategies they have taught.

Strategic readers share two important characteristics: They are independent readers, and they find reading entertaining and satisfying (Paris, 1987). In Chapter 1 of this book, we offered ideas and strategies to help students become more favorably disposed to reading so they receive joy and satisfaction from text. We also offered ideas to help students become independent readers in other parts of this book.

In our work with students experiencing difficulty in reading, it has become quite clear that many students are not strategy users. They do not possess important knowledge about reading. Three types of knowledge are important: declarative, procedural, and conditional (Paris, Lipson, & Wixson, 1983).

Declarative knowledge can be thought of as factual knowledge that deals with what is involved in reading. Students, for example, may know that meaning is critical in reading. They may also know that novels and textbooks are organized in different ways. Other kinds of declarative knowledge include realizing that phonics and context can be used to help identify unknown words, that the main idea is the most important idea, and that different kinds of reading rates (study, skim, scan, pleasure) can be used to achieve different purposes.

Procedural knowledge is knowing *how* to approach and carry out a wide variety of reading tasks. Such knowledge can be gained from experience or instruction. Students who have procedural knowledge may know how to use context to help determine the meaning of an unknown word. They may have the ability to find or infer the main idea of a passage. They may also be able to sound out a word to arrive at its pronunciation or to use prefixes, suffixes, and root (or base) words to pronounce a long word.

Conditional knowledge is knowing *why* a particular strategy works and/or when to use it (or when to abandon one strategy and move to another). One example is students who know that rereading may be necessary when they are not understanding and how to use this strategy when appropriate. Another example is a student who tries to use context to determine the meaning of an unknown word only to discover that the surrounding context is not helpful. The student then decides to use a dictionary, because the word's meaning is judged to be important for understanding. This student is exhibiting metacognition.

Metacognition refers to the knowledge and control students have over their reading and learning activities (Baker & Brown, 1984; Royer, Cisero, & Carlo, 1993). The student who tried to use context but was unsuccessful was able to abandon the strategy and move to the dictionary. The student recognized that context was not working and knew what to do about it. Garner (1987) has reported that many young readers and students who have difficulty with reading perceive reading as decoding, not seeking meaning. For example, Max, a poor reader, was asked, "What is reading?" He responded, "It's a bunch of words. If you don't know them, sound them out." Students experiencing difficulty in reading may not know when they are not understanding what they are reading. Even if they possess declarative and procedural knowledge, they are often unable to put their knowledge into action. They lack resourcefulness and the ability to monitor their reading. Some key features of strategy instruction are presented here (adapted from Winograd & Hare, 1988).

Key Features of Strategy Instruction

1. Define the strategy, describe its critical features, label it, and make it sensible for students.

2. Explain why the strategy should be learned and the major advantages of using it.

3. Demonstrate how to use the strategy by modeling, thinking aloud, and other techniques so students can understand what is involved.

4. Explain the circumstances under which different strategies should be used so students understand the flexible and selective use of strategies.

5. Help students evaluate whether a particular strategy was useful.

6. Provide students with ample opportunities to use strategies, reinforce their efforts, and give plenty of encouragement. Responsibility for strategy use ultimately needs to be assumed by students and become spontaneous.

6.1   The Concept of Monitoring Reading

Behavior Observed	The student does not know what it means to monitor his or her reading.
Anticipated Outcome	The student will begin to grasp the concept of monitoring reading.

Background

Monitoring reading involves the concepts of strategic reading and metacomprehension. Both concepts are complex; therefore, the ideas we present are concrete and visual in an effort to help students begin to grasp the concept of monitoring. You should feel free to adapt the ideas and substitute actual examples from students or from your experiences to make the concept clear and relevant. Remember to keep your students' maturity in mind.

Teaching Strategy 1

1. Tell students that you are a good reader and that good readers still experience difficulty in reading. If possible, select an actual example from your own reading that represents a genuine instance of monitoring. You may also want to begin developing a file of such ideas to help with appropriate strategy lessons.

2. Share areas in which you have had difficulty, such as failing to understand a text or mispronouncing a word. Invite students to share difficulties they have experienced during reading, and write their ideas on the chalkboard.

3. Encourage discussion of the ideas presented and help students realize that:

   ■ All readers (not just poor readers) experience difficulty in reading.

   ■ Better readers keep watch over their reading to make sure they are understanding.

   ■ Readers fix up their reading to ensure understanding.

4. Ask students to share some of the things they do to keep watch over their reading. Encourage specific examples and discussion. Then share an example from your own reading. You could also use the following example. The actual words in the newspaper article are in italics.

5. Print *Lewis slows up; so do admirers* on the chalkboard and say something like the following: "I read the title to the newspaper article you see and then began reading the article. *Carl Lewis appeared Friday at the Olympic Village, nearly starting a riot in the food court. He was reading his messages on a computer when a mob of 100 athletes and passersby surrounded him for autographs and photos.* As I finished that part of the article, I thought there were quite a few people around Carl Lewis. The headline had said that admirers had slowed up because Carl Lewis had slowed up. Although I was a bit confused because of all the people around Lewis, I continued reading. *"Carl, Carl," the controlled mob screamed, following Lewis out the double doors of the Olympic Village.* At this point I was quite certain that the title and the article were not telling me the same thing. I decided to check over my

reading by going back to the title. As I reread the title, I saw my mistake; I had initially read *slows* instead of *shows*. When I read the headline correctly, the content of the article made sense. I was watching over my reading and realized that the title and the article did not seem to agree. I then decided to go back and read the title again. That's when I found my mistake. Now the article makes sense."

6. Take time to discuss this example with students and be sure they understand that rereading is one strategy that good readers sometimes use to overcome a difficulty in understanding. Use the items from number 2 and invite students to share what they have done to overcome or resolve their problems.

7. Remember that numerous lessons and modeling are needed to develop the concept of monitoring. One follow-up activity invites students to record their actual encounters with difficulties in reading. Such examples could be shared and discussed by volunteers in large or small groups to further develop the concept of monitoring.

Book or story	Name		
Page/Paragraph	**Problem I Had**	**What I Did**	**How It Worked**

Teaching Strategy 2 *(For Older Students)*

1. Write the word *monitor* on the chalkboard and ask students to share meanings and examples for the word.

2. Explore various definitions of *monitor* by using class dictionaries, an overhead transparency with the definitions, or by distributing the definitions. A thesaurus may also be useful. Have students verify their definitions with those you provide and add new definitions. Some definitions, like a computer monitor or hall monitor, may be common. Other definitions for monitor, like a lizard or a heavily ironclad warship, may broaden students' concept for the word.

3. Ask students to focus on what it might mean to monitor one's reading and identify appropriate words or phrases from the various definitions. Some examples might include:

   - keep track of
   - check
   - keep watch over
   - control
   - oversee
   - supervise

4. Invite students to share what actions they take to monitor their reading to ensure that they are understanding the text. Add appropriate examples from your own reading or the example used in Teaching Strategy 1.

5. Help students realize that a characteristic of good readers is that they monitor their reading. Many poor readers are under the mistaken notion that good readers always know the words, read fast, and never encounter difficulty in comprehension. Take time to list some of the more important actions students can take to monitor their reading. Specific items from the list could become the focus of future lessons.

6. Consider using a sheet similar to that in Teaching Strategy 1 (number 7) so students can begin to see concrete examples of how they monitor reading. These examples could also be used in future lessons and discussions.

Teaching Strategy 3

1. Use the notion of a "critter" to help get students thinking visually about the concepts of strategic reading and metacomprehension. Enlarge and present a critter on an overhead transparency (or draw one of your own):

The Critter

2. Tell students that similar critters were drawn by students who used the picture to help them remember that there is something in their heads to help them understand what they are reading. The term "inner voice" may be helpful to students.

3. Invite students to visualize a critter that they have in their heads to help them read. You may wish to give students time to draw and color their critters. You could also draw your critter on an overhead transparency or use the sample provided.

4. Use your critter to help develop important questions with the class. Some possible questions your critter asks to help your reading make sense could include:

   ■ Do I understand what I'm reading? If yes, great! If no, what should I do about it?

   ■ What do I already know about this topic?

   ■ How is this chapter organized?

   ■ How can I figure out this unknown word?

   ■ What is my purpose for reading?

   ■ Have I achieved my purpose for reading?

5. A single question could be the focus of one or more lessons to develop important ideas related to strategic reading. Have students add the questions and strategies to the sheet containing their critter. For example, if the answer to "Do I understand what I'm reading?" is "no," some possible actions could include:

   ■ I need to concentrate on what the author is trying to tell me and visualize the message.

   ■ I'll reread the last paragraph.

   ■ I'm tired so I'll take a short break.

   ■ I need to ask someone for help.

   ■ I think I need to look up the meaning of a word.

6. Remind students to use the important ideas their critters are telling them so they understand what they are reading. The important point is for students to take control of their reading and to monitor their comprehension. A critter may help provide a concrete, visual image toward that end.

Practice and Reinforcement Activities

1. Ask students to take out a book that they have just read and to think about the strategies they used as they read. To find out how aware students are of their reading strategies, you may want to interview them individually or reproduce the Reading Strategies Questions below and have students answer on separate sheets.

Reading Strategies Questions

Before I began reading, I _____.

When I get stuck on a word, I _____

_____.

When I don't understand what's happening, I _____

_____.

After I finish reading, I _____

_____.

2. After students have answered questions about their reading (above), ask them to read their answers and write goals for improving their monitoring. If they are not sure of the goals they could choose, use some of the suggestions from the following example, and write them on the chalkboard. Then ask students to discuss their reading goals in small groups and with you.

   Emily was a voracious reader of easy books but was not able to verbalize any strategies for understanding reading. Before she read a book, she looked at the title and began reading. You might suggest that Emily also do any of the following:

- look to see how hard or easy the book is
- read the book jacket
- preview the pictures or chapter titles
- make a prediction about the book
- look to see what genre the book is

Because Emily usually chooses easy books, she rarely comes to a word she doesn't know. When she does come to a word she doesn't know, Emily just skips it and reads ahead. You might suggest that Emily do any of the following:

- skip the word, read to the end of the sentence, then go back to the beginning and try again
- read ahead to connect the word with other ideas
- try to use word parts she knows
- substitute a word that makes sense
- use a picture clue
- reread and connect the word to the sense of the sentence
- ask someone what the word is
- look up the pronunciation of the word in a dictionary
- cross check by asking if it sounds right, if it makes sense, and if it looks right

Sometimes Emily does not have a high degree of comprehension when she reads. However, she normally continues reading without using any fix-up strategies. You might suggest that Emily:

- reread the confusing part
- use pictures or subheading to make sense of the text
- read ahead and try to connect the information
- use signal words in the text to understand

After reading, Emily usually writes the name of the book in her book log, but does little else to process the text. You might suggest that she:

- tell a friend about the book
- videotape a book talk
- read the book again
- look for a similar book
- write about the book in her journal
- write a letter to the author

6.2 Failure to Activate Background Knowledge

Behavior Observed	The student does not seem to activate background knowledge to create possible links between what is known and the information in the text.
Anticipated Outcome	The student will actively use his or her background knowledge before, during, and after reading.

Background

Background knowledge provides the storehouse of experiences that are the basis for meaning. It is important, therefore, that students use this knowledge before, during, and after reading. A number of related ideas may be found in Chapter 5.

Teaching Strategy

1. Get some file folders and ask students to share what they know about them. Help students realize that each file folder contains information about a topic or subject and that the file folders could be related to each other. For example, if you use portfolios in file folders, students would know that each student has a different file folder containing information about a particular student. Discuss how the information in a file folder can be used to help understand the student or topic.

2. Relate the concept of file folders to the way the human brain may hold information. Stress that the brain is efficient at "filing" large amounts of information in an organized fashion and that this information is vital if we are to understand what we are reading. The important point is to use this information before, during, and after reading.

3. Use an actual file folder or have students make one and write in the folder what they know about a particular topic. Choose a topic about which practically all students have knowledge. Some possible topics include a particular animal (dog or cat), an area in the community, a sport, a game, or a famous person.

4. Give students sufficient time to write what they know about the selected topic. Stress that words or phrases, not complete sentences, can be written. Charts and/or drawings may also be used.

5. Invite students to share their knowledge and create a master file folder on the chalkboard or an overhead transparency. As some students share, other students may say, "I knew that but I didn't write it down." These students can add the information to their file folders. Encourage all students to share their knowledge.

6. Ask students how the information in their file folders could be used if they were asked to read a story, chapter, or book about the topic. Lead students to understand that such knowledge can help them link what they already know about a topic to what they are reading. It can help them make predictions about what might be in a book or story. It can help them make

sense of and raise questions about what they are reading. And it can help them evaluate what they have read within the context of their existing knowledge.

7. To encourage students to use their background knowledge, have them pretend to take out their file folders prior to reading about a particular topic.

Practice and Reinforcement Activities

1. Invite students to use their background knowledge (file folders) to make predictions before reading. Remind them to use the title, pictures, chapter headings, and so on.

2. Use the K-W-L or SQ3R strategy described in Chapters 5 and 8, respectively.

3. Model the think-aloud strategy to show students how you use your background knowledge to make predictions about a selection to be read. For example: "The title of this story is 'All About Fish.' Because we are studying science, I think this is not really a story but a selection that will present some information and facts about fish. I know that fish [you give known knowledge] . . . and I wonder if this passage will talk about goldfish. I have two at home and [share knowledge]. . . . I wonder if the passage will talk about sharks. I really would like to know more about them." Use similar think alouds to help students learn how you link knowledge in your head with the passage while reading and after reading. Remind students to use a similar strategy while they read.

4. Develop lessons that model what you do when the information in your head is different from what you are reading or have read in the text. You may sometimes need to go back and reread to clarify something that does not match your existing knowledge. You may have to consider whether what you know is, in fact, accurate. You may also need to go to another source (person or text) for additional information that will help clarify the conflicting information. Try to provide actual examples from your experiences for each situation.

5. Help students come to understand some of the basic differences between narrative and expository texts. See section 8.1 for additional information and strategies. Use actual examples from students' reading and develop a list of characteristics. For example:

Narrative Texts	Expository Texts
setting	possible cause and effect relationships
characters	likenesses and differences between ideas
present, past, or future	description presenting attributes or explanations
actions or problems	ideas are related to each other by a common factor or factors
solutions	

6. Use a variety of cloze activities in which students can use their background knowledge to make reasonable predictions about the missing word(s). Help students come to understand that predictions are possible because of their background knowledge and that it is useful in reading. Discuss the various words predicted and their appropriateness. Some possible items to use include the following:

Jack and Jill _____.

Last _____, I went to the show.

Yesterday _____, I went to the show.

The _____ had nearly finished building the house.

The older person walked _____ to the car with a _____ in hand.

7. Based on the title of a book, chapter, or selection, have students brainstorm possible words that might be encountered. Discuss the reasons behind certain choices that may appear strange.

8. Use anticipation guides (see the sample entitled "Chomping Champs" on the following page) to get students more actively involved in reading by using their background knowledge. Begin by identifying the major concepts presented in the selection. Then create a series of statements to challenge or support students' beliefs. Present the statements to students on an individual sheet, the chalkboard, or an overhead transparency. Students should work independently and then discuss their reactions to the statements (drawing on their background knowledge). Following active discussion, students read the selection silently to verify or change their initial predictions. Post-reading assessment (see "after you read" column on "Chomping Champs") and discussion provide students with an opportunity to clarify the accuracy of their predictions and to verify information. The anticipation guide on "Chomping Champs" is based on an article in the February 1982 issue of *Ranger Rick's Nature Magazine*. Another example of an anticipation guide for pyramids (along with the passage) is also included. This example may be appropriate for use with older students:

CHOMPING CHAMPS

Directions: The article you will be reading is about fuzzy little insects called dermestid (dur-MES-tid) beetles. Pretend you are one of these tiny beetles. Read the statements below and check the items you think are true about yourself. After reading the article go back and check those items that the author agrees with.

Before You Read   **After You Read**

❑ 1. I help museums save money by cleaning the bones of dead animals for their exhibits. ❑

❑ 2. My favorite food is raw flesh. ❑

❑ 3. I work for my room and board in museums all around the world. ❑

❑ 4. My house is made of metal. ❑

❑ 5. I can eat and eat and never get full. ❑

❑ 6. After 3 days of eating, I spin a cocoon and turn into a butterfly. ❑

❑ 7. Baby dermestid beetles are called dermies. ❑

Chomping Champs*

In a dark room in a museum lie the bodies of a monkey, a fox, a deer, and fifty bats. The skeletons of these animals soon will be used for studies and displays. But first the bones must be perfectly cleaned by a team of the museum's hardest workers.

These workers, fuzzy little insects called *dermestid* (dur-MES-tid) beetles, keep busy at their job nearly 24 hours a day. Dermestids are smaller than your thumbnail, but they have mighty appetites. They can scurry in and out of a skeleton's every nook and cranny—no matter how small—leaving no flesh on the bones. Just sixty larvae can make a small bird's bones spotless in only three days.

It would take loads of time and hard work for a person to do the same job by hand. By using hungry beetles, museums save money—and get spanking-clean skeletons.

Most of the eager eaters are the beetles' young, or *larvae*. They love to feast on dried flesh and almost anything else! That's why they always must be kept in boxes made of metal.

Scientists cut most of the extra meat off an animal's body, then let the remaining meat dry. As soon as they put the body into a beetle box, the chompers get busy. Adult females lay their eggs in the dried flesh right away providing a steady supply of food from the moment the larvae hatch. After stuffing themselves for many days, they burrow into a layer of cotton on the bottom of their box, change into adults, and come out ready to lay their own eggs. (Dermestids live only about a month.)

One museum put its beetles to work on elephants and whales. Even though it will take years, they know they can count on the chomping champs.

*Adapted from Fred Johnson

Reaction Guide for Pyramid Article

Before you read the article on pyramids, read each statement below. Depending on what you believe, circle true or false for each statement.

After you read the article, decide if the statement is true or false based on the article. Circle the word to the right of each statement.

Before Reading				**After Reading**	
True	False	1.	Some pyramids are located near Cairo.	True	False
True	False	2.	The pyramids are over 10,000 years old.	True	False
True	False	3.	The three pyramids of Giza are quite famous.	True	False
True	False	4.	The Great Pyramid is called Khafra.	True	False
True	False	5.	The Great Pyramid is made of granite and is the biggest stone building in the world.	True	False
True	False	6.	There are over 3 million blocks of stone in the Great Pyramid.	True	False
True	False	7.	The blocks of stone weigh between two-and-one-half and five tons each.	True	False
True	False	8.	The Great Pyramid is taller than the Leaning Tower of Piza.	True	False
True	False	9.	Mortar was used to hold the blocks of stone together.	True	False
True	False	10.	The sides of the pyramid face almost exactly north, south, east, and west.	True	False

Pyramids

The Ancient Egyptians built many pyramids, but the most famous of these are the three pyramids of Giza, near Cairo, the capital of Egypt. Over the years, the city has gradually crept closer. Now there are new houses almost at the feet of the pyramids. But if you look at the pyramids across the city, they still rise up, silent and mysterious, on the edge of the great desert. For more than four thousand years, they have stood there, barely changed by the passage of time.

The largest of the three pyramids was built by King Khufu or King Cheops, to use his Greek name. This is called the Great Pyramid. It was the first to be built at Giza, in about 2500 B.C. The second largest is only a few feet lower and was built by Khafre (or Chephren in Greek), the son of Khufu. The third pyramid in this group is much smaller, and was built by King Menkaure (or Mycerinus in Greek). All three pyramids were built in the space of about eighty years.

The Great Pyramid is made of limestone and is the same color as the sand and rock of the desert around it. There are no trees or other plants on this plain—just dry, open spaces. The pyramid soars to 137 meters above this—about as high as a forty-story modern skyscraper. A total of 2,300,000 blocks of stone, weighing between $2\frac{1}{2}$ and 5 tons each, were used to build the Great Pyramid. It is still the biggest stone building in the world. Assuming that the pyramid was completed within Khufu's twenty-three year reign, this means that some 100,000 of these huge blocks of stone had to be prepared and put into position each year—or 273 every day. The Great Pyramid was the most ambitious of the pharaoh's many great building works; in view of its huge size it is not surprising that is has been called "Pharaoh's Mountain."

Enormous though this monument is, the stone blocks are so accurately cut and so carefully fitted together (without mortar) that in many cases the joints will not allow even a sheet of paper to be inserted. The actual position of the Great Pyramid is also remarkably precise: its sides face almost exactly north, east, south and west. How was all this done? How could a people, who lived so long ago and who only had very simple tools, plan and carry out such a great project?

6.3   Lack of Clear Purpose(s) for Reading

Behavior Observed	The student appears to approach reading tasks without purposes or goals.
Anticipated Outcome	The student will develop purposes or goals to guide his or her reading.

Background

When students have a clear purpose for reading, comprehension is enhanced. The trouble is that many students' purposes for reading may be dominated by thinking such as "the teacher said to read this," "so I can answer the questions," or a surprising "I don't know." Although external purposes are a reality of classroom instruction, students should also learn how to set their own purposes for reading.

Recognizing that there are externally-imposed purposes for reading as well as internally-generated purposes in both school and life, two principles should guide your actions when asking students to read. First, be sure you set clear purposes and expectations for students when making reading assignments. Second, model how to read to fulfill purposes. Strategies such as taking notes, summarizing, outlining, answering questions, and mapping may need to be taught, preferably within the context of your lessons (see Chapters 5 and 8). Students may sometimes be able, with your help, to fuse your expectations with their purposes. The following ideas should help students develop purposes for reading. Keep in mind that students can have more than one purpose for reading even though we generally use the singular form.

Teaching Strategy

1. Choose one or more sports (for example, soccer and softball), and encourage students to share reasons why players participate in that sport. Students could write their responses individually or in groups. If groups are used, be sure someone serves as a recorder.

2. Invite students to share their ideas and write responses on the chalkboard. Some possible responses include:

for fun	to be with friends	to improve skills
to win	to stay fit	to be outside

3. Help students realize that players participate in sports for different reasons. Then make the connection to reading and suggest that there are different purposes for reading.

4. Have students share purposes for reading. It may be helpful to have them think of different types of reading material (books, stories, magazines, recipes, road signs, newspapers, television guide, and so on) when they are suggesting purposes.

5. Spend time discussing some of the advantages for setting purposes for reading. Be sure that students realize that reading can be done for different purposes and that their purpose should guide their reading.

6. Model a few situations in which you set a purpose, read, and then evaluate whether your purpose was achieved. Here is one example: "I want to find out which movies are playing in town. I'll use today's newspaper to help me. Let's see . . . from the index on the front page, I know that the movies are in section 2, page 6. Okay, I've found the page in that section, and I can see that the following movies are playing [read movies]. I think I might like to see _____ because I read a good review of it a few days ago. My purpose was to find out which movies were playing, and I was successful in achieving my purpose. I know I was successful because I found the movies." Other situations to model include:

- beginning a short story
- reading a textbook
- finding a TV show
- looking up a word
- using an encyclopedia
- reading a memo
- finding a telephone number
- browsing a newspaper
- reading a magazine

7. Encourage students to think aloud and model some of the purposes they have for reading. Be sure they also explain how they went about achieving their purpose and whether they were successful.

8. Transfer purpose setting to ongoing reading activities taking place in the classroom.

Practice and Reinforcement Activities

1. Use the K-W-L procedure described in Chapter 5.

2. Have students write down their purposes for reading and, if necessary, refer to their purposes while reading to see whether they are being achieved. After reading, students could determine the degree to which their purposes were achieved by reflecting on these questions:

- What were my purposes for reading?
- Did I achieve my purposes?
- How do I know whether I was successful?

3. Develop class purposes for reading and return to the purposes after reading to evaluate success in light of the purposes.

4. Use the Directed Reading-Thinking Activity described in Chapter 5 and SQ3R described in Chapter 8.

6.4   Inflexible Rate of Reading

Behavior Observed	The student appears to read everything at the same rate.
Anticipated Outcome	The student will vary reading rate to match his or her purpose.

Background

Strategic readers have a flexible silent reading rate that is determined by their purposes. Some ideas and strategies related to setting purposes for reading were presented in section 6.3. Now, we focus on ways to help students become more strategic in selecting a reading rate that is commensurate with their purpose.

Rate of reading is better thought of as rate of comprehension to achieve the reader's purposes. It does little good to consider rate apart from comprehension; moreover, comprehension may suffer when rate is too fast or too slow. For many students experiencing difficulty in reading, lack of automaticity in identifying words may require so much of students' attention that meaning suffers. One teacher observed that it takes Jada so long to decode that she forgets what the beginning of the sentence is about by the time she gets to the end. Jada may be preoccupied with decoding. Another student is excellent at decoding but does not have the slightest idea what the passage is about. This student is a word caller. Between these two extremes are students who seldom practice flexibility in reading—quite possibly because it was never an instructional focus.

Strategic readers know that there are several factors that help determine the rate at which they read, and they know how to take these factors into account while they are reading. The major factors include:

➤ purpose

➤ type of material

➤ familiarity with content and/or background knowledge

➤ motivation and/or mood (for example, preparing for a test, relaxing with a novel)

➤ reading environment (for example, light quality, presence or absence of distractions)

➤ size of type, amount of figures, illustrations, and so on

These factors influence each of the major kinds of reading such as study-type reading, rapid reading (like skimming and scanning), and technical reading. Within each of these major types of reading, rate may sometimes be faster or slower. The important point to keep in mind is whether the readers' purposes are being achieved.

Teaching Strategy *(For Younger Students)*

1. Be sure students understand that meaning is what reading is all about. If needed, refer to section 2.1 for helpful strategies.

2. Ask students to name some of the reasons they read and to offer examples of that kind of reading. A chart similar to the following might be developed on the chalkboard.

What We Read	Why We Read
Clifford books	For fun
Our own stories	To read better
	To learn words
Lunch menu	To see what we will eat
Science book	To learn things

3. Use the chart to help students realize that they read for different purposes, especially for fun and to learn things.

4. Tell students that good readers know why they are reading something and that they should always know why they are reading a book or story. Refer to the chart as necessary, and use other examples as appropriate.

5. Then tell students that sometimes they will read faster and sometimes they will read slower. Help students develop a list of times when they might speed up or slow down, for example:

I speed up my reading when I

■ already know the story.

■ am reading the story I've already practiced.

■ understand the meaning of the story.

I slow down my reading when I

■ don't understand.

■ am mixed up.

6. Spend time helping students realize that good readers will reread if they are not understanding. They also stop reading and try to get help if they are not understanding.

7. Use subsequent lessons or instructional opportunities to foster a greater awareness and understanding that everything is not read at the same speed.

Teaching Strategy (For Older Students)

1. Begin by inviting each student to compile a list of the various kinds of reading accomplished within the last day or two and the purposes for reading. A chart like the following might be helpful.

Day	Time	What Was Read	Why It Was Read (Purpose)

2. After students have had sufficient time for individual reflection, have them form small groups to compare their answers. Ask them to identify both common and unique items. Each group can list common and unique items on an overhead transparency or the chalkboard.

3. Engage students in a total group activity in which volunteers can share overhead transparencies or write responses on the chalkboard.

4. After responses are shared, lead students in a discussion of the rate at which the reading occurred to fulfill the intended purpose(s). Help students realize that there is a connection between purpose and rate. For example, Roger may have used a television program guide to find out whether any TV movies were showing Tuesday evening at eight o'clock. He said it took him longer to find the guide than to find out the titles of the movies by scanning the guide. Ami not only located the movies in her guide but she read the brief blurbs about each of them. Actually, she didn't read the entire blurb for a movie once she decided that she wasn't interested. After her initial reading, she went back and reread one of the movie blurbs because she thought it might be worth watching.

5. Use the previous example or a similar one to help develop the notion of a flexible rate of reading that is governed by purpose. For example, both Roger and Ami scanned the guide to find specific information to fulfill their purpose for reading. Once the information was found, Roger and Ami read. Roger read the movie titles; Ami read the titles, blurbs, and even reread one of the blurbs. Each student's reading was successful because their purposes were achieved.

Practice and Reinforcement Activities

1. Give students a newspaper article and develop a purpose for reading the article (to find who, what, when, where, or why). Have students read at a rate that is comfortable to fulfill purposes. After reading, determine whether those purposes were achieved. Invite individual students to share insights about their reading. Possible examples include:

   "I just skimmed to find each of the answers."

   "I reread the questions so I'd know what to read for."

   "I only had trouble remembering the answer to one of the questions so I scanned the article for that specific information. Then I reread that sentence."

2. Use a selection from one of your classroom texts and model how you set purposes for reading and read flexibly to achieve those purposes.

3. Secure classroom quantities of various reading materials (telephone books, driver's license study manuals, product information sheets, maps, and so on). Identify some of the major purposes for reading each type of material and how the material might be read to fulfill particular purposes. Then have students use the material to fulfill one or more of the purposes and share how the material was read.

4. Have students share their anticipated rate of reading prior to reading one of the materials mentioned in activity 3. Then have the students think aloud to share what they will do. For example, "I want to know the phone number for Sports of All Sorts. I'll look toward the back of the phone book and find the *s*. Then I'll use my knowledge of guide words to find the right page. I'm not really very good at using guide words, so I'd better take my time. I'll look on that page until I find the entry and phone number. If I can't find it, I might try the Yellow Pages under sports or sporting." Then have a student actually perform the task and think aloud. Use this general procedure with other types of reading materials.

5. Give students opportunities to write down some of their insights about reading rate. For example, the following chart might be developed:

I can usually speed up my reading when

- it is easy and I'm understanding.
- I already know a lot about the topic.
- the book is repeating what was said before.
- the information is not related to my purpose.

I should usually slow down my reading when

- the information is related to my purpose.
- the book has ideas that I'm interested in.
- I'm confused.
- the writing is complicated.

6. Timed silent reading exercises with comprehension questions may give students opportunities to see whether they are able to comprehend information at a faster rate. After scoring the comprehension questions, have students reinspect the text to find the correct answer or the information that formed the basis for the inference or conclusion that they drew.

7. Remember to keep the emphasis of your instruction on various rates of reading linked to purpose. Helping students practice flexibility in their reading is the key.

6.5   Lack of Comprehension Monitoring

Behavior Observed	The student does not appear to actively monitor his or her comprehension.
Anticipated Outcome	The student will use appropriate strategies to monitor comprehension.

Background

"Frankly, the naiveté of even 10- and 12-year-olds often astonishes teachers when they teach students such simple tactics as thinking about the title and topic before reading, declaring reading goals, stopping periodically to paraphrase the text, checking to see if new information makes sense, and skimming or rereading as a review technique" (Paris & Oka, 1986, p. 31). To help students become strategic readers, it soon becomes clear that, as strategic teachers, we must make some changes in our approach to teaching. First, we do not automatically assume that students know a lot about strategic reading. Disallowing that assumption, we focus some of our initial efforts on important foundations for strategic reading. Some of the important foundations have already been developed in this chapter as well as in other parts of this book (for example, section 2.1). In addition, Maria and Hathaway (1993) offer a useful way to help us develop greater self-awareness of our thinking before, during, and after reading.

Second, our teaching becomes more intentional. We often begin by modeling a particular strategy. That is followed by guided practice and feedback to students. Group discussion (both large and small) helps students see how others have responded to the task and gives a greater opportunity for ownership. A cooperative attitude is fostered among everyone in the class.

Third, our teaching takes on some of the characteristics of a coach who responds to student confusion with advice about how to think strategically. Our support gradually fades as responsibility shifts more and more to the student. Questions also take on a different flavor within the context of strategy lessons and the ongoing instructional program, for example:

- What is the strategy?

- When should you use it?

- Why is it useful?

- When might it be inappropriate?

- How did you use it in your recent reading?

- How well did it work? Why?

Fourth, we help students learn to use the strategies to aid reading comprehension in such a manner that the students become convinced about the value of using the strategies long after the lesson has ended. In short, we want students to know how and when to use strategies and then choose to use them because they perceive themselves as independent problem solvers. Ultimate ownership and responsibility for strategic reading becomes an integral part of the student's reading repertoire.

Following are some strategies that students can use as they read to help monitor their comprehension. We elected to use a number of think alouds to give you a better idea of how you can model the strategies with your students.

Teaching Strategy 1 (*Using Text Structure, Titles, and Predictions*)

1. Invite students to take out a library book and one of their content area texts.

2. Talk about the similarities and differences between the content in the two types of books. Refer, if necessary, to some of the basic differences between narrative and expository texts presented in sections 6.2 and 7.1. You may want to use a Venn diagram (see Chapter 5).

3. Ask students how knowing about some of these differences might help them in their reading. After discussion, tell students that the strategy is called text structure (or textbooks and other books) and that such knowledge will give some ideas about how the information is presented or organized.

4. Model how you use text structure by using their books. For example, "I'm going to show you how knowing about different books can help me use the title to make predictions so I will be a better reader. Here's a book called *The Egypt Game* (Snyder, 1967). I can tell—just from the picture and title on the cover—that this book is probably going to be a story about some children who dress up like Egyptians. It will have several characters and it looks like it takes place in a neighborhood. In stories like this, the main characters often run into some problems and try to solve them."

    "Here's another book, *Mummies, Tombs, and Treasure: Secrets of Ancient Egypt* (Perl, 1987). It doesn't look like a story; the word *ancient* in the title makes me think that I will be learning information about Egypt of long ago. From the title, I predict that the information will be about mummies, tombs, and treasures. If there are characters, they will probably be real. This book may be organized like my social studies book."

5. Discuss characteristics of text structure and write them on the chalkboard. Then invite some student volunteers, using their books, to model your behavior. They may already be reading the book so they could have considerable previous knowledge. Coach the students as necessary.

6. Use two new books (one narrative and one expository) that students are unlikely to have seen before, and ask for a volunteer to model the process of using the title and cover to make predictions. Guide the student as appropriate.

7. Gather and share different types of reading materials (for example, encyclopedia, dictionary, poetry, comics, newspaper, magazine, bus schedule, lunch menu, student handbook) so students can begin to see that they are structured in different ways. Students should note that a book's structure, the title, and illustrations can help students quickly form a mental set for what the reading task is likely to entail and how the content is probably going to be organized.

8. Use these strategies in class assignments and evaluate the degree to which they were useful.

9. Encourage students to share personal notes with you in which they describe their strategy use and its usefulness. Particularly helpful descriptions could be shared with the entire class if the student who wrote the note agrees.

Teaching Strategy 2
(Purpose Setting, Background Knowledge, and Previewing)

1. Refer, if necessary, to sections 6.2 and 6.3 for information about activating background knowledge and setting purposes for reading.

2. If possible, secure a narrative and expository book on the same general topic (like *The Egypt Game* and *Mummies, Tombs, and Treasure*) to model setting purposes, activating background knowledge, and previewing.

3. Tell students which strategies you will be modeling and how they can help the students become better readers. For example, "I always have a purpose when I read. It helps me focus my attention, and I know why I'm reading. While reading, I can ask myself whether my purpose is being achieved. I also try to ask myself what I already know about the topic. Some of what I know will probably help me understand. I may also be able to link what I already know to what I'm reading. Before actually reading, I often preview the book or selection. That helps me see how the book is organized and how long the reading may take me."

4. Model a preview for a narrative book (for example, *The Egypt Game*). "The teacher said I have to read a book for sharing with my literature circle, so I guess that's my major purpose for reading. Of course, I did have lots of books to choose from, and I chose *The Egypt Game* because the title sounded interesting. I suppose I want to know what this Egypt game is. I can see that I have at least two purposes for reading, and I'll probably have more once I start reading the book. I've got to keep in mind that I'll be sharing the book in a literature circle and so I need to learn about the characters and have a good idea about the major events that happened in the book. I don't really know much about Egypt, but I do know how books like this are organized [describe]."

   "Now, I'll preview the book. Wow! It's more than 200 pages long, so reading it will take me some time. I can see from the contents page in the front of the book that there are quite a few chapters, and the chapters are about 10 pages long. Perhaps I'll read a chapter or two at a time. The first chapter is called 'The Discovery of Egypt.' From the illustration on the cover of the book, I don't think the characters will discover the real country of Egypt. I think they may discover something that will eventually lead to the Egypt game. I'd better get started reading."

5. Encourage students to react to your think aloud by writing the words *setting purposes, using background,* and *previewing* to form column heads across the chalkboard. Have students recall what you did and write key words or phrases in the appropriate column. Ask students to share some of their relevant experiences and add them to the list within each column. Remember to ask questions such as, "Why is that useful?" and "How does that help you become a better reader?"

6. Model a preview for an expository selection (for example, *Mummies, Tombs, and Treasures*). "I'm choosing this book because I want to know about some of the secrets of ancient Egypt. That's part of the title, and I want to know more so that's my main purpose. I know some things about mummies and tombs [describe]. As I page through the book, I see a lot of interesting illustrations and photographs. On page 40 is a real photograph of a mummy without the cloth wrappings. Under the photograph, it says that the mummy's face and shoulders are packed with sawdust. The eyes are painted stone. I'll certainly want to know more about why and how those things were done. It sure sounds strange to me. The contents page shows seven chapters. I can see from the chapter titles that the book is mostly about mummies."

7. Elicit responses from students using a procedure similar to the one in step 5, and encourage students to relate their experiences with expository materials.

8. Guide students in using these strategies in their classroom reading assignments. Invite students to confer with you to share their successes and problems using the strategies you have taught. When appropriate, offer advice, ask questions, and help solidify the strategies taught. Remember to give recognition for effort.

Teaching Strategy 3 (*Monitoring and Fix-ups*)

1. Tell students that good readers monitor their reading (refer to section 6.1 for background and strategies). Although each of the following strategies will be dealt with, you may want to use separate lessons for particular strategies so that they are fully developed:

   ■ Summarize

   ■ Identify confusions

   ■ Look back or reread confusing parts

   ■ Read ahead to possibly clarify confusions

   ■ Ask myself questions

   ■ Use *like a*

   Write the strategies on the chalkboard and explain each of them briefly. Encourage students to share specific instances from their reading when they might have used the strategies. Have students share why the strategy did or did not work. Most of the strategies are probably familiar except *like a* (Davey, 1983). In this strategy, the reader links part of the text with something from his or her background. For example, the student might say, "The mummy being described in the text is *like a* mummy I saw when I was at the museum last summer." The *like a* approach helps the student relate relevant background experiences to better comprehend the text.

2. Tell students that you are going to use some or all of these strategies as you read *The Saga of Shakespeare Pintlewood and the Great Silver Fountain Pen* (Lehman, 1990). Thanks to the kindness of the author and illustrator, the title page and two actual pages have been reproduced here in black and white. You may make copies or overhead transparencies for classroom use. The actual words in the story are in italic. You might want to audiotape or videotape yourself modeling the strategies and then use the tape for the lesson. It can be replayed to help make your major points.

3. Begin by reading the title and thinking aloud. "The title is *The Saga. . . .* Wait a minute; I don't know what *saga* means, but I'll read ahead to see if I get any help . . . *of Shakes-peare/ Shakespeare Pin-tle-wood/Pintlewood.* Let's see, I think this is a story about Shakespeare Pintlewood, so perhaps *saga* means "story." I could look it up in the dictionary, but I'll just read on for now. I can look it up later if I can't figure it out soon. I'll finish the title . . . *and the Great Silver Foun-tain/Fountain Pen.* I can see from the picture that there is an ant holding a pen. I guess that must be a fountain pen. It looks like a pen my dad has. It's not like the ball-point pen I use. My dad even has a bottle of ink he uses to fill the pen when it runs out of ink. From the title and picture, I think this is a story about an ant named Shakespeare Pintlewood who might use the pen. I know ants can't write, so this story is not real. I have heard the name Shakespeare before, but I don't know much else. Maybe my mom will know."

4. Give students an opportunity to identify and comment on the strategies you have used. If necessary, replay parts of the tape to help clarify the discussion. Note specific strategies on the chalkboard and take time to explain why you used a particular strategy. The chart on the chalkboard might look something like the following:

Summarize	Identify Confusions	Look Back; Reread	Read Ahead	Ask Questions	Use Like a
what is known based on the title and picture	*saga unknown some words*	*sentence with garage*	*when saga wasn't known*	*about saga about garage*	*fountain pen like Dad's*

5. Continue reading the title page (which lists the author and illustrator) and then move on to the text. *"Once upon a time there was an ant who made up stories for children.* I know from 'once upon a time' that this is not a true story. Another thing is that real ants do not make up stories. *His name was Shakespeare Pintlewood, but all the other ants called him Shakey for short.* I'm glad the ant has a nickname, because I have trouble saying his name. *Because he was very small, Shakey saw things the way little girls and boys do. To him people looked like giants and gar-āge doors.* . . . No, that's not right; I've never heard of gar-āge doors. Let me finish the sentence . . . *looked like castle gates, and so he was able to make up good stories.* Now, what kind of doors look like castle gates and begins with 'gar'? It has to be a big door because castle gates are big. At our house, we have a front door, but that isn't the word because front doesn't begin the same way as the word in the book. We also have a garage door and it begins the same way as the word in the book. I'll reread the sentence to see whether it makes sense [reread sentence]. Yes, the word makes sense. So far, I know this is a story about an ant named Shakey who was able to make up good stories for children. I think I'm understanding everything so far."

6. Refer students to the chart and discuss the reading. As they tell you appropriate behaviors from your think aloud, fill in the chart. Point out that all your thinking aloud actually happens very quickly when you are reading. This might also be a good time to refer students to the critter developed in section 6.2. It is your critter or inner voice that helps you monitor or keep track of your reading.

THE SAGA OF
Shakespeare Pintlewood

AND THE
GREAT SILVER FOUNTAIN PEN
by James H. Lehman
illustrated by Christopher Raschka

Once upon a time there was an ant who liked to make up stories for children. His name was Shakespeare Pintlewood, but all the other ants called him Shakey for short.

Because he was very small, Shakey saw things the way little girls and boys do. To him people looked like giants and garage doors looked like castle gates, and so he was able to make up good stories.

7. Develop subsequent lessons in which you expand and refine the strategies using materials being read by your students. Plenty of carefully guided opportunities are needed to make the strategies automatic. Ultimately, students need to value the strategies and use them independently. Some possible questions for students to ask themselves include the following:

Before Reading

- What are my purposes for reading?

- Why am I reading this?

- What will I be doing with the information?

- What do I already know about this topic?

- What do I think I will learn?

- What are my predictions?

- What reading strategies will I have to use to read this?

- How is this selection organized?

During Reading

- Am I meeting my purposes for reading this?

- Am I understanding what I am reading?

- Does my reading make sense?

- Do I have a clear picture in my head?

- Is this what I had expected?

- What parts are similar to or different from my predictions?

- What can I do to increase my understanding?

- Do I agree with the author?

After Reading

- Have I learned what I wanted to learn?

- Should I go back and reread portions of the selection for better understanding?

- What new information did I learn, and how does it fit with what I already know?

- Should I get another point of view? What else do I still need to know about this topic?

- How do I feel about what I read? Do I agree or disagree? Why? Do I like it or not? Why?

6.6   Preoccupation with Decoding

Behavior Observed	The student seems too occupied with decoding to devote sufficient attention to comprehension.
Anticipated Outcome	The student's decoding will become more automatic.

Perspective and Strategies

Some students view reading as a process of getting all the words correct. With all their attention devoted to word-perfect reading, the students fail to take many risks. Other students have not acquired a large sight vocabulary and must devote considerable attention to sounding out words. In either case, students are focusing so much attention on words that comprehension may suffer. The following strategies may be useful:

1. Be sure that the student has a concept of reading where meaning is the critical element. Some of the strategies and activities found in section 2.1 may be especially useful.

2. Excessive preoccupation or concern with decoding is often a sign that the student is being asked to read materials that are too difficult. Ensure that the student is given materials that are easy to read. A good guideline to use is that the student will make five or fewer mistakes (miscues) in each 100 words. That means that the student will know 19 out of every 20 words. It is not uncommon for students experiencing difficulty in reading to make 8 or more miscues in each 100 words. Less effort devoted to figuring out words means that the student will be able to devote more attention to comprehension.

3. Create language experience stories by having the student dictate to you. Record the student's words on paper and have the student read the story back to you. Talk about the story. Provide ample opportunities for the student to reread the story to gain confidence and fluency.

4. Using books without words (see Appendix A), have the student "read" the book silently. Then have the student read the story to you and tape the reading. Have the student listen to the reading and emphasize the fluency with which it was read. Write or type the story so the student can follow the words as he or she listens. Then have the student read along with the recording. Later, the student can practice reading the story to a partner, friend, or someone at home. The goal of this activity is to build fluency, automaticity, and confidence.

5. Continue to foster automaticity and confidence by using pattern books (see Appendix C). The structure of the books makes it quite easy to predict the words. With repeated readings, the student has an excellent opportunity to gain sight vocabulary and automaticity.

6. Use Structured Repeated Readings found in Resources for Chapter 3. This simple strategy is easy to use and has helped students become confident, motivated readers who are able to recognize words automatically.

7. Refer to Chapter 4 for other strategies that may be useful. Particular attention could be focused on sight vocabulary and context. These two areas should help the student increase his or her storehouse of sight words and learn to use context to help anticipate or predict words.

8. Consider the strategies in Chapter 1 (especially sections 1.2 and 1.3) for building greater confidence toward reading and helping students view themselves as readers.

6.7 Ineffective Use of Word-Identification Strategies

Behavior Observed	The student knows word-identification strategies but does not use them effectively.
Anticipated Outcome	The student will become more effective in using word-identification strategies.

Background

One student always seems to sound out unknown words. Another student substitutes a word which makes sense but changes the author's meaning. A third student stops reading completely when confronted with an unfamiliar word. These and other reading behaviors, when observed consistently, can work against students becoming proficient readers.

The basic problem is that often the student has not learned why a particular strategy works and/or when to use it for figuring out unfamiliar words. It is also possible that the student does not know when to abandon one strategy and move to another. Usually, the student is overreliant on one word-identification strategy even though he or she may have learned other strategies. This situation usually occurs because the student has not been taught how to use a *combination* of strategies flexibly when confronted with an unknown word. Your primary responsibility in such a situation is to help the student use word-identification strategies in combination with one another to produce a word that makes sense in the sentence and has graphic characteristics similar to the word printed in the text. Students might be told that this is the "sound-sense strategy." If a specific strategy like context or phonics needs to be taught, refer to the ideas presented in Chapter 4. The following should help you begin to refine the process of teaching students to develop a set of flexible word-identification strategies.

Teaching Strategy

1. Invite students to share some of the strategies they use when they come across an unknown word. Typical responses may include sounding it out (phonics), skipping it, trying to figure it out from the other words in the sentence (context), breaking it into parts (syllabication), looking it up in a dictionary, and asking someone. Acknowledge that all these strategies may be used at one time or another and encourage students to provide examples of times when they have used each of them. List all of them on the chalkboard.

2. Tell students that strategic readers are flexible in terms of how they try to recognize unfamiliar words. This means that they know several strategies and use the most efficient and/or effective one(s) to figure out unknown words. Provide several examples where context can be used to figure out the unknown word. Have them identify the strategy that is used.

    The man put a _____ on his head. (hat)

    The color of milk is _____. (white)

3. Help students recognize that there are times when context can be used; moreover, stress that skilled readers also rely on context clues. Guide students to realize that context clues are used to help answer the question, "What word would make sense in the sentence?"

4. Provide another sentence for which context clues can be used to predict more than one word that may sound right or make sense in the sentence.

    Jake climbed a tree and picked a red _____. (for instance, apple, cherry)

    After the words have been given by students, list them on the chalkboard and ask, "Does *apple* make sense in this sentence? Why?" Repeat this question for each word listed on the chalkboard. Then use a word that does not make sense and have students explain why the word would not be a good choice.

5. Ask students whether the word the author used in step 4 can be correctly predicted from context. Because it cannot, provide an initial letter clue.

    Jake climbed a tree and picked a red a_____.

    Students should now be able to determine that the word is *apple*. If additional clues are necessary, supply another letter or two. Once the correct word is supplied, help students realize that they used context and some letter clues to figure out the word. Stress that context and phonics were used in combination. Use other examples and have students think aloud. For example:

    I like _____.

    The game lasted more than _____ hours.

    In the first example, a student might say, "I like. . . . Let's see. There are many words that make sense here: *soccer, candy,* and *music.* From the context or words provided, I can't really know the word so I need some letters in the word (teacher writes in a *b*). The word could be *bears,* a girl's name like *Brenda* or *Barb,* or. . . . No wait, it can't be *Brenda* or *Barb,* because a small *b* is there and people's names begin with capital letters. It must be *bears* or *beans* or something like that. I still need more information (teacher writes *ban*). Well, I guess it can't be *bears* or *beans* because they are not spelled that way. Perhaps the word is *bands.* I need more letters (teacher writes *banan*). No, it isn't *bands; ban-na, ba-nan* (student tries different pronunciations). Oh, *banana* could be the word; I mean *bananas,* because it makes sense, and I think that's the way the word is spelled."

6. After several similar examples, remind students that in reading all the words are always there, but the same basic strategies can be used. It is easier to make predictions because both context and letter clues are readily available in natural text.

7. Provide another example in which the missing word is difficult for students to pronounce and have them try to predict the unknown word. With context clues, many words are possible.

    The story was _____. (unbelievable)

    Supply the initial letter and the student may still not know the word. Sometimes it is possible to find prefixes, suffixes, endings, and a root word. Write the word in the sentence and encourage students to use this knowledge. Draw lines between the major word parts and have students try to pronounce the word. Encourage discussion about how affixes can be used to determine the word's meaning. Then ask whether it sounds like a word they know and whether it makes sense in the sentence.

8. When numerous activities such as the foregoing have been completed, help students develop a flexible approach to use when figuring out unknown words. Two possible charts that might be adapted follow.

Strategies to Figure Out Unknown Words

1. Use the words around the unknown word to help think of a word that makes sense in the sentence.

2. Use the letters, and the sounds associated with the letters, along with the words around the unknown word to say a word that makes sense in the sentence.

3. Look for root words, prefixes, suffixes, and endings. Try to pronounce the various word parts to see whether you have heard it before. Try various pronunciations, especially for the vowels.

4. Continue reading. Later sentences may help you figure out the unfamiliar word.

5. As a last resort, use the dictionary, ask someone, or skip the unknown word.

Questions for Figuring Out Unknown Words

1. What makes sense here?

2. What sound does it start with?

3. Are there root words, prefixes, suffixes, or endings that I know?

4. Should I skip the word and keep reading?

5. Can a dictionary help me?

6. Should I ask someone?

---

9. Help students realize that *flexibility* is essential to identifying unknown words. Good readers don't keep trying something that doesn't work; they move to another strategy. Teaching Strategy 3 in section 6.1, where the notion of a critter was developed, may be useful in helping students monitor the effectiveness of the strategies they use to identify unknown words.

Practice and Reinforcement Activities

1. Have students share a word they are unable to figure out, along with the context in which it is found. If the student is unable to share his or her strategies, model how a combination of strategies might be used to figure out the unknown word. Help students refine the effectiveness of their strategies.

2. Encourage students to record and share their successful attempts at figuring out unknown words by verbalizing the various strategies they used.

3. Develop exercises where a modified cloze procedure is used to refine students' ability to use context and letter clues. Discuss the word choices with the students, for example:

She left a _____ on the table.

She left a p_____ on the table.

She left a p ___ ___ on the table.

She left a p __ n on the table.

Students may request another letter to determine whether the word is *pin, pen,* or *pan.*

4. Younger students may profit from picture clues in cloze exercises, for example:

There is a _____.

5. Have students write sentences with space for a word that is missing. Students can exchange papers with one another and attempt to fill in the missing word. Papers are returned to the authors for verification. If students have difficulty, the authors can supply the first letter or two of the missing word. This activity may also lead students to an understanding of synonyms.

6. Have students keep a log in which they record unfamiliar, unknown words, the context (a phrase or sentence), and the strategies used to pronounce the words and determine their meanings. Provide opportunities for small group sharing. Be sure especially useful efforts are shared with the entire class.

Date	Book/Page	Underlined Word in Sentence	What Was Done
3-12-97	*Sitting Bull,* p. 1	But inside the cone-shaped, buffalo-hide <u>tipi</u> on the south bank of the river . . .	From the words buffalo hide and cone-shaped, I decided it was a tepee. When I looked up the word tipi, I was correct.

7. Apply strategies for identifying unknown words within the ongoing instructional program.

6.8   Using Mental Pictures

Behavior Observed	The student has trouble comprehending and may not make use of mental pictures to organize and remember information.
Anticipated Outcome	The student will use mental pictures to help organize and remember information read.

Background

In recent years, educators have renewed their interest in mental pictures and how they can be used to aid comprehension. Making mental pictures can facilitate the ongoing comprehension of text. Gambrell and Jawitz (1993) suggest using mental pictures along with text-relevant illustrations as complementary reading comprehension strategies. They can also be used by the strategic reader when comprehending is difficult, and the student activates the "read, picture; read, picture" strategy. Try some of the following ideas with students who could benefit from forming mental pictures while reading.

Teaching Strategy 1

1. Introduce the concept of forming mental pictures by telling students that mental pictures can help them comprehend what they read. Be sure they understand that the lesson is focused on how mental pictures can aid comprehension.

2. Explain why making pictures is useful. For example, "When we read, we can sometimes make pictures in our minds about what we're reading. These pictures of characters, where the story takes place, or what's happening can help us understand and remember what we read."

3. Model the strategy by thinking aloud and telling how you would use the strategy. For example, "I am going to read two sentences and try to make pictures in my mind about what I read. *The air was warm and fragrant with the perfume of flowers. There were roses of various colors and fire bush.* In my mind, I am picturing some red, pink, and white roses. The name fire bush makes me think of fire, and I picture a bush that is red or yellow."

4. Use some brief passages (see Practice and Reinforcement Activities) with students and encourage them to describe their pictures. Discuss how their pictures of the same material are similar and different.

5. Introduce other brief passages and give students opportunities to use mental pictures independently. Encourage students to help locate passages that are good for using mental pictures.

6. Several good guidelines for using mental pictures have been suggested by Cramer (1992).

   ■ Expect wide variation in students' pictures.

   ■ Explain that pictures are likely to be "hints and flashes." Rarely will students' pictures be as complete as motion pictures or TV.

   ■ Foster appreciation and tolerance for students' unique pictures.

Teaching Strategy 2

1. Tell students that good readers may picture what they are reading in order to understand and remember text. You may want to use the idea of taking pictures with a camera or camcorder. Picturing or visualizing is probably best done with books rich in description.

2. Invite students to share some of the things that they have pictured in their minds. Make the point that recalling pictures can help students remember something that may have taken place long ago.

3. Write a short, evocative passage on the chalkboard or overhead projector that is likely to foster discussion and create pictures in the students' minds, for example:

   It was noon and the sun was at its hottest. The sand was scorching my bare feet. I could see nothing but dust and glaring sand for miles and miles. I was all alone.

4. After students have read the passage, have them elaborate on the scene using their five senses. Ask questions such as:

   ■ How do you feel?

   ■ What do you smell?

   ■ Where are you?

   ■ What are you going to do next?

   After each response, have the student expand on it. If Barbara says she feels thirsty, have the class focus on thirst and how it feels. The idea is to help students physically experience being in the setting. You may want to use other selections such as an experience at a beach, in the middle of a deep forest, a musty barn, a crowded city street, or attempting to climb a rocky cliff.

5. Tell students that you are going to read them a passage and you want them to try to picture the scene in their minds. They should be told that this is a strategy they can use during reading. Have students listen carefully as you read:

   I slept late again today. My mom was at my grandmother's house next door, so the house was quiet—so quiet that I could hear the refrigerator humming. I was just about to roll over and get a few more hours of sleep when I heard a soft whining noise. I sat up on my elbow and tried to listen, but I didn't hear it again. Then I heard a scratching sound. I thought of mice and winced, burrowing my head under the covers. Finally, I heard the whining noise again and a short bark. I remembered. I was supposed to let the new puppy outside this morning.

6. Engage students in a discussion to share all that they can remember about the passage. Write their thoughts on the chalkboard. Then discuss how creating a picture of what you read can aid comprehension. Remember that not all students organize, store, and retrieve information in the same way.

7. Conclude the lesson by discussing the types of material for which thinking of pictures may work best, and encourage students to consider creating pictures in their minds during reading to help them understand and remember. Tell students that there are no "correct" answers, and pictures vary depending on prior knowledge and experience.

Practice and Reinforcement Activities

1. From a catalog, cut out the pictures and descriptions of various sets of articles (bikes, games, jewelry, clothes, and so on). Pass out the descriptions of one particular set of items (for example, bikes) to a group of students. Each student should have a different description of some similar item. Instruct students to read the description and to form a picture of the article in their mind. After they have fixed the description firmly in their mind, ask students to go to a table containing cutout pictures of similar articles. Their task is to match their picture of the item with the appropriate cutout picture.

2. Take advantage of what may be on your students' minds. For example, ten minutes before lunch, have them read about food. Tear out food articles from magazines accompanied by pictures. Have students discuss their favorite menu selections from the assortment of articles. The rationale for this activity is that because students are hungry, it will be easy for them to imagine food. Associating reading with their already-present pictures may help reinforce the habit of using mental pictures during reading.

3. Be prepared for unusual days by having an appropriate story or poem on hand. If it is a rainy, windy day, read your students a relevant story or poem. Try to take advantage of whatever may be on their minds by reinforcing it with a complementary reading passage. If a field trip is planned, be sure to read something related to the trip both before and after the excursion.

4. Use selected passages from literature to give students an opportunity to practice forming mental pictures. For example, *Charlotte's Web* (White, 1952) contains an excellent description of a barn, and *A Wrinkle in Time* (L'Engle, 1962) offers a rich description of a kitchen. Share parts of your reading with students that are appropriate for mental pictures. Here are two examples we have used with students (sources unknown):

   I allowed myself to walk out back yesterday afternoon when I returned to the farm. The air was warm and fragrant with the perfume of flowers, and I hoped that I wasn't too late to see the blooming of what Ozarkers call fire bush. All over these hills there are foundations of long-gone cabins—overgrown stone walls that show where families lived back in the days when the big timber was cut in this part of the country. Beside most of them, like the one at the back of my place, there are also flowers. Iris, bridal bush, and fire bush were planted, I think, by women who put them there to brighten their harsh homesteading lives.

   Early in the morning, after making a fire in the wood stove, I step outside my cabin while the bacon is frying to get a feel for the day in the darkness before dawn. There are no clouds in the sky, and the last stars are shining brightly. The day promises to be fair. It is too cool to have my breakfast outside and watch the sun rise, so I sit near the wood stove on an old rocking chair and watch the eastern sky through the large, inviting kitchen window.

5. Have students draw pictures based on something you have read from the pictures they formed in their minds as you read. Students can talk about their pictures in small groups. You can also have students draw pictures of a scene from a book or story they have read recently.

6. Have students imagine that they are involved in a particular activity and describe it (for example, reading a book in a comfortable location; flying a kite; swinging in the park).

7. Ask one student to leave the classroom. The remaining students are asked to describe the student in writing (clothes, physical attributes, interesting details like rings, and so on). When the student comes back into the classroom, the other students can compare their descriptions to the actual student.

8. Remember to have students use text-relevant illustrations along with mental pictures as complementary strategies.

6.9   Varying Reading Choices

Behavior Observed	The student does not vary reading choices.
Anticipated Outcome	The student will monitor his or her reading choices and vary those choices.

Background

Many students get in a rut when they read. They often begin reading a book series and spend months reading only those books. They may feel they need the stability of the characters and plots that a series has to offer. Teachers often ask us what to do to encourage students to vary their reading choices and how to discourage this "narrow reading." While it may be disquieting for teachers to spend time encouraging varied reading when students do not seem to respond, we must honor our students' reading choices while nudging them to sample other types of reading selections.

As professionals, we need to make sure our students know about the kinds of literature available at their reading and interest levels. We need to provide students with experiences in all genres with all types of books. After we have helped students learn about the books available, we need to let go and trust our students to make appropriate book selections.

Teaching Strategy 1 (Books Talks)

1. One good way to interest students in books is by giving a book talk. A book talk is a brief talk about a book with the purpose of enticing others to read it. There are several formats for sharing books through book talks:

   ■ Schedule a regular book talk every few days when you can share one book you have read.

   ■ Read books about a theme and share them with the class before you begin the unit.

   ■ Share several books from the same author.

   ■ Share different versions of the same story (e.g., Cinderella).

2. Read the book and prepare a short talk that will motivate your students to read the book. As you prepare a book talk, remember that you do not want to give away the end of the story. If you tell the end of the story, you will destroy the students' suspense as they read it. Second, try to get the attention of the students during the first sentence. Third, try to make the book talk as appealing to your students as possible. A book talk is not a report on a book, but a motivational technique to encourage students to read the book. Finally, make the book talk short. Three to five minutes is best.

3. There are several ways you can organize your book talk. Different books require different methods. Do whichever organizational pattern fits you and the book.

- **Relate the book to a personal experience.**

Ruckman, Ivy. (1984). *Night of the Twisters*. New York: Harper Collins.

I've always been afraid of tornadoes. Whenever the siren rings out, I run to the basement with my radio, a bottle of water, and a hammer. My fear stems from a tornado that hit without warning in a nearby town. As I read *Night of the Twisters*, I felt what it would really be like to be caught in a tornado and what I would hear and see. Now I run to the basement whenever there's a tornado watch!

- **Use quotations or excerpts from the book.**

Paulsen, Gary. (1987). *Hatchet*. New York: Puffin Books.

Imagine flying in a small airplane over the vast north woods of Canada. You are on your way to visit your father when suddenly something happens to the pilot, and he slumps over in his seat. *[Read pp. 9-12 where the pilot has a heart attack.]* You are the only one aboard to land the airplane, and when you land, you are all alone far away from civilization trying to survive with only a hatchet and your own wits.

- **Use props whenever appropriate.**

Hesse, Karen. (1992). *Letters from Rifka*. New York: Henry Holt.

[*Wear a scarf, apron, and/or shawl*]

Have you ever been to a new school? Remember how you felt: new, different, lonely? Rifka left Russia during the height of the Russian Revolution in 1919. She arrived in America sick and not knowing English. This diary shows how she felt and how she coped with the newness of America.

- **Dramatize the book talk by telling the book in the first person, using the main character's speech and dialect when appropriate.**

Gardiner, John Reynolds. (1980). *Stone Fox*. New York: Thomas Y. Crowell.

If only I had enough money to save my granpappy's farm. It's only $500, that's all I need. But $500 is a heap of money, more than I could git in a lifetime. Thar's only one way I can be fixin' to git the money, and that's not goin' to be easy. My dog, Searchlight, is the onliest chance I got. If he kin jist beat that ole Stone Fox, my granpappy's farm might be saved.

- **Prepare a short interview with the main character or the author.**

Paterson, Katherine. (1978). *The Great Gilly Hopkins*. New York: Thomas Y. Crowell.
Interviewer: Gilly, how did it feel to be put in a foster home again?
Gilly: Man, I get sick of all these new places. Here I'm with this crazy lady, name of Maime Trotter, and William Ernest.
Interviewer: Why are you here?
Gilly: Well, my mom has had some trouble and couldn't take care of me.
Interviewer: What will you do?
Gilly: I'm going to find my mom and get out of here.

■   **Prepare a script for a scene from the book. Ask students to read it, practice it, then perform it for the class.**

Lowry, Lois. (1989). *Number the Stars*. New York: Bantam Doubleday, Dell.

Annemarie walks outside where Uncle Henry is milking the cow.
Annemarie: Uncle Henry, you're lying to me.
Uncle Henry: You're angry.
Annemarie: Yes. Mama has never lied to me before. Never. Why now?
Uncle Henry: How brave are you, Annemarie? Are you brave enough to know the truth?
They return to the house together. Several people are gathered around a casket.
Mama: Remember, Annemarie, this is Great-aunt Birte. If anyone asks you, you must convince them. It could mean the safety of our family and our friends!
Pounding on the door, boots stomping in.
Officer: Why are all of you gathered here?
Annemarie: *(trembling)* My Great-aunt Birte has just died.

Teaching Strategy 2 (Self-monitoring of Book Selections)

1. Ask students to record the types of books they read during the year on a Book Record Chart. Include a place for them to record the genre of the book.

Book Record Chart

Name _Roger_

Title	Author	Date	Genre
Hatchet	Paulsen	9/7/97	Realistic Fiction
Stone Fox	Gardiner	9/15/97	Realistic Fiction

2. Every two or three months, ask your students to update a Reading Genre Chart. For each square, the students should color in one grid per book.

Reading Genre Chart

Name _Roger_

Number of Completed Books

	1	2	3	4	5	6	7	8	9	10	11	12
Informational books	▓	▓										
Picture books												
Historical fiction	▓	▓	▓									
Science fiction												
Biographies												
Fantasy	▓											
Realistic fiction	▓	▓										
Folk tales												
Plays	▓											
"How-to" books												

3. After several months, ask your students to study their book list and answer the following questions:

> Which genres did I read the most?
>
> Which genres did I omit?
>
> What do my selections tell about me?
>
> What do my selections tell about me as a reader?
>
> What reading goals do I have for the next month?

Practice and Reinforcement Activities

1. When students self-select books, encourage them to ask themselves why they have chosen the book. Ask them occasionally to write about their book selections in their journals. You might ask some students to keep track of their reasons for choosing their books on a book choice chart.

2. In literature circles have students discuss self-selected readings and why they chose each book.

3. Encourage students to present their own book talks. Video tape them to play back when students are inside during recess or when you want to reinforce the idea of varying book selections.

4. Ask students to prepare a poster advertising a genre of books.

5. Ask the librarian to highlight new books in the library that would be appropriate for your grade level.

6. Prepare individual bingo sheets with the different genres printed in each block. As a motivational tool, ask students to keep track of their self-selected reading. When they get four down or across, award them with additional free reading time.

Book Genre Bingo			
historical fiction	fantasy	"how-to"	folk tales
realistic fiction	plays	biographies	science fiction
realistic fiction	picture books	folk tales	historical fiction
picture books	realistic fiction	fantasy	informational books

Resources for Chapter 6

Strategy Questionnaires

➤ Metacomprehension Strategy Index

➤ Index of Reading Awareness

➤ The Reader Self-Perception Scale

Student Checklists

➤ Student Self-Check List

➤ What I Did While Reading

➤ Student Checklist

➤ Book Record Chart

➤ Reading Genre Chart

➤ Self-Monitoring Questions

➤ Book Choice Chart

Teacher Resource

➤ Checklist for Comprehension Strategies

Metacomprehension Strategy Index

Maribeth Cassidy Schmitt

Purpose

To help teachers in the middle and upper grades evaluate students' knowledge of strategic reading processes with narrative materials.

Administration

1. Reproduce enough copies of the "Metacognitive Strategy Index" for students.

2. Explain how students should mark their answers (see directions on the index).

3. Have students read and answer the items silently. If students' reading abilities are believed to interfere with their performance, read the questions and possible answers aloud to students.

Scoring and Interpretation

1. Score the Metacomprehension Strategy Index by using the following key.

1. C	6. B	11. D	16. B	21. C
2. A	7. B	12. A	17. A	22. B
3. B	8. A	13. C	18. A	23. C
4. C	9. C	14. B	19. D	24. D
5. A	10. C	15. D	20. A	25. A

2. Total the students' responses that indicate metacomprehension strategy awareness and interpret the results both quantitatively and qualitatively. Use the results in conjunction with your observations and other sources of information.

3. The six item clusters shown here may be used informally. Use extreme caution in interpreting the clusters, because they can be highly unreliable.

   ■ Predicting and Verifying

   Predicting the content of a story promotes active comprehension by giving readers a purpose for reading (that is, to verify predictions). Evaluating predictions and generating new ones as necessary enhances the constructive nature of the reading process.

   Items: 1, 4, 13, 15, 16, 18, 23

   ■ Previewing

   Previewing the text facilitates comprehension by activating background knowledge and providing information for making predictions.

   Items: 2, 3

   ■ Purpose Setting

   Reading with a purpose promotes active, strategic reading.

   Items: 5, 7, 21

- Self-Questioning

   Generating questions to be answered promotes active comprehension by giving readers a purpose for reading (that is, to answer the questions).

   Items: 6, 14, 17

- Drawing from Background Knowledge

   Activating and incorporating information from background knowledge contributes to comprehension by helping readers to make inferences and generate predictions.

   Items: 8, 9, 10, 19, 24, 25

- Summarizing and Applying Fix-up Strategies

   Summarizing the content at various points in the story serves as a form of comprehension monitoring. Rereading or suspending judgment and reading on when comprehension breaks down represents strategic reading.

   Items: 11, 12, 20, 22

4. Refer to the original article for further information on the construction, use, and interpretation of the index.

Adapted from Schmitt, M.C. (1990). A questionnaire to measure children's awareness of strategic reading processes. *The Reading Teacher, 43*(7), 454–461. Reprinted with permission of the International Reading Association.

Metacomprehension Strategy Index

Maribeth Cassidy Schmitt

> **Directions:** Think about what kinds of things you can do to help you understand a story better before, during, and after you read it. Read each of the lists of four statements and decide which one of them would help *you* the most. *There are no right answers.* It is just what *you* think would help the most. Circle the letter of the statement you choose.

I. In each set of four, choose the one statement which tells a good thing to do to help you understand a story better *before* you read it.

1. Before I begin reading, it's a good idea to:

   A. See how many pages are in the story.

   B. Look up all of the big words in the dictionary.

   C. Make some guesses about what I think will happen in the story.

   D. Think about what has happened so far in the story.

2. Before I begin reading, it's a good idea to:

   A. Look at the pictures to see what the story is about.

   B. Decide how long it will take me to read the story.

   C. Sound out the words I don't know.

   D. Check to see if the story is making sense.

3. Before I begin reading, it's a good idea to:

   A. Ask someone to read the story to me.

   B. Read the title to see what the story is about.

   C. Check to see if most of the words have long or short vowels in them.

   D. Check to see if the pictures are in order and make sense.

4. Before I begin reading, it's a good idea to:

   A. Check to see that no pages are missing.

   B. Make a list of the words I'm not sure about.

   C. Use the title and pictures to help me make guesses about what will happen in the story.

   D. Read the last sentence so I will know how the story ends.

5. Before I begin reading, it's a good idea to:

   A. Decide on why I am going to read the story.

   B. Use the difficult words to help me make guesses about what will happen in the story.

   C. Reread some parts to see if I can figure out what is happening if things aren't making sense.

   D. Ask for help with the difficult words.

6. Before I begin reading, it's a good idea to:

   A. Retell all of the main points that have happened so far.

   B. Ask myself questions that I would like to have answered in the story.

   C. Think about the meanings of the words which have more than one meaning.

   D. Look through the story to find all of the words with three or more syllables.

7. Before I begin reading, it's a good idea to:

   A. Check to see if I have read this story before.

   B. Use my questions and guesses as a reason for reading the story.

   C. Make sure I can pronounce all of the words before I start.

   D. Think of a better title for the story.

8. Before I begin reading, it's a good idea to:

   A. Think of what I already know about the things I see in the pictures.

   B. See how many pages are in the story.

   C. Choose the best part of the story to read again.

   D. Read the story aloud to someone.

9. Before I begin reading, it's a good idea to:

   A. Practice reading the story aloud.

   B. Retell all of the main points to make sure I can remember the story.

   C. Think of what people in the story might be like.

   D. Decide if I have enough time to read the story.

10. Before I begin reading, it's a good idea to:

    A. Check to see if I am understanding the story so far.

    B. Check to see if the words have more than one meaning.

    C. Think about where the story might be taking place.

    D. List all of the important details.

II. In each set of four, choose the one statement which tells a good thing to do to help you understand a story better *while* you are reading it.

11. While I'm reading, it's a good idea to:

    A. Read the story very slowly so that I will not miss any important parts.

    B. Read the title to see what the story is about.

    C. Check to see if the pictures have anything missing.

    D. Check to see if the story is making sense by seeing if I can tell what's happened so far.

12. While I'm reading, it's a good idea to:

   A. Stop to retell the main points to see if I am understanding what has happened so far.

   B. Read the story quickly so that I can find out what happened.

   C. Read only the beginning and the end of the story to find out what it is about.

   D. Skip the parts that are too difficult for me.

13. While I'm reading, it's a good idea to:

   A. Look all of the big words up in the dictionary.

   B. Put the book away and find another one if things aren't making sense.

   C. Keep thinking about the title and the pictures to help me decide what is going to happen next.

   D. Keep track of how many pages I have left to read.

14. While I'm reading, it's a good idea to:

   A. Keep track of how long it is taking me to read the story.

   B. Check to see if I can answer any of the questions I asked before I started reading.

   C. Read the title to see what the story is going to be about.

   D. Add the missing details to the pictures.

15. While I'm reading, it's a good idea to:

   A. Have someone read the story aloud to me.

   B. Keep track of how many pages I have read.

   C. List the story's main character.

   D. Check to see if my guesses are right or wrong.

16. While I'm reading, it's a good idea to:

   A. Check to see that the characters are real.

   B. Make a lot of guesses about what is going to happen next.

   C. Not look at the pictures because they might confuse me.

   D. Read the story aloud to someone.

17. While I'm reading, it's a good idea to:

   A. Try to answer the questions I asked myself.

   B. Try not to confuse what I already know with what I'm reading about.

   C. Read the story silently.

   D. Check to see if I am saying the new vocabulary words correctly.

18. While I'm reading, it's a good idea to:

   A. Try to see if my guesses are going to be right or wrong.

   B. Reread to be sure I haven't missed any of the words.

   C. Decide on why I am reading the story.

   D. List what happened first, second, third, and so on.

19. While I'm reading, it's a good idea to:

   A. See if I can recognize the new vocabulary words.

   B. Be careful not to skip any parts of the story.

   C. Check to see how many of the words I already know.

   D. Keep thinking of what I already know about the things and ideas in the story to help me decide what is going to happen.

20. While I'm reading, it's a good idea to:

    A. Reread some parts or read ahead to see if I can figure out what is happening if things aren't making sense.

    B. Take my time reading so that I can be sure I understand what is happening.

    C. Change the ending so that it makes sense.

    D. Check to see if there are enough pictures to help make the story ideas clear.

III. In each set of four, choose the one statement which tells a good thing to do to help you understand a story better *after* you have read it.

21. After I've read a story it's a good idea to:

    A. Count how many pages I read with no mistakes.

    B. Check to see if there were enough pictures to go with the story to make it interesting.

    C. Check to see if I met my purpose for reading the story.

    D. Underline the causes and effects.

22. After I've read a story it's a good idea to:

    A. Underline the main idea.

    B. Retell the main points of the whole story so that I can check to see if I understood it.

    C. Read the story again to be sure I said all of the words right.

    D. Practice reading the story aloud.

23. After I've read a story it's a good idea to:

    A. Read the title and look over the story to see what it is about.

    B. Check to see if I skipped any of the vocabulary words.

    C. Think about what made me make good or bad predictions.

    D. Make a guess about what will happen next in the story.

24. After I've read a story it's a good idea to:

    A. Look up all of the big words in the dictionary.

    B. Read the best parts aloud.

    C. Have someone read the story aloud to me.

    D. Think about how the story was like things I already knew about before I started reading.

25. After I've read a story it's a good idea to:

    A. Think about how I would have acted if I were the main character in the story.

    B. Practice reading the story silently for practice of good reading.

    C. Look over the story title and pictures to see what will happen.

    D. Make a list of the things I understood the most.

Adapted from Schmitt, M.C. (1990). A questionnaire to measure children's awareness of strategic reading processes. *The Reading Teacher, 43*(7), 454–461. Reprinted with permission of the International Reading Association.

Index of Reading Awareness

Janis E. Jacobs and *Scott G. Paris*

Purpose

To help provide data about students' reading awareness in the third and fifth grades with grade-equivalent reading abilities from second to seventh grade.

Administration

1. Reproduce sufficient copies of the "Index of Reading Awareness" for students.

2. Explain how students should mark their answers (see directions on the index).

3. Have students read and answer the items silently. If students' reading abilities might interfere with their performance, read the questions and possible answers aloud to students.

Scoring and Interpretation

1. Award points to the Index of Reading Awareness by using the following key

	a	b	c		a	b	c		a	b	c		a	b	c
1.	0	1	2	6.	1	0	2	11.	1	2	0	16.	1	2	0
2.	2	0	1	7.	1	0	2	12.	2	0	1	17.	1	2	0
3.	2	1	0	8.	1	0	2	13.	1	0	2	18.	1	0	2
4.	0	2	1	9.	2	1	0	14.	1	2	0	19.	0	1	2
5.	1	2	0	10.	2	1	0	15.	1	2	0	20.	1	2	0

2. Total the points and interpret the results quantitatively and qualitatively. Use the results in conjunction with your observations and other sources of information.

3. Although the index includes five items to measure four aspects of students' metacognition about reading (evaluation, planning, regulation, and strategy utility), these four constructs were not found to be independent; therefore, only a total score should be used.

Index of Reading Awareness

Janis E. Jacobs and Scott G. Paris

> **Directions:** Read the sentences carefully and circle the best answer for you. There are no right or wrong answers.

1. Which of these is the best way to remember a story?

   a. Repeat every word.

   b. Think about remembering it.

   c. Write it in your own words.

2. If you are reading for science or social studies, what would you do to remember the information?

   a. Ask yourself questions about important ideas.

   b. Skip the parts you do not understand.

   c. Concentrate and try hard to remember it.

3. What do you do if you come to a word and you do not know what it means?

   a. Use the words around it to figure it out.

   b. Ask someone else.

   c. Move to the next word.

4. If you could read only some of the sentences in the story because you were in a hurry, which ones would you read?

   a. The sentences in the middle of the story.

   b. The sentences that tell the most about the story.

   c. The interesting, exciting sentences.

5. Why do you go back and read things over?

   a. It is good practice.

   b. You did not understand it.

   c. You forgot some words.

6. What would help you to become a better reader?

   a. More people helping when you read.

   b. Reading easier books with shorter words.

   c. Checking to ensure that you understand what you read.

7. What do you do if you do not know what a whole sentence means?

    a. Read it again.

    b. Sound out all of the words.

    c. Think about the other sentences in the paragraph.

8. What is special about the first sentence or two in a story?

    a. They always begin with "Once upon a time…"

    b. The first sentences are the most interesting.

    c. They often tell what the story is about.

9. If the teacher told you to read a story to remember the general meaning, what would you do?

    a. Skim through the story to find the main parts.

    b. Read all of the story and try to remember everything.

    c. Read the story and remember all of the words.

10. How can you tell which sentences are the most important ones in a story?

    a. They are the ones that tell the most about the characters and what happens.

    b. They are the most interesting ones.

    c. All of them are important.

11. How are the last sentences of a story special?

    a. They are the exciting, action sentences.

    b. They tell what happened.

    c. They are harder to read.

12. When you tell other people about what you read, what do you tell them?

    a. What happened in the story.

    b. The number of pages in the book.

    c. Who the characters are.

13. If you had to read fast and could only read some words, which ones would you try to read?

    a. The new vocabulary words, because they are important.

    b. The words you could pronounce.

    c. The words that tell you the most about the story.

14. If you are reading a library book to write a book report, which would help you the most?

    a. Sound out words you do not know.

    b. Write it down in your own words.

    c. Skip the parts you do not understand.

15. If you are reading for a test, which would help you the most?

    a. Read the story as many times as possible.

    b. Talk about it with somebody to make sure you understand it.

    c. Repeat the sentences.

16. What parts of the story do you skip as you read?

    a. The hard words and parts you do not understand.

    b. The unimportant parts that do not mean anything for the story.

    c. You never skip anything.

17. What is the hardest part about reading for you?

    a. Sounding out the hard words.

    b. When you do not understand the story.

    c. Nothing is hard about reading for you.

18. If you are reading a story for fun, what would you do?

    a. Look at the pictures to get the meaning.

    b. Read the story as fast as you can.

    c. Imagine the story like a movie in your mind.

19. Before you start to read, what kind of plans do you make to help you read better?

    a. You do not make any plans. You just start reading.

    b. You choose a comfortable place.

    c. You think about why you are reading.

20. What things do you read faster than others?

    a. Books that are easy to read.

    b. Stories that you have previously read.

    c. Books that have a lot of pictures.

Adapted from Jacobs, J.E., & Paris, Scott G. (1987). Children's metacognition about reading: Issues in definition, measurement, and instruction. *Educational Psychologist, 22*(3 & 4), 255–278. Reprinted by permission of Scott G. Paris.

The Reader Self-Perception Scale

Listed below are statements about reading. Please read each statement carefully. Then circle the letters that show how much you agree or disagree with the statement. Use the following:

SA = Strongly Agree
A = Agree
U = Undecided
D = Disagree
SD = Strongly Disagree

Example: **I think pizza with pepperoni is best.**   SA   A   U   D   SD

If you are *really positive* that pepperoni pizza is best, circle SA (Strongly Agree).
If you *think* that it is good but maybe not great, circle A (Agree).
If you *can't decide* whether or not it is best, circle U (Undecided).
If you *think* that Pepperoni pizza is not all that good, circle D (Disagree).
If you are *really positive* that pepperoni pizza is not very good, circle SD (Strongly Disagree).

1.	I think I am a good reader.	SA	A	U	D	SD
2.	I can tell that my teacher likes to listen to me read.	SA	A	U	D	SD
3.	My teacher thinks that my reading is fine.	SA	A	U	D	SD
4.	I read faster than other kids.	SA	A	U	D	SD
5.	I like to read aloud.	SA	A	U	D	SD
6.	When I read, I can figure out words better than other kids.	SA	A	U	D	SD
7.	My classmates like to listen to me read.	SA	A	U	D	SD
8.	I feel good inside when I read.	SA	A	U	D	SD
9.	My classmates think that I read pretty well.	SA	A	U	D	SD
10.	When I read, I don't have to try as hard as I used to.	SA	A	U	D	SD
11.	I seem to know more words than other kids when I read.	SA	A	U	D	SD
12.	People in my family think I am a good reader.	SA	A	U	D	SD
13.	I am getting better at reading.	SA	A	U	D	SD
14.	I understand what I read as well as other kids do.	SA	A	U	D	SD

Henk, W. A., & Melnick, S. A. (1995). The Reader Self-Perception Scale (RSPS): A new tool for measuring how children feel about themselves as readers. The Reading Teacher, 48(6), 470-482. Reprinted with permission.

The Reader Self-Perception Scale, *cont.*

15.	When I read, I need less help than I used to.	SA	A	U	D	SD
16.	Reading makes me feel happy inside.	SA	A	U	D	SD
17.	My teacher thinks I am a good reader.	SA	A	U	D	SD
18.	Reading is easier for me than it used to be.	SA	A	U	D	SD
19.	I read faster than I could before.	SA	A	U	D	SD
20.	I read better than other kids in my class.	SA	A	U	D	SD
21.	I feel calm when I read.	SA	A	U	D	SD
22.	I read more than other kids.	SA	A	U	D	SD
23.	I understand what I read better than I could before.	SA	A	U	D	SD
24.	I can figure out words better than I could before.	SA	A	U	D	SD
25.	I feel comfortable when I read.	SA	A	U	D	SD
26.	I think reading is relaxing.	SA	A	U	D	SD
27.	I read better now than I could before.	SA	A	U	D	SD
28.	When I read, I recognize more words than I used to.	SA	A	U	D	SD
29.	Reading makes me feel good.	SA	A	U	D	SD
30.	Other kids think I'm a good reader.	SA	A	U	D	SD
31.	People in my family think I read pretty well.	SA	A	U	D	SD
32.	I enjoy reading.	SA	A	U	D	SD
33.	People in my family like to listen to me read.	SA	A	U	D	SD

The Reader Self-Perception Scale
Directions for Administration, Scoring, and Interpretation

The Reader Self-Perception Scale (RSPS) is intended to provide an assessment of how children feel about themselves as readers. The scale consists of 33 items that assess self-perceptions along four dimensions of self-efficacy (Progress, Observational Comparison, Social Feedback, and Physiological States). Children are asked to indicate how strongly they agree or disagree with each statement on a 5-point scale (5 = Strongly Agree, 1 = Strongly Disagree). The information gained from this scale can be used to devise ways to enhance children's self-esteem in reading and, ideally, to increase their motivation to read. The following directions explain specifically what you are to do.

Administration

For the results to be of any use, the children must: (a) understand exactly what they are to do, (b) have sufficient time to complete all items, and (c) respond honestly and thoughtfully. Briefly explain to the children that they are being asked to complete a questionnaire about reading. Emphasize that this is not a *test* and that there are no *right* answers. Tell them that they should be as honest as possible because their responses will be confidential. Ask the children to fill in their names, grade levels, and classrooms as appropriate. Read the directions aloud and work through the example with the students as a group. Discuss the response options and make sure that all children understand the rating scale before moving on. It is important that children know that they may raise their hands to ask questions about any words or ideas they do not understand.

The children should then read each item and circle their response for the item. They should work at their own pace. Remind the children that they should be sure to respond to all items. When all items are completed, the children should stop, put their pencils down, and wait for further instructions. Care should be taken that children who work more slowly are not disturbed by children who have already finished.

Scoring

To score the RSPS, enter the following point values for each response on the RSPS scoring sheet (Strongly Agree = 5, Agree = 4, Undecided = 3, Disagree = 2, Strongly Disagree = 1) for each item number under the appropriate scale. Add each column to obtain a raw score for each of the four specific scales.

Interpretation

Each scale is interpreted in relation to its total possible score. For example, because the RSPS uses a 5-point scale and the Progress scale consists of 9 items, the highest score for Progress is 45 ($9\times5 = 45$). Therefore, a score that would fall approximately in the middle of the range (22–23) would indicate a child's somewhat indifferent perception of her or himself as a reader with respect to Progress. Note that each scale has a different possible total raw score (Progress = 45, Observational Comparison = 30, Social Feedback = 45, and Physiological States = 40) and should be interpreted accordingly.

Henk, W. A., & Melnick, S. A. (1995). The Reader Self-Perception Scale (RSPS): A new tool for measuring how children feel about themselves as readers. *The Reading Teacher, 48*(6), 470–482. Reprinted with permission.

As a further aid to interpretation, Table 2 presents the descriptive statistics by grade level for each scale. The raw score of a group or individual can be compared to that of the pilot study group at each grade level.

Table 2
Descriptive Statistics by Scale and Grade Level

Grade level	n	Progress			Observational Comparison			Social Feedback			Physiological States		
		Mean	SD	SE	Mean	SD	SE	Mean	SD	SE	Mean	SD	SE
4	506	39.6	4.8	.21	20.7	4.7	.21	33.2	5.3	.24	31.8	5.9	.26
5	571	39.5	5.2	.22	21.0	4.8	.20	32.7	5.4	.22	31.0	6.4	.27
6	402	39.0	5.1	.25	21.3	4.6	.23	32.0	5.5	.27	30.5	6.2	.31
Total	1,479	39.4	5.0	.13	20.9	4.7	.12	32.7	5.4	.14	31.2	6.2	.16

Note: Total possible raw scores are Progress (45), Observational Comparison (30), Social Feedback (45), and Physiological States (40).

The Reader Self-Perception Scale Scoring Sheet

Student Name _____

Teacher _____

Grade _____ Date _____

Scoring key: 5 = Strongly Agree (SA)
4 = Agree (A)
3 = Undecided (U)
2 = Disagree (D)
1 = Strongly Disagree (SD)

Scales

General Perception	Progress	Observational Comparison	Social Feedback	Physiological States
1. ____	10. ____	4. ____	2. ____	5. ____
	13. ____	6. ____	3. ____	8. ____
	15. ____	11. ____	7. ____	16. ____
	18. ____	14. ____	9. ____	21. ____
	19. ____	20. ____	12. ____	25. ____
	23. ____	22. ____	17. ____	26. ____
	24. ____		30. ____	29. ____
	27. ____		31. ____	32. ____
	28. ____		33. ____	

Raw score   ____ of 45   ____ of 30   ____ of 45   ____ of 40

Score interpretation

High	44+	26+	38+	37+
Average	39	21	33	31
Low	34	16	27	25

Student Self-Check List

Before you began reading, did you: Yes No

1. Ask yourself what the reading was going to be about?   ❏   ❏

2. Think about what you already knew about the topic?   ❏   ❏

3. Make a prediction about the contents of the passage?   ❏   ❏

As you were reading, did you:

4. Know if you didn't understand something?   ❏   ❏

5. Stop and read again if you didn't understand?   ❏   ❏

6. Read ahead if you didn't know a word to see if you could figure   ❏   ❏
   it out from the words around it?

7. Try to put yourself in the story?   ❏   ❏

8. Check to see whether your prediction was correct?   ❏   ❏

9. Make a new prediction?   ❏   ❏

After you finished reading, did you:

10. Think about what the passage was mostly about?   ❏   ❏

11. Think about your predictions? Were they proven correct? Why   ❏   ❏
    or why not?

12. Think about how you might use the information in the future?   ❏   ❏

Adapted from Roberta L. Berglund and Richard J. Telfer.

What I Did While Reading

Name _____ Date _____

Here's my self-evaluation of what I did while I was reading _____

(name of book or story)

I checked (✔) those things I did.

Strategies	Not Much	A Little	Most of the Time	Almost Always
Used text structure				
Made predictions				
Made pictures in my mind				
Found problems like hard words and not understanding				
Fixed problems by rereading, looking ahead, and checking the dictionary				
Summarized				
Asked myself questions				
Here are other strategies I used:				

Adapted from Davey, B. (1983). Think-aloud—Modeling the cognitive processes of reading comprehension. *Journal of Reading,* *27*(1), 44–47.

Student Checklist

Name_____ Grade _____ Date _____

Please draw a face to show how you feel about the following sentences.

If you feel this way often, draw: ☺

If you feel this way sometimes, draw: 😐

If you feel this way never, draw: ☹

I like to find things out for myself. I am curious.
I like to read.
I understand what I read.
I try to figure out new words by myself.
I use what I already know.
I have lots of trouble with words.

Book Record Chart

Name _____

Title	Author	Date	Genre
_____	_____	_____	_____
_____	_____	_____	_____
_____	_____	_____	_____
_____	_____	_____	_____
_____	_____	_____	_____
_____	_____	_____	_____
_____	_____	_____	_____
_____	_____	_____	_____
_____	_____	_____	_____
_____	_____	_____	_____
_____	_____	_____	_____
_____	_____	_____	_____
_____	_____	_____	_____
_____	_____	_____	_____
_____	_____	_____	_____
_____	_____	_____	_____
_____	_____	_____	_____
_____	_____	_____	_____

Reading Genre Chart

Name_____

Number of Completed Books

	1	2	3	4	5	6	7	8	9	10	11	12
Informational books												
Picture books												
Historical fiction												
Science fiction												
Biographies												
Fantasy												
Realistic fiction												
Folk tales												
Plays												
"How-to" books												

From Jerry L. Johns and Susan Davis Lenski, *Improving Reading: A Handbook of Strategies* (2nd ed.). Copyright © 1997 Kendall/Hunt Publishing Company (1-800-228-0810). May be reproduced for noncommercial educational purposes.

Self-Monitoring Questions

Name _____

1. Which genres did I read the most? _____

_____

_____

_____

2. Which genres did I omit? _____

_____

_____

_____

3. What do my selections tell about me? _____

_____

_____

_____

4. What do my selections tell about myself as a reader? _____

_____

_____

_____

5. What reading goals do I have for the next month? _____

_____

_____

_____

Book Choice Chart

Date	Title	Genre	Why I chose the book:
___	_____	_____	_____
___	_____	_____	_____
___	_____	_____	_____
___	_____	_____	_____
___	_____	_____	_____
___	_____	_____	_____
___	_____	_____	_____
___	_____	_____	_____
___	_____	_____	_____
___	_____	_____	_____
___	_____	_____	_____
___	_____	_____	_____
___	_____	_____	_____
___	_____	_____	_____
___	_____	_____	_____
___	_____	_____	_____
___	_____	_____	_____
___	_____	_____	_____
___	_____	_____	_____
___	_____	_____	_____

Checklist for Comprehension Strategies

Student _____ Teacher _____ Grade _____

Comprehension Strategies	Date _____			Date _____		
	Yes	Sometimes	No	Yes	Sometimes	No
1. Uses prior knowledge						
2. Makes reasonable predictions						
3. To understand what has been read, the reader						
■ uses meaning (context)						
■ uses sentence structure						
■ uses sounds of words (phonics)						
4. Uses story elements						
5. Gathers and compares information from several sources						
6. Reacts critically to what has been read						
7. Applies strategies with non-fiction/content areas						
■ previewing						
■ mapping						
■ brainstorming						
■ asking questions						
8. Monitors comprehension and uses fix-up strategies						
■ knows that reading has to make sense						
■ previews and predicts						
■ thinks aloud						
■ recognizes when meaning breaks down						
■ stops to assess (uses fix-ups)						
9. Processes chunks of language (good phrasing)						
10. Can explain author's purposes						

Strengthening Reading Through Writing

Laurie Elish-Piper

Overview

Good writers tend to be good readers, and struggling writers tend to struggle with reading as well (Stotsky, 1983). By looking at the nature of reading and writing processes, many connections and instructional implications can be identified (Shanahan, 1990; Tierney & Shanahan, 1991).

Reading and writing are both acts of making and interpreting meaning for communication purposes. In reading, students use background knowledge and information from the text to construct meaning. Writing requires students to use background experience and knowledge about written texts to compose meaning that can then be communicated to those who read the text (Atwell, 1987; Graves, 1983; Tierney & Pearson, 1983).

Because there are many connections between reading and writing, writers can learn much from reading. Students learn about style, genres, and how to effectively use conventions in their writing. In addition, writing gives students meaningful opportunities to respond to and reflect on what they read. Written response and reflection allow students to relate to characters and events in narrative texts and to clarify their learning in expository texts (Pappas, Kiefer, & Levstik, 1995).

When designing an effective reading-writing program which supports students, some important principles to consider include the following:

- Students learn to become better readers and writers by reading and writing.

- Students of all ages need time for exploration and opportunities to choose what they read and write.

- Students learn a great deal when reading and writing are modeled for real purposes.

- Sharing and interaction are essential for students because both reading and writing are social processes which focus on the communication of ideas.

- Reading and writing are critical components of learning, and they are important across the curriculum, not just as separate subjects.

- Students need easy access to varied reading and writing materials.

In classrooms where the reading-writing connection is well-developed, writing is viewed as a process which involves rehearsal or prewriting, drafting, revision and editing, and publishing. The steps of the writing process are not sequential or orderly; they are recursive. As students write, they get new ideas, receive feedback from others, and clarify their own thinking. Such new information often sends a writer back to earlier stages of the process (Routman, 1991). The major stages of the writing process are briefly described below:

Rehearsal or Prewriting	This stage can be thought of as the "Getting It Out" phase. During this stage, the focus is on activating prior knowledge and experiences, getting ideas out into the open, and making plans for writing. These plans include determining the purpose and audience for writing. Many activities help students rehearse for writing. They may include talking, reading, brainstorming, role playing, drawing, taking notes, interviewing, visualizing, listening, and viewing.
Drafting	This stage can be thought of as the "Getting It Down" phase. The student writes a complete draft during this stage.
Revision and Editing	The student seeks response to what has been written. Teachers and peers who respond to a student's writing during conferences are very important during this stage. Revision focuses on content, ideas, audience, and purpose of the writing. Editing is the final step in revision. Editing focuses on mechanics such as spelling and punctuation.
Publishing	Students "Go Public" with their finished writing during this stage. Publishing can include making books, reading pieces aloud to the class from the author's chair, and displaying writing in the classroom.

This chapter will present teaching strategies and activities which develop and support the reading-writing connection.

Behavior Observed	The student has difficulty choosing topics for writing and preparing to write.
Anticipated Outcome	The student will be able to choose topics for writing and prepare to write.

Background

Writers need to prepare before beginning to write. The prewriting stage of the writing process allows the writer to generate and explore ideas, recall and rehearse ideas, relate and probe ideas, plan, and think about writing (Pappas, Kiefer, & Levskik, 1995). Such prewriting typically results in more complete, cohesive writing. The following strategies provide suggestions which may be helpful as you assist students with preparing to write.

Teaching Strategy
(Adapted from Routman, 1991)

1. Tell students you will all be writing about something you are an expert at doing. Discuss that writers often write best about things they know well. Explain to students that you will model for them how you would write your own paper.

2. Using the overhead or chalkboard, brainstorm things at which you are an expert. Make a list of items. For example, your list might contain:

sleeping late on Saturdays	shopping for bargains
needlepoint	making chocolate chip cookies
playing with my cat	growing house plants

3. Ask students to make their own brainstorming lists of things at which they are experts. Provide a few minutes for them to independently complete their lists. A sample student brainstorming list is provided below:

playing video games	playing soccer
fighting with my brother	solving the mystery in books
running	building models

4. Tell students that you need to narrow down your list so your paper focuses on only one of your expert areas. Tell them why you selected one idea over the others. For example, you might say, "I picked playing with my cat because it is a fun topic to write about, and I think that readers would enjoy it." Tell students that you will keep the other ideas on the list because you might use them for future writing topics.

5. Model for students how to brainstorm ideas related to the topic of "playing with my cat." The list may include ideas such as:

when she was a kitten	how to tell when she wants to play
the toys she likes and doesn't like	it's fun
teaching her to play fetch	

6. Tell students to return to their own brainstorming lists. Ask them to select one of their ideas and brainstorm what they could write about that area of expertise. Provide time for students to write on the topic they selected. Encourage students to keep the other ideas on their brainstorming lists for ideas for future writing topics.

Practice and Reinforcement Activities

1. Encourage students to rehearse before writing. Writing processes differ from writer to writer, and by providing options, students can choose strategies which work best for them. Some suggested activities which may help students rehearse before drafting are:

   - Talking with a peer, a group, or an expert on the topic.

   - Interviewing peers, the teacher, a writer, or an expert on the topic.

   - Brainstorming ideas alone, with a partner, or as part of a larger group.

   - Making a graphic representation of ideas by constructing a map or web.

   - Role playing or creative dramatics.

   - Mental exercises such as visualizing or quiet reflection.

   - Experiencing the situation or topic by actually engaging in an activity.

   - Reading to locate information, find a model, or gather inspiration.

   - Free writing or stream-of-consciousness writing to help identify or clarify a topic.

   - Focused free writing on an intended topic to help clarify ideas and feelings related to the topic.

   - Writing leads by drafting 3-5 possible opening sentences. This may help to clarify ideas and "get the ball rolling."

   - Doodling, drawing, or cartooning to help see how the topic "takes shape."

   - Listing ideas which relate to the topic.

   - Viewing pictures, videos, movies, or paintings related to the topic.

2. Create a file of unusual, thought-provoking magazine pictures which invite students into writing. If students are having difficulty identifying writing topics, encourage them to peruse the pictures in the file.

3. Introduce brainstorming for writing topics as a class activity. Ask students, "What are some things that might make good writing topics?" Record their ideas on the chalkboard. If necessary, guide students with questions such as: "What do you know a lot about? What concerns you? What interesting things have you done lately? What are some of your special memories?" Tell students to think about the suggestions on the chalkboard and select one to write about. Ask students to discuss their ideas with a partner. After several minutes of partner discussion time, ask volunteers to share their writing plans.

4. Provide students with a pocket notebook to record possible writing topics. During class time and conversations with students, point out possible writing topics. For example, "Your trip to the zoo this weekend would make a great writing topic." When students have time to write but express frustration that they have "nothing to write about," direct students to their writing topic notebooks.

5. Implement a writing workshop to help students engage in all the stages of the writing process. Providing regular time and opportunities for peer interaction during writing will support students in identifying meaningful writing topics and help them prepare to write.

Behavior Observed	The student has difficulty revising and editing writing.
Anticipated Outcome	The student will revise and edit writing effectively.

Perspectives and Strategies

Revision focuses on clarifying content, ideas, audience, purpose, and organization of writing. Editing focuses on mechanics such as spelling and punctuation. These processes require students to look closely at their writing to identify its strengths and weaknesses and make changes to improve the writing and its effectiveness. The following suggestions may be useful in helping students develop skills and strategies for revising their writing.

1. Invite published writers to come in the classroom to discuss their writing processes. If possible, ask the writers to bring copies of their notes, rough drafts, revised drafts, and published writing. Newspaper reporters, advertising writers, technical writers, and local children's authors are possible choices.

2. Engage students in a discussion of the personal and public types of writing. For example, discuss how a journal does not need to be revised and edited because it is a personal type of writing. Discuss which types of writing are public and should go through all the stages of the writing process. Discuss why it is important to revise, edit, and proofread public types of writing before publishing them. Make a list of the types of writing which are personal and public, and display this list on a bulletin board in the classroom for reference.

3. Use think-alouds to model revision for students. Place a piece of writing on the overhead projector or chalkboard. Read the piece aloud and explain how you would revise and edit the paper. Demonstrate how you would make the changes, and write a final copy of the paper for students to see how the piece changed through revision.

4. Teach students how to self-evaluate their own writing using a checklist. The checklist can be developed collaboratively by the teacher and students. Self-evaluation of writing helps students take more responsibility for monitoring, revising, editing, and proofreading their own writing. A sample checklist follows.

Self-Evaluation Checklist for the Writer

Title of Writing _____

Review your writing carefully. Then circle your answer.

Purpose and Audience

1. Does the piece fit my audience?	YES	NO
2. Is the purpose of my piece clear?	YES	NO
3. Will the reader learn new information or be entertained?	YES	NO
4. Is the title informative and appropriate for the piece?	YES	NO

Content and Organization

5. Are the ideas in the piece interesting and clear?	YES	NO
6. Does the piece have a good lead-in?	YES	NO
7. Does the piece have a good conclusion?	YES	NO
8. Are my ideas organized in a logical way?	YES	NO
9. Did I write exactly what I meant?	YES	NO

Mechanics

10. Did I use capital letters correctly?	YES	NO
11. Did I use periods at the end of each sentence?	YES	NO
12. Did I use commas correctly?	YES	NO
13. Did I use quotation marks correctly?	YES	NO
14. Did I use other punctuation correctly?	YES	NO
15. Are all words spelled correctly?	YES	NO

*If you answered "NO" to any of these questions and want some help, set up a conference with a peer or the teacher.

From Jerry L. Johns and Susan Davis Lenski, *Improving Reading: A Handbook of Strategies* (2nd ed.). Copyright © 1997 Kendall/Hunt Publishing Company (1-800-228-0810). May be reproduced for noncommercial educational purposes.

5. Use guiding questions when conferencing with students about their writing. These questions help students take more responsibility for revising and editing by leading them back into their writing. The following questions (Adapted from Atwell, 1987) may be helpful:

Situation	Conference Questions
The writing is unfocused.	• Do you have more than one story here?
The writing covers several events or ideas.	• What is the most important thing you want to say? • What do you think is the best part? How can you build on that?
The writing lacks depth and information.	• I don't understand. • Can you tell me more about this? • What else do you know about… ? • How can you find out more about… ?
The writing contains too much information.	• Is all the information needed by the reader? • What information isn't necessary?
The piece just lists information and doesn't contain the writer's thoughts and feelings.	• How did you feel when this happened? • What do you think about this?
The lead does not draw the reader into the writing effectively.	• Does this lead draw the reader right in? • How do some of the authors you are reading draw the reader in? • Will any of their techniques work here?
The conclusion is too sudden or drags on.	• What do you want your reader to know or feel at the end of reading this? • Does this conclusion do that well? • Where does the piece really end?
A narrative piece makes limited use of dialogue.	• What can you do to show the reader who the characters really are? • How do some of the authors you are reading use dialogue?
The writing is poorly organized.	• How do the parts of your piece fit together? • Do you think your organization makes that clear to the reader?
Bringing closure to the conference.	• What do you plan to do next with your writing?

6. Teach students how to effectively conference with peers during the writing process. Peer conferences consist of two to four students who respond to a writer's draft. The writer reads the piece aloud. The other students respond to the draft. Through teacher modeling in teacher-student conferences and focus lessons, students can be taught to use prompts such as:

   ■ What did you like best about this piece?

   ■ What worked well in this piece?

   ■ Was there anything in the piece that you wanted to hear more about?

   ■ Was there anything about this piece that was unclear?

   ■ Does the piece need more detail? Where?

   ■ Does the piece need more description? Where?

   ■ Does the piece have a good beginning or lead?

   ■ Does the piece have an appropriate ending?

7. Using the following steps, model for students how to use peer conferencing to assist with revision.

   ■ Listen to the first reading of the paper.

   ■ Listen critically to the second reading of the paper. Jot down notes as you listen. (Your notes can be written on the overhead or chalkboard so students can see what you notice about the paper.)

   ■ Start with a positive comment such as, "I liked how you described…"

   ■ Share your suggestions and questions. For example, you might say, "I wondered why you… ? or "Have you considered trying… ?"

8. Engage students in editing activities to help them develop an understanding of revision and proofreading. For younger students, place a sentence on the chalkboard. The sentence should contain one or more errors such as leaving out a capital letter, leaving a word out, misspelling a word, or forgetting a period. Provide time for students to locate and correct the errors. Discuss the errors and corrections as a whole group. With older students, provide a paragraph or two which contains multiple errors. Select the sentences and paragraphs based on the types of errors you have noticed in students' writing.

7.3　Sharing and Publishing Writing

Behavior Observed	The student has difficulty sharing and publishing writing.
Anticipated Outcome	The student will share and publish writing.

Perspective and Strategies

By having many opportunities to share and publish their writing, students can experience the social and communication purposes of writing. The following strategies may be helpful for teachers who wish to engage students in meaningful opportunities for sharing and publishing their writing.

1. Provide many opportunities for publishing student writing. Publishing can include volunteers reading their work aloud, binding books, displaying writing in the classroom writing center, performing written scripts as plays or reader's theater, and newsletters containing student writing. Specific publishing ideas and formats are provided in the Resources section of this chapter.

2. Write a classroom newspaper. Students can publish their stories, poems, and informational writing. Students can also write about classroom, school, and community happenings and upcoming events. The newspaper can be distributed to students' families, the school office, and other classrooms in the school.

3. Hold a writing fair to celebrate writing. At the fair, each student may choose to read a piece of self-selected writing. Student-made books and class-made books can be displayed and shared. Copies of student writing can be assembled into a booklet for each person who attends the writing fair. The emphasis of a writing fair should be to celebrate all students' writing, not to compete for prizes.

4. Establish an author's chair in the classroom. A rocking chair, stool, or any other specially designated chair can be used. The author's chair is a special location in the room where an author (student, teacher, or guest) reads his or her writing aloud for sharing and response purposes.

5. Develop a "Writer of the Week" bulletin board. Rotate the honor of being writer of the week throughout the class, and collaborate with students to help them select things to share as writer of the week. The bulletin board display may include a photograph of the writer, self-selected pieces of writing, and interesting information about the writer. Time should be set aside each week to allow the writer of the week to discuss his or her favorite pieces of writing and to answer questions other students may have.

7.4 Organizational Patterns of Writing

Behavior Observed	The student has difficulty organizing writing for specific purposes.
Anticipated Outcome	The student will effectively organize writing for specific purposes.

Background

Mature writers are able to compose and organize writing for many different purposes. The term "genre" refers to the different categories and organizational patterns of written texts. A genre of text has a specific purpose, type of audience, and style of writing. The following chart provides background information for the teacher about the narrative, descriptive, persuasive, and expository genres of writing. In addition, this section presents teaching strategies and activities which may help teachers support and engage students in learning to organize writing for specific purposes.

Genre of Writing	Purpose of Writing	Examples
Narrative Specific strategies are provided in Section 7.5	■ To tell a real or imaginary story ■ To recreate a series of events	■ Personal Stories ■ Fictional Stories ■ Poems ■ Ballads ■ Personal letters
Persuasive	■ To convince the reader to accept a belief, position, or opinion ■ To convince the reader to take a specified action	■ Editorials ■ Letters to the editor ■ Reviews ■ Position papers
Descriptive	■ To create a verbal portrait ■ To show the reader through words what an experience, event, person, or place is like	■ Character sketches ■ Descriptive paragraphs ■ Descriptions of people, places, and/or things ■ Poems
Expository Specific strategies are presented in Section 7.6	■ To inform the reader ■ To explain factual information to the reader ■ To tell the reader how to do something	■ Research reports ■ How-to instructions ■ Directions ■ Newspaper articles ■ Essays

Teaching Strategy 1: Persuasive Writing

1. Show students an editorial. It can be an editorial from the local newspaper or a sample editorial the teacher has written. Give students photocopies or make an overhead transparency of the editorial. The editorial should be related to an issue on which students will have some background knowledge. For example, the editorial might argue against building a new shopping mall on a piece of farm land in the community. A short, sample editorial on this topic is presented below. Provide time for students to read the editorial silently.

> We do not need another mall in Middletown. We already have a convenient, busy downtown shopping area which provides many goods and services for the people of Middletown. The downtown area is easily accessible by car or public transportation. Downtown is a safe area where families feel comfortable and welcome. Middletown doesn't need all of the undesirable elements that a new shopping mall will bring to our town.

> The proposed shopping mall on the site of Miller's farm will be a disaster for the community of Middletown. The roads are not wide enough for all of the outsiders and traffic coming into a mall. Traffic jams would become a daily event in our community. We would need to spend millions of our tax dollars to build new roads and put in stop lights. That is money that will come from honest, hard-working tax payers.

> Crime is always a problem at a mall. Because of the crime, many of our own families here in Middletown may not feel safe shopping at the new mall. If the mall is not going to benefit us, I say we don't need a mall here in Middletown. I urge you to tell your neighbors, the mayor, and the city council members that a new mall is a TERRIBLE idea for Middletown. We need to make our voices heard now, or our quiet little city could be a thing of the past.

2. Tell students that the editorial they read is an example of persuasive writing. Write the words "Persuasive Writing" on the chalkboard. Tell students that the purpose of persuasive writing is to persuade or convince the reader to believe and/or do something.

3. Ask students what they think the author's purpose was for composing the editorial. Guide students to discover that the main purposes of the editorial were:

   ■ To persuade the reader that the mall is bad for Middletown.

   ■ To persuade the reader to tell the mayor and others that the mall should not be built.

4. Tell students that an author has a specific audience in mind when writing. Explain that the audience is the person, group of people, or type of person for whom the author is writing. Ask students to identify possible audiences for the editorial. Write their ideas on the chalkboard.

5. Discuss clues that helped students identify possible audiences. Guide the students to see that the audience for the editorial is tax payers with families in Middletown.

6. Explain to students that authors of persuasive writing use many words and phrases that are persuasive or convincing. Provide time for students to reread the editorial. Tell them to jot down any words or phrases that were very persuasive or convincing to them as readers.

7. Have students share their findings. Discuss why these words or phrases were persuasive or convincing to them. If necessary, direct students' attention to words and phrases such as, "undesirable elements," "disaster," "outsiders," "traffic jams," "crime," and "TERRIBLE" to describe the proposed mall. If necessary, point out how the author used positive words and phrases such as "convenient, busy downtown," "easily accessible," "safe area," and "comfortable and welcome" in conjunction with not building the mall.

8. Tell students that persuasive writing presents an argument. The author identifies his or her position, provides evidence, and encourages the reader to reach a specific conclusion or take action.

9. Tell students that the class will be writing its own editorial in response to the one they just read.

10. Ask students if they agree or disagree with the editorial. Have students vote on the position they should take in their editorial. For the purpose of this example, the students will be writing an editorial which supports building a mall.

11. Have students identify the purpose of their writing and their audience. An example of a purpose and an audience is the following:

   Purpose: To convince the reader that building the mall is a good idea

   Audience: Editor and readers of the newspaper

12. Tell students they can use ideas from the original editorial and their own opinions and knowledge to write the new editorial. Ask students to brainstorm their arguments. Record their ideas on the chalkboard. Encourage students to suggest facts, examples, and reasons to support their ideas.

13. Create a semantic map to organize students' ideas. An example follows.

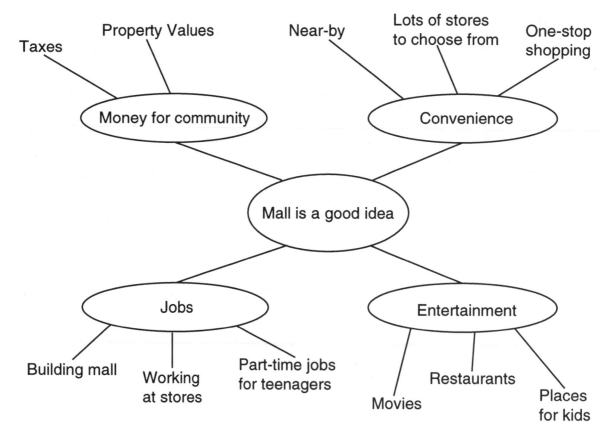

380

14. Explain to students that each of the key ideas of the semantic map will become a paragraph in the editorial. Discuss how the key ideas will be presented in their editorial. Discuss the order of ideas to be presented. Tell students that editorials often present the most convincing ideas last so the reader will remember them. Ask students to prioritize the ideas from the semantic map.

15. Tell students the center part of the semantic map should become their first sentence. Encourage them to think of persuasive ways to state their position in support of the new mall. For example, students might write, "Building a new mall in Middletown will benefit every single person in the community" or "The new mall in Middletown is the best thing to happen in this community in many years."

16. Refer to the semantic map to determine what information will be presented next. Encourage students to suggest persuasive, convincing language and facts as they contribute to the class editorial.

17. After a first draft has been written, provide time for students to work with a partner to read, discuss, and suggest revisions to the editorial. Discuss students' suggestions as a group. Make revisions as appropriate.

18. Engage students in reading and writing editorials on multiple occasions. Provide opportunities for students to send their editorials to the local paper, school newspaper or newsletter, or read the editorial over the school intercom.

19. This strategy can be adapted for other types of persuasive writing such as letters to the editor, position papers, and reviews.

Teaching Strategy 2: Descriptive Writing

1. Place a large stuffed toy on a table in front of the classroom. Provide time for students to look at, touch, and closely examine the toy.

2. Tell students that descriptive writing paints pictures in the reader's mind. Tell them that writers use descriptive words to help the reader see, hear, taste, touch, and smell what the author is writing about.

3. Ask students to brainstorm words and phrases that describe the stuffed toy. Record the words on the chalkboard. Encourage students to suggest interesting words they have seen or read in books in addition to the words they often use. Record their ideas on the chalkboard. This can be done in a semantic map.

4. Write the following prompt on the chalkboard to provide students with a start for their paragraph.

    We have a stuffed toy in our classroom. It is...

5. Ask students to suggest sentences to add to the paragraph. Write their ideas on the chalkboard. As ideas have been used in the paragraph, mark them off of the semantic map.

6. After the first draft is written, ask students to make suggestions for revisions. Encourage students to use more descriptive words and phrases, reorganize the paragraph so it is clearer, add more details, and so on.

7. Tell students that good descriptive writing creates a picture in the reader's head. Present the class's paragraph to another teacher, the principal, the librarian, or another class of students, and ask the reader(s) to draw the subject of the paragraph.

8. If the reader's drawing is not accurate, guide students back to their paragraph to see if they can make it clearer and/or more accurate.

9. Guide students through writing other descriptive paragraphs about objects, people, or events. Encourage students to incorporate elements of descriptive writing into their own writing.

Practice and Reinforcement Activities

1. Consult section 7.5 for ideas to help students write fictional stories.

2. Consult section 7.6 for ideas to help students write in the expository genre.

3. Consult Chapter 8, "Fostering Study and Test-Taking Strategies," for additional ideas about using graphic organizers to assist students with writing the five main types of expository text: description, sequence, comparison, cause/effect, and problem/solution.

4. Refer to Chapter 5, "Promoting Comprehension," for additional ideas about understanding and organizing writing around a main idea and supporting details.

5. Provide texts and time for students to read widely in various genres.

6. Read aloud to students from various genres.

7. Engage students in a "scavenger hunt" for samples of writing in a specific genre. For example, students can search for samples of persuasive writing. Provide time for students to share their findings. Students can compile a class scrapbook or 3-ring binder of examples of writing in the persuasive genre. Add to this collection as students read and write in the genre. Make the collection accessible to students by placing it in the classroom library or writing center. This activity can be used for any genre of writing.

8. Share models of writing in various genres with students. Be sure to include your writing in various genres so you can discuss your purpose, audience, and choices about writing style and techniques.

Behavior Observed	The student has difficulty effectively using the elements of fiction when writing stories.
Anticipated Outcome	The student will effectively use the elements of fiction when writing stories.

Background

Effective writers tend to read widely which provides them with many models of how to write stories. In addition, good readers and writers have a clear understanding of story elements and how they fit together. The following strategies and activities provide suggestions for helping students understand the elements of fiction and incorporating them into the stories they write.

Teaching Strategy 1 (For Younger Students)

1. Pick a story which has clear plot elements: characters, goal, problem, and solution. *Jamaica Tag-Along* by Juanita Havill (1990) works well for this strategy.

2. Read the story aloud to the students, asking them to predict and confirm their predictions throughout.

3. Place a blank copy of the plot relationships chart (Schmidt & Buckley, 1991) on the overhead, chalkboard, or chart paper. Tell students they will be using this chart to help them learn the parts of a story and how the parts fit together.

Plot Relationships Chart

Somebody	Wanted	But	So

4. Guide students through identifying the major story elements of main character, goal, problem, and solution. Use the cue words **somebody, wanted, but,** and **so** to prompt students to identify the elements. You may ask questions such as, "Who is the important **somebody** in this book?" When students answer, "Jamaica," write it on the chart. To elicit the goals, present the statement, "In the story, Jamaica **wanted**…" Follow this pattern of using the cues and students' responses to identify the problem and solution in the story.

5. Explain to students that there are special words to tell the parts of a story. They are main character (somebody), goal (wanted), problem (but), and solution (so). Write these words on the chart below the cue words.

6. Discuss with students how these important elements of stories fit together so the reader can understand the story.

7. Tell students that you will be writing a group story which is related to *Jamaica Tag-Along*. Provide students with the title, "Tag-Along Berto." Ask students to brainstorm what the story might be about. Record students' ideas on the overhead projector, chalkboard, or chart paper.

8. Show students a blank copy of the plot relationships chart and ask them to decide who the important **somebody** in the story will be. Guide students through identifying the goal, problem, and solution for the group story.

9. Discuss how the parts of the story fit together. Do they make sense? Does it seem like this will be an interesting story?

10. Using the information on the plot relationships chart, ask the children to dictate the basic story line to you. Prompt students as needed by providing the cues, "somebody… wanted… but… so…" Once the basic story line has been identified, ask students to dictate details, suggest changes, and consider the sequence of the story.

11. After the story is written, ask students to point out the important elements of the story. Tell students that the plot relationships chart will be helpful to them as they read for understanding and work to write clear stories.

12. Repeat this basic procedure for other stories.

Teaching Strategy 2 (For Older Students)

1. Consider the approach designed for younger students. By selecting an age-appropriate book or story, the plot relationships chart will provide a clear structure for reading and writing stories. This can serve as a good introduction to the more complex task outlined beginning in step 2.

2. Read a short story, such as *Slower than the Rest* by Cynthia Rylant (1985), aloud to students or ask them to read it silently. After discussing students' responses to the story, present a blank story map on the overhead projector or chalkboard. Ask students to identify the key elements of the story. Record their responses on the story map. Discuss how the elements fit together to make a story. Discuss what would happen to the story if there was no problem in the plot.

3. Present students with a title such as "Never Give Up." Ask them to brainstorm possible elements for a story with this title. Record their ideas on a blank story map. Discuss how the various ideas fit together. Ask students to clarify ideas, make modifications, consider sequencing of events, and provide details to make the story clearer.

4. Using the notes on the story map, ask a student to tell the story to the group. Ask a second student to tell the story adding more details and description. While students are telling the story, the teacher takes notes on the story map.

5. Using the story map as a guide, model how to write the story the students just developed. Cue students into the important elements of the story as you are writing. For example, you

might say, "The setting seems to be very important to the problem in the story. I wonder how I can show the reader that?" These types of observations followed by questions will guide students through the process of including and connecting important elements when writing a story.

6. After the story is written, ask students to identify the story elements. Discuss how story mapping will help students as they read and write stories.

Teaching Strategy 3 (For Younger Students)

1. Display the "Getting to Know My Character" chart (Richards & Gipe, 1993). Explain to students that this strategy will help them recognize how authors tell readers about story characters.

2. Read the following summary of *The Balancing Girl* by Bernice Rabe (1981) (adapted from Richards & Gipe, 1993). The teacher should display the passage on the overhead projector or on the chalkboard. As the teacher reads the passage aloud, the students follow along.

> Margaret was good at balancing. She could balance a book on her head while gliding along in her wheelchair. She could balance herself on her crutches, too. One day Margaret went to a quiet corner in the classroom. She worked hard all morning and made a big domino castle. When Margaret came back to the classroom after lunch, she saw that her castle had been knocked down. "I DIDN'T DO IT!" shouted Tommy. Margaret yelled, "Yes, you did Tommy, and you better never knock down anything I balance again, or YOU'LL BE SORRY!" Later, Margaret made a new domino castle. When she finished, six dominoes fell down. "Oh no!" she thought, but just then, the dominoes stopped falling. "Thank goodness," Margaret thought to herself.

3. Tell the students that the author provides some very important facts about Margaret. Ask the students to identify some of these facts. As students identify important facts, the teacher highlights the appropriate portions of the passage on the overhead or chalkboard. Ask questions as needed to help students identify important facts.

4. After the important facts have been identified, place a blank copy of the "Getting to Know My Character" chart (found in the Resources section of this chapter) on the overhead projector or chalkboard. Fill out the facts section of the chart. Guide students to make inferences about Margaret based on the facts presented in the summary. You can do this by asking questions such as "Why do you think Margaret balances books on her head?" or "Why might Margaret be in a wheelchair?"

5. Tell students that the author also helps the reader learn about Margaret by describing her actions. Guide the students through locating portions of the passage that provide descriptions of Margaret's actions. Highlight these portions on the overhead or chalkboard.

6. Record the information which describes Margaret's actions on the overhead or chalkboard. Guide the students to make inferences about Margaret by considering her actions. Model how you make inferences to aid students in making their own inferences. For example, you might state, "The story says Margaret 'worked hard all morning and made a big domino castle.' That makes me think Margaret was a careful, hard worker who had a lot of patience. I know that making something from dominos or blocks can be very hard and take a lot of concentration and patience." Encourage students to make other inferences by using information about Margaret's actions.

7. Discuss how authors also tell readers about a character by what the character says and thinks. Tell the students that by looking at conversations the character has with others in the story, the reader can learn a great deal about the character. Point out that authors also provide information about a character's thoughts, and the reader can make inferences about what the character is thinking. Guide the students to find examples of conversations Margaret had with other story characters. Highlight these on the passage on the overhead or chalkboard. Model your inference-making techniques for students. For example, you might say, "I think Margaret was really angry when she yelled, 'YOU'LL BE SORRY!' to Tommy. I know that when people yell they are usually very angry. I bet she was thinking that Tommy knocked down her castle." Encourage students to make other inferences about Margaret, guiding them as necessary. Ask students to support their inferences with examples and clues from the story.

8. As an application activity, students can use the information on the chart and their inferences to write the rest of the story. Younger students can dictate the story. Older students can write the story on their own or with a partner. Students should be reminded to provide facts, actions, conversations, and thoughts to tell about Margaret in their story. A sample of the completed chart follows:

"Getting to Know My Character" Chart
(Adapted from Richards & Gipe, 1993)

Facts about my character	My character's actions
Margaret was good at balancing.	Margaret found a private corner.
She balanced books on her head.	She made a big domino castle.
She had wheelchair.	She was a careful worker.
She had crutches.	She had good concentration.
My character's conversations	**My character's thoughts**
Margaret yelled at Tommy.	Margaret thought, "Oh no," when some dominoes fell.
She thought Tommy knocked down her castle.	She was concerned and upset.
She was mad when she yelled at Tommy.	Margaret said to herself, "Thank goodness," when the dominoes stopped falling. She was relieved.

Practice and Reinforcement Activities

1. Encourage students to read widely. Provide a classroom library with books and stories representing a variety of genres and levels.

2. When planning stories, have students draw story boards to show the major story elements. For example, students can draw the main character, the setting, the problem situation, important events, and the solution. Older students can write phrases and details on their story boards to prepare for writing the story. Once students have prepared their story boards, they can tell their story to a partner to confirm effective use of story elements, clarity, and details. Students can then write a draft of their story.

3. Prepare a set of cards which contain information about story elements. Have students tell a story using the elements presented on the cards. Encourage them to add details and consider the sequence of events. Students can then write stories using the story line they have created from the cards. To show students how story elements are related to each other within a story, substitute one of the cards. Ask students how the story will be changed. Sample story element cards are shown below.

Setting: A small town in the United States	**Main Character:** A shy, quiet boy named Billy
Problem: Billy's best friend has moved away, and Billy is very lonely.	**Solution:** Billy learns he has a special talent that helps him make new friends.

4. Use wordless picture books to help students "read" pictures to discover the story line and identify the main story elements. Wordless books with clear, familiar patterns and story lines such as *Deep in the Forest* (Turkle, 1976), a modification of the "Three Little Bears," work well with younger or struggling students. After identifying the elements, younger students may dictate the story. Older students may write their own stories based on the pictures. Students can then analyze their stories and their peers' stories to determine if major story elements are present and used effectively in the story. A list of wordless picture books is provided in Appendix A.

5. Students can complete story frames for stories they have read. Story frames can also be used with stories students have written. Students can analyze their own stories, analyze peers' stories, or work in teams to analyze each other's stories. See Chapter 5 for sample story frame formats.

6. Help students make a visual plan for a main character before they begin writing a story. Tell students to visualize their main character. Prompt them to draw a picture of the character and write notes, descriptive words, and important details about their character. Students can share their drawings with a partner to clarify their plans before they begin writing.

Behavior Observed	The student has difficulty constructing meaning from content texts.
Anticipated Outcome	The student will construct meaning from content texts.

Background

While students can learn a great deal from their own experiences, they cannot get all of their knowledge from first-hand experience. Content area texts allow students to expand their experiences and knowledge. Reading informational texts becomes increasingly important as students progress from the primary grades to the intermediate grades and beyond. Unfortunately, many students encounter difficulty with content texts. These texts and informational trade books generally include vocabulary, concepts, and organizational patterns which are new to students. The strategies students have learned for reading narrative texts such as stories, poems, and plays do not work well when reading content texts. Additional strategies for reading content texts are found in Chapter 8.

By connecting content reading and writing, students can explore concepts, clarify their understanding, and connect their learning to their own lives. "Writing to learn" before reading promotes learning by increasing students' motivation, arousing their curiosity, activating their prior knowledge, and focusing their attention on important information. Writing during and after reading allows students to focus on and document their own thinking, organize information, and identify points of confusion (Moore, Readance, & Rickleman, 1989). The following strategies and activities connect content reading and writing and may be helpful as you guide students toward constructing meaning from content texts.

Teaching Strategy 1 (For Younger Students)
(Adapted from Smith & Bean, 1980)

1. Use the guided writing procedure after students have been studying a topic for a period of time. For example, the topic could be plants.

2. Draw a picture of a plant on the center of the chalkboard. Write the word "plants" in the middle of the drawing. Tell the students you will be thinking and writing about plants.

3. Ask the students to share important things they have learned about plants. Write their ideas on the chalkboard. Cluster their ideas with other similar ideas to make a structured overview similar to the one included in the example on page 390.

4. After several items are present in a cluster, ask students to identify the main idea for that cluster. For example, the cluster which contains "dirt," "water," "sun," "rain," and "no snow" could be given the category name "what plants need." Write the category name above the cluster. Continue with this pattern until students are unable to share more ideas.

5. Direct students to content texts they have been reading about plants. These may include their science textbook, informational trade books, and student-written materials. Divide students into groups of two, and ask them to look for other important information they have learned about plants. Remind them to look at the pictures, titles, captions, and text. Provide 5-10 minutes for students to locate information. Circulate around the room to assist students as they look for new information.

6. Ask students to suggest other important information about plants. Add the new information to the chart.

7. Select one of the clusters on the chart. Encourage students to suggest sentences based on the ideas on the chart. Tell students that they can suggest sentences that tell about one piece of information from the cluster, or they can combine several pieces of information into one sentence. As students suggest sentences which contain information from the cluster, cross it off the chart. Guide students to suggest sentences by posing questions as necessary. For example, for the section "parts of plants," the teacher might ask students an open-ended questions such as, "What should we write about the parts of plants listed on the chalkboard?" To provide more direction, the teacher may ask a question such as, "Can you think of a sentence to tell about how plants have leaves and stems?" Write the students' sentences on another piece of chart paper or the chalkboard. Continue this procedure until all of the clusters have been crossed off of the chart.

8. Explain to students that the sentences they wrote for each cluster combine to make a paragraph with one main idea. Show students how each paragraph begins with an indentation and a capital letter. Use the students' language from the sentences to model writing a paragraph based on one cluster. Ask students, "Does that sound right?" and "Should we make any changes?" as you write the paragraph. Continue this pattern until a paragraph has been written for each cluster.

9. Read and discuss the entire piece. Encourage students to make suggestions to improve the piece.

10. Eventually, students can use the steps of this strategy for small group or individual writing activities.

Guided Writing Procedure: Structured Overview

Parts of plants	Kinds of plants
leaf	trees
stem	bushes
twig	grass
petal	pine trees
seeds	flowers
branches	tomato plants

What plants do for us	What plants need
give us food	dirt
give us wood	water
help us make our houses	sun
give animals places to live	rain
make shade	no snow
look pretty	

Teaching Strategy 2 (For Older Students)

1. Ask students to brainstorm what they already know about an upcoming topic of study. For this example, the topic will be the presidential election process in the United States. Record their responses on the chalkboard. A possible list is shown below.

vote	candidate
republican	commercials
democrat	president
campaign	debates
vice president	independent

2. Explain to students that their responses can be categorized by looking at how the ideas are similar. Identify categories that encompass the brainstormed terms. List the category titles on the chalkboard. Sample category titles may include:

political parties
election procedures
elected offices
candidates

3. Guide the students through dividing the brainstormed ideas into the appropriate categories. Display this information in a web format or as an outline. A sample web and outline are shown below.

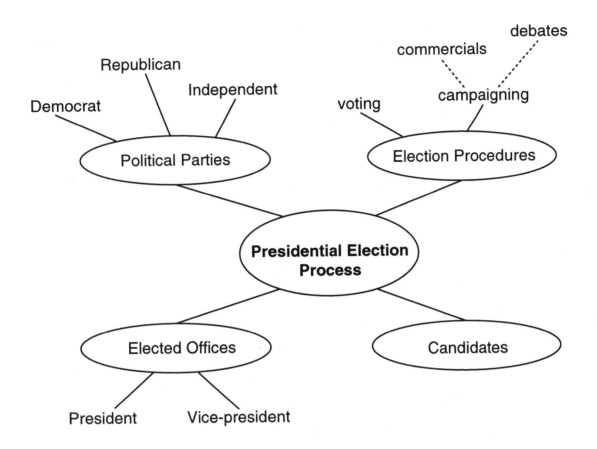

Outline for Presidential Election Process

    I. Political Parties
        A. Republican
        B. Democrat
        C. Independent

    II. Election Procedures
        A. Voting
        B. Campaigning
            1. commercials
            2. debates

    III. Elected Offices
        A. President
        B. Vice-President

    IV. Candidates

4. Ask students to write about the topic using the information from the web or outline. Provide approximately 10 minutes for students to complete this task. Ask students what types of information they need to make their writing clearer and more informative. Ask them what types of information are missing from their papers. List this information on the chalkboard.

5. Provide students with a short passage about presidential elections. The passage can be from their social studies textbook or other informational text. Tell students to look for additional information to add to their web or outline. Ask them to concentrate on looking for the types of information that are missing from their web or outline. Incorporate new information into the map or web.

6. Revisit the map or outline several times during the study of presidential elections. Ask students to keep an ongoing list of new information which can be added. Incorporate the new information into the map or web on a regular basis.

7. Near the end of the unit of study, ask students to write a paper which incorporates the information from the map or web. This can be done as a teacher-led, whole class activity for review, or it can be completed by small groups or individual students.

Teaching Strategy 3 (For Older Students)

The Hennings Sequence (Hennings, 1982) provides eight steps for teachers to use to help guide students through understanding informational text. The eight steps are presented below.

1. *Factstorming:* Help students become familiar with a new topic, such as vertebrates, by exposing them to videos, teacher read-alouds, reading materials, field trips, hands-on materials, and guest speakers. Next, ask students to "factstorm" what they know about the topic of vertebrates. Record the information on the chalkboard.

2. *Categorizing facts:* Explain to students that they will be organizing their ideas by creating a data chart. Ask students to look at the results of their factstorming and suggest categories or "big ideas" which describe some of their ideas. Write these possible categories on the chalkboard. Organize this information onto a blank data chart. Provide time for students to work in groups to fill in the data chart. Encourage them to use the information from their factstorming, but also provide additional resource materials, including content texts to help students fill in the data chart. Share and discuss the information students included on their data charts. A sample data chart format for vertebrates is shown below.

Data Chart for Vertebrates

	Where they live	What they eat	Natural enemies	Warm or cold-blooded	Examples
Fish					
Amphibians					
Reptiles					
Birds					
Mammals					

3. *Drafting cohesive paragraphs:* Discuss the characteristics of a good paragraph. Remind students that a paragraph focuses on one main idea, includes details and examples about the main idea, and contains at least 4-5 good sentences. Guide the students through writing a paragraph about fish. Next, divide students into groups of 2-3. Ask each group to write a paragraph about one of the types of animals. For example, one group will write about amphibians using the information from the data chart.

4. *Sequencing paragraphs into a logical whole:* Provide time for each group of students to share its paragraph. Tell students that the class will be writing a report about vertebrates based on the data chart. Discuss how to order and organize the paragraphs into a report. Encourage students to consult the data chart for ideas about how to organize the paragraphs.

5. *Drafting introductions and conclusions:* Guide students through writing an introduction and conclusion for the report. Explain to them that the data chart and organization of the paragraphs will help them write the introduction and conclusion. This can be done as a teacher-guided, group writing activity.

6. *Organizing the parts into a cohesive report:* Discuss how to determine a good title for the report, how headings and subheadings can be used to make the report clearer, and how illustrations can enhance the report. Encourage students to make revisions which will make the report clearer or more informative. Divide students into groups of two to write a final copy of the report, including titles, headings, and illustrations.

7. *Interpreting similar pieces of discourse:* Provide opportunities for students to use data charts to organize ideas after they have read content texts. Explain that data charts are helpful as a post-reading strategy as well as a pre-writing strategy.

8. *Summarizing, synthesizing, and evaluating:* Help students connect some of the steps in the Hennings sequence to their independent reading by having them engage in writing. Ask students to read a content text selection related to vertebrates. Have them write a summary of key ideas from their reading. Encourage them to use the data chart to focus their writing.

Practice and Reinforcement Activities

1. Implement learning logs so students can reflect on and document their own learning. Learning logs can be used in conjunction with any area of the curriculum. Teachers may provide daily or weekly opportunities for students to write in their learning logs. A list of learning log prompts is provided below:

   - Something important I learned is…

   - I am having a hard time understanding…

   - I want to learn more about…

   - I wonder why…

   - What do I already know about…?

   - What was the point of today's lesson or reading?

   - In the lesson or reading, I got confused when…

2. Incorporate informational trade books into the content areas. Trade books are generally more appealing to students than textbooks. In addition, most trade books provide more complete treatments of topics and concepts than textbooks. Book lists such as *A to Zoo* (Lima & Lima, 1993) and *Adventuring with Books* (Jett-Simpson, 1989) are arranged by subject and can be helpful in locating appropriate informational trade books for use in the classroom.

3. Students can become editors and experts on a specific topic by creating skinny books (Epstein, 1996). Individually or in small groups, students select a specific topic related to the unit of study in the classroom. Students gather articles, pamphlets, pictures, interviews, letters, and other resources related to their topic. They identify key ideas related to their topic and develop an outline or semantic map to organize their material. They become the editor of their book as they cut, paste, write headlines, create headings and subheadings, write introductions, and create connecting information for their skinny book. Students can also highlight key vocabulary words and create a glossary, develop a table of contents, and make an index for their skinny book. Students can add illustrations, charts, graphs, tables, and other graphics to clarify their topics. Students can do presentations on their topics, and their skinny books can be added to the classroom library.

4. Encourage students to write "wish you were here" letters to clarify their learning about new places, important events, and important people. For example, students could write "wish you were here" letters about meeting with Abraham Lincoln after hearing the Gettysburg Address, traveling to Jupiter, visiting the rain forest, or participating in the Battle of the Alamo.

5. Share content-related alphabet books with students. Examples include *The Icky Bug Alphabet Book* (1987), *The Bird Alphabet Book* (1987), and *The Flower Alphabet Book* (1988) by Jerry Pallotta. Using these books as samples, ask students to create alphabet books related to content reading and studies. For example, students can make ABC books about the civil war, solar system, chemical elements, or nutrition. Additional alphabet books can be found in Appendix B.

6. Consult Chapter 8, "Fostering Study and Test-Taking Strategies," for related strategy ideas dealing with text structure, summary writing, and notetaking.

Behavior Observed	The student has difficulty reading like a writer as evidenced by limited ability to observe, understand, analyze, and use authors' styles and content for inspiration and models when composing text.
Anticipated Outcome	The student will read like a writer as evidenced by observing, understanding, analyzing, and using authors' styles and content for inspiration and models when composing text.

Background

Students learn to write effectively by "reading like a writer" (Smith, 1983). Atwell (1987) described this connection between reading and writing as looking at texts from the inside, from a writer's point of view, so students may "look at their own texts from the outside, from a reader's point of view" (p. 227).

As students read a variety of literature and engage in thoughtful discussion, reflection, and interpretation of what they read, they come to know how authors create feelings, ideas, and responses in readers. This knowledge enables students to analyze their reading closely and critically. In addition, such knowledge allows students to "borrow" genres, topics or themes, and writing techniques or styles for their own writing (Atwell, 1987). The following strategies focus on creating opportunities to help students become aware of how writers evoke desired responses in readers and how students can use the techniques of other authors in their own writing.

Teaching Strategy

1. Introduce the phrase, "reading like a writer," to students by placing it on the chalkboard. Ask students what they think the phrase means. Guide their thinking by asking questions such as:

   How are reading and writing alike?
   How are they different?
   How might reading help you when you are writing?
   What kinds of things might a writer look for when reading something?

2. Record students' ideas on the chalkboard. Then tell students that when "reading like a writer," a person pays close attention to how the author writes and how this affects them as a reader. Refer to students' ideas as appropriate. Explain that by doing this, students can get new ideas for topics, techniques, and genres they can "borrow" for their own writing.

3. Select a page from a book students have recently read or one they are currently reading. Prepare a transparency of the page or copy the text onto the chalkboard. Tell students they will be learning how to "read like a writer" during this activity. Read the passage aloud to the students.

4. Ask students to discuss what they liked and disliked about the passage. Ask students to explain why they think they responded as they did. Guide them to cite specific words, phrases, images, topics, themes, or writing styles which influenced their responses.

5. Direct students' attention to a particular aspect of the passage. For example, how the author used descriptive words, introduced a character, wrote dialogue, or created suspense.

6. Ask students how they might "borrow" ideas from the author for their own writing. Encourage students to jot down notes about how they might "borrow" from the author for their own writing.

7. Ask students to "read like writers" and pay special attention to how other authors approach the same aspect of writing in their books and stories. Encourage students to include "borrowed" ideas in their writing.

Practice and Reinforcement Activities

1. Encourage students to read widely from many genres. Provide a well-stocked classroom library. Do brief "book talks" to introduce students to new books in the classroom library. Provide daily silent reading time, daily teacher read-aloud time, and regular opportunities for students to discuss and share books.

2. When reading aloud to students, draw their attention to how an author has created a mood, setting, or character. Ask students to think of possibilities for how they might use similar ideas and techniques in their own writing.

3. Implement literature response journals for students to reflect on what they have read. Ask students to respond to open-ended prompts about what they have read. Encourage them to cite specific examples or thoughtful explanations to support their responses. With such activities, students can begin to become "insiders" who read like writers. For students to become comfortable with responding to literature, they should write in their journals several times a week. Teachers are cautioned, however, to not over-use these journals so students begin to view them as a burden rather than a useful tool for connecting literature to real life. A list of literature response questions to promote "reading like a writer" is provided in the Resources section of this chapter.

4. Ask students to close their eyes as they listen to you read a descriptive passage aloud. Tell students to visualize the picture the words paint for them. Younger students can draw the picture they "see" in their mind's eye. Next, re-read the text and ask students to identify words, phrases, and literary techniques which helped create the pictures and images for students. Encourage students to use descriptive words in their writing and to analyze their own writing in this manner.

5. Share your own writing. Explain to students how you "borrowed" from authors you have read. Show examples of the author's writing which influenced your writing. Discuss how and why you "borrowed" elements of the author's writing for your own writing.

6. Engage students in writing response groups. Encourage them to respond to peers' writing by "reading like a writer." Encourage them to analyze their peers' writing and their own writing closely to see what does and does not work well. Students can use questions such as those for literature response journals to guide their groups. Sample questions are provided in the Resources section of this chapter.

7. Discuss author biographies with students so they can begin to understand how authors' life experiences impact their writing. Many author biographies also discuss how other writers influenced the author's writing and desire to write. Brief biographical sketches of many popular children's authors are included in the following books:

Hill, S. *Books Alive!* Winnipeg, Manitoba: Peguis, 1994.

Kovacs, D. *Meet the Authors.* New York: Scholastic, 1995.

Kovacs, D., & Preller, J. *Meet the Authors and Illustrators.* New York: Scholastic, 1991.

Silvey, A. (Ed.). *Children's Books and Their Creators.* Boston: Houghton Mifflin, 1995.

8. Writing letters to favorite children's authors allows students to ask questions about how and why authors write as they do. Addresses for many popular children's authors can be found in *Books Alive!* (Hill, 1994).

9. Engage in author studies wherein students read, critique, analyze, and respond to multiple pieces written by one author. This process will help students develop a depth of knowledge about an author's style which should lead students to "borrowing" ideas, formats, and techniques for their own writing.

10. Students can rewrite the final chapter or section of a book or story while attempting to use the author's style. Students can exchange their rewrites and try to guess who the author is.

7.8 Promoting Positive Attitudes Toward Writing

Behavior Observed	The student does not like to write or exhibits a negative attitude toward writing.
Anticipated Outcome	The student will gain a more positive attitude toward writing.

Perspectives and Strategies

Many students who exhibit negative attitudes toward writing do not understand or appreciate the personal and social dimensions of writing. They tend to see writing as handwriting, copying from the board, and answering questions posed by teachers (Graves, 1991). These students often get bogged down in the mechanics of writing which causes them to view writing as drudgery rather than an exciting process of preserving and then sharing their ideas. By showing students that writing is a powerful personal and social tool for communicating thoughts, feelings, and personal experiences, student attitudes toward writing should improve. The following strategies provide ideas for teachers who wish to encourage positive attitudes toward writing.

1. Provide daily journal writing time. Plan for at least 5-10 minutes for primary students and 10-15 minutes for older students. Younger students can use both words and pictures to convey their ideas in journals. Use prompts initially, but work toward encouraging students to write about things which are of interest to them. Prompts might include open-ended statements such as those in the box.

Journal Prompts

- I remember when…
- I like to…
- I wish that…
- I wonder about…
- The person I admire most…
- My favorite memory is…
- The best present I ever got…
- The best present I ever gave…
- If I had three wishes…
- If laughed so hard when…
- My favorite movie is… because…
- My favorite song is… because…
- My favorite book is… because…
- My favorite place is…
- I would like to be famous for…

- If I could travel anywhere in the world…
- If I could change one thing about myself…
- I had the greatest day when…
- I had the most horrible day when…
- When I grow up, I want to…
- When I was little, I…
- I want to be remembered as a person who…
- A good friend is someone who…
- If I had a time machine, I would travel to…
- If I suddenly became an adult, I would…
- I would love to meet…
- I wish I could trade places with…
- If I had a million dollars…
- The best thing about school is…
- The worst thing about school is…

---

2. Implement dialogue journals in your classroom. Dialogue journals are letters written back and forth between two students or the teacher and a student. Set aside time each day for partners to read and write letters to each other in their dialogue journals.

3. Encourage students to write about what they know best – themselves. Younger students can write and illustrate "All About Me" books which include pages devoted to favorite foods, books, colors, and television programs. In addition, students can write about their plans for when they are adults. Students' "All About Me" books can be bound, shared, and displayed in the classroom. Older students can write autobiographies which also make predictions about their futures. Photographs and illustrations can be incorporated into the autobiographies.

4. Establish a classroom post office or message board. These systems provide real-life opportunities for students to write and read. Many students find writing notes fun and motivating. A post office can be as simple as a set of cardboard boxes with dividers and name labels. Students rotate the responsibility of letter carrier. The teacher can send mail to students, and they can send mail to the teacher and to each other. A bulletin board (with an assortment of paper and note cards and push pins) or a dry erase board can serve as a classroom message board. The teacher can write messages to students, and students can write messages to the teacher, class, or specific students.

5. Set up a writing workshop to provide regular opportunities for students to write on self-selected topics and engage in responding to writing. By having choice and control over their own writing, many students will begin to view writing more positively.

6. Establish a pen pal program with students in other schools, cities, states, or countries. College undergraduates studying to become teachers will also make excellent pen pals for students. Provide class time for students to write to their pen pals. Students can also write to pen pals via electronic mail (E-mail).

Behavior Observed	The student lacks confidence in writing.
Anticipated Outcome	The student will gain greater confidence in writing.

Background

Students who are confident writers are willing to take risks with language and learning. They are willing to try new words, formats, and organizational patterns in their writing. Students who view themselves as writers tend to make more progress in writing than students who do not see themselves as writers (Atwell, 1987). The following teaching strategies and practice activities may be helpful for enhancing students' confidence as writers.

Teaching Strategy 1 (For Younger Students)

1. Use "text tapping" to help students write in a particular format or genre. "Text tapping" taps into students' existing knowledge and links what students have read and heard with what they can write (Turbill, Butler, Cambourne, & Langton, 1991). Select a format or genre which is very familiar to the students. Nursery rhymes and fairy tales may be good initial selections.

2. Begin with two nursery rhymes which are familiar to many students (e.g., "Humpty Dumpty" and "Hey Diddle Diddle"). Place each on the overhead projector (chart paper or the chalkboard can also be used for this teaching strategy). Read through each nursery rhyme several times with the students. Ask students to point out patterns they notice in the nursery rhymes. These patterns may include rhyming, short words and phrases, and repetition.

3. Show a transparency which has sections of "Humpty Dumpty" deleted. For example,

   Humpty Dumpty sat on a _____ .

   Humpty Dumpty had a great _____ .

   All the _____ .

   And all the _____ .

   Couldn't put Humpty _____ .

   Ask students to brainstorm words and phrases which could fit into a new version of "Humpty Dumpty." Record students' suggestions on the transparency.

4. Discuss the new version of the nursery rhyme, paying special attention to the patterns students identified as part of nursery rhymes (e.g., rhyming, short words and phrases, and repetition).

5. Place a transparency of "Hey Diddle Diddle" on the overhead. Key words and phrases should be deleted. Ask students to brainstorm words and phrases which would fit into a new version of the nursery rhyme. The procedure may be repeated with other nursery rhymes.

6. After students understand the process, ask pairs of students or individual students to create new versions of other nursery rhymes. New versions of the nursery rhymes can be recited chorally. They can also be illustrated and bound into class books or big books.

7. After students become comfortable with this form of "text tapping," introduce other familiar formats of text such as fairy tales, poems, and predictable books. By being able to tap into what students already know about a text genre, they will be more able and confident to write their own versions. Appendix C contains a list of predictable pattern books for possible use.

Teaching Strategy 2 (For Older Students)

1. Consider the approach used with younger students. Present "text tapping" in a fun, non-threatening manner to encourage students to participate. Using nursery rhymes, poems, or traditional songs such as "Row, Row, Row Your Boat" may invite reluctant students into this type of activity.

2. Select a text format which is familiar to students. For example, most students know the story of "Hansel and Gretel." Tell the students they are going to write their own fairy tales. Ask how many of the students know "Hansel and Gretel." You may want to read the story aloud so all students are familiar with it.

3. After reading and discussing the story, ask students how the story begins (e.g., Once upon a time…). Ask students what patterns and elements are found in fairy tales. Their list may include magic, evil character, good character, took place long ago, and so on. Write their suggestions on the chalkboard and invite comment and discussion.

4. Tell the students they will be writing an updated version of "Hansel and Gretel." Provide a new title such as "Hansel and Gretel in the Big City." Ask students to brainstorm places, events, words, and names that would fit into the story "Hansel and Gretel in the Big City."

5. Guide students to include the major patterns and elements found in all fairy tales (e.g., magic, evil character, good character). Provide time for students to write in pairs or individually. Additional time can be given for students to illustrate their stories. Share the stories in small groups or as a whole class.

6. Use "text tapping" with other familiar formats such as mysteries, folk tales, legends, myths, and fables.

Practice and Reinforcement Activities

1. Create opportunities for success with writing. These can include writing about topics students know well, capitalizing on students' interests, and using a writing workshop format in the classroom.

2. Administer a writing survey to determine how students view the writing process and themselves as writers. This information will help teachers plan appropriate activities and provide opportunities for success in writing. A possible survey form is provided on the following page.

Writing Survey

1. Are you a writer?

2. How did you learn to write?

3. How do people learn to write?

4. Why do people write?

5. What do you think a good writer does in order to write well?

6. In general, how do you feel about your writing?

Adapted from: Atwell, N. (1987). *In the Middle: Writing, reading, and learning with adolescents.* Portsmouth, NH: Heinemann.

3. Focus on the positive when discussing students' writing. Phrase suggestions for improvement in the positive, and offer specific steps students can take to strengthen their writing. For example, say, "You have introduced an interesting character. I really want to learn more about her. I'd like to know what she looks like. I'd also like to read some of the things she might say." Such statements are much more helpful than, "You didn't develop your character fully."

4. Share books which invite students into writing. Students can write their own version of pattern books such as *Each Peach Pear Plum* (Ahlberg & Ahlberg, 1978), *Mary Wore Her Red Dress and Henry Wore His Green Sneakers* (Peek, 1985), and *Dear Zoo* (Campbell, 1982). Wordless picture books also provide a non-threatening opportunity to write the story told by the pictures. A list of wordless picture books can be found in Appendix A.

5. Set-up a cross-age writing project between older and younger students. Older students can publish their writings for the younger students' classroom library. Older students may also serve as classroom helpers and assist their younger partners with writing. With very young students, older partners may serve as scribes who write down the young students' words in a format similar to a language experience activity.

6. Dramatizing student's writing with reader's theater, plays, puppet shows, or skits shows students that their writing is important and valued. Students can dramatize their own writing, or a local theater company, high school drama class, or college acting class may be willing to dramatize the children's writing.

Resources for Chapter 7

Audiences and Formats for Sharing Student Writing

➤ Ideas for Publishing Student Writing

➤ Making a Book

➤ Magazines That Publish Student Writing

➤ "Real Life" Audiences for Student Writing

Elements of Fiction Resources

➤ Plot Relationships Chart

➤ "Getting to Know My Character" Chart

➤ Literature Response Questions to Promote "Reading Like a Writer"

Teacher Resources

➤ Kinds of Writing Students Can Explore

Ideas for Publishing Student Writing

Students can make individual bound books to take home, put in the classroom or school library, present to a special person as a gift, or donate to a younger grade class.

Book Binding Formats

Type of Book	Directions	Sample
Shape Book	Make pages and cover in the shape of book. For example, make a fish shape for a book about fish. Fasten together with staples, duct tape, or lace with yarn or ribbon.	THE PUMPKIN PATCH / FUN FACTS / The Day I Turned Into a Pencil!
Ring Book	Punch holes in pages and cover and fasten together with chicken rings (available at a feed supply store), shower curtain rings, or metal binder rings (available at office supply stores).	OUR POEMS
Stapled Book	Staple together pages and cover. Then use duct tape along the spine for added strength and durability.	Outer Space Race
Flip Book	Fold three sheets of 8 1/2 by 11 inch paper so one sheet has a 3 inch flap, one has a 4 inch flap, and one has a 5 inch flap. Line up the folds and use a long-arm stapler to fasten the pages.	
Fold-out Book	Fold paper accordion-style. Then staple or glue to covers.	My number Book 1 2 3 4 5

Making A Book

Materials Needed:

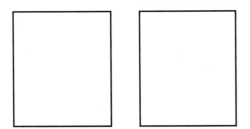

2 pieces of heavy cardboard

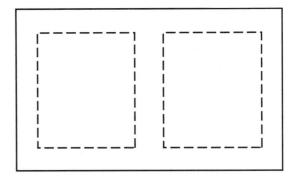

1 piece of fabric
(allow 1" on all sides)

Pieces of white paper (slightly
smaller than the 2 cardboards
laid together).

Button
thread

2 pieces of drymount (one
slightly smaller than the fabric
and one slightly smaller than
the white paper pages) or
rubber cement.

Procedure:

1.

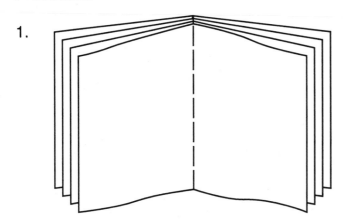

Fold sheets of white
paper in half.

Sew together with button
thread on the fold.

Making A Book (continued)

2.

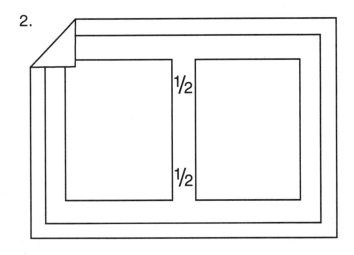

Cover
Lay drymount on the fabric, then cardboard pieces. Leave about 1/2" space between the cardboard pieces.

Fold corners down, as illustrated, and press with a warm iron. Next, fold the four sides over and press onto cardboard. Turn and press on the other side.

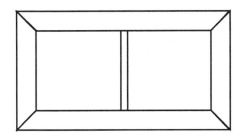

After pressing

3.

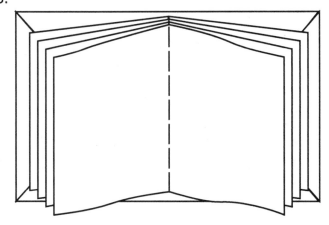

Place another sheet of drymount between cover and first and last page. Press.

Fold to make a book.

Magazines That Publish Student Writing

Children's Album. This magazine publishes creative writing by students ages 8-14. Contact the magazine at 1320 Galaxy Way, Concord, CA 94520.

City Kids. This magazines publishes writing by students ages 11-14. Contact the magazine at 1545 Wilcox, Los Angeles, CA 90028.

Cobblestone: The History Magazine for Young People. Each issue of this magazine is devoted to a particular theme. The magazine publishes writing by students ages 8-14. Contact the magazine at 20 Grove Street, Peterborough, NH 03458.

Creative Kids. This award-winning magazine publishes stories, poems, and reviews by students ages 6-18. Contact the magazine at P.O. Box 637, 100 Pine Avenue, Holmes, PA 19043.

Cricket. This magazine publishes winning pieces from their writing contests for students ages 5-13. Contact the magazine at Box 100, LaSalle, IL 61301.

Shoe Tree. This literary magazine is published by the National Association for Young Writers. The magazine publishes essays, creative fiction, poems, and reviews for students ages 6-14. Contact the magazine at P.O. Box 452, Belvidere, NJ 07823.

Sprint. This magazine publishes writing by students ages 9-11 based on writing "assignments" given in the magazine. Contact the magazine at Scholastic Inc., 730 Broadway, New York, NY 10003.

Stone Soup. This magazine is devoted to publishing writing from students ages 6-12. Contact the magazine at P.O. Box 83, Santa Cruz, CA 95063.

"Real-Life" Audiences for Student Writing

Each other

Students in other classes

Students in other local schools

Students in schools in other states or countries

Students in lower grade classes

Principal or other school administrators

School personnel

Parent organization at school

Family members

Community leaders

Local politicians

Candidates for office

Community newspaper and its readers

State and federal representatives and senators

Business people

Corporations

Civic, fraternal, service, and other local organizations

Chambers of commerce

Historical societies

Pen pals

E-mail pals

Nursing home residents

People with specific jobs or careers

    firefighter

    police officer

    lawyer

    judge

    doctor

    musician

    dancer

    artist

    secretary

    and so on

Newspaper editor

Newspaper reporter

Local television personalities

Local radio personalities

Plot Relationships Chart

Somebody	Wanted	But	So

Adapted from: Schmidt, B., & Buckley, M. (1991). Plot relationships chart. In J.M. Macon, D. Bewell, & M. Vogt (Eds.). *Responses to literature: Grades K-8*. Newark, DE: International Reading Association.

"Getting to Know My Character" Chart

Story _____

My Character _____

Facts about my character	**My character's actions**
My character's conversations	**My character's thoughts**

Adapted from: Richards, J.C., & Gipe, J.P. (1993). Getting to know story characters: A strategy for young and at-risk readers. *The Reading Teacher, 47*(1), 78-79.

Literature Response Questions
to Promote "Reading Like a Writer"

1. What is the best or most memorable thing about this book? Why do you think so?

2. What is the worst thing about this book? Why do you think so?

3. How do you feel about the main character? How did the author's writing influence how you felt about the main character?

4. How does the author help the reader get to know the main character's personality?

5. What particular words does the author use that "paint a picture" of the setting?

6. What has the author done to build suspense in the story?

7. What does the author do to make you want to continue to read?

8. How does the author organize the book? Do you think it is effective?

9. How does the author create humor in the book?

10. Why do you think the author wrote the ending this way?

11. How is the author's style of writing like other authors you have read?

12. Why do you think the author selected the title? Can you think of a better title? Why do you think it is better?

13. Why do you think the author wrote this book?

14. What audience do you think the author wrote this book for? What clues in the writing helped you decide?

15. What are some of your favorite words, phrases, or sentences from the book? What do you like about these examples of the author's language?

16. What startling/effective words, phrases, expressions, or images did you come across during your reading? Which do you want to try in your writing? Why?

17. How does the author draw the reader into the story?

18. As you read the book, write down your favorite examples of how the author uses descriptive language. Why do you like these examples?

Adapted from: Routman, R. (1991). *Invitations: Changing as teachers and learners K-12*. Portsmouth, NH: Heinemann.

Kinds of Writing Students Can Explore

Advertisements
Advice columns
Alphabet books
Agendas
Announcements
Autobiographies
Biographies
Book jackets
Books
Brochures
Bumper stickers
Captions
Cartoons
Character sketches
Children's books
Comics
Commentaries
Commercials
Conversations
Debates
Diaries
Editorials
Essays
Experience stories
Fact sheets
Fictional narratives
   realistic fiction
   fables
   fairy tales
   folk tales
   historical fiction
   science fiction
   short stories
   tall tales
Fortune cookies
Games
Greeting cards
Guidebooks
Instructions
Interviews
Invitations
Itineraries
Jingles

Jokes
Journals
Jump rope rhymes
Learning logs
Letters
   to pen pals
   to E-mail key pals
   to the editor
   to friends
   to family members
   requesting information
   requesting permission
   celebrating holidays
   marking special occasions
   registering complaints
Lists
Lyrics
Memoirs
Memos
Menus
Minutes of meetings
Mottoes
Newsletters
Newspaper articles
Notes
Parodies
Petitions
Poetry
   ballads
   limericks
   rhymed couplets
   acrostics
   free verse
   haiku
   other formats
Post cards
Public notices
   posters
   bulletin board displays
   intercom announcements
   flyers
Prophecies and predictions
Questionnaires

Recipes
Research reports
Responses to literature
Reviews
   book
   record
   movie
   television show
Riddles
Rules and regulations
Satire
Science writing
   observations
   lab reports
   procedures
Scripts
   skits
   plays
   radio plays
   puppet shows
   speeches
   reader's theater
Slogans
Songs
Stories
Study guides
Summaries
Surveys
Thank you notes
Thumbnail sketches
   of famous people
   of places
   of historical events
   of characters in literature
Time lines
   Travelogues
Want ads
Written debates
"You are there" scenes

Fostering Study and Test-Taking Strategies

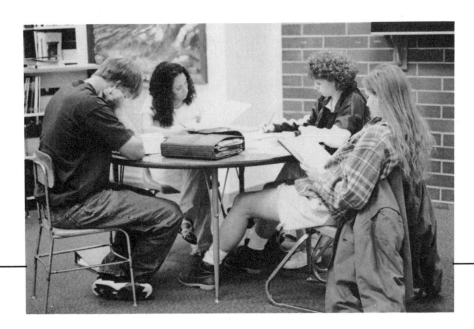

Overview

One of the continuing complaints of intermediate, middle, and secondary school teachers is that students don't know how to study. We've often heard teachers of students as young as third grade ask their students to study for a test without giving them any specific instructions and then be surprised when the students do poorly. This is probably because teachers don't realize that the strategies students use when studying are different from those students use when reading for other purposes. Study strategies differ because studying is reading for the purpose of performing a specific task (Anderson & Armbruster, 1984).

If you think about what you are asking students to do when you ask them to study, you'll realize that you really want them to identify important ideas, remember new material, and apply their learning to a variety of situations. These thinking tasks take as much or more effort than does reading a good story or identifying unknown words. The strategies students need for studying can be taught. That's because studying is an intentional act in which students set out to read and remember when they study (Vacca, 1981). Therefore, teachers need to take time to teach study strategies to students.

Teachers often ask us what the best study strategies are to use in the classroom. Obviously, a teacher won't be able to teach every study strategy there is, so the question is an appropriate one. The truth is, however, that no one study strategy is effective for every situation. If we want our students to learn how to study, we need to provide them with a repertoire of strategies from which they can choose and integrate into their individual approach. We also need to teach students how to choose study strategies appropriate to their study task.

As you develop a program to teach study strategies, therefore, keep in mind the various components of studying. According to Anderson and Armbruster (1984), studying has two main variables: state and processing variables. State variables are related to the student, such as the students' knowledge of the task, knowledge of the content, and motivation. State variables also include the text: how well the text is organized and how reader-friendly it is. Processing variables include the kinds of things the reader must do to process the information, such as focusing attention, encoding information, and retrieving the information during the task.

The variables of studying can be best taught if you consider the following principles as you teach a study strategy (Readence, Bean, & Baldwin, 1992):

➤ Help students focus attention on important information.

➤ Provide students with meaningful study goals.

➤ Help students organize information.

➤ Cause students to practice.

➤ Encourage deep processing of text.

The lessons that follow have been developed with these principles in mind. Remember that as you choose lessons for your students, the widest variety of strategies will be most helpful to your students as long as you instruct them to choose the strategy that best fits the type of studying they need to do.

Before you begin, however, you may want to have your students fill out a self-report on their study habits. A study survey (Davis, 1990) and a test-taking survey (Ritter & Idol-Maestas, 1986) are included in Resources for Chapter 8. For additional monitoring suggestions, refer to Chapter 6.

8.1   Understanding Text Structure

Behavior Observed	The student does not understand how texts are organized.
Anticipated Outcome	The student will apply knowledge of text structure during studying.

Background

Texts are written in a variety of organizational patterns, depending on the author's purpose. An author may choose to write a fictional story that is narrative (a sequence of events leading to a solution of a problem). Another author may decide to write expository text (text that explains ideas or provides information). Readers who can identify the elements in narrative text and who can discern the organizational pattern in expository text will have an easier time comprehending the selection and studying it.

When you teach text structure, it's a good idea to first review the information yourself. Then model how you identify text organization, and help students recognize organizational patterns. Finally, ask students to write text with different organizational structures. Only after students have had instruction and practice with different text structures can you expect students to use text structure as a tool for studying.

Narrative text is a more formal name for a story. Stories have seven main elements in them: beginning-middle-end, repetition, plot, setting, characters, theme, and point of view (Tompkins & Hoskisson, 1991).

➤ *Beginning-middle-end.* All stories have a beginning, a middle, and an end. Often the beginning contains information about the characters and the setting. A problem or a conflict is also introduced in the beginning. In the middle of the story, events are described that advance the conflict until it is finally resolved at the end of the story.

➤ *Repetition.* Repetition is a writing device to make stories more interesting. Books for young children often use repetition to advance the plot. See Appendix C for a list of pattern books.

➤ *Plot.* The plot is the sequence of events that happen in the story. The characters in the story have a conflict (problem), and that conflict is explained by a series of events. The plot includes all of the events that take the characters through the conflict to the resolution.

➤ *Setting.* The setting is the story's time and place. The time may be past, present, or future. The setting can be real or imaginary.

➤ *Characters.* The characters are the people or animals in the story.

➤ *Theme.* The theme is the main point of the story, the idea the author wants to get across to the reader.

➤ *Point of View.* Stories are written from a variety of points of view. Two common ways authors write are using the first-person and the omniscient points of view. First-person viewpoint tells the story through the eyes of the author. In the omniscient viewpoint, the author knows everything about the characters and action.

There are five main types of expository text: description, sequence, comparison, cause/ effect, and problem/solution (Tompkins & Hoskisson, 1991).

➤ *Description.* The author of descriptive writing lists characteristics, features, and examples to describe a subject. Cue words for description include *for example* and *characteristics.* To map a descriptive passage, you might use the following graphic organizer.

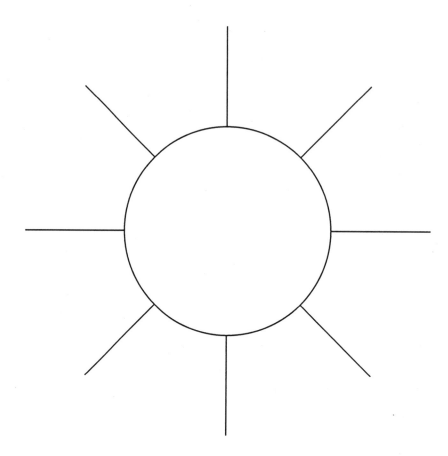

➤ *Sequence.* Writers who use sequence in a text list events in chronological or numerical order. Some cue words are *first, second, third,* or *next, then,* and *finally.* To map a sequential passage, you might use the following graphic organizer.

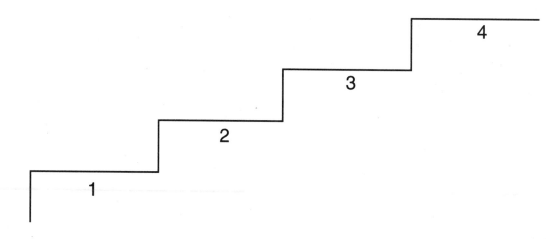

➤ *Comparison.* In comparison text, the writer is explaining how things are alike or different. Cue words include *different, in contrast, alike, same as,* or *on the other hand.* The graphic organizer that best depicts a comparison passage is the following:

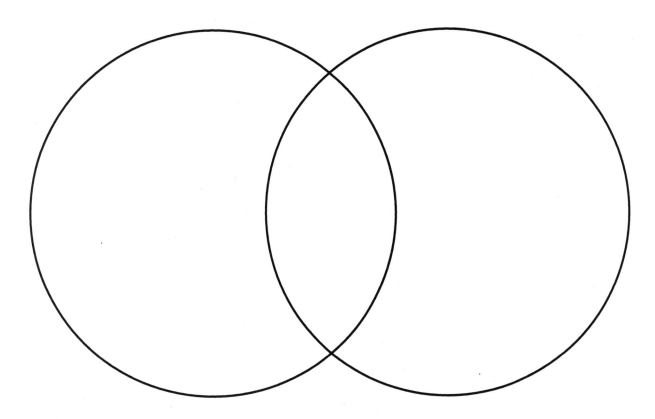

➤ *Cause and Effect.* The author describes a cause and the resulting effect. Cue words are *reasons why, if … then, as a result, therefore,* and *because.* The most common graphic organizer used in cause and effect writing is the following:

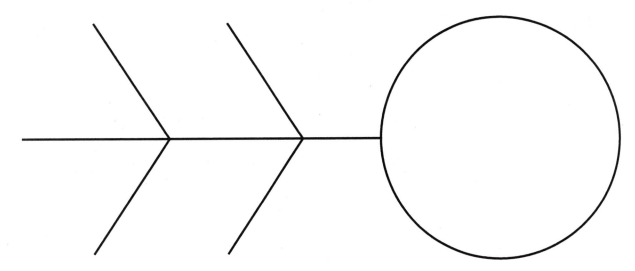

➤ *Problem and Solution.* The author describes a problem and lists solutions for that problem. Some cue words are *the problem is*, *solved*, and *the dilemma is*. A graphic organizer used for problem and solution texts is the following:

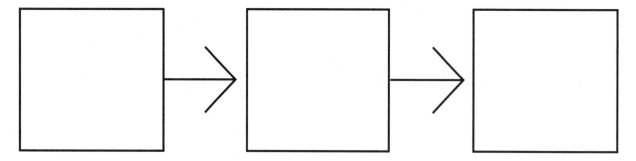

The following strategies should help students learn about text structure.

Teaching Strategy 1 *(Narrative Text)*

1. Collect stories that illustrate each element. You might use some of the following children's books as examples of the story elements (adapted from Tompkins & Hoskisson, 1991).

Repetition

Anderson, H. C. (1979). *The Ugly Duckling.* New York: Harcourt.

Gag, W. (1956). *Millions of Cats.* New York: Coward.

Sendak, M. (1963). *Where the Wild Things Are.* New York: Harper and Row.

Plot

Galdone, P. (1973). *The Little Red Hen.* New York: Seabury.

Kellogg, S. (1985). *Chicken Little.* New York: Morrow.

McGovern, A. (1967). *Too Much Noise.* New York: Scholastic.

Characters

McCloskey, R. (1969). *Make Way for Ducklings.* New York: Viking.

Van Allsburg, C. (1981). *Jumanji.* Boston: Houghton-Mifflin.

White, E. B. (1952). *Charlotte's Web.* New York: Harper and Row.

Theme

Lobel, A. (1970). *Frog and Toad Are Friends.* New York: Harper and Row.

Piper, W. (1953). *The Little Engine That Could.* New York: Platt and Munk.

Van Allsburg, C. (1985). *The Polar Express.* Boston: Houghton Mifflin.

Point of View: First Person

Howe, D., and Howe, J. (1979). *Bunnicula.* New York: Atheneum.

MacLachlan, P. (1985). *Sarah, Plain and Tall.* New York: Harper and Row.

Viorst, J. (1977). *Alexander and the Terrible, Horrible, No Good, Very Bad Day.* New York: Atheneum.

Point of View: Omniscient

Grahame, K. (1961). *The Wind in the Willows.* New York: Scribner's.

Lewis, C. S. (1981). *The Lion, the Witch, and the Wardrobe.* New York: Macmillan.

Steig, W. (1982). *Doctor De Soto.* New York: Farrar.

2. Read stories to the class, explaining which story element is emphasized. For example, if you had read the book *The Little Engine That Could* (Piper, 1953) to the class, you might say: "This story is a fun story, but it also tells us something important. When an author writes a story, he or she usually wants to convey a point to the readers. The point the author is conveying is told through a story, but it's up to the reader to try to understand. In *The Little Engine That Could*, the author is trying to tell us that if we think we can accomplish something and try really hard, we can. That main point is called the theme of the story."

3. Read another story to the class and ask them to identify the specific story element. For example, if you read *Frog and Toad Are Friends* (Lobel, 1970), you should ask students some possible main ideas that the author wanted to convey. Students should be able to answer something about the value of friendships.

4. Create a chart listing the seven story elements (e.g., point of view, plot, theme) as you teach them. Under the story elements, write information from the books you discuss. The partial chart that follows is an example:

Story	Setting	Characters
Make Way for Ducklings	Boston	Mr. and Mrs. Mallard
Frog and Toad Are Friends	Forest	Frog and Toad

5. After students read narrative passages, discuss the elements of the story. You may want to choose from the following questions (adapted from Tompkins & Hoskisson, 1991) to form the basis for the discussion:

Beginning-Middle-End

■ What kinds of information does the author include at the beginning of the story?

■ What happens in the first part of the story?

■ Does the author add new characters in the middle of the story?

■ What happens to the story at the end?

■ How do you feel about the end of the story?

Repetition

■ What words are repeated in the story?

■ Is an event repeated?

■ How does the repetition make you feel?

Setting

■ What is the setting?

■ Is the setting described in detail?

■ Does weather play an important role in the story?

■ Could the characters be found in other kinds of settings?

■ Does the author use the setting to provide important action?

Characters

■ What is the character's goal?

■ What problems do the characters face?

■ Are there minor characters in the story?

■ What do the characters look like?

■ What do the actions of the characters tell us about them?

■ Are the actions of the characters consistent throughout the story?

Theme

■ What does the story mean?

■ Is the main idea stated in the story?

■ How does the author get the theme across?

Point of View

■ Who is telling the story?

■ Do we know what the characters are thinking?

■ Does the story have a narrator?

Teaching Strategy 2 *(Expository Text)*

1. Identify texts with different text structures that are at the appropriate reading levels for your students. To teach expository text structure, choose a passage that exemplifies the type of structure you want to teach. The following is an example of description:

> People have always been fascinated by gold. Gold is one of the metallic elements. Because it is found in such small quantities on earth, gold is very expensive. In fact, its rarity gave rise to the practice of alchemy, the object of which was to turn base metals into gold. Throughout history, gold has been the preferred substance for money and jewelry. Other examples of its use are that it has been woven into fabric and hammered thin for bracelets, drinking vessels, and body coverings such as breastplates.

> As a metal, gold has some unique characteristics. Because it does not react with oxygen, it will neither rust nor corrode. It has a low melting point, so it can be heated and then reshaped. Although gold is heavy, it is very soft. This makes it easy to work with. However, gold's softness makes it impractical for use. Therefore, gold is often combined with other metals that give it strength and help to prevent scratching.

2. Explain that you will be discussing the descriptive text structure. Tell students that descriptive writing is when an author lists characteristics, features, or examples of a topic.

3. Ask students to read the passage about gold. Model how you would identify the text structure of this passage. You may say something like the following: "As I read the first sentence, I saw that the topic of the passage was gold. Because the main idea seems to be the fascination people have with gold, I'm going to predict that the author will be describing gold. The

first paragraph does describe gold. Another clue I find in the second paragraph is the word *examples*. Often, descriptive writing uses examples. As I continue to read, I find out the characteristics of gold. Again, the word *characteristics* is a clue that the passage is descriptive."

4. Ask students to discuss other cues from the text that might signal text structure.

Practice and Reinforcement Activities

1. Ask students to retell a story, emphasizing one of the seven elements. You may choose a story that you have read to the entire class or one that students have read independently. For additional information about retelling, see Chapter 5.

2. Ask students to dramatize stories with puppets or by acting out a play. They may want to focus on making the characters believable, on making the setting realistic, or any combination of story elements.

3. Have students compare the beginning-middle-end of different versions of the same story. Fairy tales are especially appropriate to use.

4. Make up a list of the characters and settings of a story. Ask the students to predict what the story will be about using the following story frame before they read. Additional story frames can be found in Chapter 5.

The event takes place _____ .

_____ is a character in the event

who _____

_____

_____ . A problem occurs when

_____ .

After that, _____

_____ . The

problem is solved when _____ .

The event ends _____ .

5. Have your class write a story together focusing on the story elements that you have taught.

6. Ask students to write their own stories. If you have focused on writing with a first-person point of view, for example, ask students to write using that element.

7. Ask students to work in groups to try to find out the text structure of a selected passage. Ask them to underline words or phrases that give them clues about the structure.

8. Have students diagram a passage using the graphic organizer suggested for the specific text structures. A partial example from the passage on gold follows:

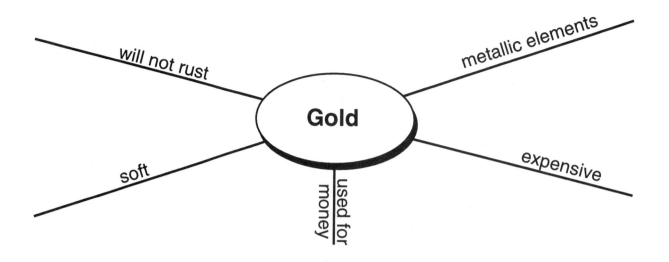

9. Give students a blank graphic organizer and ask them to organize other information they know into the same pattern. Then ask them to write a passage similar to the passage they had read.

10. Discuss monitoring strategies with students (see Chapter 6). Students trying to identify text structure need to monitor their reading carefully.

11. After you have taught narrative text structure and expository text organizations, give students passages at random and ask them to identify the type of text organization the writer used. Remember, not all texts are easy to identify, so give your students good examples of each type. Discussion should help students clarify their understanding of various organizational structures.

8.2 Previewing Text

Behavior Observed	The student does not preview text material before reading.
Anticipated Outcome	The student will preview text as an aid to studying and reading.

Background

When students are assigned texts to read and study, many think they should begin reading with the first sentence and continue reading until the chapter is finished. Students who proceed in this manner are not usually using the most efficient means of reading. If students preview the text before reading, they can gain a better idea of the organization of the text, and they can begin to activate their prior knowledge about the subject (Brozo & Simpson, 1991). Understanding the text organization and making connections to what is known can help facilitate readers' comprehension as they read and study. You should, therefore, encourage your students to preview text material before they read or study.

One of the most popular textbook previewing strategies is SQ3R (Robinson, 1946). Students who use SQ3R will begin to think about their reading before they actually read. You should not assume, however, that just discussing the stages of SQ3R will enable students to use it. Research indicates that most students will not use SQ3R independently unless you give them many guided opportunities (Caverly & Orlando, 1991). We have described the steps of SQ3R (see the following Teaching Strategy 1) and the value of each step. We also explain how to incorporate it in your lessons (adapted from Richardson & Morgan, 1990).

Because many of the texts your students will be using contain illustrations and graphs, students should preview the pictures along with the text. You can include pictures and illustrations in the survey part of SQ3R, or you can teach the Picture and Text Survey (Lamberg & Lamb, 1980).

Another method of teaching students to preview text, is the Textbook Activity Guide (TAG) (Davey, 1986). TAG is a teacher-directed activity that guides students through a preview of the text.

Another strategy described in this chapter is SCROL—a strategy developed by Grant (1993) to assist students in using headings before they read. She identified four advantages to using a strategy such as SCROL:

1. Students activate their background knowledge before reading which increases comprehension.

2. Using SCROL helps students understand the relationships between the ideas in the text.

3. Students identify content cues that help them remember the information.

4. SCROL is motivating for many students.

To encourage students to preview books before reading, Davis (1989) developed the nonfiction book scan. It is a strategy you can teach students so they do not think they have to read all books from beginning to end. Students can learn valuable information from scanning a book and should be encouraged to use this technique when they are looking for a book about a particular topic or when they want a small amount of general information about a topic.

Teaching Strategy 1 (SQ3R)

1. Introduce the entire strategy, explaining what each step means. Just as in surveying a passage, giving the students an overview of the entire study strategy is important. Then explain to students that you will be showing them how to use the SQ3R strategy, but that you will be expecting them eventually to be able to use SQ3R on their own. Provide guided practice so students can use each step of the strategy as you introduce it.

2. Introduce one step of the strategy at a time. Explain how to do each step and explain the value of the step. You may want to use the following as an example:

   S = Survey. Ask the students to survey the chapter by reading the opening paragraph, headings and subheadings, and the chapter summary. Surveying the chapter will give students an idea of the main points covered in the text. As they survey, direct them to ask the following questions: "From the survey, what is the chapter about?" or "What do I already know about the topic?" or "How much time do I think it will take to read and understand this material?" Explain that the value of the survey is to help students focus on the main points of the chapter. The chapter headings give the general idea, and the subtitles help students realize what is included as subpoints. Understanding what is included under the main heading is important. As students make predictions about a general topic, they may think of points that may not be included in the text. If they have not surveyed the text, they may be distracted while reading as they look for the ideas they thought might be in the chapter.

   Q = Question. Tell students to convert chapter headings into questions in their head, in discussion, or in writing. Because the headings of the passage are already developed by title and subtitle, students may also write their questions in the form of an outline.

   Explain that the value of questioning before reading is that it arouses curiosity and helps to set a purpose for reading. Questioning also helps students to focus on the material in the text by becoming actively involved in trying to answer the questions the students have formulated.

   R = Read. Next, direct students to read the text looking for the answers to their initial questions and perhaps posing additional questions. While they read, students should use comprehension monitoring strategies such as those described in Chapter 6. As they read, tell students to continue thinking about the questions they asked. If they are not able to answer their questions, they may have to reread the passage or use other fix-up strategies. They should also consider the possibility that they may have asked inappropriate questions. Explain that reading to answer self-generated questions has the advantage of holding students' attention during reading. If students are reading for their own purpose to answer their own questions, they will be more attentive while reading.

   R = Recite. The next step is to explain to students that they should think about the answers to their questions and recite them in their minds or write them down. They can then decide whether they answered the questions about the text and, if they had, students should decide what information is important to remember. Tell students that it is impossible to remember everything they read. After they read, they should make some judgments about prioritizing the information in the text. They may want to use memorization strategies (see section 8.5) to process the information.

Tell students that reciting is an important aspect of SQ3R. If information is not processed, it will not be stored in the long-term memory of the student. Processing information directly after reading increases the chance that students will remember it. Tell students that reciting also helps them personalize the material by thinking about it in their own words.

R = Review. After reading, ask students to review what they have learned. Tell them that they should begin by reviewing the headings and the questions the students asked. They should look for connections between the information they read and what they already know about the topic. They should then try to recall the main points of the passage. Finally, students may want to write a brief summary (see section 8.3).

Explain that students need to review what they have read to remember information. Reviewing is another way to process text so that it will be stored in students' long-term memory. Tell students that reviewing text is also valuable because they can look for relationships between the new information and their background knowledge.

3. After you have introduced one of the steps of SQ3R, model how you would use the strategy using one of the student's texts. An example of modeling SQ3R follows: If you were surveying the "Identifying and Understanding Words" chapter from this book, you would read the chapter title, the first sentence or paragraph of the overview, and then the subtitles. You would find out what types of reading behaviors are covered in that chapter and which are not. You would then be ready to ask questions.

4. You may decide to model question-asking with the same passage or a different one. For example, you could ask "What are some strategies recommended for helping students learn basic sight words?" or "How do I help students expand their concepts of words?" Try to ask a question for each part of the chapter. You might even write them down.

Because the passage you surveyed is relatively long, you might want to choose one part of it to read. Let's say you have chosen the part "Identifying Sight Words." Read the part about using good reading strategies. In this instance, a good plan would be for you to determine what teaching strategies and practice activities would be most helpful to you in your teaching. You should make a mental note of the strategies you think will be useful to you.

5. After reading, recite the activities you intend to put into practice. Tell yourself which ones have the highest priority and which ones you will consider for another time.

6. To review the material, reread the questions you wrote, looking for additional strategies you wish to remember. If there are activities from the text that you think would also be helpful, reread them. Then consider how the strategies you have chosen relate to what you are already doing in the classroom. For example, you may be using one of the activities, and the suggestions from the text will be added to your lesson plans. You may also be using different strategies to teach the same concept. Then you might add the strategy to your own repertoire of teaching tools.

Teaching Strategy 2 (*Picture and Text Survey*)

1. Ask students to preview the pictures and text to get a general idea of the subject. For example, if students are going to read a chapter on insects, you would ask them to read the title of the chapter, the subtitles, the first sentence, and then look at each picture. As the students look at the pictures, tell them to read any captions under the pictures and think about why the picture is included.

2. Next, tell students they should organize the information in their minds by writing a sentence describing the topic. In the case of a chapter on insects, students might write a sentence similar to the following: *This chapter will be discussing the life cycle of insects.*

3. After organizing the information, ask students to predict questions they think the text will answer. The pictures will give them a clue. The following questions could be asked on the insect chapter. *What are the stages of the life cycle of an insect? What happens to an insect in the egg cycle? What is larva and what does the insect look like at the larva stage? What is a pupa and what is happening to the insect in the pupa stage? How long does it take for the insect to become an adult?*

4. Before they begin reading, ask students to try to answer their questions. This helps them to access their background knowledge. As they read, then, students will be better able to comprehend the information. In the example of the life cycle of insects, students can discuss the times they have seen insect larva. They may know something about the stages of development of frogs, and the teacher can relate this knowledge to the life cycle of insects.

5. Next, ask students to read the text to locate answers to their questions. If they have carefully formulated questions for the text, they will be able to find answers to their questions. Many times, however, students will not be able to find answers to their questions because they did not ask good questions. If students were not able to find their answers, help them revise their questions. If students are able to locate information, tell them to think about their predictions to the questions and revise answers they had given.

Teaching Strategy 3 (*TAG: Textbook Activity Guide*)

1. Decide on your objectives for the lesson. Then choose chapters from the text that relate to those objectives.

2. Decide which text features you want to include in the preview. Students may not need to read each chapter of a passage. Choose the ones that meet your objectives to emphasize in the TAG.

3. Choose a different task for each chapter of the guide. Even though students will be interacting with each chapter of the text, you should recommend a different strategy for each one. This will encourage students to use a variety of strategies as they read. Some strategies you might consider are predicting, reading and discussing in a small group, skimming the text (looking for the main ideas only), reading and retelling (explaining the gist of the text to a partner), and writing. Writing can take the form of a summary, a response by explaining how the passage made the student feel, a fictional account of the passage, or comments on the passage in a journal.

4. Design TAGs so that students learn to interact with their texts in a variety of ways. A sample TAG follows so you can see what one looks like.

5. After students complete their TAG, spend time discussing each part of the guide. Encourage students to share problems or difficulties they encountered as well as insights gained from using the guide.

Teaching Strategy 4 (SCROL)

1. *S = Survey the headings*. Have students read the headings in the chapter and ask themselves what they already know about the topic. For example, if students are reading a text on the Civil War with the headings battles and generals, they may bring to mind all they already know about the topic. You might ask students to share some of their ideas and write them on the chalkboard. List everything they say whether it is correct or not. Examples might include Grant, Sherman, Meade, Shiloh, Antietam, Gettysburg, and Vicksburg.

2. *C = Connect*. Direct students to ask themselves how the headings connect to one another. They may use key words in the headings to help them make the connections. In the example on the Civil War, students will most likely predict that the battles were battles of the Civil War, and the generals were famous leaders in that conflict.

3. *R = Read the text*. Ask students to read the text, looking for words and phrases that explain the headings. As students read about the battles of the Civil War, for example, they try to put them in order and understand their relative importance to the war as a whole.

4. *O = Outline*. Explain to your students that they should then write the headings and details under the headings that they remember from their reading, for example:

    Battles

    Gettysburg   July 1-3, 1863

                        Under General Meade

                        Lee retreated

                        Both sides lost about 25% of their soldiers

5. *L = Look back*. Finally, direct students to look back at the text to determine the accuracy of their outlines or notes. If they have incorrect information, they should revise what they have written. In looking at the outline for the Battle of Gettysburg, it would seem unlikely that each side lost so many men, yet the Union won the battle. Checking back in the text, however, shows the outline to be correct.

Teaching Strategy 5 (*Nonfiction Book Scan*)

1. Ask students to identify a topic of interest and find a book on the topic. You might model how you would go about this task. For example, you might say: "If I were looking for a book on improving my running time, I would look in the card catalog under the subject of running. If the "card catalog" is on a computer, model appropriately. Then I would write down the Dewey decimal number of the subject and go to the library stacks. After locating the number, I would find several books about running. I would then choose one of the books to scan. I might make my decision based on the title, the front cover, the author's qualifications, or the summary on the book jacket."

2. After finding the book, students should scan through the table of contents to find a single area of interest. In this example, you might add: "If I were looking at improving my time for running a marathon, I would look in the table of contents for the chapter on long runs or the marathon."

3. Students should scan the chapter, looking only for the part of the chapter that interests them. "In the marathon chapter, I would survey the chapter using the survey strategy from SQ3R (Teaching Strategy 1). I have already asked myself the question and have a purpose for reading, that being to improve my time in running a marathon. After surveying the chapter, I should be able to locate the passage that discusses marathon times."

4. After scanning the chapter, direct students to read the part of the text that interests them, looking for the main ideas. For the example of improving marathon time, you could say: "I would next look at the subchapters. They may be nutrition, a pacing chart, and speed workouts. I would read each chapter looking only for information that tells me what I need to do to improve my running time."

5. Tell students they should then decide whether to read the book more carefully. After scanning the book and finding relevant information, they should decide whether other chapters of the book would be helpful. If so, they can check out the book and read the chapters that interest them.

Practice and Reinforcement Activities

1. Ask students to try each step of SQ3R on their own with a passage from your text. You may want them to work in groups and think aloud as they proceed.

2. Give students a chance to practice SQ3R independently. You'll need to remind them to use this strategy when you give an assignment to read and study. You may also develop an SQ3R guide similar to the one that follows (adapted from Gall, Gall, Jacobsen, & Bullock, 1990).

SQ3R Guide

Name_____ Date_____

Text _____ Pages_____

1. Survey the chapter. As you survey, answer the following questions.

What is the title of the chapter? _____

What are the main headings?

a. _____

b. _____

c. _____

d. _____

Describe in a sentence or two what you think the chapter will be about.

_____

_____

2. Question

List questions for each of the main headings and subheadings. Use who, what, when, where, why, and how in each question.

a. _____

b. _____

c. _____

d. _____

3. Read

Read one chapter of the text at a time. Think about what you have read. List any points that surprise you or that you think you don't understand.

_____

_____

_____

4. Recite

Recite what you learned from the passage. Use memory techniques to remember what you learned. List what you think you need to remember here.

_____

_____

_____

5. Review

Review the entire chapter. Were you able to answer your questions? If not, reread that part. Then write the main points of the passage without looking at your text.

_____

_____

_____

_____

From Jerry L. Johns and Susan Davis Lenski, *Improving Reading: A Handbook of Strategies* (2nd ed.). Copright © 1997 Kendall/Hunt Publishing Company (1-800-228-0810). May be reproduced for noncommercial educational purposes.

3. Give students a passage containing pictures. Ask them to apply the Picture and Text Survey.

4. Ask students to select five texts with pictures. In groups of two, have them discuss the importance of the pictures to the text. Students might rank the texts according to the importance of the pictures.

5. Give students a passage without pictures. Ask them to illustrate the text to provide clearer meaning.

6. Put a list of strategies used in TAGs on the chalkboard. Ask students to use two of the strategies (for example, predict and write) on the same passage. Discuss which strategy was more useful in helping students understand the text.

7. Have students rank order the strategies used in TAG by their favorite to the least favorite. Ask them to share reasons for their opinions.

8. Ask students to develop a TAG for a passage in your text. They may want the students to work in groups for this activity. Then ask them to trade TAGs with other groups.

9. Ask students to use the SCROL strategy on a passage. Then ask them to compare SCROL with SQ3R. Discuss which strategy they prefer and ask them to explain why they made their decision.

10. Ask students to do a book scan independently. Discuss what they learned from their scan and what situations would be appropriate for a book scan. Answers might include scanning books for a report, finding information for an essay test, and locating information for personal learning.

11. Encourage students to evaluate the various strategies they have used, and share the situations in which a strategy was particularly useful or ineffective.

8.3 Summary Writing

Behavior Observed	The student has difficulty writing summaries of texts.
Anticipated Outcome	The student will be able to write summaries and use them in studying.

Background

Before students can be effective at studying, they need to be able to identify important information and condense that information into a few short sentences. This process is called summarizing. Summary writing is an important study strategy, one that is difficult for many students. Summaries are important to teach, however, because they help students organize information into its relational components.

We will describe three ways to teach students to write summaries. The first strategy will be writing summaries by finding the main idea and deleting unimportant information. The second strategy is GRASP: Guided Reading and Summarizing Procedure (Hayes, 1989). The purpose of teaching GRASP is to help students learn how to write summaries independently, to help students recall text, to encourage students to self-correct, and to help students develop organizational skills (Hayes, 1989). The third strategy is the summary microtheme (Brozo & Simpson, 1991) which encourages students to write the main point of a portion of text.

Teaching Strategy 1 *(Writing Summaries)*

1. Provide students with short passages at their instructional level of reading. An example follows:

   Zebras are one of the most attractive animals in nature. Zebras come from the horse family so they look much like horses you would see at a farm or zoo. Just like horses, baby zebras are called foals, and mothers are called mares. The difference between horses and zebras, of course, is in their appearance. Zebras have black and white stripes, unlike domesticated horses. Their stripes cover their entire body including their mane. Each zebra has its own unique pattern of stripes.

2. Guide students to underline the main idea of the passage and to cross out unimportant or redundant information. An example follows:

   <u>Zebras are one of the most attractive animals in nature</u>. Zebras come from the horse family ~~so look much like horses you would see at a farm or zoo. Just like horses,~~ baby zebras are called foals and mothers are called mares. ~~The difference between horses and zebras, of course, is in their appearance.~~ Zebras have black and white stripes, ~~unlike domesticated horses. Their stripes cover their entire body including their mane.~~ Each zebra has its own unique pattern of stripes.

3. Help students make a graphic organizer with the remaining information, for example:

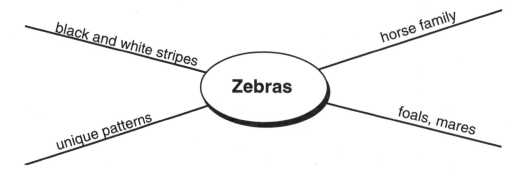

4. Together, write a short paragraph from the information on the graphic organizer, for example:

   Zebras come from the horse family. Babies are called foals, and mothers are called mares. Each zebra has its own pattern of black and white stripes.

5. Review the procedure and provide students with an appropriate passage so they can begin to gain competence with the strategy. After they have completed their summaries, go through each of the above steps, and discuss students' strategies. Provide guidance as needed.

Teaching Strategy 2 (GRASP)
(Guided Reading and Summarizing Procedure)

1. Provide students with a short passage at their instructional level of reading. Explain that the students will be writing a summary of the passage. If your students do not understand the term *summary,* explain that a summary is a brief description of a longer text.

2. Ask students to read the passage independently with the purpose of remembering all that they can. After they are finished reading, they should put the passage on their desk and wait for others in the group.

3. After all students are finished reading, ask them to tell you what they remembered. List on the chalkboard all of the items they suggest.

4. Ask students to reread the passage with the purpose of making additions and deletions to the list on the board.

5. After rereading, have the class suggest changes to the list on the chalkboard. Revise the list as needed.

6. Then ask students to suggest categories for the information. List the categories and ask students to divide the items on the list into the categories.

7. Using the outline generated by categorizing the information, write the summary. You might suggest that students begin with a main idea statement for the first main heading with their details as the subheadings. An example of the GRASP strategy based on an adapted encyclopedia entry follows.

   Otters are aquatic or semiaquatic carnivores of the weasel family. The body of the otter is lithe and muscular and covered with thick fur. Their paws are generally webbed. Otters often shut their nostrils and eyes to swim underwater. Their prey consists of small fish, eels, crayfish, and frogs. The sea otter's diet is more specialized. They have powerful teeth that are perfect for crushing sea urchins, abalones, and mussels. The sea otter floats on its back, breaking open the ur-chin—or mussel—shell on a stone anvil balanced on its chest. Unlike most other wild animals, otters remain playful as adults.

Teacher: Today we are going to read a paragraph about otters. I'd like you to read it care-fully trying to remember as much of the passage as you can. After you're done reading, put your paper on your desk and wait for the other students.

Teacher: Now that you have finished reading, what can you remember from the passage?

Students: Otters like to play.   Otters eat snakes.   Otters are weasels.

                   They have fur.   They swim underwater.   They eat fish and frogs.

                   Sea otters eat seaweed.   Sea otters eat sea animals.   Their paws are webbed.

Teacher: Now reread the paragraph and think if you would like to add any more ideas, erase some of them, or change some of them.

Student: Otters shut their eyes underwater just like we do!

Teacher: Let's add that one to the list.

Student: We have some wrong things on the chalkboard. Otters don't eat snakes or seaweed.

Teacher: What do you think, class? Raise your hands if you agree that otters don't eat snakes or seaweed. I see everyone's hand up, so I'll erase those two ideas. Now let's try to put some of the information into categories. What categories can you think of?

Student: How they look.

Teacher: What would fit under How Otters Look?

Student: They have fur and webbed feet.

Teacher: Let's make an outline with categories and information under them.

Otters in General
weasels
swim under water with eyes shut
like to play

How Otters Look
fur
webbed feet

What Otters Eat
fish
frogs
sea animals

Teacher: Let's try to write a summary using this information.

Otters are playful weasels who like to swim under water with their eyes shut. They have fur and webbed feet. Otters like to eat fish, frogs, and sea animals.

Teaching Strategy 3 (*Summary Microtheme*)

1. Explain to students that a summary microtheme is a short sentence or two that expresses the main point of a text or a lecture. A microtheme can be used to help students know whether they are understanding a passage.

2. After students have read a paragraph or two, ask them to think about the main idea of the passage. You might ask students to refer to the title and/or subheadings of the text to help them understand the main idea.

3. Distribute 5 × 7 note cards to each student and ask students to write the main idea on the card in a sentence or two. For example, with the preceding paragraph about otters, a main idea sentence can be one of the following:

   Otters are in the weasel family but they can swim underwater.

   Otters are playful animals who like to swim.

4. Ask students to evaluate their responses by determining whether they understood the main point of the passage. Those students who are unsure whether they have an accurate summary should reread the text.

5. After the students have completed a final reading of the text and have written a summary sentence, give them an example that does not express the main idea of the text but is one of the details. An example might be the following: *Otters eat frogs.*

   Explain that this is one of the details of the passage and that students sometimes confuse details with main ideas. Then write an example that is too broad, such as the following: *Otters are wild animals.*

   Explain that although students need to think in general terms, students should also try to have some specific information in their summary microtheme.

6. Invite students to make changes in their response if needed to express the summary of the text in a sentence or two.

Practice and Reinforcement Activities

1. After teaching all three summary writing strategies, give students a passage and ask them to use all three strategies. After they have finished, ask them which strategy they preferred, which was most useful, and when they could use each one.

2. When students are studying for tests, ask each student to summarize two important sections from the chapter. Combine the chapters into a booklet that students could use for study purposes.

3. Give students five minutes to discuss their hobbies with a partner. Then ask them to write down a summary of what their partner said. Share the summaries with the class.

4. Ask students to summarize their favorite television program. Give them an opportunity to read their summaries to a partner.

5. Have students listen to a story on tape by a storyteller. Then have them summarize the story. They can share their summaries with the class by illustrating them and placing them on a bulletin board.

Behavior Observed	The student has difficulty taking notes from texts or lectures.
Anticipated Outcome	The student will be able to take and use notes for studying.

Background

Taking notes from texts and from lectures is expected in schools today. Notes have a real purpose. They serve as external storage for information that cannot be held in memory. When students study, they refer to the information listed in their notes to trigger other ideas that were thought or read. In addition, notes serve an encoding function. When students take notes, they process that information and personalize it. Therefore, taking notes is a good way to process text, and reading notes is a good way to remember text.

As with all study strategies, there is no one best way for students to take notes. There are, however, some basic principles in notetaking that you should consider:

➤ Assess your students' ability to take notes before you expect them to do it. Then teach several notetaking strategies to those students who are not proficient notetakers.

➤ If you expect students to take notes from lectures, speak slowly and clearly, pausing every few minutes to give students time to write.

➤ Write important material on the chalkboard, an overhead, or a handout.

➤ Encourage students to use abbreviations in their notes.

➤ Help students attend to clues in your lecture that would alert them to the main ideas you are presenting.

Many of your students will probably need instruction in taking notes. The strategies that follow should give you some ideas on useful notetaking strategies.

Teaching Strategy 1 (*Distinguishing What Is Important*)

1. Explain to students that what they take in their notes depends on their purpose for reading. Before they begin taking notes, students should decide on the purpose for reading and think about the kinds of information that they might find. Explain to students that not all information should be included in their notes.

2. Distribute to all students an appropriate passage from a text. Discuss the purpose for reading, then read the passage aloud. You might use the passage that follows as an example.

Teacher: Today we're going to read about one of the important discoveries in history. Some of you have been asking me how we know what life was like in ancient civilizations. This passage will help us understand how scientists and historians have been able to work together to understand life of long ago.

Frozen in Time

One of the most fascinating discoveries in history was the buried city of Pompeii. Pompeii was a city in Italy that flourished approximately 2000 years ago. Apparently, life was proceeding as usual when, with little warning, Mt. Vesuvius erupted. People who had been at the markets, in their homes, or in the surrounding countryside panicked but could not escape from the rush of lava that flowed from the mountain. The lava covered the town in a brief period so that no one who had not escaped in boats was saved.

Across the bay, Pliny, a young boy, saw the destruction of Pompeii. When he grew older, Pliny wrote about the volcanic eruption and tragedy of helplessly watching the town being covered with lava and ashes.

Years passed and Mt. Vesuvius erupted again, covering the place where Pompeii was buried with more ash. The ash turned to soil during the next centuries, and a town was built on the site that was once Pompeii.

Centuries later, people began reading Pliny's writing and began talking about the missing city that was once Pompeii. One day as some workmen were digging a tunnel, they found an ancient wall. One of the men found a stone with the name Pompeii carved on it. The discovery was greeted with great excitement by scientists. They began digging where the workmen had found the wall and were able to uncover many treasures. The biggest treasure, though, was that they were able to understand how people in ancient Italy lived. The people of Pompeii were frozen in time when they were covered by the volcanic eruption of Mt. Vesuvius..

3. After you read the passage to students, ask them to discuss the important points in the passage. It's important that you accept all answers at this point, even if you consider them incorrect. Students will get a chance to revise their thinking after rereading the passage.

   Teacher: What do you think is important in the passage?

   Student 1:   Pompeii was covered by lava and then discovered 2000 years later!

   Student 2:   The people of Pompeii couldn't escape so they were found just as they were the day they were killed. It's like the animals that were covered by the glacier.

   Student 3:   Pliny wrote about Pompeii but no one paid attention to his writing at first.

   Student 4:   People were going to the store when the volcano erupted.

   Teacher: These are all good observations. Let's reread the passage to find out more.

4. Ask students to reread the passage. Then think aloud about how you came up with the important points. "I'm going to give you an example of how I would decide on the important points of the passage. Usually, I go through each section of the passage something like this: The first sentence tells me that Pompeii was discovered and that it existed about 2000 years ago. I think that's important. It tells me the main idea of the passage. Then it says that Mt. Vesuvius erupted. That's also important. The passage then gives details about what the people were doing at the time. That's interesting, but I don't think it's important for my purpose in reading. The final sentence is interesting. It says that no one escaped except those who had escaped in boats. That must mean that some people escaped. I wonder what happened to them? Well, anyway, that might be interesting, but I don't think it's important to list in my notes."

5. Ask students to compare what you decided was important with their own predictions. Ask them to discuss in what ways your decisions were similar to theirs and how they were different.

Teacher: How was my version the same as the ideas you thought were important?

Student: We found most of the same things.

Teacher: What specifically do you think was the same?

Student: That Pompeii was covered by lava 2000 years ago.

Teacher: That's right. Now tell me what was different.

Student: You didn't think what the people were doing was important.

Teacher: Why do you think I made that decision?

Student: You said that it was interesting but that it didn't fit your purpose for reading.

Teacher: That's right. We need to choose only information to list that fits our purpose.

6. After you have guided students through finding important information, give them many opportunities to practice in groups and independently use instructional materials from appropriate texts.

Teaching Strategy 2 *(Telegraphing)*

1. Explain that when students take notes, they need to write as little as possible and still retain the main thoughts.

2. Have students pretend they are journalists. They must describe a story to an editor with as few words as possible. Tell them each word will cost $1. Here's an example using the passage in Teaching Strategy 1.

POMPEII FOUND BURIED UNDER LAVA AFTER 2000 YEARS

3. Have students take notes on a story. Count the number of words to determine who was able to keep the story line with the fewest number of words.

Teaching Strategy 3 *(T-notes)*

1. Explain to students that there are many types of notetaking strategies and that you will be modeling several of them. They can then use the ones they prefer.

2. Explain that most textbooks contain a variety of information: main ideas, details, vocabulary words, examples, and general information.

3. Divide a piece of notebook paper down the middle and across the top margin to form a large *T.* Use the different regions of the paper for the different types of information. The main ideas are placed on the left side of the line and details on the right. Any unfamiliar vocabulary words are placed on the center line with definitions on the right side of the line. Any examples or written information are written across both columns of the page, for example:

Main Ideas	Details
Main idea	1. Detail 2. Detail 3. Detail
Main idea	1. Detail 2. Detail

New vocabulary definitions

Examples and illustrations

Teaching Strategy 4 *(Cornell Method)*

1. After students understand the different types of information found in the text, they should draw a vertical line down the notebook page approximately 2 inches from the left margin. Another line should be drawn across the top to place the date and the page number of the notes.

2. Ask students to record notes from the lecture or text on the right side of the line. Tell them to write down everything. Tell them not to make judgments about what information is important and what information is extraneous while they are writing.

3. After the lecture is finished, ask students to read the notes they had written on the right side of the paper. As they read, tell them to decide what key words or phrases are present. Have them write the key words on the left side of the line.

4. Invite the students to reflect on the information in their notes and write any observations at the bottom of the page.

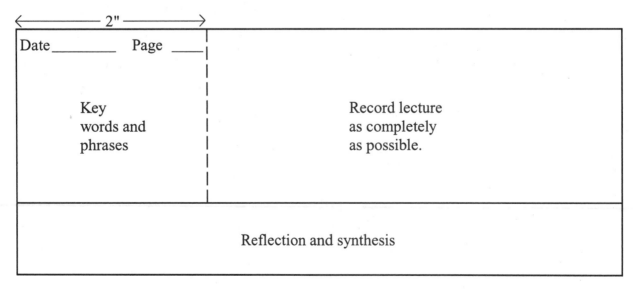

Teaching Strategy 5 (*REST*)

1. Explain to students that REST (Record, Edit, Synthesize, Think) is a notetaking strategy that helps them integrate both text material and lectures. Because students often need to study from both texts and lectures, REST is an easy way for them to remember the steps they need to take during notetaking.

2. Explain the first step, *Record*. Tell students that they will first be writing down notes from their teacher's lecture. They can choose any of the notetaking strategies they feel best suits them.

3. After students have taken notes on a lecture, ask them to *Edit* their notes. You might review Teaching Strategy 1 (distinguishing what is important), or say something like the following: "After you write notes, you might find that there are several things you have written down that aren't important. For example, if you were taking notes on a lecture about Pompeii [see section 8.4 for text] and you had written that the workmen who found the site were digging a tunnel, you might edit that point from your notes."

4. Next, explain to students that the material teachers often discuss in class and the text material have overlapping points, but that doesn't mean that they should disregard the text. Usually, text explains points the teacher has not discussed in class. Therefore, explain to the students that they should review the text, adding notes from the text to their lecture notes. This is the third step: *Synthesize*.

5. Finally, encourage your students to *Think* about the information they have in their notes. Have them think about ways the information from the lecture and the text fit into what they already know about the topic. Explain that they need to look through their notes as a whole, to decide whether they have complete information. If they have missing ideas, they might decide to reread the text.

Practice and Reinforcement Activities

1. Ask students to silently read a passage such as "Animal with a View." Then ask them to return to the paragraph finding pertinent information relating to the specific topics that follow the passage. After completion, discuss how the information for each of the topics was located. Use sentence numbers to indicate information.

Animal with a View

(1) The giraffe, native to Africa, is the tallest animal in the world. (2) When fully grown, the giraffe's height ranges from 480 to 600 centimeters. (3) Even at birth, it is taller than most adult humans. (4) The giraffe's legs may seem too slender to support its weight, but they are very strong. (5) In fact, the giraffe relies on kicking as its only means of defense. (6) Yet the height of the giraffe's legs creates a bit of a problem for the animal. (7) The giraffe cannot simply lower its head to drink from a water hole because its neck is shorter than the distance from toe to shoulder. (8) The giraffe shortens the distance from toe to shoulder by spreading its legs far apart. (9) This lowers its body just enough so that when the animal bends its neck, its head reaches the ground. (10) Needless to say, the giraffe is in a vulnerable position whenever it is drinking water.

Advantages of a giraffe's legs _____

Giraffe's height _____

Drinking habits _____

2. Have students pair off for "Inquiring Reporter." One student in each pair will be the reporter who will interview his or her partner, "the person on the street." Explain that a reporter's job is to get the facts, but sometimes it is difficult for a reporter to write as fast as the person being interviewed. Therefore, it is important to pick out only the important words and phrases and fill in the story later. For example, the person might say: "When I run fast in a race, I like the feel of the wind against my face. I sort of like that hot feeling I get. I try to keep my breathing from getting too fast, but I usually stop because I get winded." The reporter's notes might resemble the following: "Likes wind in face when running, likes hot feeling. Tries to keep breathing slow. Usually stops because winded."

Ask students to form pairs and take turns choosing one of the following topics, with one talking about it while the other acts as reporter, jotting down the essence of what the partner says. Have the students dictate for five minutes and then ask the reporter to read back his or her notes.

Possible Topics:

- Describe your favorite sport.

- What hobbies do you have?

- Describe how you would get from your house to school.

- Describe how to make your favorite recipe.

After the reporters have finished their notes, they can write the article and share it with the class.

3. Ask students to take notes on a television program or a sports event. Explain that they should take down only the main action. They should use the five W's and an H (who, what, where, when, why, and how) as a frame of reference for their decisions. After the program is finished, students should review their notes and fill in spots that don't make sense. Then students can give their notes to a partner to write a report from their notes. The success of their partner's report will correlate with how complete the notes were. After students have written their reports, they should evaluate their ability to take notes.

Behavior Observed	The student is not prepared for tests.
Anticipated Outcome	The student will learn how to study for tests and will become aware of general test-taking principles.

Background

One of the ways teachers assess student learning is by giving tests. Tests are a sampling of what students know; they do not measure all student knowledge but merely the parts the teacher thinks are most important. Sometimes, however, students are hindered in exhibiting what they know on tests because they are not familiar with the testing format. If students do not know how to study for tests or how to take tests, you as a teacher will get a false picture of students' knowledge.

Several factors can prevent students from doing well on tests. Sometimes students won't see the connection between the information they are studying and what is on the test. In this case, some of the study strategies and test preparation strategies should help. Other students may misinterpret test questions. Again, helping these students prepare for specific tests may help. Finally, students may exhibit test anxiety, where they are afraid of tests. Preparing for tests by using the study strategies in this chapter should help these students overlearn the information so that they can be confident test-takers.

Teachers often ask us what test-taking practices are ethical. VanLeirsburg (1993) outlined practices that will not pollute test results and those that will (see box).

Ethical Test Preparation Activities

1. Instructing, in general, to objectives that have not been selected in relation to the objectives measured on the tests.
2. Training in test-wiseness or general test-taking skills.
3. Increasing student motivation to perform well on tests.
4. Explaining to students the purpose of the test.

Unethical Test Preparation Activities

1. Developing a curriculum that is based on the content of a test.
2. Preparing objectives for skills based on items from a test.
3. Presenting items similar to those on the test as classroom practice if they are not usual instructional practice.
4. Presenting items verbatim from the test as practice.

The test preparation strategies that follow have been designed to be ethical so that they do not pollute test scores (adapted from Readence, Bean, & Baldwin, 1992; Rubin, 1993).

Teaching Strategy 1 *(General Test-Preparation Principles)*

1. In preparation for a test, tell students that they should plan to do well. Having a positive attitude about a test-taking situation can influence their study plan. Even if they have done poorly in the past on tests, students should approach each testing situation as a positive experience.

2. Explain that tests are a learning experience. Students can make determinations from tests about what they have learned and what they still need to learn. Even though a test may be given at the end of a unit, students can still continue learning about the topic after the unit is complete.

3. Tell students that it is their responsibility to find out as much as they can about the test itself. Because there are different methods of studying, they will need to ask their teachers about the kind of tests they will be giving. They also need to know what the test will cover, when the test will be given, and the testing format. Give students the chance to ask you questions at this point rather than telling them about the test you will give. An example of questioning follows:

Student: When is the test?

Teacher: Next Thursday.

Student: How long will we have to take the test?

Teacher: You will not be timed, but you need to have the test done within the hour. Most of you will probably finish the test in 30 minutes.

Student: What are some of the questions?

Teacher: I can't tell you the questions. Can you ask something different?

Student: What kinds of questions will be on the test?

Teacher: The test will have 10 true/false questions, 25 multiple choice questions, and 1 essay.

Student: How do I study for the test?

Teacher: I will be giving you some study tips each day for the next five days.

4. Tell the students that it is helpful if they try to predict questions that could be on the test. Put them in groups and ask them to think of true/false questions. Explain that these questions should not just be literal, but also inferential and evaluative. See Chapter 5 for an explanation of the different kinds of questions. After students have practiced writing true/false questions, give them the opportunity to write multiple choice questions and essay questions. Discuss the questions with the class. You might invite students to write their questions on an overhead transparency so they can be discussed.

5. Five to ten days before the test, explain to students that they should divide the amount of material they need to learn into study sessions. The amount of time for each study session will vary from grade to grade. Then they should decide which facts or vocabulary words should be memorized. After that, tell them to schedule study sessions for each day and plan what they will be studying on each day. Emphasize that students need to monitor their study

sessions. They should record what they have accomplished each session and decide what they still need to do. You might do a think aloud as in the following example to clarify what you would do to monitor your studying. For example: "I just spent 30 minutes reading about the battles of the Civil War. I think I remember the battles, but I believe the teacher will want me to know what role they played in the outcome of the war. I don't know that. I'm sure the text doesn't give that information, but it should be in my notes. I remember that I was absent during one of the class sessions about the battles, so I'd better check with Jerry. His notes are always complete."

6. The night before the test, you should remind students to go over their notes one last time. Tell them that additional studying at this point is probably superfluous. If they have been following their study plan, they should be prepared for the test. They may only become confused if they try to study at the last minute.

7. Tell students that they should make sure they have all of the materials they need for the test. Students who are rushing around in the morning to find a sharpened pencil will have a good chance of becoming flustered before the test. After gathering the material they need, students should get a good night's sleep. Tell students that the best way to do well on tests is to be prepared and well rested.

8. Just before the test, remind students that they should concentrate on the test questions. To keep from becoming anxious, students can take a deep breath and tell themselves that they will do fine. Then they should pay attention to the test and not allow other thoughts in their mind. Suggest that students use SCORER (see Practice and Reinforcement Activities in section 8.5) or other test-taking strategies while they are taking the test.

9. After the test has been graded, give the test back to students and tell them to look over the results and determine which study strategies were most effective. They might find that they do well on factual questions but poorly on essay questions. Then encourage students to make a plan about ways to improve their studying in the future. For example, students who identify their study weakness as not scheduling enough study sessions, should plan to study longer. Students who did poorly on the essay questions, should review the PORPE strategy and plan to work on predicting essay questions (see section 8.5 for a description of PORPE). You might even encourage your students to keep a study journal. They can chart how they have studied and write down how to study in the future. Teach students test-taking strategies that may not have been previously taught. Refer to the strategies that follow.

10. Teach key words to students. For example, the word *probably* in a test question usually means that the student will be unable to find the correct response in the text. Instead, the student will have to make an inference that uses information in the text. Some representative key words that may be helpful to discuss with students have been categorized by Antes (1989). For example, the phrase *most likely* implies that there may be several possible answers, but the student must select the best of the choices. Provide an example and think aloud to show students how you choose the *most likely* answer.

Generic Key Words

of the following	possible	imply
maximum	means	story
probably	most likely	infer
minimum	shows	one may conclude

Main Idea Key Words

good name for story	mostly about
mainly about	good title for story

Sequence Key Words

first	after	next
before	last	in order
second	following	

Because key words vary according to the type of test, the grade for which the test is intended, and the specific content of the test, be selective in the words you choose for tests. Integrate the words into the ongoing instructional program.

Teaching Strategy 2 (*True/False Tests*)

1. Begin by discussing the following tips for taking true/false tests.

   - Tell them that they should never leave a true/false question unanswered, because they have a 50% chance of getting the answer correct.

   - Explain that they should read the questions carefully. Questions that contain *never, always, all, none, impossible,* or *nothing* are usually false.

   - Tell students that they should also look for questions that are partially true. Because they are not completely true, the answer should probably be false.

   - Explain that long statements are more likely to be true than are short statements.

   - Be sure the *T* and *F* are written neatly so there is no problem in scoring the test.

   - Finally, tell students to assume that teachers are asking straightforward questions and not to read too much into them.

2. Model how you would put these tips into practice with several questions based on materials you have been using for instruction. For example, you might use these questions which are based on the reading passage, "Frozen in Time," from section 8.4, Teaching Strategy 1:

   Test Question 1. Pliny wrote about the destruction of Pompeii.

   Thought process for answer: "I remember someone wrote about Pompeii being destroyed, but I can't remember the name. I remember he was a young boy and his writing wasn't read for many years. Pliny could be his name, but I really don't know. I won't lose anything by trying, but if I leave it blank, I'll get it wrong for sure. I think I'll mark this answer *true.*

   Test Question 2. Volcanoes always erupt so quickly that people in their path can't escape.

   Thought process for answer: "I think that's what happened to Pompeii, but I'm not sure it always is that way with volcanoes. I think I heard that Mt. St. Helens in Washington erupted, and the people were warned to get off of the mountain in time. I don't think volcanoes *always* erupt that quickly, and I know that I should be cautious about answering *true* for a question that has the word *always.* I think the answer is *false.*"

Test Question 3. Pompeii was destroyed by a hurricane 2000 years ago.

Thought process for answer: "I know Pompeii was destroyed, and I remember that it was about 2000 years ago. The reason I remember the date is because my house address is 2000. We saw pictures of Pompeii after it was discovered again, and I remember a mountain in the background. Pompeii was also by the sea, but I'm sure it wasn't destroyed by a hurricane. That means the answer is false because the part about the hurricane is false."

Test Question 4. Pompeii was discovered when some workmen were digging a tunnel and found an ancient wall.

Thought process for answer: "This question has a great deal of specific information and is longer than most of the questions. I remember that Pompeii was discovered by some local people, and I think the question is *true*."

Test Question 5. The people of Pompeii were frozen in time when they were covered by the volcanic eruption of Mt. Vesuvius.

Thought process for answer: "There's part of the question that I know for sure, and that is that Pompeii was covered by the volcanic eruption of Mt. Vesuvius. I'm not sure, however, what 'frozen in time' means. That might mean something about a glacier or an ice flow, but I don't see how that could have happened. Maybe it means that all of their clocks stopped. That doesn't make sense. They didn't have clocks back then. Perhaps 'frozen in time' doesn't mean anything special, just that people were stopped at what they were doing. That would be the simplest answer, and I know we're not supposed to read anything into the test question. I think I'll just answer *true*."

Teaching Strategy 3 *(Multiple Choice Tests)*

1. First, tell students that multiple choice tests are usually more difficult than true/false tests, so the students need to read the stem before reading the choices and try to predict a correct response. If necessary, clarify *stem* and stress that it will usually set a definite task. Also, tell students to read all the choices carefully before making a final choice. Sometimes a response may be partly correct, but it is not the best choice. Make a sample question based on the material being taught, and model the process by "thinking aloud."

2. As they read, tell students to note any negatives because they can look for the wrong answer by skipping an important word in the question. An example of a negative follows:

   Which of the following was *not* a cause of the Civil War?

3. Explain that students should also look for clues in the tests. Tell them that if a choice is much longer and more detailed than the others, it is usually the correct answer. If a word in a choice also appears in the statement, it is probably the correct choice.

4. Tell them that they should try to eliminate incorrect choices. Stress that if they eliminate an unreasonable answer such as C, they have a greater chance of choosing a correct answer. For older students, you could say something like, "My chance of selecting the correct response increases if I can eliminate one or more possible answers. If there are four choices, my chance of selecting correctly by guessing is 25%. If I can eliminate two of the choices, my chance of selecting correctly is 50%." You might model this type of thinking similar to the following:

The speed of sound through air is

    A. 3700 feet per second

    B. 1085 feet per second

    C. 2 feet per second

    D. 186 miles per second

"I'm really not sure about the speed of sound. Let me see. I know it's really fast. Looking at the answers, I can tell that one answer is definitely false. There's no way C could be correct because I know sound travels more than 2 feet per second. I'm ruling out C, and I'm not thinking about it again."

5. Explain that when two choices are similar, they are both probably incorrect. Again, modeling the thinking behind this principle might be helpful.

The universal donor is

    A. O

    B. H_2O

    C. AB

    D. water

"I think I know which type of blood is the universal donor, but I'm not sure. The answers have two types of blood, answers A and C. The other two answers are the same. H_2O (answer B) is the same thing as water (answer D). Because I can choose only one correct answer, neither B nor D could be correct because they both say the same thing."

6. Explain that when two of the choices are opposites, one of them is always wrong and the other is usually correct. See A and B in the following example.

A molecule is

    A. the largest part of something.

    B. the smallest part of something.

    C. always solid.

    D. invisible.

7. Finally, remind students that the answer must be grammatically correct. If they find answer choices that do not fit grammatically with the question, they would probably be incorrect. For example:

The largest land animal is an

    A. whale.

    B. elephant.

    C. horse.

    D. hippopotamus.

8. Tell students that a viable choice that includes one or more of the others is likely to be correct. Use an example from material being taught and share your thought processes with the students.

9. Remind students that there may be clues in the stems of other items that may be helpful in resolving a question with which they are experiencing difficulty.

10. Tell students to skip a difficult question and go to the next question. Be sure students make a mark beside the question so they can find it more easily. This strategy has four advantages: 1) it does not waste time; 2) the correct answer may come to the student while thinking of something else; 3) helpful clues may occur in the stems of other questions; and 4) the student will not become overly frustrated about any single item.

11. Additional clues that may be useful to students are offered by Antes (1989, p. 20).

   ■ If the word *none* or *all* is used in a response, it is usually incorrect.

   ■ If *some* or *often* is used in a response, it is likely to be correct.

   ■ If *all of the above* is a response, determine whether at least two of the other responses seem appropriate before selecting *all of the above*.

   ■ If one response is more precise or technical, it is more likely to be correct than a general response.

   ■ If you are unsure about a response, and the correct response for many items on the test tends to be longer, select the longer response.

Teaching Strategy 4 (*Essay Tests*)

1. Explain that essay tests are difficult mainly because students do not know what to include in their answers and what is extraneous information. Tell students they can improve their essay-writing abilities through this lesson.

2. Tell students that the first rule in essay writing is to read the question carefully. Tell them to make sure they understand the entire question, for example:

   Compare and contrast the main characters from two of the books you have read.

3. Remind students that essay questions usually begin with a key word. Write the key words and their meanings on the chalkboard. Explain what each one means, and if you have an example of an essay question using each key word, read them to the students. Some key words and their definitions follow:

Key Word	Meaning
enumerate	to name one at a time
illustrate	to explain with examples
trace	to tell the history or development
compare	to point out similarities and differences
contrast	to point out differences
summarize	to give a brief description of important points
evaluate	to give the merits of
justify	to give reasons for
critique	to summarize and evaluate

4. Tell students that after they read the question, they should immediately write down any relevant information that comes to mind.

5. Then tell them to think about the question, rereading it several times.

6. Next, explain that they should plan their answer, writing a brief outline.

7. As they are planning, remind students to budget their time. Explain how you would budget your time during an essay test. The following example may be useful: "I've read the essay question and jotted down a few ideas. Let's see, I have 20 minutes to answer the question and I've already spent 5 minutes reading, thinking, and jotting down notes. I really need to outline the answer, but I also need to have a good 15 minutes to write. I think I'll just write a topical outline and get writing."

8. Tell students that there are a few additional techniques that will help them improve their essay answers. Explain that they need to use their best handwriting; they should try to elaborate each point; and they should use any technical vocabulary from the material of the text that they know.

Teaching Strategy 5 *(Matching Tests)*

1. Tell students that in a matching test, you must often match the items in one column with those in another.

2. Provide instruction in using the process of elimination with sample items or vocabulary words from various content areas.

3. Consider using the following example and reasoning:

_C_	an animal with a backbone	A. butterfly
_D_	an amphibian	B. starfish
_B_	a spiny-skinned animal	C. snake
_A_	an animal without a backbone	D. alligator

"After reading all of the items, it seems that a spiny-skinned animal is the starfish. An amphibian can live in and out of the water. Only an alligator can do that; I know that a butterfly and starfish can't. I also know a snake and an alligator have backbones, but if I use alligator as an amphibian, that would leave snake as the animal with a backbone. I think the butterfly is the animal without a backbone. Even though I don't know if the starfish has a backbone, it is the only spiny-skinned animal."

Teaching Strategy 6 *(Memorization Techniques)*

1. Tell students they will need to memorize certain facts for both objective and essay tests and that there are methods for remembering information.

2. Explain that the first thing students should do is plan to remember. Tell them that their minds will react differently to information that they have consciously intended to commit to long-term memory. To model how you would plan to remember, you might try the following: "I've got to read this section in my science book on the habitat of dolphins. I know Ms. Linder said this section was important both for our test and for a project we will be working on. I'm going to remember this information as I read it and not just gloss over it."

3. Remind students that they need to schedule time in their studying for memorization. Many students prefer to memorize information and facts last in their schedule. Ask students to write down when they will be studying for their test and to write in times for memorizing information and facts.

4. Tell students as they memorize that they should read the entire chapter that discusses the points they want to remember. This will help them understand the relationship of the facts to other information they know.

5. Give students a chance to talk about the things they want to remember. During science class, for example, provide students with several minutes to discuss the ideas that they have been memorizing with a partner.

6. Explain the use of mnemonic devices. A mnemonic device is a memory strategy that helps you retain bits of information. The following are examples of mnemonic devices that you can teach to your class:

➤ *Rhyme*

Create a rhyme or a song that includes the points you have to learn.

"Thirty days hath September ..."

➤ *Acronyms*

Form words by using the first letter from each of the words to be recalled.

HOMES (Names of the Great Lakes: Huron, Ontario, Michigan, Erie, Superior)

➤ *Pegwood*

Memorize a short rhyme and then create the images that link the nouns in the rhyme with the items to be remembered.

➤ *Method of Loci*

Select a spatial layout, such as your home. Mentally place the items to be recalled in each room.

➤ *Clustering*

Memorize the material in categories and learn them as a pattern.

➤ *Silly Sentences*

Make up a silly sentence from the first letter of each word to be remembered.

Even After Dinner, Giraffes Bend Easily (guitar strings E, A, D, G, B, E).

➤ *Numbering*

When you are memorizing a group of words, remember how many items there are to avoid missing any when you need to recall them.

Teaching Strategy 7 (*Test Anxiety*)

1. Tell students that everyone probably experiences some anxiety when approaching a testing situation or taking a test. Invite students to share some reasons for test anxiety, and write their responses on the chalkboard. Typical responses might include:

   That's just the way I am.

   I'm not sure I know the material.

   I've always done poorly on tests.

   A lot is based on this test.

   I didn't study very much.

2. Discuss their responses, and perhaps develop lessons that focus on the development of test-taking strategies or help students develop positive self-concepts as learners and test takers. For example, if a student says, "That's just the way I am when I take a test. I get very nervous." You could ask students to share techniques they use to relax. You might also say something like, "When I feel anxious about tests or other areas of my life, I close my eyes, take a deep breath, and hold it while I slowly count to ten. Then I let out the breath slowly as I let my body relax."

3. Foster good rapport with students and be sure students know what to expect on a test. Be as explicit as you can.

4. Take time to meet with individual students or a small group of students who may be experiencing a similar difficulty. For example, if the anxiety is partially caused because students think they don't know the material, schedule a review session or invite students to write questions on note cards about areas of concern so you can respond to specific areas.

5. Review the ethical test preparation activities at the beginning of this section. Use them to develop appropriate responses to students' anxieties. For example, standardized tests are usually quite different from classroom tests. One difference is that some of the items on standardized tests are likely to be difficult for all students, while your classroom test may be more of a mastery test where students get almost all of the items correct. You could take the time to explain such a difference to students, especially those who may be taking a standardized test for the first time.

6. Provide quality, ethical instruction in test-taking preparation using other strategies in this section. Remember, too, that test anxiety may manifest itself in various ways and personal or small group interactions may be especially helpful.

7. Encourage students to memorize material in small, frequent doses, and spread out the information to be learned over several sessions. Pace the items to be memorized eight to ten seconds apart to increase retention level.

8. Have students color code information in their notes that they want to remember. Different colors could signify various clusters of information.

9. Use music to match the syllables to be learned to the beat of the music. The multiplication tables, for example, can fit "I'd Like To Teach the World to Sing" or "Yankee Doodle."

10. Have students relate words and their definitions to an image to help retrieve the information. For example, *circumvent* means to go around. A key image might be a merry-go-round that has vents instead of horses.

11. Practice making up test questions students would expect to be on the test. This can be done in small groups with other groups answering the questions. Thorough preparation may help to allay some anxiety.

Practice and Reinforcement Activities

1. It may be helpful as your students study for essay tests for them to use PORPE, a study strategy for essay tests (Simpson, 1986).

   P = Predict. Students should predict potential essay questions that may be asked on the test.

   O = Organize. Students should organize the information they know that matches the predicted question.

   R = Rehearse. Students should recite the information that would be included in the essay answer.

   P = Practice. Students should practice writing their essay answer.

   E = Evaluate. Students should evaluate the quality of their answer. They may ask their teacher or another student to help them determine the quality of their work.

   Teach students the PORPE strategy and ask them to use it to practice for essay tests.

2. Ask students if they need help remembering the strategies for taking objective tests. If they have trouble remembering what to do, teach them SCORER (Ritter & Idol-Maestas, 1986). Explain that SCORER is a memory device to help them as they take tests.

   S = Schedule your time

   C = Use Clue words

   O = Omit difficult questions

   R = Read carefully

   E = Estimate your time

   R = Review your work

3. Encourage students to use a variety of memory devices. Ask them to use several different devices on the same information. Explain that different students will find some strategies more effective than others. Ask them which ones they thought worked best for them and why.

4. Have students keep a study journal. Ask them to chart what they do to study for a test, how they did on the test, and what plans they have for improvement.

5. Use the test-preparation checklist in the Resources for Chapter 8 to help students accept greater responsibility for their test-preparation behavior.

8.6 Charts and Graphs

Behavior Observed	The student has difficulty interpreting charts and graphs.
Anticipated Outcome	The student will use graphic aids to study.

Background

Graphs and charts are an integral feature of most texts because they can communicate information quickly, effectively, and persuasively. For some students, graphs and charts are a mystery rather than a source of information. Teachers need to be certain that students have the proper background in the interpretation of graphs and charts. The following strategies may provide some assistance.

Teaching Strategy 1

1. Explain that charts are ways of simplifying data to make it easy to read at a glance. Then hand out individual-size bags of M&M candies to each student. Let them open the bags and put the candy on their desks. Ask them to think about the aspects of the candies (weight, color, number).

2. Hand out a blank chart and ask students to record their data for the different colors and the number of each. An example might be the following:

blue candies	3
green candies	5
brown candies	6
yellow candies	4
orange candies	7
red candies	4
Total	29

3. Discuss the importance of developing a descriptive title for the chart. Ask students to suggest titles for the M&M chart. Some student responses might include: M&Ms, Number of M&M Candies, and Types of M&M Candies. Explain that someone reading the chart needs to know exactly what information is listed. Then ask students to write a title for their chart (perhaps Number of Colors in M&Ms).

454

4. Ask students to compare their charts with each other, noting similarities and differences.

5. Synthesize the individual charts into a class chart. Discuss the information that the class found.

6. Explain that information listed on a chart can also be expressed in a pictorial form using a graph. Show students an example of a bar graph and ask them whether they are able to understand the information given more readily than by using a chart. Explain that many people find graphs a quick method of understanding information.

7. Create a bar graph on the chalkboard or an overhead transparency from the information gathered from the class chart on M&M candies. As you write, explain the different features of the graph.

From the example that follows, for instance, you could say something like this: "This bar graph has its title at the top. The title tells me exactly what I can find on the graph. I see that this graph compares the number of individual colors of M&M candies that were gathered from our class project. I see the number of candies is on the left side of the graph and the colors are listed at the bottom. Looking at the graph, I can see that the most colors found in the class were brown. We had a total of 56 brown candies. The next highest number was 50 orange. We had 45 green candies, 44 yellow candies, 40 red candies, and 35 blue candies."

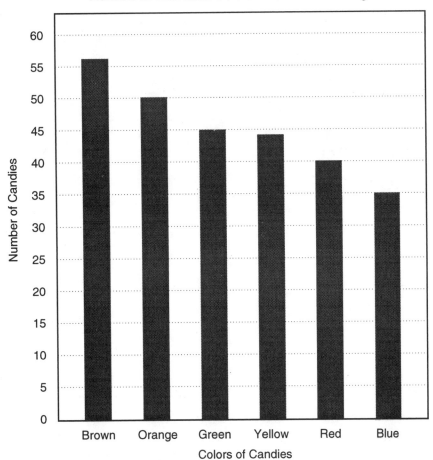

Number of Individual Colors in 10 M&M Packages

8. Provide students with graph paper and ask them to create a bar graph for their individual data. They may want to color the bars in the graphs with colored pencils or markers for effect.

9. Ask students to share their graphs with each other. Discuss the similarities and differences between the graphs.

10. Then groups of students could combine their data into group bar graphs. The final activity could be a single bar graph for the total group data.

11. Refer to a bar graph in your text and help students transfer their skills. Guide students through an interpretation of the graph by asking questions and thinking aloud. Model how you go about understanding a portion of the graph and invite students to share their thinking.

Teaching Strategy 2 (*Charts and Graphs*)

1. Explain to students that graphs and charts are visual methods of presenting information, making comparisons, and showing relationships, rather than using lots of words.

2. Brainstorm the similarities and differences between charts and graphs. Answers might include that charts show the relationship among several parts. They may show the order in which things happen or the cause and effect, but they always show how one part relates to the others. Graphs are similar to charts in that they show relationships, but they use points and lines rather than pictures or symbols.

3. Create a chart and a graph illustrating the months when students have birthdays.

4. Demonstrate how to read the chart and graph.

   Ask questions for which the students will have to use the graphic aids to answer, for example: Which month has the most birthdays?

Teaching Strategy 3 (*Line Graphs*)

1. Explain that a line graph is another way of arranging information that can be read at a glance. Ask students whether they have seen graphs other than bar graphs in their readings. Discuss the kinds of graphs students have seen.

2. Show students an example of a line graph on the overhead projector. Tell students about the feature of the line graphs including the title, the numbers, the lines, and the labels. An example of a line graph follows:

Temperature at 9:00 from Sept. 1 – Sept. 5

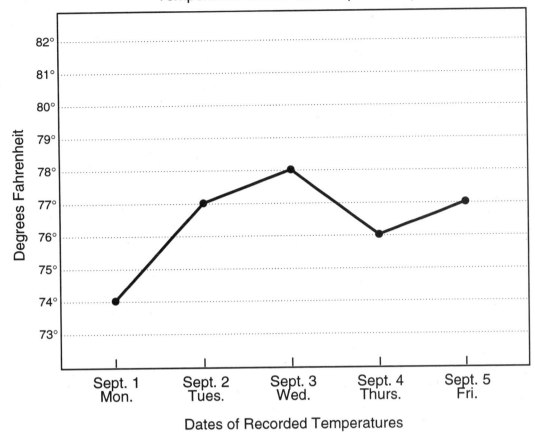

Dates of Recorded Temperatures

3. Ask the students to discuss the information they found on the graph. Some guiding questions and answers might be:

Teacher: What does this graph tell us?

Student: The temperature.

Teacher: Where did you find that information?

Student: From the title.

Teacher: What else do we know from this graph?

Student: How hot it was during the last week.

Teacher: Can you tell me how hot it was last Wednesday?

Student: Yes, it was 78 degrees.

4. Provide students with graph paper and help them construct a sample line graph using information from the birthday charts. See Teaching Strategy 2.

5. Ask students to compare line graphs with each other noting similarities and differences. Give them an opportunity to discuss how effective they think line graphs are at representing information.

Teaching Strategy 4 (*Pie Charts*)

1. Remind students that graphs and charts are visual ways of presenting information, comparisons, and relationships using few numbers and words. Explain that one of the uses of charts and graphs is that they give information in a brief form and help students visualize the data without a great deal of reading.

2. Tell students that they will be learning a new kind of chart, a pie chart. Put an example of a pie chart on the overhead projector. Tell students that the information from the chart was gathered from the class family heritage unit. An example of a pie chart follows:

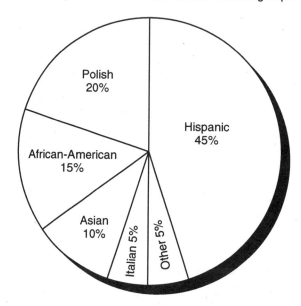

Mr. Thompson's Class
Percentage of members from different cultural groups

3. Ask students whether they have seen a pie chart in their reading or on television. Give students a chance to discuss the pie charts they have seen. If possible, refer to a pie chart in one of their texts.

4. Ask students what information they found on the pie chart. Remind them of the features of any graph or chart: the title, the labels, and the numbers.

5. Model for the students how you would read a pie chart for information. You might say something like this: "The first thing I look for when I see a chart is the title. This title says that the chart is the percentages of members from different cultural groups from a classroom. From looking at the chart, I see the largest area on the graph is made up of Hispanics. We see that 45% of the class has Hispanic origins. The second largest ethnic group in the class is made up of students of Polish ancestry. There are 20% of students who make up this group. We also see 15% of students who have an African-American background; 10% of students with Asian backgrounds; 5% of students with Italian backgrounds, and 5% in a category that says other."

6. Ask students whether they were able to understand the information from the pie chart as you described it. Provide students with an opportunity to discuss difficulties they had with interpreting the chart. Students may ask about the category *other* on the chart. Explain that when there are too few members in a group to be represented on the chart, they may be placed together in one category.

Practice and Reinforcement Activities

1. Ask students to think of some information they would like to know. It might be how many students wear a certain brand of clothes, the methods students use to get to school, or the number of rabbits in their backyard. Have students record their data for a period of time, several days at least. Ask students to make a graph for their data. All the points on the graph should be neatly plotted and connected. Share the data with the class by writing a story about it or explaining it to a group of older students.

2. Divide the class into groups of two. Distribute two graphs to each pair of students. Ask each student to read one graph with the purpose of explaining that graph to their partner. Give the students time to read and think about the graphs. Then ask them to share what they have learned with their partner. After the discussions are finished, ask students whether they have questions about the information on the graphs that they were unable to understand. Answer any questions students might have.

3. Ask students to look for bar graphs, line graphs, and pie charts in newspapers and magazines. Invite them to bring in samples of these graphs to class. Give students an opportunity to explain the graph either to the entire class or to a small group. Post the graphs on a poster or bulletin board.

4. Locate information from the texts used in class that would be appropriate to chart or graph. Ask students to develop a graph for the information.

5. Convert some of the information you record on a daily or weekly basis to be converted into a graph. For example, you might graph the number of books the students have read, the number of books they have written, or the number of sunny days in the month. Ask a group of students to chart the information and another group to graph it on poster board for the class.

6. Integrate graph learning activities with the ongoing curriculum. Pay particular attention to graphic aids in textbooks.

Resources for Chapter 8

➤ Study Skills Self-Report

➤ Test-Taking Skills: Self-Assessment

➤ Test-Preparation Checklist

Study Skills Self-Report

Name_____

Please answer the following questions by circling the appropriate number.

	Always	Usually	Sometimes	Rarely	Never
1. I read material more than once if I don't understand it the first time.	5	4	3	2	1
2. I try to pick out the most important points as I read.	5	4	3	2	1
3. I survey new reading assignments.	5	4	3	2	1
4. I recite facts to learn them.	5	4	3	2	1
5. I review for a test more than one day before it is given.	5	4	3	2	1
6. I concentrate when I try to study.	5	4	3	2	1
7. I get all of my homework done.	5	4	3	2	1
8. I study with a friend.	5	4	3	2	1
9. I finish my test before the time is up.	5	4	3	2	1
10. I try to "overlearn" material before a test.	5	4	3	2	1
11. I plan in my mind the answer to an essay question before starting to write.	5	4	3	2	1
12. I pay attention in class.	5	4	3	2	1
13. I take notes that help me when we have a test.	5	4	3	2	1
14. I take the required materials to class.	5	4	3	2	1
15. I really try to get good grades.	5	4	3	2	1

From Davis, S.J. (1990). Applying content study skills in co-listed reading classrooms. *Journal of Reading, 33*(4), 277-281.

Test Taking Skills: Self-Assessment

To be completed before teaching a test-taking strategy.

Student's Name: _____ Grade _____ Date_____

Teacher's Name: _____

Please read each statement and circle (Yes) or (No), according to your test-taking behaviors.
Be sure to mark every item.

---

1. I am aware of how much time I have to take tests.   Y   N

2. I answer questions that I know first.   Y   N

3. I go back to more difficult, time-consuming questions.   Y   N

4. I check my answers after I finish my test to avoid careless mistakes.   Y   N

5. I know what type of questions that I answer.   Y   N

6. I look for clue words to determine what information is given and what information I need to answer myself.   Y   N

7. I spend less time on questions I know, saving my time for those that I am unsure of.   Y   N

8. I read all the directions before beginning the test.   Y   N

9. When I don't understand directions, I ask for help.   Y   N

10. I read the entire questions and answers when they're given.   Y   N

11. I read over my answers.   Y   N

12. I ask myself if my answers make sense.   Y   N

13. I guess only after an honest attempt at an answer.   Y   N

14. I use information given to help me estimate my answer.   Y   N

15. I check over my answers before handing in my test.   Y   N

16. My work is neat and legible on my tests.   Y   N

17. I check to make sure all questions are answered before handing in my test.   Y   N

18. I always make sure my name is on my test.   Y   N

From Ritter, S., & Idol-Maestas, L. (1986). Teaching middle school students to use a test-taking strategy. *Journal of Educational Research, 79*(6), 350-357.

Test-Preparation Checklist

Name_____

Here are some tips to help you organize textbook information as you get ready for a test. Circle *yes* or *no* for each item. If you are able to answer *yes* to each question, then you are probably ready for the test. Work on those areas where you have circled *no*.

1. Do I know what type of test I'll be taking? (multiple choice, essay, matching, etc.)   Y   N

2. Do I know which subject areas will be covered?   Y   N

3. Have I studied a little at a time, not waiting for the last minute?   Y   N

4. Have I reviewed my notes carefully?   Y   N

5. Have I looked up hard vocabulary words in order to understand them?   Y   N

6. Do I know important words that are printed in **bold** or *italics*?   Y   N

7. Have I skimmed chapter headings to recall the overall ideas in each chapter?   Y   N

8. Can I recall the main ideas listed in the chapter summaries?   Y   N

9. Have I looked at charts, diagrams, or illustrations for important information?   Y   N

10. Can I answer the questions at the end of the chapter?   Y   N

CHAPTER 9

Strengthening the Home-School Partnership

Overview

Parents and care givers have an important role in the development of their children's literacy (Morrow, 1995). They are their children's first teachers. From the moment of birth, parents consciously and unconsciously model the values and knowledge they want their children to learn. Parents spend a great deal of time with their children showing them how to develop into successful adults who can care for themselves, earn a living, function in society, and—we hope—read.

Students who stay in school from kindergarten through twelfth grade will have spent only 9% of their time in school (Kearns, 1993). That leaves an astounding 91% of time out of school; therefore, parents are responsible for a great deal of their children's education. Clearly, schools and parents need to work together to foster continuity in the lives of children.

A literacy-rich home can make a difference to the reading development of children. There are ten general characteristics of a home that are associated with positive reading growth (Baker, et al., 1994). They include:

- Reading guidance and encouragement
- Books and other reading material for children
- Print materials for adults
- Space and opportunities for reading
- Adults reading in the home
- Trips to the library
- Regular outings with parents
- Parents who have positive attitudes toward reading
- Parents who converse with their children
- Children who are read to regularly

Parents want to know how to best help their children learn to read. Joyce Epstein and her colleagues at the Center on Families, Communities, Schools and Children's Learning have been studying the effects of parent involvement on school success (*Making Parents Your Partners,* 1993). Epstein finds that parents want to become actively involved in schools but believes that there is not enough clear direction from teachers and school administrators. According to Epstein, concern about education is a feeling that cuts through class and socioeconomic groups.

Parental involvement in schools is a vital issue in education today. Teachers and school administrators are willing to involve many parents in reading programs and to sustain that involvement (Rasinski & Fredericks, 1989). Often, however, articles and other resources give only a list of ideas to follow or home activities that teachers may suggest to parents. These are helpful, but they may be difficult to use as a basis for plans and development of well-articulated programs for parents.

We believe that it would be useful for you to have information about five levels of increasing parent involvement as you develop a comprehensive home-school partnership. In this chapter, there is a section on each type of parental involvement: parenting, communicating, volunteering, learning at home, and representing other parents. For each type of parental involvement, there is a goal, outcomes for parents, students, and teachers, and suggested practices (*Making Parents Your Partners*, 1993). Most of the sections also have letters to parents. Please feel free to reproduce or adapt any of these pages and send them home to parents. We hope the information provided will help you design effective programs to strengthen the home-school partnership.

9.1   Parenting (Level 1)

> ***Goal***   To help all families establish home environments to support literacy learning.

Anticipated Outcomes

For Parents

Parents will increase their self-confidence in parenting and knowledge of ways to support their children's literacy acquisition.

For Students

Students will gain respect for their parents and will have improved attendance when they perceive home and school working together.

For Teachers

Teachers will learn more about understanding and accepting family cultures and values.

Suggested Practices

One of the best services that a school can offer parents is suggestions about how they can make their homes conducive to reading. At this point, there is no other societal structure that lets parents know how to help their child learn. Perhaps the need for a literacy-rich environment was not quite as important to past generations as it is for children today. Many families in our society do not know what to do to support their child's learning at home because they did not experience it in their growing-up years. The literacy demands for your students are much higher than they were for their parents, and by the time your students graduate from high school, the demands for reading, writing, and using technology will have increased even more. To help students in our classrooms meet the literacy demands of our present society, we need to offer suggestions to parents about ways to make their home a place of literacy learning and then encourage them to take action.

One of the best ways parents can help their children learn to read is to have their home conducive to learning. There are several things parents can do to make their home a place of learning. They include the following (Lalas, 1993):

A Learning Home

- an inviting area or corner for reading

- a wide variety of books and magazines for all family members

- a regular time for reading

- a collection of "how to" books

- shelves, crates, or boxes for storing books
- places for writing messages
- places to display notes, writings, and drawings
- different kinds of paper for writing
- crayons, markers, pencils, and pens
- comfortable chairs for reading
- a library card for checking out books

There are many ways parents can help their children read at home. All homes are filled with reading material, and not just books. We all rely on reading. Parents may not be aware of the literacy-rich environments their homes already are. You may want to make them aware of the many reading activities that can go on in their homes. The following ideas are some examples of real reading at home (Lalas, 1993):

Real Reading at Home

write family diaries

cook together and read recipes

collect grocery coupons

read video game directions

design cards and invitations

write letters to relatives

videotape family events

read TV guide and discuss good choices

make a pictorial biography

read and discuss news articles

write thank you notes

prepare a calendar of activities

tape record stories

create original stories

write messages to each other

read bulletins from school

create photo album captions

sing together

write and file addresses

write a family history

make shopping lists

read menus

read bus schedules

write a family vacation journal

create a family bulletin board

Many parents want to know how they can help their children learn in school. Learning in school can be different from other types of learning children experience. There are several ways parents can help their children become better learners in school (Jones, 1991).

Tips for Learning

- Talk with your child about daily events and take time to listen to what your child wants to tell you.

- Read aloud to your child—every day—and let your child read to you. The more children read, both in school and at home, the more they will improve their reading abilities. Read with children of all ages.

- Encourage children to draw and scribble stories at home. This will increase confidence at school.

- Take your child to new and different places such as museums, historical sites, and nature centers. Talk about what you've seen.

- Supervise television viewing. Choose good programs and set some time limits. Talk to your child about what you have watched.

- Establish a regular time and place for doing homework, encourage your child's efforts, and offer praise when assignments are completed.

- Be generous in showing affection and express interest in your child's everyday activities and accomplishments.

- Instill self-confidence by encouraging your child to believe in his or her self-worth and abilities.

- Encourage good health practices by making sure your child has three nutritious meals a day, gets plenty of sleep and exercise, and has regular dental and medical checkups.

- Monitor how your child spends his or her time out of school. Limit video games and television viewing. Encourage reading, hobbies, scouts, and other activities that provide learning and social opportunities.

- Make sure your child attends school regularly. Show an interest in what is being learned at school, and communicate that school is important. Belief in the value of hard work, personal responsibility, and the importance of education all contribute to greater success in school.

- Be a role model for your child. Children will imitate what they see their parents doing. If you read, your child will want to read.

Helping children develop self-esteem is one of the more important jobs a parent has. Self-esteem means appreciating one's own worth, being accountable for one's own actions, and acting responsibly toward others. Children with high self-esteem take pride in their accomplishments, make good decisions, demonstrate responsibility, and have high self-expectations. Here are some ways to develop self-esteem in your children (Jones, 1991):

Helping Children Develop Healthy Self-Esteem

- Seek out opportunities to praise and encourage your child.

- Recognize the things your child does well.

- Treat your child with love, respect, and courtesy.

- Nurture a positive attitude in all situations.

- Give your child opportunities to assume responsibility appropriate for his or her age.

- Encourage your child to participate in activities that will be successful.

- Listen attentively to your child's ideas, fears, feelings, and concerns.

- Reward good behavior and accomplishments.

- Encourage decision making whenever possible.

- Spend time together and share favorite activities.

Children are subject to many influences outside their home, but parents have the most lasting influence when it comes to success in school. Motivation is the key to becoming a successful learner. Here are some ways you can help to motivate your children (Jones, 1991):

Motivating Your Child to Succeed in School

Show interest in your child's learning. Ask about what is happening in school. Ask to see papers and projects.

Work with your child on setting daily goals that are attainable. Write the goals and post them in a prominent place.

Help your child envision and formulate long-term goals.

Instill in your child that achievements are usually the result of persistence and hard work, not luck or ability.

Show caring and love if your child makes a mistake or fails, and help him or her see mistakes as opportunities to learn and grow.

Demonstrate through your words and actions faith in your child's ability to learn and achieve.

Look for successes in your child's efforts and acknowledge them.

Recognize, praise, and celebrate your child's successful completion of a goal.

Model for your child language that conveys positive expectations, such as *I can, I will, I want to, I understand, my goal is,* and so on.

Stress to your child the importance of learning and education.

One way to communicate the information in this section to parents is to send home parent letters. This section contains six letters to parents with information about making their home supportive to literacy learning. You may want to send these letters near the beginning of the school year or spread them out throughout the year, whichever is appropriate for your parent population. If at all possible, however, try to follow-up these suggestions with other ways of communicating about the home environment, such as making telephone calls, conducting conferences, and offering parent workshops. Some parents do not or cannot read every letter that comes home from school.

Parent letters included in this section are:

- Creating a Learning Home
- Real Reading at Home
- Tips for Learning
- Helping Children Develop Healthy Self-Esteem
- Motivating Your Child to Succeed in School
- Magazines for Children

Dear Parents,

One of the best ways you can help your child in reading is to have your home conducive to learning. There are several things you can do to make your home a place of learning. I've listed some of them here.

Please read this list and circle "yes" for those you have and "no" for those you do not have. Then think about which ones you would want to add to your home routine. You should try to do as many as possible, but I know that there are times when some of them probably won't work in your family situation. You should consider your home a Learning Home if you are able to accomplish many of the items on this list.

Sincerely,

Creating A Learning Home

Does the place where you live have:

➤ an inviting area or corner for reading?	Yes	No
➤ a wide variety of books and magazines for all family members?	Yes	No
➤ a regular time for reading?	Yes	No
➤ a collection of "how to" books?	Yes	No
➤ shelves, crates, or boxes for storing books?	Yes	No
➤ places for writing messages?	Yes	No
➤ places to display notes, writings, and drawings?	Yes	No
➤ different kinds of paper for writing?	Yes	No
➤ crayons, markers, pencils, and pens?	Yes	No
➤ comfortable chairs for reading?	Yes	No
➤ a library card for checking out books?	Yes	No

Dear Parents,

There are many ways you can help your child read at home. Your home is filled with reading material. You would be surprised at how much we all rely on reading. You may read directions when you cook, clip coupons from the newspaper, read cards or letters from friends, and read junk mail. You read all of the time! And the reading you do is important. It is reading for a real purpose. For example, you need to read the directions to microwave popcorn correctly or you will burn the popcorn. Your child needs to know that reading outside school is still reading.

Invite your child to read with you during these reading times at home. At least once a day, think about one of these reading events, and ask your child to join you. Read the directions (or whatever) to your child, then ask your child to read them with you. Finally, ask your child what the words are saying. This will help your child on the road to reading!

Sincerely,

Real Reading at Home

➤ write family diaries

➤ cook together and read recipes

➤ collect grocery coupons

➤ read video game directions

➤ design cards and invitations

➤ write letters to relatives

➤ videotape family events

➤ read TV guide and discuss good choices

➤ make a pictorial biography

➤ read and discuss news articles

➤ write thank you notes

➤ prepare a calendar of activities

➤ create original stories

➤ write messages to each other

➤ read bulletins from school

➤ create photo album captions

➤ sing together

➤ write and file addresses

➤ write a family history

➤ make shopping lists

➤ read menus

➤ read bus schedules

➤ write a family vacation journal

➤ create a family bulletin board

➤ tape record stories

Dear Parents,

Many parents have asked me how they can help their children learn in school. Learning in school can be different from other types of learning your child experiences. There are several ways you can help your child become a better learner in school.

The ideas presented here are general ideas that can help your child learn. Try to incorporate as many of them as possible into your home.

Sincerely,

Tips for Learning

➤ Talk with your child about daily events and take time to listen to what your child wants to tell you.

➤ Read aloud to your child—every day—and let your child read to you. The more children read, both in school and at home, the more they will improve their reading abilities. Read with children of all ages.

➤ Encourage children to draw and scribble stories at home. This will increase confidence at school.

➤ Take your child to new and different places such as museums, historical sites, and nature centers. Talk about what you've seen.

➤ Supervise television viewing. Choose good programs and set some time limits. Talk to your child about what you have watched.

➤ Establish a regular time and place for doing homework, encourage your child's efforts, and offer praise when assignments are completed.

➤ Be generous in showing affection and express interest in your child's every day activities and accomplishments.

➤ Instill self-confidence by encouraging your child to believe in his or her self-worth and abilities.

➤ Encourage good health practices by making sure your child has three nutritious meals a day, gets plenty of sleep and exercise, and has regular dental and medical checkups.

➤ Monitor how your child spends his or her time out of school. Limit video games and television viewing and encourage reading, hobbies, scouts, and other activities that provide learning and social opportunities.

➤ Make sure your child attends school regularly. Show an interest in what is being learned at school, and communicate that school is important. Belief in the value of hard work, personal responsibility, and the importance of education all contribute to greater success in school.

➤ Be a role model for your child. Children will imitate what they see their parents doing. If you read, your child will want to read.

Dear Parents,

Your child is an important person, but many children don't realize how special they are. Everyone struggles with uncertainty about themselves at some time in their lives; it's part of being human. But the better children feel about themselves, the more attention they can give to learning. Children who have low self-esteem often are so worried about themselves, that they do not do as well as they could in school.

As a parent, you can help your child have healthy self-esteem. Having healthy self-esteem doesn't mean your child will be stuck up. It just means that your child will be able to take pride in accomplishments, make good decisions, and be responsible.

Here are ways to help your child develop healthy self-esteem. I know you do many of these already, but try to add a few more. It will help your child in school.

Sincerely,

Helping Children Develop Healthy Self-Esteem

➤ Seek out opportunities to praise and encourage your child.

➤ Recognize the things your child does well.

➤ Treat your child with love, respect, and courtesy.

➤ Nurture a positive attitude in all situations.

➤ Give your child opportunities to assume responsibility appropriate for his or her age.

➤ Encourage your child to participate in activities that will be successful.

➤ Listen attentively to your child's ideas, fears, feelings, and concerns.

➤ Reward good behavior and accomplishments.

➤ Encourage decision making whenever possible.

➤ Spend time together and share favorite activities.

Dear Parents,

One of the most important qualities of a good student in school is high motivation. I know your child may be motivated to do many things well, and I want your child also to be highly motivated at school. There are many things you can do at home to increase your child's motivation. I know you do many of these already, but please think about adding a few more to what you already do. They can play a major role in increasing your child's motivation to succeed in school.

Sincerely,

Motivating Your Child to Succeed in School

➤ Show interest in your child's learning. Ask about what is happening in school. Ask to see papers and projects.

➤ Work with your child on setting daily goals that are attainable. Write the goals and post them in a prominent place.

➤ Help your child envision and formulate long-term goals.

➤ Instill in your child the idea that achievements are usually the result of persistence and hard work, not luck or ability.

➤ Show caring and love if your child makes a mistake or fails, and help him or her see mistakes as opportunities to learn and grow.

➤ Demonstrate through your words and actions faith in your child's ability to learn and achieve.

➤ Look for successes in your child's efforts and acknowledge them.

➤ Recognize, praise, and celebrate your child's successful completion of a goal.

➤ Model for your child language that conveys positive expectations, such as *I can, I will, I want to, I understand, my goal is,* and so on.

➤ Frequently stress to your child the importance of learning and education.

Dear Parents,

One of the most important ways you can help your child become a better reader is to have reading material at home that is appropriate for your child. You can get books and other reading materials from your public library. You might also choose to purchase magazines that are written with children in mind. Many parents have asked me what magazines they could get for their children. In response to that question, I have devised a list. If you do not wish to use this list, please pass it on to another parent who may be interested.

Sincerely,

Magazines for Children

Child Life
1100 Waterway Blvd.
Indianapolis, IN 46202
12 issues a year
Ages: 5-12
Stories, poems, arts and crafts

Creative Kids
P.O. Box 637
Holmes, PA 19043-9937
8 issues a year
Poems, stories, photos, artwork by children

The Electric Company Magazine
P.O. Box 2926
Boulder, CO 80322
12 issues a year
Activities for beginning readers

Highlights for Children
P.O. Box 269
Columbus, OH 43272
11 issues a year
Ages: 5-12
Stories, poems, arts and crafts, activities

Jack and Jill
P.O. Box 567B
Indianapolis, IN 46206
12 issues a year
Ages: 8-12
Stories, poems, art

Sesame Street Magazine
P.O. Box 52000
Boulder, CO 80321
10 issues a year
Ages: 3-7
Stories, games, and activities

Ranger Rick
National Wildlife Federation
1400 16th Street N.W.
Washington, D.C. 20036-2266
12 issues a year
Stories, photos, activities about animals and wildlife

Sports Illustrated for Kids
P.O. Box 830
Birmingham, AL 35282-9487
12 issues a year
Ages: 8-14
Sports articles and photos

Your Big Backyard
National Wildlife Federation
1400 16th Street N.W.
Washington, D.C. 20036-2266
Ages: 3-5
Stories, puzzles, games, arts and crafts, and photos about animals and nature

---

9.2   Parenting (Level 2)

> ***Goal***   To design more effective forms of communication to reach parents.

Anticipated Outcomes

For Parents

Parents who look closely at their children's work may develop an understanding of school programs and procedures. They can monitor their child's progress.

For Students

Parents who are informed can guide their children to make better decisions about courses and programs that are suited to the child's needs and abilities.

For Teachers

Teachers who send home student work frequently receive communications that offer few surprises. Parents are aware of student progress because they have seen daily work and will likely readily communicate more effectively, rather than feeling "on the spot."

Suggested Practices

Parents are interested in what you are doing at school. They want to keep informed at some level about how and what you are teaching and how their child is doing in your classroom. There are many ways to keep parents informed about your classroom. They might include several of the following (Jones, 1991):

Keeping Parents Informed About Schooling

- welcome packets for new families delivered to the home
- class and individual letters and messages sent home
- back-to-school nights and open houses
- parent/student handbooks
- school and program information brochures
- parent interest surveys
- "happy grams" reporting good news
- principal-parent coffees
- newsletters (program, class, school)
- teacher-parent lunches, teas

- special occasion cards/recognition messages
- student work sent home frequently with a sheet for parent response
- personal handwritten notes
- progress/success reports
- letters and notes from the principal/superintendent
- monthly event and activity calendars

Of course, you cannot do everything in one school year. Instead, try to incorporate one new method of communicating what you are doing in your classroom every few months. That way, the amount of information you send to parents will increase at a steady pace.

One idea that can provide you with valuable information about your students' reading is to ask parents for information. Parents can tell you about their child's reading habits at home, interests their child has, and books their child likes. Asking parents to share this information can give parents a chance to provide you with input and can save you the time it takes to find out this information from each of your students. To help gather this information, we have provided two sources: a Parent Checklist that you can send home and a Parent Survey in letter form. Either of these sources will be helpful as you make instructional decisions.

Parent Checklist

Name _____

Grade _____

Date _____

> Please indicate your observation of your child's learning in the following areas and comment where appropriate.

	Yes	No	Comments
My child likes to listen to me read to him or her.			
My child likes to read to me.			
My child attempts to read in daily situations, that is, signs, labels, and other print.			
My child understands books I read to him or her.			
My child attempts to figure out words.			
My child sometimes chooses to write.			
My child shares what he or she writes.			
My child is provided with the opportunity to visit the public library often.			

Parent Survey About Reading

Dear Parents,

Please take a few minutes and reflect on what you have observed about your child's reading at home. Your information can help me provide more appropriate instruction to your child. I appreciate your help.

Sincerely,

Child's Name _____

Parent or Care Giver's Name _____

1. What strengths do you think your child has in reading?

_____

_____

2. Please list your child's interests.

_____

_____

3. What books or authors does your child like?

_____

_____

4. What concerns do you have about your child's reading?

_____

_____

5. What magazines, books, or newspapers do the adults in your home generally read?

_____

6. What hobbies or interests does your family have?

_____

From Jerry L. Johns and Susan Davis Lenski, *Improving Reading: A Handbook of Strategies* (2nd ed.). Copyright © 1997 Kendall/Hunt Publishing Company (1-800-228-0810). May be reproduced for noncommercial educational purposes.

Many teachers regularly send home a weekly class newsletter. Class newsletters are a great way to keep parents informed about the day-to-day events in your classroom. Of course, if you have to write the newsletters, they can be very time-consuming. Instead, we recommend that the students (if they can) either write the copy for their own personal newsletter, called a Weekly Review, or copy items you have listed from the chalkboard. Asking students to write their own Weekly Review has additional benefits. Learning in the classroom is reinforced in each student's mind if they write the Weekly Review themselves. Second, many students can use free time to decorate the Weekly Reviews and make them attractive for their parents. Third, parents love to read what their children have written. A sample Weekly Review form is included that you may use or adapt.

Another thing to keep in mind is that if you have specific changes in your classroom curriculum, you should inform the parents of your students. In addition, alerting parents to changes in your teaching can prevent misunderstandings that escalate into problems. An example might be an increase of literature-based teaching in your classroom. If you are using fewer worksheets and workbooks, parents may think you are not teaching your students to read. You need to inform them of any instructional changes you make, and let them know the good reasons for these changes. That way you will be keeping parents informed as you are strengthening your reading program.

Sample Letter Only
(Not to be Sent)

Dear Parents,

I have been pleased with the reading program that I have used in the past, but during the summer I spent some time thinking about how to make reading more exciting for my students without omitting any of the reading skills that I teach. I signed up for a course on using literature in the classroom, and did I ever learn a lot! I learned how I could use literature in the classroom, thus increasing the children's interest in reading, while keeping my program of skill instruction. During the class, I revised my reading program, and under the direction of the professor, developed a literature-based reading program that I will be implementing this fall.

The main difference between the way I will be teaching reading this year, and the way I have taught it in previous years, is that I will be using more whole books to teach, rather than using excerpts of the books that are found in our basal reader. The administration in our district is in favor of this change, and I know my students will love it.

I will also make a few changes in how I teach reading skills. Instead of teaching them from the workbook, I will teach them using real books. For example, I usually teach my students how to find the main idea of a paragraph. Previously, I used workbook pages. This year I will use the paragraphs from class sets of real books.

I am confident that this change in my reading program will help your child learn to read more effectively. I will be providing you with updates about this program change, beginning with our first open house. Please feel free to call me if you have any questions.

Sincerely,

Weekly Review

Name _____   Date _____

Here are some things I've done this week:

_____

_____

_____

Here are some things I've learned:

_____

_____

_____

I've read these books:

_____

_____

_____

I've worked on these reading skills:

_____

_____

Teacher comments:

_____

_____

Parent comments:

_____

_____

There are several pieces of information about classrooms that we think are essential for parents to have. These we have included as parent letters. You might decide to adapt and send the parent letters that are appropriate for your grade level and classroom.

Parent letters include:

- Unity poem
- Parent/Teacher Conference Letter
- Conference Summary Form

Dear Parents,

    I'm looking forward to this year and having your child in my classroom. To begin the year, I'd like to share a poem with you. It's one that explains how I feel about the dual role teachers and parents have in the lives of children. I hope you enjoy the poem.

Sincerely,

Unity

I dreamed I stood in a studio
And watched two sculptors there.
The clay they used was a young child's mind
And they fashioned it with care.

One was a teacher—the tools he used
Were books, music, and art.
The other, a parent, worked with a guiding hand,
And a gentle, loving heart.

Day after day, the teacher toiled with touch
That was careful, deft, and sure.
While the parent labored by his side
And polished and smoothed it o'er.

And when at last their task was done,
They were proud of what they had wrought.
For the things they had molded into the child
Could neither be sold nor bought.

And each agreed they would have failed
If each had worked alone.
For behind the parent stood the school
And behind the teacher, the home.

Author Unknown

From Jerry L. Johns and Susan Davis Lenski, *Improving Reading: A Handbook of Strategies* (2nd ed.). Copyright © 1997 Kendall/Hunt Publishing Company (1-800-228-0810). May be reproduced for noncommercial educational purposes.

Dear Parents,

I am looking forward to seeing you at Parent/Teacher Conferences this year. Parent conferences provide you with an opportunity to learn about your child's progress in school. They allow me to learn from you how to help your child. The following tips will help you get the most from our upcoming conference.

- Focus on your child before coming to the conference. Jot down any questions you have for me.

- Feel free to take notes during the conference. Don't hesitate to ask me to clarify anything that seems unclear.

- If there are factors at home that you wish to discuss with me, the conference would be a good time. It is helpful for me to know if anything at home might be interfering with your child's learning.

- Since we can only meet a short time, try not to bring young children to the conference.

Sincerely,

Conference date _____   Time _____

Questions you have: _____

_____

_____

Notes during conference: _____

_____

_____

_____

Conference Summary

Name _____ Date _____

Participants _____

_____

Parent Concerns _____

_____

_____

Teacher Concerns _____

_____

_____

Decisions _____

_____

_____

Goals _____

_____

_____

Follow-up _____

_____

_____

_____

_____   _____
Teacher's Signature   Parent's Signature

9.3 Volunteering (Level 3)

> **Goal** To recruit and organize parent help and support for the classroom and the school.

Anticipated Outcomes

For Parents

Volunteering provides an understanding of the day-to-day duties and responsibilities of teachers and an appreciation of their job. Parents who are in the school frequently have an increased comfort in school interactions.

For Students

Students will increase their ability to communicate with adults as they relate to various volunteers within their classroom and their school.

For Teachers

Teachers may become more confident that parents who are volunteering are serious and consistent in their desire to help at school. Teachers may gain confidence in trying programs that involve parents in new ways.

Suggested Practices

There are many ways parents can become involved in your classroom. Parent volunteers in your classroom can be the added boost that help you accomplish your instructional goals. To get parents involved, you might consider setting up a parent center where volunteers can meet and where resources for parents are located. Volunteers will feel more welcome and a part of the school if they know where things are and do not have to ask someone for help. Annually, survey all parents, perhaps with a postcard, to find out who is willing to volunteer, in what area, and the times volunteers are available.

In order to facilitate greater consistency and willingness on the part of parents, school personnel must remember that parents are coming on their own time. Parents decide what is the best time for them or if they can be available. Often, child care is a concern. Parents may bring toddlers if a child care alternative is not offered. Some parents need transportation, and often car pools of volunteers can be arranged or supported. These problems are not insurmountable; if you can help solve them, you will be rewarded with increased parent involvement.

Some ways parents can become involved in volunteering may include:

■ parent visitation days

■ assisting teachers with special projects such as cooking, making books, chaperoning field trips, and so on

■ having parents or grandparents read to the class

- having parents tell about their occupations or special expertise to enrich the curriculum

- working with small groups to hear students read, record students' dictated stories, or help write stories on the computer

- helping with special musical programs or plays

- cutting paper or preparing for special projects

- supervising before-school or after-school programs

- helping with school-wide projects such as book fairs, meet the author programs, or awards programs

One of the most successful uses of parent volunteers is asking them to become involved in paired reading. Paired reading is when a parent (or any adult) and a child sit together and read a book. The parent can assist the child in reading the text, can read along with the child, or can listen to the child read without interference.

As parents listen to students from your class read, they may appreciate some guidelines for times when students make miscues. Here are a few guidelines for parents who are listening to students read.

Guidelines for Listening Parents

- Don't jump in and help right away. Silently count to 5 first.

- If the child is silent ask:

  "What word would make sense there?"

  "What is the first sound of the word?"

  "What do you think that word could be?"

- If the child still misses the word, say:

  "Start the sentence again."

  "Read on to the end of the sentence; then we'll go back and try the word again."

- If the child still misses the word, say the word, and ask the child to reread the sentence saying the word this time.

- If the child misses several words on a page or in a small book, encourage the selection of an easier book.

If you ask parents to volunteer for paired reading, you might find the following parent letters useful:

- Letter for Listening Parents

- Tips for Listening Parents

- Discussion Guide for Listening Parents

Dear Parent,

In the past, I have had parents come to school to give students an opportunity to talk on a one-to-one basis with an adult about the books they read.

The children in my room this year are looking forward to this activity and suggested your name as someone who might be interested in coming to our room. A guide for the discussion you might carry on with students will be provided. If you would like to be a "listening parent," please indicate on this note and check the day and time period best for you. You may check more than one day and time if you wish.

Sincerely,

- -

I'd like to be a "listening parent". I can come to school on the following times:

Day   Time

Monday   _____

Tuesday   _____

Wednesday   _____

Thursday   _____

Friday   _____

_____
Signature

_____
Telephone

Tips for Listening Parents

As you listen to students from this class read, you will notice that they make mistakes. The way children learn to read is by trying to read words, making mistakes, and correcting those mistakes. Sometimes a child will need assistance in order to correct a reading mistake. That's where you come in.

Here are a few guidelines for those times when your reading partners make mistakes:

- Don't jump in and help right away. Silently count to 5 first.

- If the child is silent ask:

    "What word would make sense there?"

    "What is the first sound of the word?"

    "What do you think that word could be?"

- If the child still misses the word, say:

    "Start the sentence again."

    "Read on to the end of the sentence; then we'll go back and try the word again."

- If the child still misses the word, say the word, and ask the child to reread the sentence saying the word this time.

- If the child misses several words on a page or in a small book, encourage the selection of an easier book.

Discussion Guide for Listening Parents

Child's Name _____ Date _____

Parent's Name _____

1. What is the name of your book? _____

_____

2. What was this book mostly about? _____

_____

_____

3. What part did you like best? Why? _____

_____

_____

Listening Parent Comments:

1. Do you think this book was too easy, just right, or too hard for the child? _____

_____

2. Please list some of the words that the child missed. _____

_____

_____

3. Please comment on the child's understanding of the book. _____

_____

_____

4. Additional Comments. _____

_____

_____

9.4   Parenting (Level 4)

> **Goal**   To provide specific ideas to parents about how to help their child at home.

Anticipated Outcomes

For Parents

Parents will gain an understanding of their child as a student when they interact with their child doing school activities together at home.

For Students

A gain in achievement in the skills and strategies practiced at home will be evident.

For Teachers

Teachers may have a better, more efficient design of homework assignments, and they may make specific enrichment activities for families to do together. Learning will be enhanced as both parents and school work together.

Suggested Practices

Many parents are able to help their children with reading at home. However, some parents have reasons that prevent them from doing as much as they would like at this time. We need to honor the complex lives of the parents of our students while encouraging them to help with their child's reading at home whenever they can. Some parents will feel intimidated about doing school-work with their child. Some parents may not know English. Others, however, will welcome your suggestions. Remember, parents are people as diverse as the students in your classroom. We cannot expect them to do everything we want, but we can offer suggestions and provide activities that we know will help their children.

There are many ways you can involve the parents of your students in their child's reading. Here are some ideas:

1. **Book Journal.** Make or buy a blank journal for several books in your class library. Have the children check out books. Encourage families to react to the story. Keep the same journal with each book so other families can enjoy the comments.

2. **Mystery Bag.** Decorate a bag and send it home with the following directions: "Find an item from home that will fit in the bag. Write three clues about the object on the index card you will find in the bag. Bring the bag and object back to school." Have a special table to display the bag and the clues. Let the children look at the bag and read the clues during the day. Then, let them write what they think the object is and why. Have the class share their ideas, and allow the student to reveal what is in the bag.

3. **Author's Tea.** Choose a day to invite family members in to hear the children read their own writings. These may be reports, poems, songs, and individual books. Serve punch and tea, and let the children show off their accomplishments.

4. **Comment Pages.** Put blank pages in the back of class and individual books. As children check these books out to take home, encourage family members to write comments about the books.

5. **Teddy Bear Journal.** Place a teddy bear, journal, and directions in a sturdy bag. Ask families to write a journal from the teddy bear's point of view, retelling the events and feelings it experienced during its stay with the family.

6. **Backpack.** Fill a backpack with a variety of reading and writing materials. These may include a variety of short books, paper, pens, colored pencils, chalk, and construction paper. Let children earn the opportunity to take the backpack home to read and write about their choice.

Parents also are interested in how they can encourage their children to read at home. A sampling of suggestions for parents to help their children become better readers follow.

Reading At Home: How Parents Can Help

■ Read aloud to your children, young and old, every day.

■ Alternate which parent reads aloud with the children so both male and female models are given.

■ Read and write often for authentic purposes to serve as a model to your children.

■ Read a novel to your children on long car trips or tape-record books for them to listen to during the ride.

■ Set up a neighborhood Reading Circle where parents and children get together to read and discuss their favorite books.

■ Encourage your children to select books by interest and not necessarily by reading level. Children who are interested in a particular topic may enjoy a book on that subject that they might otherwise consider too easy or too difficult.

■ Discuss books with your children.

■ Encourage your children to write a journal or diary from the perspective of the main character in the book being read.

■ Have your children make hand puppets and act out a book they have read.

Many parents know they need to read with their children; however, they may not know what kinds of questions to ask after their child has finished reading. There are several questions that parents should ask their children as they read with them (Fredericks, 1991).

Questioning When Reading

- Did this story turn out the way you thought it would? Why or why not?

- What made this book interesting?

- Is the main character someone you would like to have as a friend? Why or why not?

- If you were the author, how would you have changed the ending? How would you have changed the beginning? What other events would you have changed?

- Is this a book you would recommend to a friend? Which events would your friend enjoy most?

- What other events would you like to see happen to the main character?

- How would the story change if it took place in your town?

- Have you ever experienced some of the events or feelings that the main character had? Describe them.

- Would you enjoy reading other books by this author? Why or why not?

- What do you think would happen in a sequel to this book?

Parents are also interested in how to help their child improve reading comprehension by interacting with the story material. Fetterman (1993) has suggested the following reading activities for parents who read with their children.

Story Reading Ideas

Before reading

- Look at the title and illustrations together. Predict what the story will be about.

- Discuss what you both already know about the topic of the story.

- Read the first page and then ask your child to predict what might happen next.

During reading

- Encourage your child to picture in his or her mind what is happening in the story.

- Ask what might happen next in the story.

- Have your child change his or her predictions as the story provides new information.

- Ask how a character might feel.

- Talk about the illustrations.

After reading

- Have your child retell the story and create a new ending together.

- Retell the story from another character's point of view.

- Let your child illustrate his or her favorite part of the story.

- Think about the story together.

Bernice Cullinan (1992), sensing that some parents may feel they are too busy to adequately support reading in the home, has come up with marvelous suggestions, called "Tips for Busy Parents," which are specific for different age levels.

Reading Activities

Preschoolers

- Read a bedtime story.
- Read the same books over and over.
- Give your child markers or paper and pencils.
- Give your child a chalk board and chalk.
- Write messages to your child.
- Label your child's possessions.
- Get alphabet books and make alphabet books.
- Put magnetic letters on the refrigerator.

Five and Six Year Olds

- You read to me and I'll read to you.
- Fill in the blanks. Read poetry and verse that rhymes and stop before the end of the line, having your child fill in the blank.
- Play sound games. A simple starter is, "Riddle, riddle, ree. I see something you don't see and it starts with T."
- Create a newspaper.
- Make a book.
- Write a wish list.
- Make a calendar.
- Write a fill-in-the-blank story.
- Write a biography or autobiography.
- Make a jigsaw puzzle from a poster, book jacket, or picture postcard.
- Make a board game.

- Start a memory box.
- Cook from a book.

Seven and Eight Year Olds

- Write a book about something real or imagined.
- Keep a journal.
- Write a thank-you letter.
- Write your own cards.
- Make your own valentines.
- Keep score at sports events.
- Write a letter to an author.
- Get informational books.
- Start a scrapbook.
- Interview your parents or grandparents.
- Explore your family letters and albums.

Nine and Ten Year Olds

- Read riddles.
- Play thinking games.
- Work on projects.
- Support scout activities.
- Write fractured fairy tales.
- Create a camera story.
- Write a text for wordless books (see Appendix A).

Eleven and Twelve Year Olds

- Put a book in your child's room.
- Tell about a book you enjoyed.
- Start your child on a new series.

Finally, parents frequently say they don't know how to read aloud or they feel funny reading aloud. Following are some tips for reassuring parents that they indeed know how to read aloud (Trelease, 1989):

Read-Aloud Techniques

- Select books that you'll enjoy and that will spark your child's interest.

- Read unfamiliar stories silently first to note places that may need special effects to create drama.

- Don't read too fast and adjust your pace to the story and your child.

- Be responsive to your child's actions.

- Encourage your child's participation in the reading session—joining in repeating phrases, making comments, asking questions, predicting what will happen, or actually reading parts of the material.

- Allow time after reading for a relaxed discussion. This should involve sharing reactions, not quizzing on facts.

- Both parents should take turns reading aloud. Fathers are important models, too. Make sure your child sees you read for pleasure.

- Never withdraw reading aloud as a punishment. That may destroy all the positive effects of reading aloud.

The following parent letters which you may adapt can give parents additional ideas about how to help their children at home:

- Reading At Home: How Parents Can Help
- Questioning When Reading
- Story Reading Ideas
- Reading Activities
- Read Aloud Techniques
- Homework Tips for Parents

Dear Parents,

Children need a great deal of practice reading. Whenever someone learns something new, he or she needs to learn new techniques and then practice, practice, practice. At school, I spend time teaching your child reading skills and there is time to read, but not nearly enough. It would help tremendously if you would provide a time and place for your child to read at home. Enclosed are some suggestions about ways you can accomplish reading at home.

Sincerely,

Reading At Home: How Parents Can Help

➤ Read aloud to your children, young and old, every day.

➤ Alternate parents reading aloud with your children so both male and female models are given.

➤ Read and write often for authentic purposes to serve as a model to your children.

➤ Read a novel to your children on long car trips or tape-record books for them to listen to during the ride.

➤ Set up a neighborhood Reading Circle where parents and children get together to read and discuss their favorite books.

➤ Encourage your children to select books by interest and not necessarily by reading level. Children who are interested in a particular topic may enjoy a book on that subject that they might otherwise consider too easy or too difficult.

➤ Discuss books with your children.

➤ Encourage your children to write a journal or diary from the perspective of the main character in the book being read.

➤ Have your children make hand puppets and act out a book they have read.

➤ Encourage your children to explore answers to questions by using informational books.

Dear Parents,

I appreciate the time many of you have taken to begin new ways of reading with your child at home. When your child is reading, it can help if at times you ask probing questions. This will improve your child's reading comprehension. Enclosed are some suggestions for questioning when reading.

Sincerely,

Questioning When Reading

➤ Did this story turn out the way you thought it would? Why or why not?

➤ What made this book interesting?

➤ Is the main character someone you would like to have as a friend? Why or why not?

➤ If you were the author, how would you have changed the ending? How would you have changed the beginning? What other events would you have changed?

➤ Is this a book you would recommend to a friend? Which events would your friend enjoy most?

➤ What other events would you like to see happen to the main character?

➤ How would the story change if it took place in our town?

➤ Have you ever experienced some of the events or feelings that the main character had? Describe them.

➤ Would you enjoy reading other books by this author? Why or why not?

➤ What do you think would happen in a sequel to this book?

Dear Parents,

Many of you are reading with your child at home. There are a few techniques that will make your reading time even more profitable for your child. At school, when I read a story, I use special techniques to help them understand the story. I'd like to share these story-reading ideas with you.

Sincerely,

Story-Reading Ideas

Before reading

➤ Look at the title and illustrations together. Predict what the story will be about.

➤ Discuss what you both already know about the topic of the story.

➤ Read the first page and then ask your child to predict what might happen next.

During reading

➤ Encourage your child to picture in his or her mind what is happening in the story.

➤ Ask what might happen next in the story.

➤ Have your child change his or her predictions as the story provides new information.

➤ Ask how a character might feel.

➤ Talk about the illustrations.

After reading

➤ Have your child retell the story and create a new ending together.

➤ Retell the story from another character's point of view.

➤ Let your child illustrate his or her favorite part of the story.

➤ Think about the story together.

Dear Parents,

Many of you have more than one child at home, and you have been asking me about appropriate reading activities for children of different ages. Enclosed is a list of suggestions of reading activities for children of different ages. I've decided to send this letter home with every child in my room. You can get some good ideas even if you have one child.

Sincerely,

Reading Activities

Preschoolers

➤ Read a bedtime story.
➤ Read the same books over and over.
➤ Give your child markers or paper and pencils.
➤ Give your child a chalk board and chalk.
➤ Write messages to your child.
➤ Label your child's possessions.
➤ Put magnetic letters on the refrigerator.

Five and Six Year Olds

➤ You read to me and I'll read to you.
➤ Fill in the blanks. Read poetry and verse that rhymes and stop before the end of the line, having your child fill in the blank.
➤ Play sound games. A simple starter is, "Riddle, riddle, ree. I see something you don't see and it starts with T."
➤ Create a newspaper.
➤ Write a wish list.
➤ Make a calendar.
➤ Write a fill-in-the-blank story.
➤ Write a biography or autobiography.
➤ Make a board game.

➤ Start a memory box.
➤ Cook from a book.

Seven and Eight Year Olds

➤ Write a book about something real or imagined.
➤ Keep a journal.
➤ Write a thank-you letter.
➤ Write your own cards.
➤ Keep score at sports events.
➤ Start a scrapbook.
➤ Explore your family letters and albums.

Nine and Ten Year Olds

➤ Read riddles.
➤ Play thinking games.
➤ Work on projects.
➤ Support scout activities.
➤ Write fractured fairy tales.
➤ Create a camera story.
➤ Write a text for wordless books (see Appendix A).

Eleven and Twelve Year Olds

➤ Put a book in your child's room.
➤ Tell about a book you enjoyed.
➤ Start your child on a new series.

Dear Parents,

Children love to listen to stories, even older children. And it's fun to read stories to children. You can read books your child has brought home, or you can borrow books from your public library. In any case, it would be good for your child to listen to you read aloud at least three times each week. I have some read-aloud techniques that I use that I thought you might enjoy.

Sincerely,

Read-Aloud Techniques

➤ Select books that you'll enjoy and that will spark your child's interest.

➤ Read unfamiliar stories silently first to note places that may need special effects to create drama.

➤ Don't read too fast and adjust your pace to the story and your child.

➤ Be responsive to your child's actions.

➤ Encourage your child's participation in the reading session—joining in repeating phrases, making comments, asking questions, predicting what will happen, or actually reading parts of the material.

➤ Allow time after reading for a relaxed discussion. This should involve sharing reactions, not quizzing on facts.

➤ Both parents should take turns reading aloud. Fathers are important models, too. Make sure your child sees you read for pleasure.

➤ Never withdraw reading aloud as a punishment. That may destroy all the positive effects of reading aloud.

Dear Parents,

Your child will be receiving homework this year. I would like your support by asking you to help your child do the homework, not to do it yourself. I need to see your child's best work. There are some things you can do to encourage your child to finish homework. I would like to share these homework tips with you. Attached you will also find an Assignment Chart which your child may want to use to know which homework assignments need to be completed when.

Sincerely,

Homework Tips for Parents

- Set aside a daily quiet family time when each family member is engaged in quiet activities while your child does homework. Starting quiet time when children are young establishes the expectation for doing homework and gets them into the routine of studying.

- Establish a time and place where homework is to be done. Make sure the table or desk is in a well-lighted area and that needed materials such as paper, pencils, and crayons are available.

- Make sure your child understands all assignments. If needed, work through the first question or problem together. If your child does not understand an assignment and you are unable to help, have him or her call a friend or a homework hot line, if available, for help.

- For elementary children, check over the completed assignment. You may need to sign and date it.

- Each day ask whether there is any homework. Even when there isn't any, the simple act of asking conveys that you consider homework to be an important responsibility. If no specific homework is due, this is a golden opportunity to read together, write a story, take a walk, or just talk together.

- Don't forget to praise your child for homework efforts.

Day_____   Month _____   Date _____ 19 _____

Subject	Assignments	Date Due
☐ Reading		
☐ Language		
☐ Spelling		
☐ Math		
☐ Science		
☐ Social Studies		
☐ Writing		
☐ Other		

Things To Take Home

1. _____

2. _____

3. _____

4. _____

5. _____

Things To Bring To School

1. _____

2. _____

3. _____

4. _____

5. _____

_____
Parent's Signature

9.5   Representing Other Parents (Level 5)

> ***Goal***   To recruit and train parent leaders.

Anticipated Outcomes

For Parents

Parents can help develop policies that will affect the education of the children at the school.

For Students

When parents and school personnel communicate effectively, the rights of children are protected. Education can make its greatest gains.

For Teachers

Teachers and school personnel gain an awareness of parent perspectives for policy development. Parent fund-raising activities can also bring monies into the classroom or school because PTA/PTO groups often choose to purchase items that school budgets will not permit, such as computers and book-binding machines.

Suggested Practices

Parents and school personnel become involved together in advocacy groups and participate in or lead PTA/PTO organizations. Parents will not become involved unless the school personnel—teachers as well as principals—show them they are wanted. Involving parents in cooperative governance helps to overcome the sense of alienation sometimes felt by minority or lower socioeconomic groups of parents toward schools. It is a way to make the school serve the needs of the cultures of the community in a way that is successful and meaningful for children.

In forming organizations of parents and school personnel, it is important to understand that what its effective in one school may not work in another. Groups need to reflect the culture and values of the neighborhood in conjunction with the school. Examine and assess a variety of ways to organize and assist parents in taking an active role in the education of their children. These additional strategies for involving parents were gathered from Fredericks (1991), Fredericks and Rasinski (1990a), Rasinski and Fredericks (1989), Jones (1991), and Jones and Blendinger (1988).

- Provide parents with a constant flow of interesting and timely information about upcoming events and activities. Send reminder notices and make telephone calls to parents who may need additional encouragement.

- Make parent involvement a schoolwide effort. Teachers and administrators must be committed to parent involvement. Staff enthusiasm stimulates greater parent participation.

- Maintain a warm and friendly school environment, and, above all, make it a place where parents feel comfortable, needed, and respected.

- Involve students in recruiting parents. Students can make personal invitations, plan activities, and serve as hosts. Student interest often generates parent interest.

- Whenever possible, develop activities and projects that involve the entire family.

- Create a parental-support system to make parents feel that they are part of a larger family. Enlist parents in a telephone tree to spread the word about special school activities and projects.

- Coordinate with local community organizations and agencies that offer services to families. School personnel can link families in need of social services to agencies that can offer help. Parents aren't always aware of these services.

- Demonstrate to parents that the school cares about issues affecting their welfare by becoming involved in such neighborhood projects as day care, health, and recreation.

- Whenever special events and activities are planned for parents, provide child care and transportation if needed.

- Be patient with parents. Some may be reluctant to get involved for any number of reasons. Keep trying and do not give up on any parent.

- In planning activities, provide parents with a number of scheduling options: morning, afternoons, after school, evenings, and weekends. Activities should be scheduled for the convenience of parents, not schools. Many schools adjust staff schedules in order to provide parent contacts and activities.

- Make daily efforts to communicate with parents through a brief phone call or note—especially to parents who do not participate regularly.

- Do not plan activities that are a repetition of school activities, rather, extend the natural relationship between parents and children.

- Provide parents with many opportunities to discuss their children's interests and achievements. Be sure to acknowledge those achievements. Parents like to see their children succeed.

- Use the telephone frequently for brief messages of good news. This will help parents get used to the idea that a call from school is not just to convey bad news.

- Find out why parents who are not involved choose to distance themselves. Approach them with a non-judgmental attitude to discover reasons for non-involvement. Sometimes parents just need information and encouragement.

- Consider home visits, especially for parents who, for whatever reason, do not come to school.

- Consider holding parent meetings in locations other than school. Hold neighborhood coffees in homes, churches, or community centers for parents who may be intimidated by the school environment.

Resources for Chapter 9

➤ No "Lion" I've Been Trying

➤ Reading Award Certificate

No "LION" I've Been Trying

ROARING SUCCESS MEDAL

**This Special
Achievement Award
is being presented**

to _____

for _____

date _____

official signature _____

507

Reading Award Certificate

presented to

signed by

Books
Without Words

Overview

Driving down a typical road, it is evident that understanding visual clues is crucial to reaching a destination. According to Debes (cited in Smith & Read, 1982), 80% of information must be comprehended visually. Visual literacy is a term used to describe actively using past visual experiences with incoming visual messages to obtain meaning (Sinatra, 1987). Books without words provide a meaningful way for children to become visually literate in that they peruse the material and tell their own version of the story.

One tends to think of books without words as being only appropriate for prereaders; however, such books can benefit *all* age levels and abilities. Non-English-speaking children can "read" these books without the burden of print. Young children can develop expressive verbal skills as they retell the stories repeatedly. Many children will also notice the left-to-right progression of stories as they follow the storyline. Nurss, Hough, and Goodson (1981) suggest using books without words to develop a sense of story in young readers. When a child's version of a story is transcribed, it will become apparent that speaking, writing, and reading are interrelated. If the story is then read to an audience, the listening factor is added.

Reading strategies required to comprehend text can also be represented in books without words. Smith and Read (1982) list these concepts: sequence, details, main idea, inferences, conclusions, cause and effect, and judgments. Also, story elements such as characterization, plot, and imagery are represented in the illustrations of books without words.

Books without words are available in two forms: concept and story. Concept books such as Tana Hoban's *Of Colors and Things* (1989) focus on one idea such as color. Other ideas covered may be shapes, numbers, or letters. The other type of wordless book is a story. In this form, a plot is revealed as the reader follows the progression of the illustrations. In Brinton Turkle's *Deep in the Forest* (1976), a variation of *Goldilocks and the Three Bears* unfolds as the "reader" follows a small bear through a house.

Activities for Books Without Words

Provided here are a few activities adapted from a list by Raines and Isbell (1988) to use with books without words. All the suggestions can easily be adapted to fit the needs of students at various age and grade levels.

Prereaders

- Dictate a version of the story to an adult.
- Act out a favorite scene.
- Label pictures in concept books.
- Tape record a retelling of the story using a bell when the page is turned.
- Pretend to be a specific character for a friend.
- Make pictures in sequence for a wordless book.
- Name the actions of a character.

Beginning Readers

- Write a caption for the most exciting pages.
- Retell the story to a group of classmates.
- Write a new ending for the story.
- Describe your favorite character.
- Write a group story.
- Write dialogue for the story.
- Make a story map.
- Provide words or sentences on cards, and match them to a page in the book.

Fluent Readers

- Remove a character from the story and write a new story about the character.

- Create a wordless book for a younger reader.

- Role play a new scene to be added to the wordless book.

- Discuss how the main idea is shown in a picture book.

- Discuss art elements expressed.

- Create a talking mural in a small group.

Listing of Books Without Words

Alexander, Martha. *Bobo's Dream*. New York: Dial, 1970.

————. *Out! Out! Out!* New York: Dial, 1968.

Aliki. *Go Tell Aunt Rhody*. New York: Macmillan, 1974.

Amoss, Berthe. *By the Sea*. New York: Parents' Magazine, 1969.

Anderson, Laurie. *The Package*. Indianapolis: Bobbs-Merrill, 1971.

Angel, Marie. *The Ark*. New York: Harper & Row, 1973.

Anno, Mitsumasa. *Anno's Italy*. New York: Philomel, 1984.

————. *Anno's Flea Market*. New York: Philomel Books, 1984.

————. *Anno's U.S.A.* New York: Philomel, 1983.

————. *Anno's Britain*. New York: Philomel, 1982.

————. *Anno's Journey*. Cleveland, Ohio: Collins-World, 1978.

————. *Anno's Counting Book*. New York: Crowell, 1977.

————. *Anno's Alphabet*. New York: Crowell, 1975.

————. *Dr. Anno's Magical Midnight Circus*. New York: Weatherhill, 1972.

————. *Topsy-Turvies*. New York: Walker/Weatherhill, 1970.

Ardizzone, Edward. *Look What I Can Do*. New York: Scribner's, 1971.

————. *The Wrong Side of the Bed*. New York: Doubleday, 1970.

Asch, Frank. *In the Eye of the Teddy*. New York: Harper & Row, 1973.

————. *The Blue Balloon*. New York: McGraw-Hill, 1971.

Baker, Jeannie. *Window*. New York: Greenwillow, 1991.

Bang, Molly. *The Grey Lady and the Strawberry Snatcher*. New York: Four Winds, 1980.

Banyai, Istan. *Re-Zoom*. New York: Viking, 1995.

Barton, Byron. *Elephant*. New York: Seabury, 1971.

Baum, Willi. *Birds of a Feather*. Reading, Mass.: Addison-Wesley, 1969.

Bollinger-Savelli, Antonella. *The Mouse and the Knitted Cat*. New York: Macmillan, 1974.

————. *The Knitted Cat*. New York: Macmillan, 1972.

Bonners, Susan. *Just in Passing*. New York: Lothrop, Lee & Shepard, 1989.

Briggs, Raymond. *The Snowman*. New York: Random House, 1978.

————. *Father Christmas*. New York: Coward, McCann & Geoghegan, 1973.

Brinckloe, Julie. *The Spider Web*. New York: Doubleday, 1974.

Brown, Craig. *The Patchwork Farmer*. New York: Greenwillow, 1989.

Burton, Marilee R. *The Elephant's Nest*. New York: Harper & Row, 1981.

Carle, Eric. *My Very First Book of Colors*. New York: Crowell, 1974.

————. *My Very First Book of Shapes*. New York: Crowell, 1974.

————. *I See a Song.* New York: Crowell, 1973.

————. *A Very Long Tail.* New York: Crowell, 1972.

————. *The Very Long Train.* New York: Crowell, 1972.

————. *Do You Want to Be My Friend?* New York: Crowell, 1971.

————. *One, Two, Three to the Zoo.* Cleveland, Ohio: Collins-World, 1968.

Carrick, Donald. *Drip, Drop.* New York: Macmillan, 1973.

Carroll, Ruth. *The Dolphin and the Mermaid.* New York: Henry Z. Walck, 1974.

————. *Rolling Downhill.* New York: Henry Z. Walck, 1973.

————. *The Witch Kitten.* New York: Henry Z. Walck, 1973.

————. *The Chimp and the Clown.* New York: Henry Z. Walck, 1968.

————. *What Whiskers Did.* New York: Henry Z. Walck, 1965.

Carroll, Ruth, and Latrobe, Carroll. *The Christmas Kitten.* New York: Henry Z. Walck, 1970.

Collington, Peter. *The Tooth Fairy.* New York: Knopf, 1995.

————. *The Midnight Circus.* New York: Knopf, 1992.

————. *On Christmas Eve.* New York: Knopf, 1990.

————. *Angel and the Soldier Boy.* New York: Random House, 1983.

Craig, Helen. *Mouse House Months.* New York: Random House, 1981.

Crews, Donald. *Truck.* New York: Greenwillow, 1980.

Day, Alexandra. *Carl's Birthday.* New York: Farrar Straus Giroux, 1995.

————. *Carl's Masquerade.* New York: Farrar Straus Giroux, 1992.

————. *Carl's Christmas.* New York: Farrar Straus Giroux, 1990.

De Groat, Diane. *Alligator's Toothache.* New York: Crown, 1977.

De Paola, Tomie. *Sing Pierrot, Sing.* New York: Harcourt, 1983.

————. *Flicks.* New York: Harcourt, 1981.

————. *The Hunter and the Animals.* New York: Holiday, 1981.

————. *Pancakes for Breakfast.* New York: Harcourt, 1978.

Elzbieta. *Little Mops and the Butterfly.* New York: Doubleday, 1974.

————. *Little Mops and the Moon.* New York: Doubleday, 1974.

————. *Little Mops at the Seashore.* New York: Doubleday, 1974.

Emberley, Ed. *Birthday Wish.* Boston: Little, Brown, 1977.

Espenscheid, Gertrude. *Oh Ball.* New York: Harper & Row, 1966.

Ets, Marie Hall. *Talking Without Words. I Can. Can You?* New York: Viking, 1968.

Felix, Monique. *The Further Adventures of the Little Mouse Trapped in a Book.* LaJolla, Calif.: Green Tiger, 1983.

Fuchs, Erich. *Journey to the Moon.* New York: Delacorte, 1969.

Gilbert, Elliot. *A Cat.* New York: Holt, 1963.

Gill, Madelaine. *The Spring Hat.* New York: Simon & Schuster, 1993.

Giovannetti. *Max.* New York: Atheneum, 1977.

Goodall, John S. *Little Red Riding Hood.* New York: MacMillan Child Group, 1988.

————. *Above and Below Stairs.* New York: Atheneum, 1983.

————. *Lavinia's Cottage.* New York: Atheneum, 1983.

————. *Paddy Finds a Job.* New York: Atheneum, 1981.

————. *Shrewbettina Goes to Work.* New York: Atheneum, 1981.

————. *Victoria Aboard.* New York: Atheneum, 1981.

————. *An Edwardian Season.* New York: Atheneum, 1980.

————. *An Edwardian Christmas.* New York: Atheneum, 1978.

————. *An Edwardian Summer.* New York: Atheneum, 1976.

————. *Paddy Pork's Holiday.* New York: Atheneum, 1976.

————. *Creepy Castle.* New York: Atheneum, 1975.

————. *Naughty Nancy.* New York: Atheneum, 1975.

————. *The Midnight Adventures of Kelly, Dot and Esmeralda.* New York: Atheneum, 1973.

————. *Paddy's Evening Out.* New York: Atheneum, 1973.

————. *Jacko.* New York: Harcourt, 1972.

————. *Shrewbettina's Birthday.* New York: Harcourt, 1971.

————. *The Ballooning Adventures of Paddy Pork.* New York: Harcourt, 1969.

————. *The Adventures of Paddy Pork.* New York: Harcourt, 1968.

Graham, Alastair. *Full Moon Soup.* New York: Dial, 1991.

Hamburger, John. *A Sleepless Day.* New York: Four Winds, 1973.

————. *The Lazy Day.* New York: Four Winds, 1971.

Hefter, Richard. *The Strawberry Word Book.* New York: Larousse, 1974.

Heller, Linda. *Lily at the Table.* New York: Macmillan, 1979.

Henstra, Frisco. *Mighty Mizzling Mouse.* Philadelphia: Lippincott, 1983.

Hoban, Russell, and Selig, Sylvie. *Crocodile and Pierrot.* New York: Scribner's, 1977.

Hoban, Tana. *Of Colors and Things.* New York: Greenwillow, 1989.

————. *Round and Round and Round.* New York: Greenwillow, 1983.

————. *A, B, See.* New York: Greenwillow, 1982.

————. *Take Another Look.* New York: Greenwillow, 1980.

————. *Is It Red? Is It Yellow? Is It Blue?* New York: Greenwillow, 1978.

————. *Dig, Drill, Dump, Fill.* New York: Greenwillow, 1975.

————. *Circles, Triangles and Squares.* New York: Macmillan, 1974.

————. *Over, Under and Through.* New York: Macmillan, 1973.

————. *Count and See.* New York: Macmillan, 1972.

————. *Push Pull, Empty Full.* New York: Macmillan, 1972.

————. *Where Is It?* New York: Macmillan, 1972.

————. *Look Again!* New York: Macmillan, 1971.

————. *Shapes and Things.* New York: Macmillan, 1970.

Hoest, William. *Taste of Carrot.* New York: Atheneum, 1967.

Hogrogian, Nonny. *Apples.* New York: Macmillan, 1972.

Hutchins, Pat. *Changes, Changes.* New York: Macmillan, 1971.

Keats, Ezra Jack. *Clementina's Cactus.* New York: Viking, 1982.

————. *Pssst! Doggie.* New York: Franklin Watts, 1973.

————. *Skates.* New York: Franklin Watts, 1973.

Kent, Jack. *The Scribble Monster.* New York: Harcourt, 1981.

————. *The Egg Book.* New York: Macmillan, 1975.

Knobler, Susan. *The Tadpole and the Frog.* Commack, N.Y.: Harvey, 1974.

Krahn, Fernando. *Amanda and the Mysterious Carpet.* New York: Clarion Books, 1985.

————. *The Secret in the Dungeon.* New York: Clarion, 1983.

————. *The Biggest Christmas Tree on Earth.* Boston: Little, Brown, 1978.

————. *Catch That Cat!* New York: Dutton, 1978.

————. *Earth.* Boston: Little, Brown, 1978.

————. *The Great Ape.* New York: Viking, 1978.

————. *A Funny Friend from Heaven.* Philadelphia: Lippincott, 1977.

————. *The Mystery of the Giant Footprints.* New York: Dutton, 1977.

————. *Little Love Story.* Philadelphia: Lippincott, 1976.

————. *Sebastian and the Mushroom.* New York: Delacorte, 1976.

————. *Who's Seen the Scissors?* New York: Dutton, 1975.

————. *April Fools.* New York: Dutton, 1974.

————. *The Self-Made Snowman.* Philadelphia: Lippincott, 1974.

————. *A Flying Saucer Full of Spaghetti.* New York: Dutton, 1970.

————. *How Santa Claus Had a Long and Difficult Journey Delivering His Presents.* New York: Delacorte, 1968.

————. *Journeys of Sebastian.* New York: Delacorte, 1968.

Lisker, Sonia. *Lost.* New York: Harcourt, 1975.

————. *The Attic Witch.* New York: Four Winds, 1973.

Lustig, Loretta. *The Pop-Up Book of Trucks.* New York: Random House, 1974.

McCully, Emily. *New Baby.* New York: Harper & Row, 1988.

————. *School.* New York: Harper & Row, 1987.

———. *Picnic.* New York: Harper & Row, 1984.

McTrusty, Ron. *Dandelion Year.* Commack, N.Y.: Harvey, 1974.

Mari, Iela, and Mari, Enzo. *The Apple and the Moth.* New York: Pantheon, 1970.

———. *The Chicken and the Egg.* New York: Pantheon, 1970.

Massie, Diane Redfield. *Cocoon.* New York: Crowell, 1983.

Mayer, Mercer. *Oops.* New York: Dial, 1977.

———. *Ah Choo.* New York: Dial, 1976.

———. *Hiccup.* New York: Dial, 1976.

———. *The Great Cat Chase.* New York: Four Winds, 1975.

———. *One Frog Too Many.* New York: Dial, 1975.

———. *Frog Goes to Dinner.* New York: Dial, 1974.

———. *Two More Moral Tales.* New York: Four Winds, 1974.

———. *Two Moral Tales.* New York: Four Winds, 1974.

———. *Bubble Bubble.* New York: Parents' Magazine, 1973.

———. *Frog on His Own.* New York: Dial, 1973.

———. *Frog, Where Are You?* New York: Dial, 1969.

———. *A Boy, a Dog, and a Frog.* New York: Dial, 1967.

Mayer, Mercer, and Mayer, Marianna. *A Boy, a Dog, a Frog and a Friend.* New York: Dial, 1971.

Mendoza, George. *The Inspector.* Garden City, N.Y.: Doubleday, 1970.

———. *And I Must Hurry for the Sea Is Coming In.* Englewood Cliffs, N.J.: Prentice-Hall, 1969.

Meyer, Renate. *Hide-and-Seek.* Scarsdale, N.Y.: Bradbury, 1972.

———. *Vicki.* New York: Atheneum, 1969.

Miller, Barry. *Alphabet World.* New York: Macmillan, 1971.

Olschewski, Alfred. *Winterbird.* Boston: Houghton, 1969.

Ormerod, Jan. *Moonlight.* Wooster, Ohio: Lathrop, 1982.

———. *Sunshine.* Wooster, Ohio: Lathrop, 1981.

Prater, John. *The Gift.* New York: Viking Kestrel, 1986.

Ramage, Corinne. *The Joneses.* Philadelphia: Lippincott, 1975.

Reiss, John J. *Shapes.* Scarsdale, N.J.: Bradbury, 1974.

Ringi, Kjell. *The Winner.* New York: Harper & Row, 1969.

———. *The Magic Stick.* New York: Harper & Row, 1968.

Rockwell, Anne. *Albert B. Club and Zebra.* New York: Harper Children Books, 1987.

Rohmann, Eric. *Time Flies.* New York: Crown, 1994.

Ross, Pat. *Hi Fly.* New York: Crown, 1974.

Schick, Eleanor. *Making Friends.* New York: Macmillan, 1969.

Schubert, Dieter. *Where's My Monkey.* New York: Dial, 1987.

Schweninger, Ann. *A Dance for Three.* New York: Dial, 1979.

Simons, Ellie. *Family.* New York: David McKay, 1970.

————. *Cat.* New York: David McKay, 1968.

————. *Dog.* New York: David McKay, 1967.

Sis, Peter. *Ocean World.* New York: Greenwillow, 1992.

Spier, Peter. *Dreams.* New York: Doubleday, 1986.

————. *Christmas.* New York: Doubleday, 1983.

————. *Rain.* New York: Doubleday, 1982.

————. *Noah's Ark.* New York: Doubleday, 1977.

Steiner, Charlotte. *I Am Andy.* New York: Knopf, 1961.

Sugano, Yoshikatsu. *The Kitten's Adventure.* New York: McGraw-Hill, 1971.

Sugita, Yutaka. *My Friend Little John.* New York: McGraw-Hill, 1973.

Tafuri, Nancy. *Follow Me.* New York: Greenwillow, 1990.

————. *Junglewalk.* New York: Greenwillow, 1988.

————. *Do Not Disturb.* New York: Greenwillow, 1987.

Tanaka, Hideyuki. *The Happy Day.* New York: Atheneum, 1983.

Turk, Hanne. *Happy Birthday Max.* Natick, Maine: Neugebauer, 1984.

————. *Max Packs.* Natick, Maine: Neugebauer, 1984.

————. *Goodnight Max.* Natick, Maine: Neugebauer, 1983.

————. *A Lesson for Max.* Natick, Maine: Neugebauer, 1983.

————. *Max the Artlover.* Natick, Maine: Neugebauer, 1983.

————. *Merry Christmas Max.* Natick, Maine: Neugebauer, 1983.

————. *Rainy Day Max.* Natick, Maine: Neugebauer, 1983.

————. *Raking Leaves With Max.* Natick, Maine: Neugebauer, 1983.

————. *Max Versus the Cube.* Natick, Maine: Neugebauer, 1982.

————. *The Rope Skips Max.* Natick, Maine: Neugebauer, 1982.

————. *A Surprise for Max.* Natick, Maine: Neugebauer, 1982.

Turkle, Brinton. *Deep in the Forest.* New York: Dutton, 1976.

Ueno, Noriko. *Elephant Buttons.* New York: Harper & Row, 1973.

Ungerer, Tomi. *One, Two, Three.* New York: Harper & Row, 1964.

————. *One, Two, Where's My Shoe?* New York: Harper & Row, 1964.

————. *Snail, Where Are You?* New York: Harper & Row, 1962.

Van Allsburg, Christopher. *The Mysteries of Harris Burdick.* Boston: Houghton, 1984.

————. *Ben's Dream.* Boston: Houghton-Mifflin, 1982.

Van Soelen, Philip. *A Cricket in the Grass.* New York: Scribner's, 1981.

Vasiliu, Mircea. *What's Happening?* New York: John Day, 1970.

Ward, Lynd. *The Silver Pony.* Boston: Houghton, 1973.

Weatherbee, Holden. *The Wonder Ring.* New York: Doubleday, 1979.

Wezel, Peter. *Good Bird.* New York: Harper & Row, 1966.

Wiesner, David. *Tuesday.* Boston: Houghton-Mifflin, 1991.

—————. *Free Fall.* New York: Lothrop, 1988.

Wildsmith, Brian. *Whose Shoes?* Oxford: Oxford University Press, 1984.

—————. *The Apple Bird.* Oxford: Oxford University Press, 1983.

—————. *The Nest.* Oxford: Oxford University Press, 1983.

—————. *The Trunk.* Oxford: Oxford University Press, 1982.

—————. *Animal Tricks.* Oxford: Oxford University Press, 1981.

—————. *Brian Wildsmith's Circus.* New York: Franklin Watts, 1970.

Winter, Paula. *Sir Andrew.* New York: Crown, 1980.

—————. *The Bear and the Fly.* New York: Crown, 1976.

Wondriska, William. *A Long Piece of String.* New York: Holt, 1963.

Young, Ed. *Up a Tree.* New York: Harper & Row, 1983.

Alphabet Books

Overview

When *The New England Primer* was published in 1683, the intent was to present letters of the alphabet as well as to teach the moral strictures of early American Society (Camp & Tompkins, 1990). During this period, reading was a serious subject, not to be considered interesting or fun. Alphabet books have evolved considerably in content and form over the last 300 years; they are a pleasurable literary genre that benefits *all* age levels.

As prereaders are read alphabet books, they learn several concepts about print that are crucial to emergent literacy: (1) differences between letters and words, (2) directionality, (3) orientation of letters, (4) distinctive graphic features, (5) sound-symbol relationships, (6) beginning word sounds, and (7) symbolic differences between numbers and letters (Smolkin & Yaden, 1992).

Alphabet books are represented in several formats, varying from uppercase and lowercase letters accompanied with pictures to complex rhymes discussing a specific topic. In *A Is for Angry* (Boyton, 1983), a simple phrase describes the actions of the animal in the picture, which also helps form the letter. Graeme Base's *Animalia* (1986) uses alliteration to describe a scene representing each letter, as well as several fantastic illustrations. *Chicka Chicka Boom Boom* (Martin & Archambault, 1989) tells a rhyming story of letters racing to the top of a coconut tree. When the tree topples over, the reader sees the letters in different positions and predicaments. Illustrations and paragraphs describe twenty-six African concepts in Musgrove's (1976) Caldecott-winning *Ashanti to Zulu: African Traditions*.

Activities for Alphabet Books

The following are extension activities for alphabet books. Although the activities are arranged by type of reader, they can be adapted to any age or ability level.

Prereaders

- Name pictures or objects in the book.
- Talk about your favorite letter page.
- Share an alphabet book with a friend.
- Tell the story to an adult.
- Draw a picture that shows your favorite letter.

Beginning Readers

- Make an alphabet book about yourself.
- Make an alphabet book with a group describing your favorite foods.
- Tell three differences between two alphabet books.
- Tape record your reading of an alphabet book for a younger student.
- Write a rhyme about your favorite letter.
- Make an alphabet name book of classmates and friends.

Fluent Readers

- Make an alphabet book for a young child.
- Describe an object using alliteration.
- Write riddles to represent letters. Use *Q is for Duck* (Elting & Folsom, 1980) for ideas.
- Make an alphabet book in a group that describes a historic event.
- Write about a science topic using the ABC form.

Listing of Alphabet Books

Agard, John. *The Calypso Alphabet.* New York: Henry Holt, 1989.

Alexander, Martha. *A You're Adorable.* Cambridge, MA: Candlewick Press, 1994.

Anglund, Joan Walsh. *In a Pumpkin Shell, A Mother Goose ABC.* San Diego: Harcourt, 1960.

Anno, Mitsumasa. *Anno's Magical ABC: An Anamorphic Alphabet.* New York: Philomel, 1981.

————. *Anno's Alphabet: An Adventure in Imagination.* New York: Crowell, 1975.

Ashton, Elizabeth Allen. *An Old-fashioned ABC.* New York: Viking, 1990.

Aylesworth, Jim. *Old Black Fly.* New York: Holt, 1992.

Azarian, Mary. *A Farmer's Alphabet.* Boston: Godine, 1981.

Barsam, Richard Meran. *A Peaceable Kingdom: The Shaker Abecedarius.* New York: Puffin, 1982.

Base, Graeme. *Animalia.* New York: Harry N. Abrams, 1986.

Baskin, Leonard. *Hosie's Alphabet.* New York: Viking, 1972.

Bayer, Jabe. *A, My Name is Alice.* New York: Dial, 1984.

Bender, Robert. *The A to Z Beastly Jamboree.* New York: Lodestar, 1996.

Bernhard, Durga. *Alphabeasts: A Hide & Seek Alphabet Book.* New York: Holiday House, 1993.

Blake, Quentin. *Quentin Blake's ABC.* New York: Knopf, 1989.

Bourke, Linda. *Handmade Alphabet: A Manual ABC.* Reading, Mass.: Addison-Wesley, 1981.

Boynton, Sandra. *A Is for Angry.* New York: Workman, 1983.

Bridwell, Norman. *Clifford's ABC.* New York: Scholastic, 1983.

Brown, Judith Gwyn. *Alphabet Dreams.* Englewood Cliffs, N.J.: Prentice-Hall, 1976.

Brown, Marcia. *All Butterflies: An ABC.* New York: Scribners, 1974.

Brown, Ruth. *Alphabet Time Four: An International ABC.* New York: Dutton, 1991.

Burningham, John. *John Burningham's ABC.* Bellevue, Wash.: Bobs, 1967.

Carle, Eric. *All About Arthur: An Absolutely Absurd Ape.* Chicago: Watts, 1974.

Carter, Angela. *Comic & Curious Cats.* New York: Harmony Books, 1979.

Chess, Victoria. *Alfred's Alphabet Walk.* New York: Greenwillow, 1979.

Coletta, Irene. *From A to Z: The Collected Letters of Irene and Hattie Coletta.* New York: Prentice-Hall, 1979.

Crowther, Robert. *The Most Amazing Hide and Seek Alphabet Book.* New York: Viking, 1977.

Downie, Jill. *Alphabet Puzzle.* New York: Lothrop, 1988.

Duke, Kate. *The Guinea Pig ABC.* New York: Dutton, 1983.

Duvoisin, Roger. *A is for Ark.* New York: Lothrop, 1952.

Ehlert, Lois. *Eating the Alphabet: Fruits and Vegetables from A to Z.* San Diego: Harcourt, 1989.

Eichenberf, Fritz. *Ape in a Cape.* San Diego: Harcourt, 1952.

Elting, Mary, and Folsom, Michael. *Q Is for Duck: An Alphabet Guessing Game.* New York: Clarion, 1980.

Feelings, Muriel. *Jambo Means Hello: Swahili Alphabet Book.* New York: Dial, 1974.

From Jerry L. Johns and Susan Davis Lenski, *Improving Reading: A Handbook of Strategies* (2nd ed.). Copright © 1997 Kendall/Hunt Publishing Company (1-800-228-0810). May be reproduced for noncommercial educational purposes.

Fisher, Leonard Everett. *Alphabet Art*. New York: Simon and Schuster, 1984.

Gag, Wanda. *ABC Bunny*. New York: Coward, 1933.

Garten, Jan. *An Alphabet Tale*. New York: Random, 1964.

Geisert, Arthur. *Pigs from A to Z*. Boston: Houghton Mifflin, 1986.

Grover, Max. *The Accidental Zucchini: An Unexpected Alphabet*. New York: Harcourt Brace, 1993.

Hague, Kathleen. *Alphabears: An ABC Book*. New York: Henry Holt, 1984.

Hepworth, Cathi. *Antics! An Alphabet of Ants*. New York: Putnam's Sons, 1992.

Hoban, Tana. *A, B, See!* New York: Greenwillow, 1982.

Houget, Susan. *I Unpacked My Grandmother's Trunk*. New York: Dutton, 1985.

Isadora, Rachel. *City Seen from A to Z*. New York: Greenwillow, 1983.

Jernigan, Kathleen. *Agave Blooms Just Once*. Tucson: Harbinger House, 1984.

Johnson, Audean. *A to Z Look and See*. New York: Random House, 1989.

Johnson, Stephen T. *Alphabet City*. New York: Viking, 1995.

Kellogg, Steven. *Aster Aardvark's Alphabet Adventures*. New York: Mulberry Books, 1987.

Kitamura, Satoshi. *What's Inside: The Alphabet Book*. New York: Farrar, 1985.

Kitchen, Bert. *Animal Alphabet*. New York: Dial, 1984.

Knowlton, Jack. *Geography from A to Z: A Picture Glossary*. New York: Crowell, 1988.

Lear, Edward. *A Was Once an Apple*. Cambridge, Mass.: Candlewick Press, 1992.

———. *Nonsense ABC's*. Philadelphia: Running Press, 1991.

———. *An Edward Lear Alphabet*. New York: Lothrop, 1983.

Leedy, Loreen. *The Dragon ABC Hunt*. New York: Holiday House, 1986.

Leonard, Marcia. *Alphabet Bandits*. Mahwah, N.J.: Troll, 1990.

Linscott, Jody. *Upon A to Z: An Alphabet Odyssey*. New York: Doubleday, 1991.

Lionni, Leo. *The Alphabet Tree*. New York: Dragonfly Books, 1968.

Lobel, Anita. *Alison's Zinnia*. New York: Greenwillow, 1990.

Lobel, Arnold. *On Market Street*. New York: Greenwillow, 1981.

Macdonald, Suse. *Alphabetics*. New York: Bradbury Press, 1986.

McPhail, David. *Animals A to Z*. New York: Scholastic, 1989.

Martin, Bill Jr., and Archambault, John. *Chicka Chicka Boom Boom*. New York: Simon and Schuster Books for Young Readers, 1989.

Matthiesen, Thomas. *ABC: An Alphabet Book*. New York: Platt, 1966.

Micklethwait, Lucy. *I Spy*. New York: Greenwillow, 1992.

Miller, Jane. *Farm Alphabet Book*. New York: Scholastic, 1981.

Miles, Miska. *Apricot ABC*. Boston: Little Brown, 1969.

Munari, Bruno. *Bruno Munari's ABC*. Chicago: World, 1960.

Musgrove, Margaret. *Ashanti to Zulu: African Traditions*. New York: Dial, 1976.

Neumeier, Marty, and Glaser, Byron. *Action Alphabet.* New York: Greenwillow, 1984.

Obligado, Lilian. *Faint Frogs Feeling Feverish & Other Terrifically Tantalizing Tongue Twisters.* New York: Viking, 1983.

Oxenbury, Helen. *Helen Oxenbury's ABC of Things.* Chicago: Watts, 1972.

Pallotta, Jerry. *The Extinct Alphabet Book. Watertown, MA: Charlesbridge Publishing, 1993.*

————. *The FROG Alphabet Book.* Chicago: Children's Press, 1990.

————. *The Yucky Reptile Alphabet Book.* Watertown, MA: Charlesbridge Publishing, 1989.

————. *The FLOWER Alphabet Book.* Boston: Quinlan Press, 1988.

Paul, Ann Whitford. *Eight Hands Round: A Patchwork Alphabet.* New York: HarperCollins, 1991.

Provensen, Alice, and Provenson, Martin. *A Peaceable Kingdom: The Abecedarius.* New York: Viking, 1978.

Rankin, Laura. *The Handmade Alphabet.* New York: Dial, 1991.

Rockwell, Anne. *Albert B, Cub, and Zebra.* New York: Harper, 1977.

Ruben, Patricia. *Apples to Zippers.* New York: Doubleday, 1976.

Rubin, Cynthia Elyce. *ABC Americana from the National Gallery of Art.* San Diego: Gulliver Books, 1989.

Sardegna, Jill. *K is for Kiss Goodnight.* New York: Delacorte Press/Doubleday, 1994.

Sendak, Maurice. *Alligators All Round.* New York: Harper, 1962.

Shannon, George. *Tomorrow's Alphabet.* New York: Greenwillow, 1996.

Shelby, Anne & Trivas, Irene. *Potluck.* New York: Orchard, 1991.

Simmonds, Posy. *F-Freezing ABC.* New York: Knopf, 1995.

Sloat, Teri. *From Letter to Letter.* New York: Dutton, 1989.

Steig, Jeanne, and Steig, William. *Alpha Beta Chowder.* New York: HarperCollins, 1992.

Stock, Catherine. *Alexander's Midnight Snack: A Little Elephant's ABC.* New York: Clarion, 1988.

Sullivan, Charles. *Alphabet Animals.* New York: Rizzoli, 1988.

Tarlow, Nora. *An Easter Alphabet.* New York: Putnam.

Tryon, Leslie. *Albert's Alphabet.* New York: Atheneum, 1991.

Tudor, Tasha. *A Is for Annabelle.* New York: Walck, 1954.

Van Allsburg, Chris. *The Z Was Zapped.* Boston: Houghton Mifflin, 1987.

Walters, Marguerite. *The City-Country ABC: My Alphabet Ride in the City, and My Alphabet Ride in the Country.* New York: Doubleday, 1966.

Watson, Clyde. *Applebet: An ABC.* New York: Farrar Straus & Giroux, 1982.

Wildsmith, Brian. *Brian Wildsmith's ABC.* Chicago: Watts, 1963.

Williams, Jenny. *Everyday ABC.* New York: Dial, 1991.

Wilner, Isabel. *A Garden Alphabet.* New York: Dutton Children's Books, 1991.

————. *B is for Bethlehem: A Christmas Alphabet.* New York: Dutton Children's Books, 1990.

Yolen, Jane. *All in the Woodland Early.* New York: Collins, 1979.

Pattern Books

Overview

Students who are just learning to read are exposed to a number of different approaches, and print awareness is probably the first task teachers will need to foster for emergent readers. As teachers begin exposing students to print awareness concepts, whole class or small group instruction is helpful. The use of pattern books, along with a combination of language experience and big books, should enable students to become aware of the purposes and functions of print. Observing early contact with print allows teachers to collect information about students' awareness of important concepts related to reading.

Rhodes (1981) defines a predictable book as one having text that, at times, is either sufficiently repetitive or so predictable that students can chant the text with the teacher after it has been read once or twice. One major distinction of pattern books is that of the language in the books. Some teachers confuse predictable materials in the books with consistent spelling patterns: Pat sat on that mat. Predictable language is much different from consistent spelling patterns, mainly because such sentences are an unnatural example of the way we speak.

Certain predictable language can be found in a student's speech; the distinction is that the student's pattern and rhythm of language contains a message that is also memorable. Most students find it easy to recall information that is repetitive, meaningful, and that can be chanted or read along with the teacher or other students.

Pattern books and other predictable materials are available in a variety of forms. *Brown Bear, Brown Bear* (Martin, 1970) uses catchy rhythm and rhyme to entice the reader, making recall of the material rather simple. Other books use repeated phrases and plot to hold the attention of students. An example of this type of pattern book is *Alexander and the Terrible, Horrible, No Good, Very Bad Day* (Viorst, 1972). Students can relate to the storyline of this book, and their anticipation heightens throughout the story as they gain appreciation for the way Alexander copes with his problems and catastrophes. Opitz (1995) provides strategies and activities for teaching with predictable books and provides a resource of over 800 predictable books.

With some pattern books, students can use the rhyming language to hypothesize what the author might say next. Reading will help confirm predictions as well as strengthen new knowledge of the familiar print encountered. Structured language patterns allow beginning readers to use their predictive abilities for successful reading. Modeling and role playing are essential to the success of using pattern books in the classroom.

Uses for Pattern Books

Following are a few ideas for using pattern books to develop fluent, natural reading with beginning readers. The ideas may also be adapted for use with other, more experienced readers.

- Ask students to predict what the book will be about once they have heard the title of the book and have seen the cover.

- After you have read three or four pages to them, ask students what they think will happen or what a specific character will say.

- Have students explain the reasons for their predictions.

- Allow students to confirm, reject, or revise their predictions once you have read the part of the story that pertains to their prediction.

- Read the rest of the story and ask students to join in when they can.

Activities Involving Pattern Books

- Match sentence strips to lines from the actual story. Matching individual words with target words from the story can also be done.

- Do a cloze activity with the students based on the predictable language found in the story. Omit key words from the story that would complete a phrase, thought, or rhyme.

- On a subsequent day, read the story to the students again, giving them opportunities to join in as well as to say the next line before you read it.

- Using a large wall chart, have students take turns pointing to words you read again from the story.

- When students have learned the story well, let them take home booklets that contain a copy of the story to practice reading to friends or family members.

- Have students dictate patterned language of their own to you for the composition of student-generated literature. Stress, as appropriate, the importance of familiarity of language and the use of rhythm and/or rhyming. Students will want to read books they have made and will want to share this material with parents, teachers, and other students.

■ Change the outcome of the story.

■ Have students draw a new picture that could be added to the story, following the pattern or prediction. Students could work individually or in groups.

■ Change one or two words and create a new pattern book. Rewrite the story as a class activity.

Listing of Pattern Books

Ahlberg, Janet, and Ahlberg, Allen. *Each Peach Pear Plum.* New York: Scholastic, 1978.

Alain. *One Two Three Going to Sea.* New York: Scholastic, 1964.

Alborough, Jez. *Where's My Teddy?* Cambridge, MA: Candlewick, 1992.

Aliki. *My Five Senses.* New York: Crowell, 1962.

Anholt, Catherine, and Anholt, Laurence. *What I Like.* New York: Putnam, 1991.

Archambault, John, and Bill Martin, Jr. *A Beautiful Feast For a Big King Cat.* New York: Harper Collins, 1989.

Asch, Frank. *Monkey Face.* New York: Parents' Magazine, 1977.

————. *Just Like Daddy.* New York: Prentice-Hall, 1961.

Aylesworth, Jim. *My Son John.* New York: Aladdin, 1994.

Baer, Gene. *Thump Thump Rat A Tat Tat.* New York: Harper & Row, 1989.

Baker, Keith. *Who is This Beast?* New York: Voyager/Harcourt Brace, 1990.

Balian, Lorna. *Where in the World Is Henry?* Scarsdale, N.J.: Bradbury, 1972.

Barrett, Judi. *Animals Should Definitely Not Act Like People.* New York: Antheneum, 1980.

————. *Animals Should Definitely Not Wear Clothing.* New York: Antheneum, 1970.

Baum, Arline, and Baum, Joseph. *One Bright Monday Morning.* New York: Random House, 1962.

Becker, John. *Seven Little Rabbits.* New York: Scholastic, 1973.

Beckman, Kaj. *Lisa Cannot Sleep.* New York: Franklin Watts, 1969.

Bonsall, Crosby. *The Case of the Cat's Meow.* New York: Harper & Row, 1965.

Borden, Louise. *Caps, Hats, Socks & Mittens.* New York: Scholastic, 1989.

Brandenberg, Franz. *A Robber, A Robber.* New York: Greenwillow, 1976.

————. *I Wish I Was Sick, Too.* New York: Greenwillow, 1976.

————. *I Once Knew a Man.* New York: Macmillan, 1970.

Brooke, L. Leslie. *Johnny Crow's Garden.* New York: Fredrick Warne, 1903.

Brown Marcia. *The Three Billy Goats Gruff.* New York: Harcourt, 1957.

Brown, Margaret Wise. *The Important Book.* New York: Parents' Magazine, 1964.

————. *Four Fur Feet.* New York: William R. Scott, 1961.

————. *Home for a Bunny.* New York: Golden Press, 1956.

————. *Where Have You Been?* New York: Scholastic, 1952.

————. *Goodnight Moon.* New York: Harper & Row, 1947.

Brown, Ruth. *A Dark, Dark Tale.* New York: Dial, 1981.

Byars, Betsy. *Hooray for the Golly Sisters!* New York: Harper & Row, 1990.

Bulla, Clyde Robert. *The Chalk Box Kid.* New York: Random House, 1987.

Bunting, Eve. *Flower Garden.* New York: Harcourt Brace, 1994.

Burningham, John. *Would You Rather?* New York: Crowell, 1978.

————. *Mr. Gumpy's Outing.* New York: Holt, 1970.

From Jerry L. Johns and Susan Davis Lenski, *Improving Reading: A Handbook of Strategies* (2nd ed.). Copright © 1997 Kendall/Hunt Publishing Company (1-800-228-0810). May be reproduced for noncommercial educational purposes.

Burton, Marilie. *Tail, Toes, Eyes, Ears, Nose.* New York: Harper & Row, 1988.

Butler, Dorothy. *My Brown Bear Barney.* New York: Greenwillow, 1988.

Cairns, Scharlaine. *Oh No!* Crystal Lake, Ill.: Rigby Education, 1987.

Carle, Eric. *The Very Busy Spider.* New York: Philomel, 1985.

————. *The Grouchy Ladybug.* New York: Crowell, 1977.

————. *The Mixed-Up Chamelion.* New York: Crowell, 1975.

————. *Have You Seen My Cat?* Saxonville, Mass.: Picture Book Studio, 1973.

————. *Rooster's Off to See the World.* Saxonville, Mass.: Picture Book Studio, 1972.

————. *Do You Want to Be My Friend?* New York: Harper & Row, 1971.

————. *The Very Hungry Caterpillar.* Cleveland, Ohio: Collins-World, 1969.

Cazet, Denys. *Nothing At All.* New York: Orchard, 1994.

Charlip, Remy. *Fortunately.* New York: Parents' Magazine, 1969.

————. *What Good Luck! What Bad Luck!* New York: Scholastic, 1969.

Cherry, Lynne. *Who's Sick Today?* New York: Dutton, 1988.

Coerr, Eleanor. *Chang's Paper Pony.* New York: Harper & Row, 1986.

Cohen, Caron Lee. *Three Yellow Dogs.* New York: Greenwillow, 1980.

Cohen, Miriam. *First Grade Takes a Test.* New York: Greenwillow, 1980.

Cole, Brock. *The King at the Door.* New York: Doubleday, 1979.

Cole, Joanna, and Stephanie Calmenson. *Ready . . . Set . . . Read! The Beginning Reader's Treasury.* New York: Doubleday, 1990.

Conover, Chris. *Six Little Ducks.* New York: Crowell, 1976.

Cook, Bernadine. *The Little Fish That Got Away.* Reading, Mass.: Addison-Wesley, 1976.

Cowley, Joy. *Greedy Cat.* New York: Richard C. Owen, 1988.

————. *The Jigaree.* Bothell, Wash.: The Wright Group, 1987.

————. *Meanies.* Bothell, Wash.: The Wright Group, 1987.

————. *Mrs. Wishy-Washy.* Bothell, Wash.: The Wright Group, 1987.

————. *Number One.* New York: Richard C. Owen, 1987.

————. *The Red Rose.* Bothell, Wash.: The Wright Group, 1987.

Cuyler, Margery. *That's Good, That's Bad.* New York: Holt, 1991.

DePaola, Tomie. *The Comic Adventures of Old Mother Hubbard and Her Dog.* New York, Harcourt, 1981.

De Regniers, Beatrice Schenk. *May I Bring a Friend?* New York: Atheneum, 1972.

————. *Catch a Little Fox.* New York: Seabury, 1970.

————. *Willy O'Dwyer Jumped in the Fire.* New York: Atheneum, 1968.

————. *The Day Everybody Cried.* New York: Viking, 1967.

————. *How Joe the Bear and Sam the Mouse Got Together.* New York: Parents' Magazine, 1965.

————. *The Little Book.* New York: Henry Z. Walck, 1961.

Demers, Jan. *What Do You Do With a . . . ?* Pinellas, Fla.: Willowisp, 1985.

Deming, A. G. *Who Is Tapping at My Window?* New York: Dutton, 1988.

Dodds, Dayle Ann. *Wheel Away.* New York: Harper Trophy, 1989.

Domanska, Janina. *Din, Dan, Don, It's Christmas.* New York: Greenwillow, 1975.

Dragonwagon, Crescent. *This Is the Bread I Baked for Ned.* New York: Macmillan, 1989.

Ehlert, Lois. *Feathers for Lunch.* New York: Harcourt Brace, 1990.

Ehrlich, Amy. *Leo, Zack, and Emmie.* New York: Dial, 1981.

Einsel, Walter. *Did You Ever See?* New York: Scholastic, 1962.

Emberly, Barbara. *One Wide River to Cross.* Englewood Cliffs, N.J.: Prentice-Hall, 1966.

Emberly, Barbara, and Emberly, Ed. *Drummer Hoff.* Englewood Cliffs, N.J.: Prentice-Hall, 1967.

Emberly, Ed. *Klippity Klop.* Boston: Little, Brown, 1974.

Ets, Marie Hall. *Elephant in a Well.* New York: Viking, 1972.

————. *Play With Me.* New York: Viking, 1955.

Evans, Katie. *Hunky Dory Ate It.* New York: Dutton, 1992.

Field, Rachel. *General Store.* New York: Greenwillow, 1988.

Flack, Marjorie. *Ask Mr. Bear.* New York: Macmillan, 1932.

Fleming, Denise. *In the Tall, Tall Grass.* New York: Holt, 1992.

Fox, Mem. *Shoes from Grandpa.* New York: Orchard, 1990.

Gage, Wilson. *Squash Pie.* New York: Greenwillow, 1976.

Galdone, Paul. *The Teeny, Tiny Woman.* Boston: Houghton, 1984.

————. *The Gingerbread Boy.* New York, Seabury, 1975.

————. *The Little Red Hen.* New York: Scholastic, 1973.

————. *The Three Billy Goats Gruff.* New York: Seabury, 1973.

————. *The Three Bears.* New York: Scholastic, 1972.

————. *The Three Little Pigs.* New York: Seabury, 1970.

————. *Henny Penny.* New York: Scholastic, 1968.

Gelman, Rita Golden. *I Went to the Zoo.* New York: Scholastic, 1993.

Gilman, Phoebe. *Jillian Jiggs.* New York: Scholastic, 1985.

Gerstein, Mordicai. *Roll Over!* New York: Crown, 1984.

Ginsburg, Mirra. *Good Morning, Chick.* New York: Greenwillow, 1980.

————. *The Chick and the Duckling.* New York: Macmillan, 1972.

Goennel, Heidi. *My Day.* Boston: Little, Brown, 1988.

Goss, Janet L., and Harste, Jerome. *It Didn't Frighten Me!* New York: Scholastic, 1988.

Graham, John. *I Love You, Mouse.* New York: Harcourt, 1976.

————. *A Crowd of Cows.* New York: Scholastic, 1968.

Green, Robyn, Pollock, Yevonne, and Scarffe, Bronwen. *When Goldilocks Went to the House of the Bears.* New York: Scholastic, 1987.

Greenberg, Polly. *Oh Lord, I Wish I Was a Buzzard.* New York: Macmillan, 1968.

Greenly, Valerie. *White Is the Moon.* New York: Macmillan, 1990.

Griffith, Helen, V. *Alex and the Cat.* New York: Greenwillow, 1982.

Guarino, Deborah. *Is Your Mama a Llama?* New York: Scholastic, 1989.

Hamm, Diane. *Rockabye Farm.* New York: Half Moof/Simon Schuster, 1992.

Hays, Sarah. *The Grumpalump.* New York: Clarion, 1990.

Hellen, Nancy. *Old MacDonald Had a Farm.* New York: Orchard, 1990.

————. *The Bus Stop.* New York: Orchard, 1988.

Hennessy, B. G. *Jake Baked the Cake.* New York: Viking, 1990.

Higgins, Don. *Papa's Going to Buy Me a Mockingbird.* New York: Seabury, 1968.

Hill, Eric. *Where's Spot?* New York: Putnam, 1980.

Hoban, Lillian. *Arthur's Prize Reader.* New York: Harper & Row, 1978.

Hoberman, Mary Ann. *A House Is a Home for Me.* New York: Viking, 1978.

Hoffman, Hilde. *The Green Grass Grows All Around.* New York: Macmillan, 1968.

Hogrogian, Nonny. *One Fine Day.* New York: Macmillan, 1971.

Hopkins, Lee Bennett, selector. *Good Books, Good Times.* New York: Harper & Row, 1990.

Hutchins, Pat. *The Doorbell Rang.* New York: Greenwillow, 1986.

————. *The Wind Blew.* New York: Macmillan, 1974.

————. *Good-Night, Owl!* New York: Macmillan, 1972.

————. *Titch.* New York: Collier, 1971.

————. *The Surprise Party.* New York: Collier, 1969.

————. *Rosie's Walk.* New York: Macmillan, 1968.

Johnson, Crockett. *A Picture for Harold's Room.* New York: Harper & Row, 1968.

Joslin, Sesyle. *What Do You Say, Dear?* Reading, Mass.: Addison-Wesley, 1958.

Kalan, Robert. *Jump, Frog, Jump.* New York: Mulberry, 1981.

Keats, Ezra Jack. *Over in the Meadow.* New York: Four Winds, 1972.

Kent, Jack. *The Fat Cat.* New York: Scholastic, 1971.

Kessler, Leonard. *Kick, Pass, and Run.* New York: Harper & Row, 1966.

Kirk, David. *Miss Spider's Tea Party.* New York: Scholastic, 1994.

Klein, Leonore. *Brave Daniel.* New York: Scholastic, 1958.

Kochenmeister, Cherryl. *On Monday, When It Rained.* Boston: Houghton, 1989.

Kraus, Robert. *Where Are You Going, Little Mouse?* New York: Greenwillow, 1986.

————. *Leo the Late Bloomer.* New York: Windmill, 1971.

————. *Whose Mouse Are You?* New York: Collier, 1970.

Krauss, Ruth. *The Carrot Seed*. New York: Scholastic, 1984.

————. *What a Fine Day for. . . .* New York: Parents' Magazine, 1967.

————. *The Happy Day*. New York: Harper & Row, 1949.

————. *Bears*. New York: Harper & Row, 1948.

Langstaff, John. *Oh, A-Hunting We Will Go*. New York: Atheneum, 1974.

————. *The Golden Vanity*. New York: Harcourt, 1972.

————. *Soldier, Soldier, Won't You Marry Me?* New York: Doubleday, 1972.

————. *Gather My Gold Together: Four Songs for Four Seasons*. New York: Doubleday, 1971.

————. *Over in the Meadow*. New York: Harcourt, 1957.

Lexau, Joan. *Crocodile and Hen*. New York: Harper & Row, 1969.

Lindbergh, Reeve. *There's a Cow in the Road*. New York: Dial, 1993.

Lobel, Anita. *King Rooster, Queen Hen*. New York: Greenwillow, 1975.

Lobel, Arnold. *On Market Street*. New York: Greenwillow, 1981.

————. *Mouse Soup*. New York: Harper & Row, 1977.

————. *A Treeful of Pigs*. New York: Greenwillow, 1975.

Long, Earlene. *Gone Fishing*. Boston: Houghton, 1987.

Lyon, George Ella. *The Outside Inn*. New York: Orchard, 1991.

Mack, Stan. *10 Bears in My Bed*. New York: Pantheon, 1984.

Mandel, Peter. *Red Cat, White Cat*. New York: Henry Holt, 1994.

Maris, Ron. *Is Anyone Home?* New York: Greenwillow, 1985.

Martin, Bill, Jr. *Polar Bear, Polar Bear, What Do You Hear?* New York: Holt, 1990.

————. *Chicka Chicka Boom Boom*. New York: Simon and Schuster, 1989.

————. *Monday, Monday, I Like Monday*. New York: Holt, 1983.

————. *Brown Bear, Brown Bear, What Do You See?* New York: Holt, 1970.

————. *Fire! Fire! Said Mrs. McGuire*. New York: Holt, 1970.

McDonald, Megan. *Is This a House for Hermit Crab?* New York: Orchard, 1990.

McGovern, Ann. *Too Much Noise*. New York: Scholastic, 1967.

McMillan, Bruce. *Play Day: A Book of Terse Verse*. New York: Holiday, 1991.

Memling, Carl. *Ten Little Animals*. New York: Golden Press, 1961.

Melser, June, and Cowley, Joy. *Grandpa, Grandpa*. Bothell, Wash.: The Wright Group, 1987.

————. *Hairy Bear*. Bothell, Wash.: The Wright Group, 1987.

————. *In a Dark Dark Wood*. Bothell, Wash.: The Wright Group, 1987.

————. *Lazy Mary*. Bothell, Wash.: The Wright Group, 1987.

————. *Sing a Song*. Bothell, Wash.: The Wright Group, 1987.

————. *Yes Ma'am*. Bothell, Wash.: The Wright Group, 1987.

Merriam, Eve. *Do You Want to See Something?* New York: Scholastic, 1965.

Miller, Margaret. *Who Uses This?* New York: Greenwillow, 1990.

Minarik, Else Holmelund. *Little Bear.* New York: Harper and Row, 1957. (Others in the Little Bear series: *Father Bear Comes Home,* 1959; *Little Bear's Friend,* 1960; *Little Bear's Visit,* 1961; *A Kiss for Little Bear,* 1968.)

Moffett, Martha. *A Flower Pot Is Not a Hat.* New York: Dutton, 1972.

Moore, Lilian. *I'll Meet You at the Cucumbers.* New York: Atheneum, 1988.

Numeroff, Laura Joffe. *If You Give a Moose a Muffin.* New York: HarperCollins, 1991.

————. *If You Give a Mouse a Cookie.* New York: Harper & Row, 1985.

Parkes, Brenda. *Who's in the Shed?* Crystal Lake, Ill.: Rigby Education, 1986.

Patrick, Gloria. *A Bug in a Jug and Other Funny Rhymes.* New York: Scholastic, 1970.

Peppe, Rodney. *The House That Jack Built.* New York: Delacorte, 1970.

Pigdon, Keith, and Marilyn Woolley. *Is There Room For Me?* Cleveland, OH: Modern Curriculum Press, 1989.

Pinczes, Elinor. *One Hundred Hungry Ants.* Boston: Houghton Mifflin, 1993.

Pizer, Abigail. *It's a Perfect Day.* Philadelphia: Lippincott, 1990.

Polushkin, Maria. *Mother, Mother, I Want Another.* New York: Crown, 1978.

Porte, Barbara Ann. *Harry in Trouble.* New York: Greenwillow, 1989.

Preston, Edna Mitchell. *Where Did My Mother Go?* New York: Four Winds, 1978.

Quackenbush, Robert. *Too Many Lollipops.* New York: Scholastic, 1975.

————. *She'll Be Comin' Round the Mountain.* Philadelphia: Lippincott, 1973.

Roe, Eileen. *All I Am.* Scarsdale, N.J.: Bradbury, 1990.

Rosen, Michael, reteller. *We're Going on a Bear Hunt.* New York: Macmillan, 1989.

Rylant, Cynthia. *Henry and Mudge and the Happy Cat.* Scarsdale, N.J.: Bradbury, 1990.

Sawyer, Ruth. *Journey Cake, Ho!* New York: Viking, 1953.

Scheer, Jullian, and Bileck, Marvin. *Upside Down Day.* New York: Holiday House, 1968.

————. *Rain Makes Applesauce.* New York: Holiday House, 1964.

Sendak, Maurice. *Where the Wild Things Are.* New York: Scholastic, 1963.

Serfozo, Mary. *Who Said Red?* New York: Macmillan, 1992.

Seuss, Dr. *Fox in Sox.* New York: Random House, 1965.

————. *Green Eggs and Ham.* New York: Random House, 1960.

————. *The Cat in the Hat Comes Back.* New York: Random House, 1958.

————. *The Cat in the Hat.* New York: Random House, 1957.

Shapiro, Arnold. *Who Says That?* New York: Dutton, 1991.

Shaw, Charles B. *It Looked Like Spilt Milk.* New York: Harper & Row, 1947.

Shaw, Nancy. *Sheep Take a Hike.* Boston: Houghton Mifflin, 1994.

————. *Sheep Out to Eat.* Boston: Houghton Mifflin, 1992.

————. *Sheep in a Jeep.* Boston: Houghton, 1989.

————. *Sheep on a Ship.* Boston: Houghton, 1989.

Shulevitz, Uri. *One Monday Morning.* New York: Scribner's, 1967.

Simon, Mina, and Simon, Howard. *If You Were an Eel, How Would You Feel?* Chicago: Follett, 1963.

Skaar, Grace. *What Do the Animals Say?* New York: Scholastic, 1972.

Slobdkina, Esphyr. *Caps for Sale.* New York: Scholastic, 1968. (Originally published in 1940).

Spier, Peter. *The Fox Went Out on a Chilly Night.* New York: Doubleday, 1961.

Stickland, Paul, and Henrietta Stickland. *Dinosaur Roar!* New York: Dutton, 1994.

Stover, JoAnn. *If Everybody Did.* New York: David McKay, 1960.

Tafuri, Nancy. *Spots, Feathers, and Curly Tails.* New York: Greenwillow, 1988.

―――. *Have You Seen My Duckling?* New York: Greenwillow, 1984.

Titherington, Jeanne. *A Child's Prayer.* New York: Greenwillow, 1989.

Tolstoy, Alexei. *The Great Big Enormous Turnip.* New York: Franklin Watts, 1968.

Van Laan, Nancy. *Possum Came a-Knocking.* New York: Knopf, 1990.

―――. *The Big Fat Worm.* New York: Knopf, 1987.

Van Leeuwen, Jean. *Oliver and Amanda's Christmas.* New York: Dial, 1973.

Viorst, Judith. *Alexander and the Terrible, Horrible, No Good, Very Bad Day.* New York: Atheneum, 1972.

Watanabe, Shigeo. *How Do I Put It On?* Cleveland, Ohio: Collins, 1977.

Weiss, Nicki. *On a Hot, Hot Day.* New York: Putnam's Sons, 1992.

―――. *Where Does the Brown Bear Go?* New York: Greenwillow, 1989.

Welber, Robert. *Goodbye, Hello.* New York: Random House, undated.

Wellington, Monica. *All My Little Ducklings.* New York: Dutton, 1989.

Wells, Rosemary. *Noisy Nora.* New York: Dial, 1989.

―――. *A Lion for Lewis.* New York: Dial, 1982.

Wescott, Nadine Bernard. *I Know an Old Lady Who Swallowed a Fly.* Boston: Houghton, 1980.

Winter, Jeanette. *Follow the Drinking Gourd.* New York: Knopf, 1988.

―――. *Hush Little Baby.* New York: Pantheon, 1984.

Winter, Susan. *I Can.* New York: Dorling Kindersley, 1993.

Wondriska, William. *All the Animals Were Angry.* New York: Holt, 1970.

Wood, Audrey. *The Napping House.* New York: Harcourt, 1984.

Zaid, Barry. *Chicken Little.* New York: Random House, undated.

Zemach, Harve. *The Judge.* New York: Farrar, 1969.

Zemach, Margot. *Hush, Little Baby.* New York: Dutton, 1976.

―――. *The Teeny Tiny Woman.* New York: Scholastic, 1965.

Zolotow, Charlotte. *It's Not Fair.* New York: Random House, 1976.

―――. *If It Weren't for You.* New York: Harper & Row, 1966.

―――. *Someday.* New York: Harper & Row, 1965.

―――. *Do You Know What I'll Do?* New York: Harper & Row, 1958.

References

Adams, M.J. (1990a). *Beginning to read: Thinking and learning about print.* (A summary prepared by S.A. Stahl, J. Osborn, & F. Lear). Champaign: University of Illinois.

Adams, M.J. (1990b). *Beginning to read: Thinking and learning about print.* Cambridge, MA: MIT Press.

Ahlberg, J., & Ahlberg, A. (1978). *Each peach pear plum.* New York: Scholastic.

Alvermann, D. (1991). The discussion web: A graphic aid for learning across the curriculum. *The Reading Teacher, 45*(2), 92-99.

Anderson, R.C., Heibert, E.H., Scott, A., & Wilkinson, I.A.G. (1985). *Becoming a nation of readers.* Washington, DC: National Institute of Education.

Anderson, R.C., Wilson, P.T., & Fielding, L.G. (1988). Growth in reading and how children spend their time outside of school. *Reading Research Quarterly, 23*(3), 285-303.

Anderson, T.H., & Armbruster, B.B. (1984). Studying. In P.D. Pearson (Ed.), *Handbook of reading research* (pp. 657-680). New York: Longman.

Antes, R.L., (1989). *Preparing students for taking tests* (Fastback 291). Bloomington, IN: Phi Delta Kappa Educational Foundation.

Armbruster, B.B. (1986). Using frames to organize expository text. Paper presented at the National Reading Conference, Austin, TX.

Atwell, N. (1987). *In the middle: Writing, reading, and learning with adolescents.* Portsmouth, NH: Heinemann.

Baker, L., & Brown, A.L. (1984). Metacognitive skills and reading. In P.D. Pearson (Ed.), *Handbook of reading research* (pp. 353-394). New York: Longman.

Baker, L., Sonnenschein, S., Serpell, R., Fernandez-Fein, S., & Scher, D. (1994). *Contexts of emergent literacy: Everyday home experiences of urban pre-kindergarten children* (Research report No. 24). Athens, GA: National Reading Research Center, University of Georgia.

Baer, G.T. (1991). *Self-paced phonics.* New York: Macmillan.

Base, Graeme. (1986). *Animalia.* New York: Harry N. Abrams.

Beck, I., & McKeown. (1991). Conditions of vocabulary acquisition. In R. Barr, M. L. Kamil, P. Mosenthal, and P.D. Pearson (Eds.), *Handbook of reading research* (Vol. II) (pp. 789-814). New York: Longman.

Bentin, S., & Leshem, H. (1993). On the interaction between phonological awareness and reading acquisition: It's a two-way street. *Annals of Dyslexia, 43*, 125-148.

Blachowicz, C.L.Z. (1986). Making connections: Alternatives to the vocabulary notebook. *Journal of Reading, 29*(7), 643-649.

Boning, T., & Boning, R. (1957). I'd rather read than... *The Reading Teacher, 10*(7), 196-200.

Boyton, S. (1983). *A is for angry: An animal and adjective alphabet.* New York: Workman.

Brozo, W.G., & Simpson, M.L. (1991). *Readers, teachers, learners: Expanding literacy in secondary schools.* New York: Macmillan.

Brozo, W.G., & Simpson, M.L. (1995). *Readers, teachers, learners* (2nd ed.). Englewood Cliffs, NJ: Merrill.

Burnett, F.H. (1990). *The secret garden*. New York: Dell. (Original work published 1911).

Cameron, J., & Pierce, W.D. (1994). Reinforcement, reward, and intrinsic motivation: A meta-analysis. *Review of Educational Research, 64*(3), 363-423.

Camp, D.J., & Tompkins, G.E. (1990). The abecedarius: Soldier of literacy. *Childhood Education, 66*(5), 298-302.

Campbell, R. (1982). *Dear zoo*. New York: Four Winds Press.

Carlsen, G.R., & Sherrill, A. (1988). *Voices of readers: How we come to love books*. Urbana, IL: National Council of Teachers of English.

Caverly, D.C., & Orlando, V.P. (1991). Textbook study strategies. In R.F. Flippo & D.C. Caverly (Eds.), *Teaching reading and study strategies at the college level* (pp. 86-165). Newark, DE: International Reading Association.

Clay, M.M. (1967). The reading behavior of five-year-old children: A research report. *New Zealand Journal of Educational Studies, 2*(1), 11-31.

Clay, M.M. (1985). *The early detection of reading difficulties* (3rd ed.). Portsmouth, NH: Heinemann.

Cole, J. (1990). *The magic school bus lost in the solar system*. New York: Scholastic.

Cramer, E.H. (1992). *Mental imagery and reading* (Literacy Series No. 1). Bloomington, IL: Illinois Reading Council.

Cullinan, B.E. (1992). *Read to me: Raising kids who love to read*. New York: Scholastic.

Cullinan, B., & Weiss, M. J. (1980). *Books I read when I was young*. New York: Avon.

Cummings, P. (1991). *Clean your room, Harvey Moon*. New York: Bradbury.

Cunningham, J.W., Cunningham, P.M., & Arthur, S.V. (1981). *Middle and secondary school reading*. New York: Longman.

Cunningham, P.M. (1993). Action phonics. In M.W. Olson & S.P. Homan (Eds.), *Teacher to teacher: Strategies for the elementary classroom* (pp. 9-12). Newark, DE: International Reading Association.

Cunningham, P.M. (1995). *Phonics they use: Words for reading and writing* (2nd ed.). NY: HarperCollins.

Davey, B. (1983). Think-aloud—Modeling the cognitive processes of reading comprehension. *Journal of Reading, 27*(1), 44-47.

Davey, B. (1986). Using textbook activity guides to help students learn from textbooks. *Journal of Reading, 29*(6), 489-494.

Davis, S.J. (1989). Nonfiction book scans. *Journal of Reading, 33*(3), 222.

Davis, S.J. (1990). Applying content study skills in co-listed reading classrooms. *Journal of Reading, 33*(4), 277-281.

Davis, S.J. (1994). Queen Bee Elementary School reading/language arts program: Reading as its own reward. *The Reading Teacher, 47*(6), 474-476.

DeGenarao, J.J. (1993). Where there's a word, there's a vowel. In M.W. Olson & S.P. Homan (Eds.), *Teacher to teacher: Strategies for the elementary classroom* (p. 9). Newark, DE: International Reading Association.

Deighton, L.C. (1959). *Vocabulary development in the classroom*. New York: Teachers College.

Dunn-Rankin, P. (1968). The similarity of lower-case letters in the English alphabet. *Journal of Verbal Learning and Verbal Behavior, 7*(6), 990-995.

Eanes, R. (1997). *Content area literacy*. New York: Delmar.

Elkonin, D.B. (1973). USSR. In Downing, J. (Ed.), *Comparative reading: Cross-national studies of behavior and processes in reading and writing* (pp. 551-579). New York: Macmillan.

Elting, M., & Folsom, M. (1980). *Q is for duck: An alphabet guessing game*. New York: Clarion.

Epstein, B.B. (1996). Creating skinny books helps students learn about difficult topics. *Journal of Adolescent and Adult literacy, 39*(7), 496-497.

Estes, T.H. (1971). A scale to measure attitudes toward reading. *Journal of Reading, 15*(2), 135-138.

Fetterman, L.P. (1993). Parents and children: The reading connection. *Reading Today, 10*(5), 18.

Foertsch, M.A. (1992). *Reading in and out of school.* Washington, DC: U.S. Government Printing Office.

Fowler, G.L. (1982). Developing comprehension skills in primary students through the use of story frames. *The Reading Teacher, 36*(2), 176-179.

Fox, B.J. (1996). *Strategies for word identification.* Columbus, OH: Merrill.

Fractor, J.S., Woodruff, M.C., Martinez, M.G., Teale, W.H. (1993). Let's not miss opportunities to promote voluntary reading: Classroom libraries in the elementary school. *The Reading Teacher, 46*(6), 476-484.

Fredericks, A.D. (1991). No question about it: Questions can enhance reading. *Reading Today, 9*(1), 20.

Fredericks, A.D., & Rasinski, T.V. (1990a). Involving the uninvolved: How to. *The Reading Teacher, 43*(6), 424-425.

Fredericks, A.D., & Rasinski, T.V. (1990b). Involving parents in the assessment process. *The Reading Teacher, 44*(4), 346-349.

Freeman, G., & Reynolds, E.G. (1980). Enriching basal reader lessons and semantic webbing. *The Reading Teacher, 33*(6), 677-84.

Fry, E.B., Kress, J.E., & Fountoukidis, D.L. (1993). *The reading teacher's book of lists* (3rd ed.). Englewood Cliffs, NJ: Prentice-Hall.

Gall, M.D., Gall, J.P., Jacobsen, D.R., & Bullock, T.L. (1990). *Tools for learning: A guide to teaching study skills.* Alexandria, VA: Association for Supervision and Curriculum Development.

Gambrell, L.B. (1996). Creating classroom cultures that foster reading motivation. *The Reading Teacher, 50* (1), 14-25.

Gambrell, L.B. & Jawitz, P.B. (1993). Mental imagery, text illustrations, and children's story comprehension and recall. *Reading Research Quarterly, 28*(3), 264-273.

Gambrell, L.B., Palmer, B.M., Codling, R.M., & Mazzoni, S.A. (1996). Assessing reading motivation. *The Reading Teacher, 49*(7), 518-533.

Gardner, H. (1993). *Multiple intelligences.* New York: BasicBooks.

Garner, R. (1987). *Metacognition and reading comprehension.* Norwood, NJ: Ablex.

Gillet, J.W., & Temple, C. (1990). *Understanding reading problems: Assessment and instruction* (3rd ed.). Glenview, IL: Scott Foresman.

Goodman, K.S. (1996). *On reading.* Portsmouth, NH: Heinemann.

Goodman, Y.M., & Marek, A.M. (1996). *Retrospective miscue analysis: Revaluing readers and reading.* Katonah, NY: Richard C. Owen.

Grant, R. (1993). Strategic training for using text headings to improve students' processing of content. *Journal of Reading, 36*(6), 482-487.

Graves, D.H. (1983). *Writing: Teachers and children at work.* Portsmouth, NH: Heinemann.

Graves, D.H. (1991). *Build a literate classroom.* Portsmouth, NH: Heinemann.

Griffith, P.L., & Olson, M.W. (1992). Phonemic awareness helps beginning readers break the code. *The Reading Teacher, 45*(7), 516-523.

Gunning, T.G. (1996). *Creating reading instruction for all children* (2nd ed.). Boston: Allyn and Bacon.

Haggard, M.R. (1982). The vocabulary self-collection strategy: An active approach to word learning. *Journal of Reading, 27*(9), 203-207.

Hammond, D. (1983). How your students can predict their way to reading comprehension. *Learning, 12*(4), 62–64.

Harris, A.J., & Sipay, E.R. (1990). *How to increase reading ability* (9th ed.). New York: Longman.

Harste, J.C., & Short, K. G. (1988). *Creating classrooms for authors: The reading-writing connection.* Portsmouth, NH: Heinemann.

Havill, J. (1990). *Jamaica-tag-along.* Boston, MA: Houghton Mifflin.

Hayes, D.A. (1989). Helping students GRASP the knack of writing summaries. *Journal of Reading, 33*(2), 96-101.

Heckelman, R.G. (1969). A neurological-impress method of remedial-reading instruction. *Academic Therapy Quarterly, 4*(4), 277-282.

Heimlich, J.E., & Pittleman, S.D. (1986). *Semantic mapping: Classroom applications.* Newark, DE: International Reading Association.

Henk, W.A., & Melnick, S.A. (1995). The reader self-perception scale (RSPS): A new tool for measuring how children feel about themselves as readers. *The Reading Teacher, 48*(6), 470-482.

Hennings, D.G. (1982). A writing approach to reading comprehension: Schema theory in action. *Language Arts, 59*(1), 8-17.

Hill. S. (1994). *Books alive!* Winnipeg, Manitoba: Peguis.

Hoban, T. (1989). *Of colors and things.* New York: Greenwillow.

Jacobs, J.E., & Paris, S.G. (1987). Children's metacognition about reading: Issues in definition, measurement, and instruction. *Educational Psychologist, 22*(3 & 4), 255-278.

Jason, M.H., & Dubnow, B. (1973). The relationship between self-perceptions of reading abilities and reading achievement. In W.H. MacGinitie (Ed.), *Assessment problems. in reading* (pp. 96-101). Newark, DE: International Reading Association.

Jett-Simpson, M. (1989). *Adventuring with Books: A booklist for pre-K-grade 6.* Urbana, IL: National Council of Teachers of English.

Johns, J.L. (1975). Dolch list of common nouns—A comparison. *The Reading Teacher, 28*(7), 338-340.

Johns, J.L. (1977). Children's conceptions of a spoken word: A developmental study. *Reading World, 16*(4), 248-257.

Johns, J.L. (1980). First graders' concepts about print. *Reading Research Quarterly, 15*(4), 529-549.

Johns, J.L. (1981). The development of the revised Dolch list. *Illinois School Research and Development, 17*(3), 15-24.

Johns, J.L. (1986). *Handbook for remediation of reading difficulties.* Englewood Cliffs, NJ: Prentice-Hall.

Johns, J.L. (1991). Literacy portfolios: A primer. *Illinois Reading Council Journal, 19*(3), 4-10.

Johns, J.L. (1997). *Basic reading inventory* (7th ed.). Dubuque, IA: Kendall/Hunt.

Johns, J.L., Davis, S.J., Barnhart, J.E., Moss, J.H., & Wheat, T.E. (1992). *Celebrate literacy! The joy of reading and writing.* Bloomington, IN: EDINFO Press.

Johnson, D.D., & Johnson, B.V.H. (1986). Highlighting vocabulary in inferential comprehension instruction. *Journal of Reading, 29*(7), 622-625.

Johnson, D.D., & Pearson, P.D. (1984). *Teaching reading vocabulary* (2nd ed.). New York: Holt.

Jones, L.T. (1991). *Strategies for involving parents in their children's education.* Bloomington, IN: Phi Delta Kappa Educational Foundation.

Jones, L.T., & Blendinger, J. (1988). *Reaching out to parents: Strengthening your school's parent involvement program* (A resource and planning guide for principals and school staffs). Denver: Adams #1 School District.

Kearns, D.T. (1993). Toward a new generation of American schools. *Phi Delta Kappan, 74*(10), 773-776.

Kovacs, D. (1995). *Meet the authors.* New York: Scholastic.

Kovacs, D., & Preller, J. (1991). *Meet the authors and illustrators.* New York: Scholastic.

Lalas, J. (1993). Empowering families through W.H.O.L.E. (wonderful home-oriented literacy events). *The California Reader, 26*(2), 16-17.

Lamberg, W.J., & Lamb, C.E. (1980). *Reading instruction in the content areas.* Geneva, IL: Houghton Mifflin.

Lehman, J.H. (1990). *The saga of Shakespeare Pintlewood and the great silver fountain pen.* Elgin, IL: Brotherstone Publishers.

L'Engle, M. (1962). *A wrinkle in time.* New York: Dell.

Lima, C.W., & Lima, J.A. (1993). *A to zoo: Subject access to children's picture books* (4th ed.). New Providence, NJ: R.R. Bowker.

Lobel, A. (1970). *Frog and toad are friends.* New York: Harper and Row.

Lundberg, I., Frost, J., & Petersen, O.P. (1988). Effects of an extensive program for stimulating phonological awareness in preschool children. *Reading Research Quarterly, 23*(3), 264-284.

Making parents your partners. (1993). *Instructor, 102*(8), 52-53.

Manzo, A.V. (1969). The ReQuest procedure. *Journal of Reading, 13*(7), 123-126.

Manzo, A.V., & Manzo, U. C. (1993). *Literacy disorders: Holistic diagnosis and remediation.* New York: Harcourt Brace Jovanovich.

Maria, K., & Hathaway, K. (1993). Using think alouds with teachers to develop awareness of reading strategies. *Journal of Reading, 37*(1), 12-18.

Martin, B., Jr. (1970). *Brown bear, brown bear.* New York: Holt.

Martin, B., Jr., & Archambault, J. (1989). *Chicka chicka boom boom.* New York: Simon and Schuster.

May, F.B. (1990). *Reading as communication* (3rd ed.). Columbus, OH: Merrill.

McCloskey, R. (1943). *Homer Price.* New York: Viking.

McCormick, S. (1995). *Instructing students who have literacy problems* (2nd ed.). Columbus, OH: Merrill.

McGee, L.M., & Richgels, D.J. (1996). *Literacy's beginnings: Supporting young readers and writers* (2nd ed.). Boston: Allyn and Bacon.

McGinley, W.J., & Denner, P.R. (1987). Story impressions: A prereading/writing activity. *Journal of Reading, 31*(3), 248-253.

McKenna, M.C., and Kear, D.J. (1990). Measuring attitude toward reading: A new tool for teachers. *The Reading Teacher, 43*(9), 626-639.

Miles, B. (1995). *Hey! I'm reading.* New York: Scholastic.

Miller, W. H. (1995). *Alternative assessment techniques for reading & writing.* West Nyack, NY: The Center for Applied Research in Education.

Moore, D.M., & Moore, S. A. (1986). Possible sentences. In E. K. Dishner, T.W. Bean, J.E. Readence, & D.W. Moore (Eds.), *Reading in the content areas: Improving classroom instruction* (2nd ed.) (pp. 174-179). Dubuque, IA: Kendall/Hunt.

Moore, D.W., Readence, J.E., & Rickleman, R.J. (1989). *Prereading activities for content area reading and learning* (2nd ed.). Newark, DE: International Reading Association.

Morris, D., & Perney, J. (1984). Developmental spelling as a predictor of first-grade reading achievement. *The Elementary School Journal, 84*(4), 441-457.

Morrow, L.M. (Ed.). (1995). *Family literacy: Connections in schools and communities.* Newark, DE: International Reading Association.

Musgrove, M. (1976). *Ashanti to Zulu: African traditions.* New York: Dial.

Numeroff, L.J. (1991). *If you give a moose a muffin.* New York: HarperCollins.

Nurss, J., Hough, R.A., & Goodson, M.S. (1981). Prereading/language development in two day care centers. *Journal of Reading Behavior, 13*(1), 23-31.

O'Flavahan, J., Gambrell, L.B., Guthrie, J., Stahl, S., & Alvermann, D. (1992, August). Poll results guide activities of research center. *Reading Today,* p. 12.

O'Flahavan, J.F., Hartman, D.K., & Pearson, P.D. (1988). Teacher questioning and feedback practices: A twenty year perspective. In J.E. Readence & R.S. Baldwin (Eds.), *Dialogues in literacy research* (37th Yearbook of the National Reading Conference) (pp. 183-208). Chicago: National Reading Conference.

Ogle, D.M. (1989). The know, want to know, learn strategy. In K.D. Muth (Ed.), *Children's comprehension of text* (pp. 205-223). Newark, DE: International Reading Association.

Optiz, M.F. (1995). *Getting the most from predictable books.* New York: Scholastic.

Palinscar, A.S., & Brown, A.L. (1986). Interactive teaching to promote independent learning from text. *The Reading Teacher, 39*(8), 771-777.

Pallotta, J. (1987). *The icky bug alphabet book.* Watertown, MA: Charlesbridge Publishing.

Pallotta, J. (1987). *The bird alphabet book.* Watertown, MA: Charlesbridge Publishing.

Pallotta, J. (1988). *The flower alphabet book.* Watertown, MA: Charlesbridge Publishing.

Pappas, C., Kiefer, B.Z., & Levstik, L.S. (1995). *An integrated language arts perspective in the elementary school: Theory into action* (2nd ed.). White Plains, NY: Longman.

Paris, S.G. (1987). *Reading and thinking strategies.* Lexington, MA: Heath.

Paris, S.G., Lipson, M.Y., & Wixson, K.K. (1983). Becoming a strategic reader. *Contemporary Educational Psychology, 8*(3), 293-316.

Paris, S.G., & Oka, E.R. (1986). Children's reading strategies, metacognition, and motivation. *Developmental Review, 6*(1), 25-26.

Paris, S.C., Wasik, B.A., & Turner, J.C. (1991). The development of strategic readers. In R. Barr, M. Kamil, P. Mosenthal, & P.D. Pearson (Eds.), *Handbook of reading research* (Vol. II) (pp. 609-640). New York: Longman.

Pelham, D. (1990). *Sam's sandwich.* New York: Dutton.

Peek, M. (1985). *Mary wore her red dress and Henry wore his green sneakers.* New York: Clarion.

Perl, L. (1987). *Mummies, tombs, and treasure: Secrets of ancient Egypt.* New York: Clarion.

Piper, W. (1953). *The little engine that could.* New York: Harper and Row.

Pittleman, S.D., Heimlich, J.E., Berglund, R.L., & French, M.P. (1991). *Semantic feature analysis: Classroom applications.* Newark, DE: International Reading Association.

Rabe, B. (1981). *The balancing girl.* New York: E. P. Dutton.

Raines, S.C., & Isbell, R. (1988, April). *An array of teaching ideas using wordless picture books.* Paper presented at the Annual Study Conference of the Association for Childhood Education International, Salt Lake City, UT.

Rawls, W. (1961). *Where the red fern grows.* New York: Doubleday.

Raphael, T.E. (1984). Teaching learners about sources of information for answering comprehension questions. *Journal of Reading, 27*(4), 303-311.

Rasinski, T.V., & Fredericks, A.D. (1989). Dimensions of parent involvement. *The Reading Teacher, 43*(2), 180-182.

Readence, J.E., Bean, T.W., & Baldwin, R.S. (1992). *Content area reading* (4th ed.). Dubuque, IA: Kendall/Hunt.

Rhodes, L.K. (1981). I can read! Predictable books as resources for reading and writing instruction. *The Reading Teacher, 34*(5), 511-518.

Richards, J.C., & Gipe, J.P. (1993). Getting to know story characters: A strategy for young and at-risk readers. *The Reading Teacher, 47*(1), 78-79.

Richardson, J.S., & Morgan, R.F. (1990). *Reading to learn in the content areas.* Belmont, CA: Wadsworth.

Richek, M.A., Caldwell, J.S., Jennings, J.H., & Lerner, J.W. (1996). *Reading problems: Assessment and teaching strategies* (3rd ed.). Boston: Allyn and Bacon.

Ritter, S., & Idol-Maestas, L. (1986). Teaching middle school students to use a test-taking strategy. *Journal of Educational Research, 79*(6), 350-357.

Roberts, B. (1992). The evolution of the young child's concept of word as a unit of spoken and written language. *Reading Research Quarterly, 27*(2), 124-138.

Robinson, R.P. (1946). *Effective study.* New York: Harper and Row.

Routman, R. (1991). *Invitations: Changing as teachers and learners K-12.* Portsmouth, NH: Heinemann.

Royer, J.M., Cisero, C.A., & Carlo, M.S. (1993). Techniques and procedures for assessing cognitive skills. *Review of Educational Research, 63*(2), 201-243.

Rubin, D. (1993). *A practical approach to teaching reading.* Needham Hts., MA: Allyn and Bacon.

Ruddell, M.R. (1993). *Teaching content reading and writing.* Needham Hts., MA: Allyn and Bacon.

Ruddell, R.B. (1974). *Reading-language instruction: Innovative practices.* Englewood Cliffs, NJ: Prentice-Hall.

Rylant, C. (1985). *Slower than the Rest.* New York: Aladdin Books.

Samuels, S.J. (1994). Toward a theory of automatic information processing in reading revisited. In R.B. Ruddell, M.R. Ruddell, & H. Singer (Eds.), *Theoretical models and processes of reading* (4th ed.) (pp. 816-837). Newark, DE: International Reading Association.

Schmidt, B., & Buckley, M. (1991). Plot relationships chart. In J.M. Macon, D. Bewell, & M. Vogt (Eds.). *Responses to literature: Grades K-8* (pp. 7-8). Newark, DE: International Reading Association.

Schmitt, M.C. (1990). A questionnaire to measure children's awareness of strategic reading processes. *The Reading Teacher, 43*(7), 454-461.

Scieszka, J. (1989). *The true story of the 3 pigs by A. Wolf.* New York: Scholastic.

Shanahan, T. (Ed.). (1990). *Reading and writing together: New perspectives for the classroom.* Norwood, MA: Christopher-Gordon Publishers.

Silvey, A. (Ed.). *Children's books and their creators.* Boston: Houghton Mifflin.

Simpson, M.L. (1986). PORPE: A writing strategy for studying and learning in the content areas. *Journal of Reading, 29*(5), 407-414.

Sinatra, R. (1987). *Visual literacy connections to thinking, reading and writing.* Springfield, IL: Charles C. Thomas.

Smith, F. (1983). Reading like a writer. *Language Arts, 60*(5), 558-567.

Smith, C.C., & Bean, T.W. (1980). The guided writing procedure: Integrating content reading and writing improvement. *Reading World, 19*(3), 290-294.

Smith, H.M., & Read, D. (1982). Teaching visual literacy through wordless picture books. *The Reading Teacher, 35*(8), 928-933.

Smolkin, L.B., & Yaden, D.B. (1992). O is for mouse: First encounters with the alphabet book. *Language Arts, 69*(6), 432-441.

Snyder, Z. K. (1967). *The Egypt game.* New York: Dell.

Sobol, D.J. (1981). *Encyclopedia Brown's second record book of weird and wonderful facts.* New York: Dell.

Stanfill, S. (1978). The great American one-sentence summary. In O. Clapp (Ed.), *Classroom practices in teaching classroom English, 1977-1978* (pp. 47-49). Urbana, IL: National Council of Teachers of English.

Stanovich, K.E. (1991). Word recognition: Changing perspectives. In R. Barr, M.L. Kamil, P. Mosenthal, & P.D. Pearson (Eds.), *Handbook of reading research* (Vol. II) (pp. 418-452). New York: Longman.

Stanovich, K.E. (1993-1994). Romance and reality (Distinguished Educator Series). *The Reading Teacher, 47*(4), 280-291.

Stauffer, R.G. (1969a). *Directing reading maturity as a cognitive process.* New York: Harper and Row.

Stauffer, R.G. (1969b). *Teaching reading as a thinking process.* New York: Harper and Row.

Sternberg, R.J., & Powell, J. S. (1983). Comprehending verbal comprehension. *American Psychologist, 38*(8), 878-893.

Stotsky (1983). Research on reading/writing relationships: A synthesis and suggested directions. *Language Arts, 60*(5), 627-643.

Taylor, B.M., Frye, B.J., & Maruyama, G.M. (1990). Time spent reading and reading growth. *American Educational Research Journal, 27*(2), 351-362.

Thorndike, E.L. (1941). *The teaching of English suffixes.* New York: Teachers College.

Tierney, R.J., & Pearson, P.D. (1983). Toward a composing model of reading. *Language Arts, 60*(5), 568-580.

Tierney, R.J., Readence, J.E., & Dishner, E.K. (1990). *Reading strategies and practices: A compendium* (3rd ed.). Boston: Allyn and Bacon.

Tierney, R.J., & Shanahan, T. (1991). Research on reading-writing relationships: Interactions, transactions, and outcomes. In P.D. Pearson, R. Barr, M. Kamil, & P. Mosenthal (Eds.). *Handbook of reading research* (Vol. II) (pp. 246-280). New York: Longman.

Tompkins, G.E., & Hoskisson, K. (1991). *Language arts: Content and teaching strategies.* New York: Macmillan.

Trelease, J. (1989). *The new read-aloud handbook.* New York: Penguin.

Turbill, J., Butler, A., Cambourne, B., & Langton, G. (1991). *Frameworks course notebook.* Stanley, NY: Wayne Finger Lakes Board of Cooperative Educational Services.

Tullock-Rhody, R., & Alexander, J.E. (1980). A scale for assessing attitudes toward reading in secondary schools. *Journal of Reading, 23*(2), 609-614.

Tumner, W.E., Herriman, M.L., & Nesdale, A.R. (1988). Metalinguistic abilities and beginning reading. *Reading Research Quarterly, 23*(2), 134-158.

Turkle, B. (1976). *Deep in the forest.* New York: Dutton.

Vacca, R.T. (1981). *Content area reading.* Boston: Little, Brown.

Vacca, R.T., & Vacca, J. L. (1996). *Content area reading* (5th ed.). New York: HarperCollins.

VanLeirsburg, P. (1993). Ethics and standardized testing. *Illinois Reading Council Journal, 21*(1), 35a-35d.

Viorst, J. (1972). *Alexander and the terrible, horrible, no good, very bad day.* New York: Atheneum.

Waddell, M. (1975). *Owl babies.* Cambridge, MA: Candlewick Press.

White, E.B. (1952). *Charlotte's web.* New York: Harper and Row.

Wilder, L.I. (1932). *Little house in the big woods.* New York: Harper.

Wilson, P.T. (1988). *Let's think about reading and reading instruction: A primer for tutors and teachers.* Dubuque, IA: Kendall/Hunt.

Winograd, P., & Hare, V.C. (1988). Direct instruction of reading comprehension strategies: The nature of teacher explanation. In E.T. Goetz, P. Alexander, & C. Weinstein (Eds.), *Learning and study strategies: Assessment, instruction, and evaluation* (pp. 121-140). New York: Academic Press.

Wood, K. (1984). Probable passages: A writing strategy. *The Reading Teacher, 37*(6), 496-499.

Yopp, H.K. (1995). A test for assessing phonemic awareness in young children. *The Reading Teacher, 49*(1), 20-29.

Index

to predict meanings for unknown words, 141, 173-75, 331
pronunciation and, 126-27
for unpronounceable words to correct overuse of phonics, 126-27
Contextual Redefinition, 180-81
Continuum graphic organizer, 188
Contractions, 159, 211
Contrasts, 174, 277, 287, 322
Conversations, parent-child, 81
Cornell method of notetaking, 440
Critter, 304-5
Cross-age writing project, 403
CSSR (context, structure, sound, reference) strategy for word identification, 176-77
Cues, 120. *See also* Miscues
Cyclic graphic organizer, 189

Dear Zoo, 403
Declarative knowledge, 300
Decoding, 120
preoccupation with, 330-31
unknown words and, 120, 123, 141
Deep in the Forest, 387, 510
Description Idea-Map, 277
Descriptive writing, 378, 381-82, 396, 418
Details
recalling, 225-28
in wheel-and-spoke analogy, 219-20
Dialects
African-American, 130-31
Chinese, 131
Spanish, 130
student's nonstandard language from, 67
taking account of, 130-31
Dialogue journals, 14, 399
Dictionaries, 58, 175, 194
Digraphs, 149, 150
Directed Reading-Thinking Activity (DR-TA), 256-57, 316
Directions, reading, 14
Discussion Guide for Listening Parents, 491
Discussion Web strategy, 291-92
Dolch List, Revised, 200, 201
Drafting stage of writing, 370, 393
Dramatizing
strategic reading and, 341, 342
of student writing, 403

Each Peach Pear Plum, 403
Echo reading
for improving fluency, 111, 114
sentences that use appropriate syntax, 80
Echoing, 112
Editing, 370, 373-76
Editorials, 379-81
Egypt Game, The, 322
Elementary Reading Attitude Survey
form for, 30-34
instructions for administering, scoring, and interpreting, 29
norms for, 36-37
scoring sheet for, 35
Emergent literacy. *See* Beginning reading
Enthusiasm, 11
Environment, supportive, 2. *See also* Home environment
Essay tests, strategy for, 449-50
Examples, 174
Excerpts, 341
Exclusion brainstorming, 247
Experience
in book talks, 341
inventory of, 20
unknown words and, 174
Experience stories, 113, 330
Expository texts
defined, 261, 284-85
modeling comprehension monitoring of, 322, 323
narrative vs., 309, 322
organizational pattern of, 417
retelling procedure for, 284-85
structure of, teaching strategy for, 422-23
types of, 418-20
writing, 378

Facts
categorizing, 392
opinion vs., 241-42
recalling, 225-28
Factstorming, 392
Failure, repeated, 5
Family Read Aloud program, 10, 15
Feature analysis strategy, 248-49
form for, 249
for meaning vocabulary, 182-84